CIVIL WAR

Untold Tales of the Blue and Gray

WEST
SIDE
PUBLISHING

Contributing Writers: Michael Amedeo, Ed Avis, Michael Patrick Brady, Bryan Davies, Tom DeMichael, Eric Paul Erickson, John Gorenfeld, William Gorenfeld, Martin F. Graham, Kathryn Holcomb, Sarah Milov, Richard Mueller, Nick Smith, Michael J. Varhola, Jacob Wheeler, David Wolfford

Contributing Illustrator: John Zielinski

ISBN-13: 978-1-4127-1418-1
ISBN-10: 1-4127-1418-4

Manufactured in U.S.A.

8 7 6 5 4 3 2 1

CONTENTS

★ ★ ★ ★

AMERICA'S DECISIVE CONFLICT

★ ★ ★ ★

Welcome to *Armchair Reader™: Civil War*.

The Civil War is one of the most interesting, perplexing, heartbreaking, and divisive periods in American history. We set out to create a book with a breadth of information to keep readers of all ages fascinated. There's plenty to choose from in *Armchair Reader™: Civil War*. Battles, armaments, and skirmishes are here, as are the realities of life in the regimental camps, but we try to focus on the personalities, the intriguing details, and some of the more unusual tales. Scalawags, carpetbaggers, heroes, and heroines alike are highlighted in a mix we hope you'll find interesting and educational.

Here are some of the fascinating facts and stories you'll find inside:

- Women who disguised themselves as male soldiers and spies to get in on the action
- Generals who succeeded and failed—while drunk
- Soldiers who built great reputations or destroyed them

We believe we've created a treasury of interesting information that you'll find as engrossing as we did, so kick back in your favorite armchair or other comfy reading spot, and enjoy. You'll discover that once you get started, this book will be hard to put down.

Allen Orso

Allen Orso, Publisher

P.S. If you have any thoughts, questions, concerns, or ideas about this book, or if you'd like more information about our other West Side Publishing titles, please contact us at: www.armchairreader.com.

THE BOMBARDMENT OF FORT SUMTER

★ ★ ★ ★

The first assault of the Civil War, lasting more than 34 hours,
was launched after months of standoff.

On December 26, 1860, Major Robert
Anderson and 70 Federals under his
command rowed from their garrison at
South Carolina's Fort Moultrie to the more
secure Fort Sumter in Charleston Harbor.
After South Carolina's secession from the
Union six days earlier, Anderson—a Southerner
loyal to the Union—felt the move to the more defensible fort was
necessary to ensure the safety of his soldiers.

Starting the War

Fort Sumter offered little strategic value, but it meant everything
to both sides. To the North, it symbolized the United States. To
the South, it represented the right to leave that Union.

Although President Abraham Lincoln, newly inaugurated in
March 1861, swore to defend federal property within the seceded
states, he also pledged that the Union wouldn't fire the first shot.
He announced plans to send supply boats to bring "food for hungry men." Confederate President Jefferson Davis, however, decided to wage war anyway. On April 12, 1861, four Confederate
emissaries rowed to Fort Sumter and called for surrender. Anderson refused, and the Confederates opened fire around 4:30 A.M.

The South Wins the First Battle

After more than a day of shelling leveled part of the fort and set the
interior afire, Anderson realized further defense was futile. He evacuated the fort, and the Confederates allowed him to return North.

PRESERVING THE UNION

★ ★ ★ ★

As the Civil War got started, the U.S. Congress wanted everyone to know what they were—and were not—fighting about.

One common misconception about the Civil War is that it was fought to abolish slavery. In reality, the issue was never as cut and dried as that. In fact, some people wanted to take the argument over slavery out of the discussion about the conflict altogether.

Early in the war, Congress tried to do just that. Representative John J. Crittenden of Kentucky (who had just finished his term in the Senate before running for a seat in the House) and Senator Andrew Johnson of Tennessee presented a resolution to state the North's war aims clearly. It was passed on July 25, 1861—a little more than three months after the war began.

The Official Reason for Fighting

The Crittenden-Johnson Resolution stated the war with the Southern states was being fought neither to abolish slavery nor for "overthrowing or interfering with the rights or established institutions of those States," but only to "defend and maintain the supremacy of the Constitution and to preserve the Union."

Claiming slavery had nothing to do with the war didn't sit well with abolitionists. A primary opponent of slavery in the House, Pennsylvania's Thaddeus Stevens fought against the measure. He couldn't stop it from passing, but he got it repealed in December 1861.

By that time, the resolution had served its main purpose: to discourage the slave states of Delaware, Kentucky, Maryland, and Missouri from seceding. The losses of these border states would have been devastating. If Maryland had seceded, Washington, D.C., would have been completely surrounded by Confederate territory. But by assuring residents that their slaves were not at risk, the Union gave itself a bit more protection.

Fast Facts

- On March 9, 1862, the USS Monitor *and the* CSS Virginia *engaged in a four-hour close-range battle resulting in a draw. A milestone in naval warfare, it marked the first engagement between two ironclad warships.*

- *Lieutenant Thomas Custer was the only soldier to win two Congressional Medals of Honor during the Civil War. More than a decade later, he would go to his death at Little Big Horn under the leadership of his brother General George Armstrong Custer.*

- *In 1861, Lincoln became the first president from the Republican party, which was founded in 1854 on a platform opposing the expansion of slavery into new territories. Initially, the Republican party was composed largely of former members of the Whig party, which had been in decline. Both the Whig party and today's Democratic party had their roots in Thomas Jefferson's original Democratic-Republican party.*

- *The first gun fired in defense of the Union was in Pensacola, Florida, on January 8, 1861, when state troops tried to occupy federal forts.*

- *There were no casualties during the attack on Fort Sumter. However, one day after the Union troops surrendered the fort but before they evacuated it, Fort Sumter's commander, Union Major Robert Anderson, was allowed to run up his flag for a 100-gun salute. The salute began at 2:00 P.M. on April 14 but was shortened to a 50-gun salute after Private Daniel Hough was killed when a cannon accidentally discharged while he was loading it. He was buried on the parade ground, but it is unknown if he is still buried there or if his body was relocated during the course of the war.*

THE BRAIN OF THE CONFEDERACY

★ ★ ★ ★

*Mystery surrounds the life of Judah P. Benjamin, a
Confederate leader subjected to anti-Semitism
and suspicion despite his loyalty to the Southern cause.*

Even before becoming Jefferson Davis's most trusted confidant,
Senator Judah P. Benjamin had made an exceptional career for
himself. The Sephardic Jew who devoted his powers of oratory to
the cause of slavery was a novelty in the prewar Senate. Admirers
claimed that intelligence blazed from his eyes. He enchanted allies
with his disarming wit, his old-world sophistication, and, as one
lawmaker recalled, a voice "as musical as the chimes of silver bells."

Representing Louisiana in the Senate, he withdrew from that
body when Louisiana left the Union. The newly formed Confederate government put his smiling face on its two-dollar bill and his
quick mind to work as secretary of war. The wife of Confederate
President Jefferson Davis reported that Benjamin was at Davis's
side 12 hours a day. One biography asserts that his workdays began
at 8:00 A.M. and lasted until the crack of dawn the next morning.
But even as a powerful Confederate, he remained an outsider in
his own South. Plantation society repaid Benjamin's devotion to
the Confederacy with anti-Semitism and suspicion. One way he
coped with this predicament was through humor. In one instance
when Davis was headed for a service at an Episcopal church and
Benjamin realized he was obliged to accompany his president,
Benjamin joked, "May I not have the pleasure of escorting you?"

Humble Beginnings

Judah Philip Benjamin was born in the present-day Virgin Islands
to a dry-goods seller who founded one of America's first reform
synagogues. After growing up in the Carolinas, the immigrant son
attended Yale at only 14 years old, but he was expelled under

cloudy circumstances. A newspaper piece published just before the Civil War claimed that his expulsion had been for playing cards and pickpocketing, a charge that Benjamin dismissed as libel by a man who falsely claimed to be his classmate.

Fortunately for the young Benjamin, one could become a self-trained lawyer in the 19th century. Harvard was the only law school at that time, so most lawyers—including Abraham Lincoln—were self-taught. Benjamin's facile legal mind readily cut to the heart of a case, and clients paid him handsomely. In this way, he achieved one of his aims, that of owning a plantation. His climb up the social ladder accelerated when he married Natalie St. Martin, a stunning Creole beauty from a well-to-do Catholic Louisiana family. The marriage was somewhat mysterious, characterized by long periods of separation and rumors that Mrs. Benjamin sometimes looked elsewhere for love. She spent most of her married life in Paris.

A Future in Politics

Benjamin sold off his plantation and about 140 slaves in 1850. His rising political career took him to the Senate two years later. President Millard Fillmore considered appointing Benjamin to the Supreme Court, but the senator chose to stay in Congress instead. He also wrote books and was a walking encyclopedia on everything from techniques for planting sugar to the French language, his wife's native tongue. For relaxation, he regaled friends with suspenseful ghost stories and verses by his favorite poet, Lord Alfred Tennyson.

Benjamin had a knack for enraging abolitionist enemies such as Senator Ben Wade of Ohio, who disdainfully called him "an Israelite in Egyptian clothing" for defending the right to own slaves. Benjamin took what might be called a libertarian view of slavery. To him, the pro-abolitionist positions of the Republican party were violating the sacred American right of property. In one speech, he asked how the North would like it if animal-rights fanatics, believers in "the sinfulness of subjecting the animal creation to the domination and service of man," were to steal cattle and descend on farms with torches, making "the night lurid with the flames of their barns and granaries."

There is no record of Benjamin being religious, but he was quick to confront any attack on his heritage with devastating oratorical parries. "It is true that I am a Jew," he snapped back at Wade, "and when my ancestors were receiving their Ten Commandments from the immediate Deity, amidst the thunderings and lightnings of Mt. Sinai, the ancestors of my opponent were herding swine in the forests of Great Britain." Known for his attacks, he was just as well-known for the ease with which he'd patch up the injury, using courtesy and tricks such as allowing his adversary to win a round of ten-pin bowling.

The election of Abraham Lincoln and the secession of Southern states that followed it found Benjamin declaring his enemies beyond reconciliation. In an angry farewell address to the Senate on December 31, 1860, he told Northerners to wild applause, "You may carry desolation into our peaceful land, and with torch and fire you may set our cities in flames . . . but you never can subjugate us; you never can convert the free sons of the soil into vassals, paying tribute to your power. . . . Never! Never!"

The Davis Connection

When the Confederacy was formed, Jefferson Davis tapped Benjamin to be attorney general. To anyone who saw how they bickered in the Senate, their friendship seemed unlikely. Benjamin had been speaking on an army appropriations bill when Davis snidely interrupted to complain that he'd had no idea he'd have to listen to "the arguments of a paid attorney in the Senate chamber." Benjamin demanded an apology. To avert the duel that was expected in those days, Davis admitted his error and apologized on the Senate floor. From that point, the two gradually came to be close allies in the Southern cause. From attorney general, Davis moved Benjamin over to Confederate secretary of war, but he soon ran into trouble in that post. In February 1862, Roanoke Island, off the coast of North Carolina, was lost to General Ambrose Burnside's forces after the rebel government failed to send reinforcements. Benjamin scored loyalty points by shouldering responsibility. Had he been less faithful, he might have embarrassed the President by revealing the real reason for the defeat: He had no troops to send.

Benjamin couldn't continue as secretary of war under the circumstances, but he remained in the Confederate Cabinet by sliding to a new role as secretary of state. He worked hard to lure the British into the war, an effort that ultimately failed. The Confederates hoped to entice European allies with promises of cotton, but that scheme proved no more successful than another idea he promoted. In late 1864 and early 1865, Benjamin devised a desperate plan to impress the United Kingdom and shore up Southern forces by freeing the slaves—if they joined the gray army. "Let us say to every Negro who wishes to go into the ranks, 'Go and fight—you are free!'" Benjamin said, and General Robert E. Lee agreed. It was, however, a plan that came too late in the war to come to fruition.

New Country, New Life

When the South lost the war, Benjamin disguised himself and escaped to England, where he again took up his career as an attorney. Back at home, on both sides of the Mason-Dixon line, anti-Semitic conspiracy theories had sprouted to blame "Judas" Benjamin for scuttling the Confederate war effort, running off with the Southern treasury, or plotting the death of Lincoln in his capacity as Southern spy chief. For that last accusation, Benjamin and Davis both feared that Benjamin would be arrested and hanged. Later investigation and scholarship has determined that Benjamin was not involved in the Lincoln assassination.

The popular memory Benjamin left behind was captured in poet Stephen Vincent Benet's 1928 depiction of a lonely but malevolent outsider—"Seal-sleek, black-eyed, lawyer and epicure/Able, well-hated, face alive with life"—who is haunted by the question: "I am a Jew. What am I doing here?"

Benjamin died in 1884 in Paris and was buried under a headstone that read, "Phillipe Benjamin." His personal letters had been burned, leaving historians with the mystery of what it was really like to be a Jewish leader of the Confederacy.

MYTHS AND MISCONCEPTIONS

★ ★ ★ ★

There's a certain romance to the tales that have circulated in the almost 150 years since the Civil War. Many are true, but many others are laced with falsehoods.

At the risk of bursting some American history bubbles, here is a sampling of the myths swirling around the Civil War.

Myth: The Civil War was America's first disagreement over slavery.

The founders of the United States had been concerned with the ownership of slaves, particularly as it played out in the issue of states' rights, since the Articles of Confederation were ratified in 1781. A confederation, by definition, is a loose alignment of states, each with the power to self-regulate. The Southern states favored slavery, and every time the issue of states' rights emerged on the national front, the South would threaten secession.

Other landmark Congressional acts and court judgments that influenced slavery in America before the Civil War include the Three-Fifths Compromise in the Constitution, the Missouri Compromise of 1820, the Compromise of 1850, the Kansas-Nebraska Act, and the Dred Scott Decision.

Myth: The Emancipation Proclamation freed all the slaves in America.

Lincoln wrote the edict in September 1862, and it went into effect on January 1, 1863. The language of the document was clear: Any slave that was still held in the states that had seceded from the Union was "forever free" as of January 1, 1863.

Significantly, this edict did not include border states in which slaves were still held, such as Kentucky or Missouri, because

Lincoln didn't want to stoke rebellion there. As one might expect, the Southern states paid hardly any attention to the announcement by the Union president. They'd already turned their backs on him and his nation, and as far as they were concerned, the Union president held no power over them.

Myth: The Union soldiers firmly believed in the cause of freeing the slaves.

For the most part, the soldiers had little, if any, opinion on slavery. At first, many young men enlisted in the Union army as a romantic adventure. Early opinion estimated that the war would end within a few months, and many decided they could afford that much time away from their work, school, or home life.

Myth: The South's secession was the first time in American history a state tried to leave the Union.

During the War of 1812, New England almost seceded in order to protect its trade with Great Britain. In the 1850s, President James Buchanan, who held office immediately before Abraham Lincoln, stated the federal government would not resort to force in order to prevent secession. In 1869, four years after the end of the war, the Supreme Court declared the act of state secession to be unconstitutional.

Myth: The Confederate attack on Fort Sumter was the first act of Southern aggression against Northern targets.

The attack on Fort Sumter was preceded by attacks on other forts and military installations in Confederate territory. On January 9, 1861, Mississippi followed South Carolina to become the second state to secede from the Union. Within a week, Mississippi's governor ordered an armed battery placed on the bluff above the wharf at Vicksburg. His declared intention was to force Union vessels to stop to be searched—after all, it was rumored that a cannon had been sent to a Baton Rouge arsenal. Intentions aside, the fact is the battery actually fired on a number of vessels in order to make them come about, including the *Gladiator,* the *Imperial,* and the *A. O. Tyler.*

Prior to this incident, the Confederate Congress had approved the creation of a volunteer army of 100,000 soldiers—far larger than any military force that was intended strictly for keeping the peace would presumably need to be.

Myth: Abraham Lincoln wrote his Gettysburg Address on the back of an envelope while riding the train on his way to make the speech.

Lincoln would never have waited until the last minute to write such an important oration, which was part of the consecration of the Gettysburg Cemetery in November 1863. But even if he had, the train ride itself would have prevented legible writing. The 1860s-period train cars bounced, swayed, and made horseback riding seem smooth by comparison. Several drafts of the Gettysburg Address (including what is referred to as the "reading draft") have been archived at the Library of Congress and other academic institutions. They are written—very legibly—on lined paper and Executive Mansion stationery.

Myth: The "Taps" bugle call was first used by Union Captain Robert Ellicombe after Ellicombe discovered his son dead on the battlefield wearing a Confederate uniform. The son had been a music student, and the music for "Taps" was found in the boy's pocket. Captain Ellicombe had it played as tribute during his son's funeral.

There is no proof that Captain Robert Ellicombe even existed at all, and certainly there is no record of any captain by that name in the Union army during the Civil War. "Taps" actually came from Union General Daniel Butterfield, although it is not certain whether Butterfield composed the tune or adapted it from an earlier piece of music. Not happy with the existing bugle call for lights out, which the general thought was too formal, he presented his bugler, Oliver Norton, with the replacement during the summer of 1862. Although it was soon used by both Union and Confederate armies as a funeral call, it did not become an official bugle call until after the war.

A timeline of Civil War dates will appear throughout this book.

1787
September 17
The U.S. Constitution prohibits importation of slaves after January 1, 1808; requires the return of fugitive slaves to their owners; and stipulates that five slaves are equal to three white Americans for the purposes of determining representation in the House of Representatives.

1820
March
Congress enacts the Missouri Compromise: Missouri is admitted as a slave state, Maine is admitted as a free state, and slavery is banned in the remaining Louisiana Purchase territory north of 36°30'.

1844
The Methodist Church splits into Northern and Southern branches over the issue of slavery.

1845
May 10
Baptists in the South organize the Southern Baptist Convention in response to a split with Baptists in the North over the slavery issue.

1850
September 9–20
Congress adopts the Compromise of 1850, which puts off the continuing debate over slavery.

1852
March 20
Harriet Beecher Stowe's *Uncle Tom's Cabin* is published as a book.

1854
May 30
The Kansas-Nebraska Act is signed into law, repudiating the Missouri Compromise.

1856
May 22
In response to an antislavery speech by Massachusetts Senator Charles Sumner, Representative Preston Brooks of South Carolina physically attacks Sumner with a cane in the Senate chamber.

1857
March 6
The U.S. Supreme Court issues the Dred Scott decision.

1859
October 16
John Brown and his raiders attack Harpers Ferry, Virginia. Roughly 36 hours later, most will have been killed or captured.

1860
May 16–18
The Republican convention meets in Chicago and nominates Abraham Lincoln for president.

November 6
Lincoln wins election as president.

December 18
Senator John J. Crittenden of Kentucky presents his compromise for dealing with the sectional crisis.

December 20
South Carolina secedes from the Union.

(Continued on p. 67)

GOING UNDERGROUND

★ ★ ★ ★

Under cover of darkness, thousands of runaway slaves were able to enjoy a new life of freedom, thanks to a secret network called the Underground Railroad.

Tice Davids was determined to make it. He had just plunged into the Ohio River's cold waters and was swimming across, away from his life of slavery in Kentucky and toward help and freedom in Ohio. On the shore, Davids's master kept an eye trained on the slave. The slave owner quickly launched a rowboat into the river, keeping tabs on Davids's head as it bobbed in the water. Both men reached shore, but in a flash, Davids was gone. Unable to find him anywhere, the master remarked that Davids "must of gone off on an underground railroad."

Thus in 1831 a name was given to an informal system that already existed to help runaway slaves escape their masters' shackles and attain freedom. The Underground Railroad was a network of safe houses throughout the United States that helped slaves escape to free states in the North and to Canada. For some fugitives, that was just a first stop on a journey that took them in the opposite direction, ending in Mexico or the Caribbean.

Dangerous Cargo

People had been helping slaves escape for many years, but the beginning of the 19th century saw a large increase in slaves finding their way to freedom. Some blacks were able to make the trip safely using clever disguises and outright trickery. Light-skinned Ellen Craft disguised herself as a white man traveling with a black servant—in reality, her husband William. Together, they journeyed openly to freedom in the North. In another highly publicized ruse, Henry "Box" Brown escaped by packing himself in a crate and shipping it to the Philadelphia office of an antislavery campaigner.

Not everyone had the means or ingenuity to carry out such grandiose plans. The Fugitive Slave Law of 1793 allowed slave owners to recover their escaped slaves—considered their personal property—in any state, so secrecy was essential. Sympathetic whites, Native Americans, and free blacks opened their homes to the escapees, providing supplies and directions to the next safe house. The Fugitive Slave Law of 1850 included the penalty of a six-month prison sentence and $1,000 fine for anyone convicted of aiding a fugitive slave, making the work of those on the Underground Railroad even more dangerous.

All Aboard

In an effort to maintain secrecy, the route was fraught with railroad euphemisms. Safe houses were called *stations,* escaped slaves were *parcels* or *passengers,* owners of safe houses were *stationmasters,* and the people traveling with slaves to lead the way were *conductors. The Promised Land* was Canada, while even the Underground Railroad itself had its own code names: *Freedom Train* or *Gospel Train.*

One of the most famous conductors associated with the Underground Railroad was Harriet Tubman, a fugitive slave from Maryland who returned to the South 19 times to rescue others and guide them north. During her years of experience, Tubman came up with some clever tricks to improve her chances of success. She always began her northward journey on a Saturday night, because plantation owners would have to wait until Monday's newspaper to post a runaway slave notice. She carried medicine to put a crying baby to sleep. If she encountered possible slave hunters, she'd turn south for a while, knowing they would expect escaped slaves to head north.

Rolling in to the Station

Another famous figure in the Underground Railroad was Levi Coffin, a Quaker from Indiana who helped more than 3,000 slaves find their freedom. A secret bedroom on the third floor of Coffin's large brick home could securely hide runaway slaves for weeks if they needed rest to complete their northward journey. Coffin's efforts earned him the nickname "President of the Underground Railroad."

Other famous conductors and stationmasters along the railroad included newspaper editor and prominent abolitionist William Lloyd Garrison and feminist Susan B. Anthony. William Still, a black civil rights activist, helped as many as 60 slaves a month reach safety. He carefully recorded personal information and biographies for each fugitive he harbored, information that he later published in his book *The Underground Rail Road Records.* During one interview with a fugitive slave, Still discovered the escapee was his own brother, Peter Still, from whom he had been separated in childhood.

Much Remains Hidden

Historians may never fully know all of the secrets of the Underground Railroad. In 2002, archaeologists in Lancaster, Pennsylvania, discovered a secret hiding place for runaway slaves on the property of Thaddeus Stevens, a Radical Republican who served five terms in the House of Representative, becoming a significant power broker and one the era's most important politicians.

Although the journey was incredibly dangerous, it was well worth it to the many who escaped slavery and oppression. Through the combined efforts of these brave souls, an estimated 75,000 blacks escaped to a new life of freedom.

- *The Confederacy consisted of 11 states and had a population of 9 million, which broke down to about 5.5 million whites and 3.5 million slaves.*

- *Without the states that seceded, the Union was made up of 25 states (including the border states of Missouri, Kentucky, Maryland, Delaware, and later West Virginia) and various organized territories in the West. It had a population of 22 million.*

BEING QUIRKY DIDN'T MEAN BEING UNFIT FOR COMMAND

★ ★ ★ ★

*From nervous ticks to unrelenting ambition, a few
Union and Confederate officers stood out among
the ranks—but not always in a good way.*

George Armstrong Custer

Army: Union

Major Battles: Chancellorsville, Brandy Station, Gettysburg

Eccentricities: George Armstrong Custer had a love for flamboyant uniforms and possessed a blind, unrelenting ambition that often led him to take risks. When promoted to brigadier general, Custer took the opportunity to outfit himself in an extravagant ensemble that included a black velveteen vest, sharply polished boots (which he never let get dirty), and a crisp, white shirt edged with silver trim and stars. His hair was expertly coiffed, and he often used perfumed oils and colognes to overpower the stench of the battlefield. He wanted to appear as a noble, romantic figure, and he cultivated friendships with journalists in an effort to create a positive public image. His lasting renown was ultimately achieved after the Civil War for being on the wrong side of the fighting at Little Big Horn.

James Ewell Brown "Jeb" Stuart

Army: Confederate

Major Battles: Fredericksburg, Gettysburg, The Wilderness

Eccentricities: Custer's Southern cavalry counterpart, Jeb Stuart, was no less ostentatious, also outfitting himself with a spectacularly fancy uniform that was anything but inconspicuous. Astride his horse on scouting missions, he wore a long gray cape with a red lining flowing behind him, and his hat was adorned with a large peacock feather. In his regiment, he had a personal banjo player named Sam

Sweeney who traveled with him to sing a song called "Jine the Cavalry" that detailed Stuart's daring victories. Like Custer, Stuart used colognes and was concerned with his public image. So focused was he on his wardrobe, that when he lost his cape to Union troops in 1862, he demanded revenge. He and his troops returned to confront the forces of General John Pope, not only overrunning them with ease but also capturing Pope's entire uniform in the process.

Alfred Pleasonton

Army: Union

Major Battles: Antietam, Chancellorsville, Brandy Station

Eccentricities: Alfred Pleasonton is the man who taught Custer everything he knew about flashy uniforms and shameless self-promotion. In the 1830s, his father had been involved in U.S. Treasury scandals and was fired from his job, leaving the family in shame. The younger Pleasonton was determined to overcome that reputation, but his antics and ambition instead alienated nearly everyone he met. He constantly exaggerated his role in battle. Wounded at Antietam, he argued that his division had turned the tide of the battle and he should be promoted to major general. This wasn't true, but he made such a fuss that his superiors gave in and upped his rank (though not as high as he'd wanted). At Chancellorsville, he claimed to have personally stopped Stonewall Jackson's advance—again, he hadn't, but it was enough to secure his promotion to major general. When confronted with failures, Pleasonton refused to accept responsibility.

John Bell Hood

Army: Confederate

Major Battles: Seven Days Battles, Antietam, Chickamauga, Gettysburg

Eccentricities: General John Bell Hood was perhaps the most resilient soldier of the American Civil War. At Gettysburg, he was severely wounded and lost the use of his left arm for the rest of his life. He soldiered on, however, only to have his leg amputated at Chickamauga, surviving to the surprise of his doctors. Most people would have called it quits at that point, but not Hood. He returned to duty just months later, commanding troops in the Army of Tennessee. To work around his disabilities, he strapped himself into his saddle on his horse and put on a specially designed French cork leg to dismount. Though his post-injury career was not very successful, he never stopped fighting and was on his way to Texas to raise another army before being apprehended on May 31, 1865. Once the war was over, he returned to civilian life, married, and fathered 11 children. He died of yellow fever in 1879.

Dan Sickles

Army: Union

Major Battles: Seven Pines, Chancellorsville, Gettysburg

Eccentricities: When General Dan Sickles took a cannonball to the leg at Gettysburg, he refused to drop his composure, instead trying to improve his troops' morale by smiling broadly and chomping on his lit cigar as the doctors amputated it. Once his mangled leg was removed, he donated it to the Army Medical Museum in Washington, D.C., where he often visited it after the war. It's still on display, now at the National Museum of Health and Medicine.

Richard Ewell

Army: Confederate

Major Battles: Gettysburg, Spotsylvania Court House

Eccentricities: General Richard Ewell was convinced he had digestive problems and would only eat boiled wheat with a dash of sugar. He was also besieged by nervous fits—his discomfort was so pronounced that he could not sleep in a bed and spent most nights restlessly leaning against a camp stool. Standing five-foot-eight with a bald head and a rather distracting lisp, Ewell was not sure he was cut out to be a general and openly questioned his selection to the rank.

UNDERESTIMATING THE WAR

★ ★ ★ ★

*As America started to divide, most people believed
the war would be a simple, short-lived skirmish.*

Before fighting began, many throughout the North anticipated a
quick Union victory. Shortly before blue-clad Federals marched
from the outskirts of Washington to meet the rebels outside of
Manassas Junction, Virginia, publisher Horace Greeley's *New York
Tribune* had published the following notice: "Forward to Rich-
mond! Forward to Richmond! Forward to Richmond! The Rebel
Congress must not be allowed to meet there on the 20th of July.
By That Date the Place Must be Held by the National Army!"

Excitement over this opening match at the First Battle of Bull Run
quickly dissipated, however, as the vanquished Union army fled
from the battlefield in panic. Greeley, whose paper helped to push
the North into battle, wrote the following in a letter to Lincoln:
"On every brow sits sullen, scorching, black despair.... If it is best
for the country and for mankind that we make peace with the rebels
at once, and on their own terms, do not shrink even from that."

Thimbles and Handkerchiefs

As states began seceding from the Union, many in the South also
felt the war would be quick and virtually bloodless. Some Southerners assumed the conflict would end with their victory at the
First Battle of Bull Run, and once they saw the Northern troops
fleeing, many thought the war was over. Confederate supporter
Edmund Ruffin saw in "this hard-fought battle virtually the close
of the war."

General William Sherman, who had been the superintendent at a
college in Louisiana before the war, wrote about the time in his
memoirs: "In the South, the people were earnest, fierce and angry,
and were evidently organizing for action; whereas, in Illinois,
Indiana, and Ohio, I saw not the least sign of preparation. It cer-

tainly looked to me as though the people of the North would tamely submit to a disruption of the Union, and the orators of the South used, openly and constantly, the expressions that there would be no war, and that a lady's thimble would hold all the blood to be shed." James Chesnut, husband of diarist Mary Chesnut, suggested that so little blood would be shed over secession that he could drink it all. Lucius Lamar, who wrote the bill of secession for Mississippi, made the same offer.

As the number of states joining the Confederacy increased, Leroy Pope Walker, the Confederate secretary of war, had a hard time generating enthusiasm for war preparation. The most common sentiment he encountered was that war could be avoided or, if fought, would end quickly, so there was no need to get ready for a long struggle. "At that time," Walker later wrote, "I, like everybody else, believed there would be no war. In fact, I had gone about the state advising people to secede, and promising to wipe with my pocket-handkerchief all the blood that would be shed."

The Confederate attack on Fort Sumter galvanized the North in its resolve to defeat the Confederates and forcibly bring them back into the Union. Most Northerners saw the initial defeat at Bull Run as a temporary setback. Lincoln ignored the calls for peace—the dismal battle strengthened his resolve to win the war. It didn't take very long before Southerners realized that thimbles and handkerchiefs wouldn't come close to mopping up the blood yet to be spilled.

- *Nearly half of Union soldiers were farmers before the war.*

- *As postwar president of what was then Washington College in Lexington, Virginia, Robert E. Lee innovated the first classes in business and journalism.*

- *William Tecumseh Sherman, named for a Shawnee Indian chieftain, was known to relatives and intimates as "Cump."*

THE UNION STATES

California
Connecticut
Delaware
Illinois
Indiana
Iowa
Kansas
Kentucky
Maine
Maryland
Massachusetts
Michigan
Minnesota

Missouri
Nevada (1864)
New Hampshire
New Jersey
New York
Ohio
Oregon
Pennsylvania
Rhode Island
Vermont
West Virginia (1863)
Wisconsin

THE CONFEDERATE STATES

State	Date of Secession
South Carolina	December 20, 1860
Mississippi	January 9, 1861
Florida	January 10, 1861
Alabama	January 11, 1861
Georgia	January 19, 1861
Louisiana	January 26, 1861
Texas	February 1, 1861
Virginia	April 17, 1861
Arkansas	May 6, 1861
North Carolina	May 20, 1861
Tennessee	June 8, 1861

SO THEY SAID

★ ★ ★ ★

"'A house divided against itself cannot stand.' I believe this government cannot endure, permanently, half slave and half free. I do not expect the Union to be dissolved; I do not expect the house to fall; but I do expect it will cease to be divided. It will become all one thing, or all the other. Either the opponents of slavery will arrest the further spread of it and place it where the public mind shall rest in the belief that it is in the course of ultimate extinction, or its advocates will push it forward till it shall become alike lawful in all the states, old as well as new, North as well as South."

Abraham Lincoln, June 16, 1858, address to the Illinois Republican Convention

"Let me tell you what is coming. After the sacrifice of countless millions of treasure and hundreds of thousands of lives you may win Southern independence, but I doubt it. The North is determined to preserve this Union. They are not a fiery, impulsive people as you are, for they live in colder climates. But when they begin to move in a given direction, they move with the steady momentum and perseverance of a mighty avalanche."

Sam Houston, Governor of Texas

"I can anticipate no greater calamity for the country than the dissolution of the Union. It would be an accumulation of all the evils we complain of, and I am willing to sacrifice everything but honor for its preservation."

Colonel Robert E. Lee, U.S. Army, in a letter to his son Custis, January 23, 1861

IT'S NOT ALWAYS EASY TO GET THE GLORY

★ ★ ★ ★

The most famous black regiment in the Civil War overcame incredible struggles to emerge as an indispensable link in the Union's success.

The 54th Massachusetts Infantry wasn't the first black regiment of the Civil War, and it certainly wouldn't be the last. But this regiment became the most celebrated, its fame enduring for more than a century after the last shots were fired.

Former slaves had been enlisted in military units in South Carolina, Louisiana, and Kansas before the 54th was organized, but Massachusetts Governor John Andrew fought for a different approach. Receiving permission from the War Department in early 1863, he asked fiery abolitionists such as Frederick Douglass and Sojourner Truth to recruit free Northern blacks into a showcase fighting unit. They took the charge seriously, recruiting two of Douglass's sons and Truth's grandson. The 54th Massachusetts Infantry was soon born.

Fighting More than Just the Enemy

The first foe these soldiers faced was racism. Though well trained, the thousand-strong regiment was taunted and paid less money than were white soldiers. The 54th's white commander, Colonel Robert Gould Shaw, ardently believed in his men, but many other people did not. In the North, there was prevailing doubt blacks could prove their mettle on the battlefield. In the South, meanwhile, politicians and commanders vowed that they wouldn't treat captured blacks as legitimate prisoners.

The 54th undertook its first significant military action on July 18—a frontal assault of Fort Wagner, the heavily defended sand fort at the mouth of South Carolina's Charleston Harbor. Running down a narrow causeway of sand right into a blitz of fire from Confederate guns, the troops seized the Wagner parapet and held it for an hour before being brutally pushed back.

A Moral Victory

The poorly conceived mission—ordered by white generals—was a complete disaster. The 54th lost more than a third of its troops, including Colonel Shaw. But in one of the largest ironies of the war, this military defeat ended up being a tremendous political victory for the regiment. The press and public sympathized with its heavy losses and recognized its daring heroism in what was essentially a suicide attack. The *New York Tribune* wrote that the battle "made Fort Wagner such a name to the colored race as Bunker Hill had been for ninety years to the white Yankees."

The Northern public, recognizing the courage of the 54th's valiant effort in the face of overwhelming odds, came to view the idea of black soldiers in a more positive light and appeared to show greater support for emancipation in general. Moreover, the acclaim given the 54th may have played a role in sparking widespread black enlistment in the Union army. By the following year, there would be almost 200,000 black troops, a number that became a crucial part of the Northern war effort.

The 54th's military exploits didn't end in the Carolina sand. In 1864, it covered retreating Union forces in the Battle of Olustee, Florida. Had the 54th faltered, the Federals could have been decimated.

The regiment was remembered—and honored—for years afterward. In 1900, 54th veteran Sergeant William H. Carney was awarded a Medal of Honor for his courageous act of keeping the Union flag aloft during the firestorm at Fort Wagner. Eighty-nine years later, Hollywood produced *Glory*, a major motion picture that profiled the 54th and portrayed the heartbreaking and heroic battles it fought and survived.

SARAH EMMA EDMONDS (AKA FRANK THOMPSON)

★ ★ ★ ★

This patriotic and devoted woman was determined to fight for her country—even if it meant posing as a man.

During the Civil War, women, their hearts full of worry and sorrow, watched their husbands, brothers, and sons march away to the battlefield. While such emotional partings were difficult, some women also felt deep regret that they couldn't suit up to defend their country as well. The life of the average woman in the 1860s was one of restrictions and clearly defined gender roles: They were to maintain the home and raise the children. Joining the military certainly was not an option. Still, as many as 400 women snuck into brigades from both North and South by posing as male soldiers. Some successfully maintained their disguise, while others were discovered and discharged for "sexual incompatibility." These female soldiers were trailblazers who put their lives on the line for their beliefs.

Sarah Emma Edmonds, born in 1841, believed that everyone should have the chance to fight for freedom and liberty—no matter what their gender. By age 17, she had already proven herself bold and willing to buck convention, fleeing her home in New Brunswick, Canada, to escape her overbearing father. She stole away in the night to create a new, unencumbered life for herself in the United States, settling in Flint, Michigan.

Starting Over

Edmonds knew that if she was going to experience the world in the way she wished, she'd have to reinvent herself entirely. As a woman, she could never fulfill her dreams of adventure—too many doors were closed to her on the basis of gender. But she believed those doors would open if she could become a man. Discarding the identity of Sarah Emma Edmonds, she became Franklin Thompson, a book salesman. Dressed as a man and acting with assertiveness and confidence, she was soon able to support herself independently. Edmonds saw America as a land of unlimited potential, and she was determined to make the most of it.

When war broke out, Edmonds saw another opportunity to prove her mettle and joined up with a Michigan infantry as a male nurse and courier. "I am naturally fond of adventure," she later explained, "a little ambitious and a good deal romantic and this together with my devotion to the Federal cause and determination to assist to the utmost of my ability in crushing the rebellion, made me forget the unpleasant items."

Upping the Ante

Posing as Franklin Thompson, Edmonds blended in with the men of her unit, served admirably, and aroused no suspicions during her tour of duty. Since her disguise seemed to be working so well, she volunteered to spy for General George McClellan at the start of the Peninsula Campaign. Edmonds continued to be effective in her use of disguises. She infiltrated the Confederates at Yorktown as a black slave by darkening her skin with silver nitrate and wearing a wig. After several days there, she returned to McClellan and shared the information she had gained. Edmonds's next assignment found her portraying a heavyset Irish woman named Bridget O'Shea. As O'Shea, she crossed enemy lines, peddled her wares, and returned with an earful of Confederate secrets. In August 1862, Edmonds assumed the guise of a black laundress in a Confederate camp. One day, while washing an officer's jacket, she found a large packet of official papers. After giving the jacket a thorough "dry cleaning," Edmonds returned to Union camp with the packet.

The Game's Up

All this time, army officials continued to believe Edmonds was Franklin Thompson. In the spring of 1863, she contracted malaria. She knew that she couldn't visit an army hospital for fear of being found out as a woman. She reluctantly slipped away to Cairo, Illinois, and checked into a private hospital. Although Edmonds had planned to return to her previous duty after her recovery, she discovered that during her sickness her alias, Private Thompson, had been pegged as a deserter. Edmonds couldn't reassume that identity without facing the consequences, and so she remained dressed as a woman and served as a nurse to soldiers in Washington, D.C.

After the Fighting Stopped

Two years after the Civil War ended, she married Linus Seelye, a fellow Canadian expatriate. The couple eventually settled down in Cleveland, Ohio. Determined that the world know her story and see that a woman could fight just as well as a man, she wrote the best-selling *Nurse and Spy in the Union Army,* which exposed her gender-bending ways. She also fought hard for her alter ego, petitioning the War Department to expunge Frank Thompson's listing as a deserter. Following a War Department review of the case, Congress granted her service credit and a veteran's pension of $12 a month in 1884. She died five years later and was buried in the military section of a Houston cemetery.

- *Military unit patches were not authorized by the U.S. Army for general use until 1918, but in 1862 General Philip Kearney ordered badges made of square pieces of cloth be worn on caps. General Joseph Hooker took it further by assigning different colors to the divisions within each corps. The 24th Corps wore heart-shape patches similar to what the unit wears today.*

- *Lincoln had Congressman Clement Vallandigham, a leading Copperhead, arrested, tried for treason, and thrown into a military prison for his antiwar activities, which included encouraging soldiers to desert and to avoid conscription. He was arrested during his campaign for the Ohio governorship. Lincoln changed the prison sentence to banishment behind Confederate lines after other politicians protested on Vallandigham's behalf.*

NO SPEED TO SECEDE

★ ★ ★ ★

Not every state that ultimately joined the Confederacy was in a rush to leave the Union.

The various states of the Confederacy didn't all secede from the Union at the same time, of course. A number of them even had considerable debate over whether to secede at all. So while seven Southern states—South Carolina, Mississippi, Florida, Alabama, Georgia, Louisiana, and Texas—opted to leave the Union within a period of less than a month and a half, four others—Virginia, Arkansas, North Carolina, and Tennessee—held out for longer than that.

To be truthful, support for secession was not unanimous in any of the Southern states, and significant numbers of Southern men fought for the federal cause. Much of the dissent within individual states was between the residents of different geographical regions that—like the North and South in general—differed from each other economically and culturally.

The Stragglers Secede

Virginia was the first of the second wave of states to secede, doing so on April 17, 1861. This was in reaction to President Lincoln ordering the state to deploy its militia against the rebels who had attacked Fort Sumter in South Carolina. Soon after Virginia joined the Confederacy, Richmond replaced Montgomery, Alabama, as the capital of the Confederate States of America. Despite this honor, however, Virginia was so divided between pro- and anti-Union tendencies that its westernmost regions counter-seceded from the state and were admitted to the United States as a brand new state, West Virginia, in 1863. So in addition to being ravaged by the war—more major battles were fought on its soil than on that of any other state—Virginia also permanently lost some of its territory and about 400,000 of its citizens before the fighting had finished.

Arkansas was also strongly divided between those loyal to the Union and those favoring secession. The eastern and southern parts of the state were controlled by cotton planters—whose plantations were farmed by the state's 111,000 slaves—and they opted for secession, while the northern and western portions were dominated by small farmers who opposed it. In March 1861, the state legislature voted to remain within the Union, a decision that was reversed amid much dissension on May 6, 1861, when it voted to secede. Some 13,000 of the state's residents, many black, subsequently served in the Union forces.

North Carolina was a relatively progressive, prosperous state that by 1861 was making advances in education, tax reform, transportation, and women's rights, but its economy was based largely on agriculture and slave-supported tobacco plantations. Pro-Union sentiment stalled secession, but on May 20, 1861, North Carolina nonetheless became the tenth state to leave the Union.

The Last State to Go

Tennessee also had its regional differences. It was torn by almost unanimous support for the Confederacy in its slaveholding middle and western areas but equally fervent support for the Union in its east. The Tennessee legislature ultimately voted to secede on June 8, 1861. More than 31,000 of its residents showed their loyalty to the Union, however, by fighting for it, and Tennessee was wrecked by the conflict, seeing more battles fought on its soil than any state other than Virginia. Even though the state seceded, one of its senators, Andrew Johnson, refused to withdraw from the Senate. He continued to represent the people of his state, even though they had abandoned him, until Lincoln made him military governor of occupied Tennessee in 1862.

- *The C.S.A. Furlough and Bounty Act of 1861 awarded a soldier a $50 bounty ($1,000 in today's money) in Confederate currency and a 60-day furlough at the time of his choosing for a three-year enlistment.*

IN GRANT'S SHADOW

★ ★ ★ ★

*General George Meade was the victor of Gettysburg.
No hero with the newspapers, however, he was easily
eclipsed by his superior officer.*

The fifth man to lead the most important Union army in the East, General George Gordon Meade is regarded by many to have been one of the finest Union generals of the Civil War. But Meade was certainly not subject to universal praise. Why? One reason is that, like many generals, he didn't trust journalists, and those journalists took revenge by writing little about him. He also may have been in the wrong place at the wrong time.

Meade graduated from West Point in 1835. He served in the Mexican War and the Second Seminole War, and he was a captain in the topographical engineer corps when the Civil War broke out. Completing a survey of the Great Lakes at the time, he was immediately given a position as a brigadier general in the Pennsylvania Reserves. This unit joined the Army of the Potomac after training and fought in battles at Beaver Dam Creek and Gaines' Mill.

General Meade was severely wounded in a battle at Glendale, Virginia, in June 1862. However, he recovered soon enough to lead his troops into the Second Battle of Bull Run and at Antietam. He served well in those conflicts and was promoted to major general. More success eventually led him to be named commander of the Army of the Potomac after Joseph Hooker resigned. That appointment came just three days before the Battle of Gettysburg, the largest confrontation of the war, so he had little time to prepare. Nevertheless, he masterfully commanded his forces to a major victory that turned the tide for the Union.

Yet Meade never got the attention he deserved. Journalists and the newspapers and magazines they wrote for played a dominant role in how events and people are remembered. This fact caused Meade to be suspicious of them, and he could be cruel to journalists who crossed his path—many of whom traveled with the troops to report on the war. He once even forced a newspaper reporter to leave camp riding backwards on a mule. Major Northern newspapers retaliated by only mentioning Meade's name in articles about defeats.

Although Meade remained in command of the Army of the Potomac through the end of the war, he faded into the background when General Grant came from the Western Theater to become General-in-Chief of all armies. Grant organized his own headquarters with the Army of the Potomac, which resulted in the spotlight passing from Meade to Grant. The war ended with Meade as a mere footnote to the more charismatic General Grant.

Fortunately, Grant himself appreciated Meade's abilities, and he gladly helped advance Meade's career. After the war Meade remained in the Army and commanded Southern reconstruction projects. He died in Philadelphia in 1872.

- *Later famous as the Drummer Boy of Chickamauga, nine-year-old Johnny Clem was one of the youngest Union army soldiers. He ran away from home and tried to join an Ohio regiment, but they rejected him as too young. He then tried to join the 22nd Michigan, which also rejected him, but he tagged along and served as a drummer and was allowed to enlist two years later. In 1864, he was discharged at the age of 13. In 1871 Clem rejoined the regular Army and remained in its service until 1915, retiring as a brigadier general. He is buried at Arlington Cemetery.*

SHE HAD THE PRESIDENT'S EAR

★ ★ ★ ★

Ambition turned into pestering and disappointment
for one woman of the Civil War era.

To hear her tell it, Anna Ella Carroll—pamphleteer, feminist, and gadfly—saved the Union. She had the ear of Abraham Lincoln himself, and she formulated the strategy that was to cut the Confederacy in two. To hear her tell it.

Carroll came from a blue-blooded, slaveholding Maryland family of great economic and political power. Her father, Thomas King Carroll, had been the governor of Maryland when she was a teenager. Anna Carroll had an active mind, did not lack for ambition, and was not content to sit at home in luxury. At an early age, she threw herself into controversial politics, becoming a propagandist for the American party, or as it was more commonly known, the Know-Nothing party. Then Republican Abraham Lincoln was elected president.

Despite coming from a slave state, Carroll became a Union apostle. She freed her own slaves and began writing pamphlets in support of the Lincoln administration. The President appreciated this and wrote to her about one of her pamphlets, "Like everything else that comes from you I have read...[it] with a great deal of pleasure and interest." Anna Carroll seemed to be rising in the world.

By the 19th century, women were just beginning to find their power in society. Florence Nightingale had revolutionized the medical treatment of soldiers in Europe, and Harriet Beecher Stowe's *Uncle Tom's Cabin* had likely turned many more people against slavery than any speech ever had. Tapping into this sense of possibility, Carroll aspired to her own role on the political stage. She first proposed that Lincoln send her to Europe to carry out a

U.S. propaganda campaign, which she predicted would cost the Union $50,000—a colossal sum in those days. Not surprisingly, the President decided against it.

Carroll continued writing pamphlets about the Union cause and bombarding the White House with offers of her services. Finally, perhaps to get her away from Washington for a while, Lincoln sent her out west with an army escort to record her observations about any strategic opportunities ready to be exploited. Or, so she told it later.

While traveling in the West, she had a revelation: The Union should attack the Confederacy along the twin gateways of the Cumberland and the Tennessee Rivers. Such a strategy would guard the flank of the military thrust down the Mississippi River and effectively split the Confederacy in two. This, of course, is precisely what the Union did, and Anna Carroll wrote a letter to the President claiming credit for the idea. Judging from previous behavior, she may even have sent a bill for services rendered.

The Lincoln administration resisted her claim. One argument against it is the fact that both the Union and the Confederacy were well aware of the possibilities of such a strategy. The Union navy had been sending gunboats up those rivers since the beginning of the war to keep an eye on the fortifications Confederates were building at Fort Henry and Fort Donelson. Anyone who could read a map could see that these rivers were highways of advance and supply into the South. Further, by the time Carroll wrote her letter, planning for the Union Tennessee Campaign that involved this strategy had been underway for months.

The war ended in 1865, but Carroll kept pressing her case for years afterward. As late as 1890, she was still suing Congress for what she believed was her just compensation—and she was still getting turned down. Although early feminist writers took up her cause, her claims have never been validated. Few if any of today's serious historians believe that Anna Ella Carroll's assertions about her contribution to the war effort were rooted in anything but her own self-aggrandizement.

LINCOLN'S NEPTUNE

★ ★ ★ ★

*As secretary of the Navy and a devoted diarist, Gideon Welles had
a reputation as the most effective member of Lincoln's Cabinet.*

To get an accurate picture of what life was like in the 19th century,
historians often look to the media of the time, examining newspapers and speeches. But to truly get an insider's view on how a
person felt about the state of the world—or the state of his or her
own personal life—historians turn to people's diaries. One faithful
diarist was Gideon Welles, U.S. secretary of the Navy from 1861 to
1869. His diary was published in 1911, and it provided readers
with an important view of Lincoln and his Cabinet throughout the
Civil War.

On the Rise

Before the Civil War, Gideon Welles had worked as a lawyer, later
becoming the founder and editor of two Connecticut newspapers,
the *Hartford Times* and the *Hartford Evening Press*. It was there
that he expressed his support for Lincoln.

As the war started, the U.S. Navy was in disarray. Many of its
officers had resigned to join the Southern cause, and it had fewer
than 100 ships—only 12 of which were available, as the rest were
on missions. Assembling an effective fighting force would be a
major task for anyone. Although Welles had no experience in naval
affairs, he made up for that fact by focusing on administration,
working closely with his aides and officers to increase the Navy's
power exponentially.

A Resemblance to Neptune

Journalist Noah Brooks described Welles as a "kind-hearted,
affable and accessible man. He is tall, shapely, precise, sensitive to
ridicule, and accommodating to the members of the press, from
which stand-point I am making all of these sketches." Not everyone found him genial, however; Welles often gave the impression

of being a curmudgeonly old man. Lincoln called him his "Neptune," after the surly Roman god of the sea—if nothing else, his long white beard made him look the part. The New Englander found it difficult to befriend his fellow Cabinet members. He was extremely outspoken in his dislike of everything British and in his conservative beliefs, which placed him at odds with fellow department heads William Seward, Salmon P. Chase, and Edwin M. Stanton.

Expanding the Navy

What was important to Welles was the work that he did. By 1865, the Navy had increased tenfold. Under Welles's watch, the United States had pioneered ironclad ships and had begun to gain a significant presence around the world. He was very consistent in his faithfulness to Lincoln, and he was quite sympathetic in the portrayal of the President in his diary. This attribute was never more evident than in his description of Lincoln's final hours.

On the evening of April 14, 1865, Welles was awakened and informed the President had been shot. He arrived at the house across from Ford's Theatre where the fallen President had been taken. "The giant sufferer lay extended diagonally across the bed, which was not long enough for him," Welles later wrote. "He had been stripped of his clothes. His large arms, which were occasionally exposed, were of a size which one would scarce have expected from his spare appearance. His slow, full respiration lifted the clothes with each breath that he took."

Welles remained at his post through the administration of Andrew Johnson. He wrote several books, including *Lincoln and Seward,* a study of the President and his secretary of state, prior to his death in 1878. At three volumes, *The Diary of Gideon Welles* was published posthumously in 1911, an invaluable insight into the personalities of the Civil War.

UNDERCOVER RAIDS

★ ★ ★ ★

*A few clever Confederate operatives attempted raids along
the Union's northern border or far behind enemy lines.
Some succeeded, and some didn't, but all went down
in history for their daring efforts.*

Island Dwellers

The Union housed Confederate soldiers and generals in several
island prisoner-of-war camps. Such locations were remote, difficult to reach, and disconnected from any methods of easy access—
ideal conditions if the purpose is to prevent prisoner escapes.
Johnson's Island in Ohio was extremely secluded in the middle of
Lake Erie. Many considered it an inescapable prison. The Confederate army, however, saw an opportunity. Hundreds of Southern soldiers and officers occupied the stockade on the island. If a
small force could sneak through the lines and free these prisoners,
the Confederacy would suddenly have a significant military presence deep within Union territory and the possibility of creating a
new front to the war.

Since it was far from the front lines of battle, Lake Erie was
guarded by only one major gunboat, the USS *Michigan.* Confederate Captains Charles Cole and John Beall came up with a plan to
commandeer the *Michigan,* which would allow them to take control of the lake without opposition. If they could achieve that, they
assumed the guards at Johnson's Island would quickly surrender.
Beall commandeered the *Philo Parsons,* a Lake Erie steamer, and
prepared an attack on the *Michigan.* He was waiting for a signal
from Cole, who'd made his way onto the ship. That signal never
came, however, because Cole was found out and captured by the
Michigan crew. Beall's *Parsons* crew, on the other hand, quickly
became concerned when the signal failed to appear and forced
Beall to take them to safety in Canada on the other side of the
lake, aborting the mission.

Charles Cole did ultimately reach Johnson's Island. He was imprisoned there for the rest of the war. Beall was later caught and executed, and any thoughts of forming an army of prisoners died with him.

An Unsuspecting Town

Believe it or not, the planned assault on Johnson's Island was not the most outlandish border raid of the Civil War. That honor is perhaps held by a group of Southerners who trekked all the way to the quiet town of St. Albans, Vermont, looking to make their mark. It was 1864, and the South was getting more and more desperate. Lieutenant Bennett Young, a brash rebel solider, was stationed in Canada and had been put in charge of formulating secret sabotage missions into Union territory. On October 19, 1864, he finally put his plans into action.

Young gathered 20 conspirators and silently slipped across the border and into St. Albans. He broke the relatively calm mood of the town by pulling a .38-caliber revolver from his coat and declaring they were taking possession of the town for the Confederate States of America. Initially, many St. Albanians didn't take the situation seriously, assuming that Young was drunk. They watched, bemused, as he and his crew robbed the town's bank and attempted to burn down buildings with crude incendiary bombs (not a single one of which worked). All in all, the attack lasted 20 minutes, although it did claim one life, that of Elinius Morrison, who attempted to confront the gang.

With more than $200,000 dollars—a large fortune in those days—Young and his followers slipped back across the border into Canada, where they were protected from prosecution by friends and supporters. After handing the money over to a Confederate agent who turned around and smuggled it back out of the country and into the South, Young was banned from entering the United States until 1868. He took advantage of the time to study law in Europe. When he was permitted to return home, he became a well-respected attorney in Kentucky and a minor celebrity with his fellow former rebels.

Confederates in the Big City

In the fall of 1864, the Confederacy began to hatch another assault on the Deep North, this time in the populous and important city of New York. Again, the plot involved an elaborate setup. Coded messages were published in the *Richmond Whig*, a Virginia newspaper, and secretly reprinted in many New York papers. These messages were placed by Confederate agents in Canada, who, like Bennett Young, had been ordered by President Davis to undertake secret espionage missions. One agent implicated in planning the New York assault was Jacob Thompson, a former House representative for Mississippi and U.S. secretary of the interior turned provocateur. The plan was to set a number of large fires in order to incite chaos in the city and ultimately capture it. Like the Johnson's Island raid, the New York plotters hoped to free prisoners of war from local camps and use them to sack the city.

The hotels were to be set ablaze by Confederate agents who checked in, lit their rooms on fire, and left, locking the door behind them. They actually succeeded in starting small fires in all the major hotels of New York City, as well as in P. T. Barnum's American Museum, but the flames were quickly put out by the city's experienced fire department and did not have the effect they desired. In the end, the Confederates escaped the city under cover of darkness. Only one, Robert Cobb Kennedy, was ultimately captured. He refused to sell out his coconspirators and went to the gallows by himself in March 1865.

"The dead of the battle-field come up to us very rarely, even in dreams. We see the list in the morning paper at breakfast, but dismiss its recollection with the coffee.... Mr. Brady has done something to bring us the terrible reality and earnestness of the War. If he has not brought bodies and laid them in our door-yards and along streets, he has done something very like it."
The New York Times, *on Mathew Brady's photo exhibit of Antietam battlefield dead*

Fast Facts

- *Tennessee was the last of 11 states to secede from the Union in 1861 but the first state to be readmitted when it rejoined in July 1866.*

- *The only American Indian nations that took an active part in the Civil War were the Cherokee, Creek, Choctaw, Chickasaw, and Seminole.*

- *General Henry Heth graduated dead last in his West Point class. During the Confederate Pennsylvania Campaign, he commanded a division in General A. P. Hill's corps. General Lee had ordered Hill to avoid any sort of engagement with the enemy before he could assemble his full army, but Henry Heth made history by accidentally starting the Battle of Gettysburg. He sent two brigades ahead on reconnaissance, and they encountered and engaged Union troops.*

- *Because of heavy casualties, Civil War soldiers devised a sort of makeshift "dog tag" before going into battle. The tags were handkerchiefs or pieces of paper with the soldiers' names and addresses on them. They were pinned to the soldiers' uniforms to ease identification if they didn't survive the battle.*

- *Prior to her rebuilding as an ironclad, the CSS Virginia was known as the USS Merrimack. The ship was named for the Merrimack River, but its name is often misspelled when people leave off the k.*

- *No effort was made to standardize the uniforms of Union troops until after the First Battle of Bull Run.*

- *In July 1862, David Glasgow Farragut was promoted to rear admiral, the first officer to hold that rank in the history of the U.S. Navy.*

A PLEASANT AFTERNOON RELAXING AND WATCHING THE WAR

★ ★ ★ ★

A picnic can be pleasant, but Washington, D.C., residents got more than they expected at the First Battle of Bull Run.

Some called it a "picnic battle." The First Battle of Bull Run was supposed to be a walk in the park for Union forces. They were to put down the Confederate rebellion in a quick effort and then march back to Washington as heroes.

The Union soldiers were green, mostly fresh volunteers who signed on after the Confederates captured Fort Sumter. These men had joined up for 90 days of army duty, which almost everyone assumed would be plenty of time to take care of the pesky rebels. Some signed up because they figured this would be the only battle of the war, and they didn't want to miss the excitement.

They were led by General Irvin McDowell. McDowell, a West Point graduate and veteran of the Mexican War, was less sanguine. He knew his 30,000 soldiers were not a real army. He'd had minimal time to train them, they were not particularly well equipped, and there was virtually no military experience among them or their line officers.

Keep It Quick

But the politicians in Washington wanted a quick end to the Southern uprising, so they urged McDowell to march his troops to meet the growing Confederate army near Manassas, a railroad junction in Virginia just 30 miles from Washington. McDowell fretted, but knew he had to follow orders.

On July 16, 1861, he marched his force out of Washington. The soldiers were having a grand time. "They stopped every moment to pick blackberries or get water," McDowell later wrote. "They would not keep in the ranks." Another witness recalled "the waving banners, the inspiring strains of the numerous bands, the shouts and songs of the men."

Washingtonians didn't want to miss the excitement of the battle either, so many of them followed the troops on horseback or in buggies, loaded down with picnic baskets. "I noticed about twenty barouches and carriages," recalled a Massachusetts soldier, "that contained members of Congress and their friends."

The Opposition

The new Confederate army forming in Manassas was no better trained than the Union army. They were Southern farm boys who also heard the call of war after Fort Sumter and charged into the fray. They were led by General Pierre G. T. Beauregard, who, like McDowell, was a West Point grad and Mexican War veteran. Nearby was the Army of the Shenandoah, led by General Joseph Johnston. Together they had about the same number of troops as McDowell.

It took a couple of days for McDowell's troops to make the 30-mile march. He massed his force near the town of Centerville while he planned the attack.

Meanwhile, the Confederates were still in two groups. Beauregard's army was set up in defensive positions along Bull Run—a stream—while Johnston's force was guarding Harpers Ferry in the Shenandoah Valley. The two groups were 30 miles away from each other but were connected by the Manassas Gap Railroad.

And So It Begins

On July 18, McDowell sent one division to the southeast, trying to outflank the Confederates on their right flank. He figured this would draw their attention and allow him to concentrate his attack on the left flank, which he expected would lead to a collapse of the entire enemy line.

The battle began at Blackburn's Ford, where the right-flanking division encountered the Confederates. A Boston news reporter recorded the start of the first major battle of the Civil War: "Louder, wilder, and more startling than the volley which they had fired was the rebel yell. A thousand Confederates were howling like wolves." Describing the ambulance corps collecting the wounded, he wrote, "I recall the first man brought back on a stretcher, his thigh torn to pieces by a cannon shot.... The reflection came that this was war. All its glamour was gone in an instant."

Surely the Washingtonian picnickers wondered what they had gotten themselves into.

Beauregard correctly guessed that the attack on his right flank was a diversionary tactic when he got reports about its relative mildness. When he learned that Union troops were massing near his left flank, he accurately assumed that the next thrust would come from there.

Confederate Reinforcements Arrive

Meanwhile, Johnston was ordered to hurry his army via train to Manassas. His 6,000 fresh troops arrived at noon on July 20, just in time to help defend the left flank.

McDowell himself led the main attack on the Confederate left flank. At first it succeeded, driving the rebels back to a position called Henry House Hill.

This site is where Confederate General Thomas Jackson earned the nickname "Stonewall." His brigade was anchoring the Confederate line on the heights. "There is Jackson standing like a stone wall," cried Confederate General Bernard Bee, whose own troops were wavering. "Rally behind the Virginians."

Eventually the Confederates were reinforced by more of Johnston's troops arriving by train. They pressed their advantage and drove the Yankees back across Bull Run, forcing them into a wild retreat toward Washington.

The green soldiers on both sides got their fill of battle that day. "The air is full of fearful noises," wrote a witness. "Trees are splintered.... There is smoke, dust, wild talking, shouting, hissings, howlings, explosions. It is a new, strange, unanticipated experience to the soldiers of both armies, far different from what they thought it would be."

A Mad Dash

The picnic was certainly over. The remaining civilian sightseers fled along with their defeated army. "What a scene," wrote a reporter for the *New York World*. "For three miles, hosts of Federal troops...all mingled in one disorderly rout—were fleeing.... Army wagons, sutler's teams, and private carriages choked the passage, tumbling against each other amid clouds of dust and sickening sights and sounds."

Fortunately for the Union, the Confederates were too tired to pursue them very far. Had they done so, they may have captured Washington.

When the armies finally stopped to survey the damage, they recorded about 2,900 killed, wounded, and missing among the Yankees and nearly 2,000 among the Confederates. It was a brutal end to the "picnic battle," and a dark sign of things to come.

- *An army colonel and the grandson of a fur trader, John Jacob Astor III served as a volunteer aide-de-camp to General McClellan and attained the rank of brevet brigadier general. He brought with him to his Washington post his valet, chef, and steward.*

- *Prominent theologian Horace Bushnell of Hartford, Connecticut, went on record as crediting God for every federal victory.*

- *Martha Washington was the great-grandmother of Mary Anna Custis Lee, Robert E. Lee's wife.*

THE WOMAN CALLED "MOSES"

★ ★ ★ ★

Harriet Tubman, one of America's most celebrated heroes, was responsible for ensuring the freedom of many slaves, both before and during the Civil War.

"The Underground Railroad" was a euphemism for any type of assisted escape made by slaves to the Northern states, Canada, or the British West Indies, where slavery was illegal. The Railroad was a loosely organized system of white abolitionists and free blacks who secretly worked together to move slaves through the countryside and into safe houses, and then on to freedom. Significant risks were attached to any work on behalf of escaping slaves on the Underground Railroad, as American law permitted slave owners to reclaim fugitive slaves anywhere they might be located within the United States.

Meet Moses

Harriet Tubman was often likened to the biblical character Moses for leading more than 300 slaves along the Underground Railroad to freedom between 1849 and 1860. What many people don't know is that Tubman's involvement didn't stop when the Civil War began—she continued to be active throughout the war as well. Despite the fact that she had no formal military training, Tubman researched, planned, and led a successful Union military operation with Colonel James Montgomery along the Combahee River in South Carolina on June 2, 1863.

In 1849, Tubman herself was a slave. She escaped her plantation existence in Maryland by stealing away into the surrounding forests, ultimately making her way to the free state of Pennsylvania. When the Civil War began in 1861, the 40-year-old Tubman was already the most famous black woman in America. Her diminutive appearance was rendered more unusual by her missing front teeth and a large dent in the back of her skull—the result of a blow delivered by a slave master in her youth.

Tubman's burning desire to assist her family and other slaves in the South was her motivation during the 12 years she led slaves to freedom—she did not work for reward or commercial gain. Tubman kept virtually no records of her secret missions to the South, and there is no precise accounting of the number of slaves she assisted to freedom. Some evidence suggests that Tubman made at least 20 different trips down south.

Although she was offering freedom to her Underground Railroad passengers, she was ruthless with her human cargo. If escaping slaves seemed overly fearful or were inclined to return to their owner, Tubman would brandish a loaded revolver to change their minds. She was proud that every slave she assisted was delivered to freedom.

In 1851, abolitionist John Brown declared that "slavery is war," and Tubman likely believed the same thing. She conducted her raids like a guerilla fighter, often in disguise, using the fields and forests as her cover. She used code phrases taken from the Old Testament to communicate to those awaiting rescue. "When the good ship Zion comes along…be ready to step on board" was one favorite.

Tubman's fame and success in infiltrating Southern slave holdings during the early 1850s caused blacks to revere her and the plantation aristocracy to hate her. One Maryland slave owner offered a reward of $40,000—about $1 million by today's standards—for her capture. This development prompted Tubman, somewhat wisely, to move to the small Canadian city of St. Catherines, just across Niagara Falls from Buffalo, New York, which was a popular northern terminus for the Underground Railroad. She lived there from 1851 to 1857.

Harriet the Spy

Tubman's knowledge of the South led her to a variety of wartime assignments for the Union army. After working as an army nurse,

Tubman was asked in 1862 to conduct a number of scouting and spying missions in the Southern states. Her experiences with the Underground Railroad were great training for this military spy and reconnaissance work.

Official Union records list Tubman as an "advisor" to Colonel James Montgomery in a combined gunboat and land mission against Confederate positions near South Carolina's Combahee River on June 2, 1863. In fact, the mission was the first American military engagement of any significance to be planned and directed by a woman.

As Tubman and a small Union force tracked enemy positions along the Combahee, she noted the location of deadly Confederate torpedoes, or mines, placed in the river. Tubman later led a Union company of 300 black soldiers, supported by river gunboats, toward the Confederate targets. Those gunboat crews and land forces went on a rampage, destroying Confederate supplies and confiscating valuable farm animals. The soldiers also succeeded in freeing more than 700 slaves from nearby plantations.

Tubman was never a commissioned officer, nor did she hold a rank in the Union army, but she continued to work as a spy and military scout until the war's end. She often disguised herself as a simple, middle-age slave woman as she made her military observations.

Harriet Tubman's contributions to both the freedom of slaves and the Union war effort were profound. After the war, she remained busy. During Reconstruction, she established schools to educate former slaves. She also helped found an old age home in Auburn, New York. Despite her achievements, however, Tubman received little public acclaim and lived a long life of relative poverty. Her memoir, *Scenes in the Life of Harriet Tubman,* only attracted much attention after she died in 1913 at age 93.

- *In 1864, Louisianans approve a new state constitution abolishing slavery.*

"LITTLE MAC" TO "THE YOUNG NAPOLEON"

★ ★ ★ ★

A string of increasingly embarrassing nicknames charts the Civil War career of Union General George McClellan.

A graduate of West Point in 1846, General George B. McClellan served honorably in the Mexican War and was an official observer during the Crimean War in Europe. However, throughout 11 years in the peacetime U.S. Army, he rose no higher than the rank of captain. Perhaps as a result, McClellan resigned from the Army to become chief engineer of the Illinois Central Railroad.

Back to the Front

When the Civil War broke out, McClellan eagerly put his army uniform back on. He had some success in winning a couple of skirmishes in western Virginia, and as a result of a vacuum of military leadership, he was made a major general and put in charge of all Union forces.

The first nickname given to McClellan was "Little Mac." The general was short in stature and had dark hair and penetrating eyes. His troops called him by this name affectionately, because he treated them well and used his engineering skills to organize the army effectively.

The general's rapid rise apparently went straight to his head. He believed he was the savior of the Union and began treating civilian authorities with disrespect. Once he even refused to meet with the President when Lincoln called at his house. After being kept waiting for half an hour, the President was told that McClellan had gone to bed. His second nickname took hold: "The Young Napoleon."

Cautious and Careful

General McClellan earned his third nickname because of his notorious cautiousness. He took several months at the beginning of the war to train his troops and refused to go into battle. Once he did take the field, he moved his troops at a glacial pace in battle after battle, greatly overestimated Confederate strength, and frequently held back when he should have taken the offensive. Confederate General Robert E. Lee, who had served with McClellan in the Mexican War, took advantage of McClellan's timidity to win battles in which the Southerners were greatly outnumbered. McClellan's new nickname was unleashed: "Mac the Unready."

Lincoln, who had once asked the general if he could "borrow" the army since McClellan wasn't using it to fight the Confederates, finally could stand it no longer and fired McClellan in November 1862. But the Young Napoleon wasn't yet ready to leave public life. He still believed it was up to him to save the Union, so he ran against Lincoln on the Democratic ticket in the 1864 election. The Union apparently didn't agree that he was vital to its survival— Lincoln trounced the former general to win a second term.

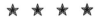

- *"File closers" was the name given to special details of soldiers who used bayonet points, when necessary, to keep stragglers in line during assaults.*

- *Confederate Captain John R. Bryan was the first to use a balloon for aerial reconnaissance when he launched a smoke balloon on April 13, 1862, to observe Union positions at York-town, Virginia.*

- *Respectable women attached to the army to perform various camp and nursing duties were know as* vivandieres. *These brave women traveled with soldiers for little or no pay as sutlers, mascots, or nurses.*

THEY MARCHED, TOO

★ ★ ★ ★

Men and boys weren't the only recruits brought into the army—animal mascots made life in camp better for soldiers.

Jack was a model soldier. A member of the 102nd Pennsylvania Infantry, he always responded quickly to bugle calls and obeyed his superiors. He served heroically in the Wilderness Campaign, the Battle of Spotsylvania, and the Siege of Petersburg. He had a big heart, and he hovered around the dead and wounded after battles. He himself was wounded at Malvern Hill and twice was taken prisoner. Nevertheless, some members of his regiment called him a dog. But he didn't mind, because he was a dog. Jack was a brown-and-white bull terrier and the regiment's mascot. He entertained the troops of the 102nd until he was sadly dognapped and never seen again.

Many regimental mascots such as Jack existed throughout the war. Dogs were most common, but some regiments adopted other animals, including raccoons, a black bear cub, a badger, and chickens. The 2nd Rhode Island took a sheep into battle, until hunger forced them to sell it for $5 to buy food. One of the most unusual mascots was a camel that trundled into battle with the 43rd Mississippi Infantry until it was killed during the Siege of Vicksburg.

Perhaps the most famous regimental mascot was Old Abe, an eagle carried into battle by Company C, 8th Regiment of the Wisconsin Volunteers. A Wisconsin family gave Old Abe—named after Abraham Lincoln, of course—to the regiment as the soldiers marched off to war. When they went into battle, Old Abe flew over the fighting and screeched at the enemy. Confederates tried to kill or capture the eagle but failed—it survived an astounding 81 battles and skirmishes. Old Abe was retired on September 28, 1864, and was given to the state of Wisconsin. It lived in a cage in the state capital until it died in 1881. Its remains were stuffed and proudly displayed there until the building burned down in 1904.

- Removed from field command after losing his left arm in fighting in Virginia and his left foot at Chancellorsville, Confederate General Francis T. Nicholls went on to serve two terms as governor of Louisiana.

- In the summer of 1861, Kentucky claimed that it was neutral. Kentuckians wanting to join the Confederacy traveled to Tennessee and formed the famed First Kentucky Brigade. But because Kentucky never seceded from the Union, Confederates considered it behind enemy lines. Therefore, the brigade could neither recruit more soldiers nor go home on furlough. They couldn't even count on receiving mail from home. Thus, they became known as the "Orphan Brigade."

- Robert Lincoln, the President's first child and the only one of the Lincolns' children to survive to adulthood, declined an offer from President Rutherford B. Hayes to serve as assistant secretary of state. He did, however, serve as President James Garfield's secretary of war in 1881. In 1889, President Benjamin Harrison appointed Lincoln minister to England, where he served for four years.

- Gail Borden's Eagle Brand condensed milk product, patented in 1856, was designed to combat food poisoning and illness related to the lack of refrigeration. It became an important part of the Union soldiers' diets and gave the brand the recognition it needed to become a household name. The brand still exists to this day.

- General Turner Ashby, second in command of the Seventh Cavalry, earned the sobriquet "Black Knight of the Confederacy" for his fearlessness coupled with his appearance—jet black hair, moustache and long beard, dark eyes, and swarthy complexion.

A TOUCH OF
FOREIGN INTRIGUE

★ ★ ★ ★

*Prince and Princess Salm-Salm were a unique duo, making
contributions to the battlefield and impressions in high society.*

Prince Felix Salm-Salm was a professional soldier from Prussia
who fought battles on both sides of the Atlantic. During the American Civil War, he served among the many European immigrants
who joined the Union army. Although he was a soldier of fortune,
his American wife, Agnes, was well connected to high-profile
decision makers.

Bad Habits

Born in 1828 in Westphalia, Prussia, Prince Salm-Salm attended
military school in Berlin and entered the Prussian army in 1846
as a second lieutenant—just in time to serve in the Schleswig-
Holstein War. He later moved over to the Austrian army. During
European conflicts, the prince proved his skills on the battlefield,
but his heroic efforts did not mask his extravagant spending habits
and card playing. Gambling debts—and possibly his attempts to
avoid them—resulted in his discharge from the Austrian army for
a lifestyle unbecoming an officer. Salm-Salm's father purchased his
son's way to the United States so he could escape that tainted
status and live a soldier's life elsewhere. With the sectional conflict
underway in his new home, Salm-Salm headed for the Union to
suit up for a new fight. The U.S. Army was happy to accept help
where they could get it, mercenary or not.

Immigrant Regiment

Salm-Salm joined the many immigrant recruits under General
Louis Blenker. He soon met his bride, Agnes Joy, a charming and
ambitious girl, who, according to one biographer, would always
overshadow her soldier husband. Agnes had a somewhat mysteri-

ous past: She worked in circus shows as a ropedancer and horse rider under the name Agnes Leclerq. In Washington, D.C., where she had apparently charmed her way into local society, she was known for daring morning rides on her wild mustang and for attending parties in influential circles. Felix Salm-Salm took note of the dashing Agnes and set up a situation in which he could meet her at a capital reception. Their romance was quick—they married in August 1862.

Salm-Salm had gained a commission in command of the 8th New York, but soon after the wedding, as a result of intended military reorganization, that position became insecure. His record in battle both abroad and in the United States was respectable enough, but by April 1863, the 8th New York was getting ready to muster out of the service. Even *The New York Times* questioned the "absurd and impolitic regulation of red-tape" that brought Salm-Salm and his troops home after a two-year tour. "The men . . . have proven themselves worthy patriots," the *Times* declared.

A New Troop

Princess Salm-Salm was able to secure her husband a new command. She had a certain reputation in political circles, but in hindsight, her degree of influence at the national level and her Washington connections were likely questionable and exaggerated, by herself as much as anyone else. She sometimes showed up at parties uninvited, and other women, including Mary Todd Lincoln, looked down on her. Despite this, she did have influence with the New York governor, and this connection landed her husband the command of the 68th New York.

On June 8, 1864, Salm-Salm became colonel of this outfit and took his troops to Nashville, where they guarded the Nashville and Chattanooga Railroad. The 68th New York then spent the next few months on an island in the Tennessee River near Bridgeport, Alabama, guarding against Confederate raids on pontoon and railroad bridges. Salm-Salm, however, had a deep desire to fight rather than simply to defend points of interest, so after hearing about Confederate General John Bell Hood's campaign into Tennessee, he convinced Union General James Steedman to include him on his staff. Reporting on one skirmish, the colonel relayed, "My men poured two well directed volleys into [the outlaw guerrillas] and they skedaddled as quick as they came." The successes in Tennessee and Alabama netted Salm-Salm a brevet promotion to brigadier general in April 1865.

"Princessly" Duties

For much of Salm-Salm's tour in the latter half of the war, he was accompanied by his wife, who didn't want to be away from him. Although the high-society women in Washington didn't like the princess, she earned respect from the troops in the field. A strong advocate for rank-and-file soldiers, she often took supplies and clothing intended for officers and gave them to the wounded enlisted. She even stole her husband's bedsheets and tore them into bandages.

Off to Mexico

After the Civil War, Prince Salm-Salm, a warrior who wasn't comfortable living in peacetime, began looking for his next fight. He and Princess Agnes traveled to Mexico, where they joined the effort to defend the regime of Emperor Maximilian in 1867. Maximilian was supported by France, and he was under attack from Mexican forces seeking to restore President Benito Juarez. Salm-Salm nearly lost his life after he was captured, but his wife saved his neck. Through tireless effort, she established an accord with the reinstated President Juarez and his generals that secured her husband's release. Salm-Salm would have been executed had it not been for her.

After fleeing Mexico, the couple headed for Europe, and the prince joined yet another fight in the Franco-Prussian War. He was killed in the Battle of Gravelotte in August 1870. His princess bride, a widow at 30, lived on to publish her diary, which details some of her adventures. She died in 1912.

THE QUITE IMAGINARY SUE MUNDY

★ ★ ★ ★

How an entire state was terrorized—and enthralled by—a fictional female operative.

Sue Mundy was a powerful fictional product of the guerrilla war in the border state of Kentucky in 1864. Even though she never actually existed, Mundy became the most feared military operative in the state, a potent symbol of Confederate stealth and resistance.

As the Civil War stretched into its fourth year, the Confederacy's military fortunes were fading on all fronts. The Union was making efficient use of its superior numbers in both soldiers and resources, and Union commanders, using their wider range of options, began to dominate the Confederate opposition. In response, some Southern fighters were resorting to guerrilla tactics.

Femme Fatale

Sue Mundy, "The Girl Guerrilla," was largely a creation of George Prentice, the pro-Union editor of the *Louisville Journal,* who intensely disliked General Stephen G. Burbridge, the Union commander in Kentucky. The ground was fertile for Prentice because guerrilla attacks were an undeniable problem for Union forces in Kentucky. Many of the raids were planned and coordinated by Jerome Clarke, whose raiders caused considerable damage in northern Kentucky throughout 1864. The son of a wealthy Kentucky landowner, Clarke joined the Confederate army in 1861 at age 17 and rode with General John Hunt Morgan's raiders until Morgan's death in 1864. Clarke was a slim, 20-year-old man with long hair and somewhat feminine features. His looks helped inspire the Sue Mundy character.

Prentice staged a public relations attack on Burbridge through a series of newspaper articles on the subject of recent hit-and-run attacks against Union targets. Prentice claimed in print that a Confederate raider named Sue Mundy had masterminded the guerrilla actions. The journalist then mocked Burbridge's army for being unable to keep Kentucky safe from the actions of a "mere woman." Prentice chose the name "Sue Mundy" on purpose—it was also the name of a notorious Louisville prostitute. The insult worked, and Prentice stirred powerful opinions in Kentucky.

Under Pressure

In early 1865, Clarke linked his Kentucky raiders to the most feared of the Confederate "bushwhackers," William Quantrill's Missouri Partisan Rangers. Quantrill's guerrillas were more renegades than soldiers. They epitomized the "Terror of the Black Flag," the no-surrender, no-prisoners, no-quarter form of warfare that was contrary to all contemporary rules of engagement.

The pressure on Burbridge's Union forces to catch and neutralize Sue Mundy swelled. In response to guerrilla operations that killed both Union soldiers and civilians, Burbridge declared that in reprisal for every Union soldier killed by a raider, four Confederates would be executed.

Mundy's notoriety peaked when Clarke and Quantrill coordinated a joint attack on a railway depot at Lair Station, Kentucky, on February 3, 1865. Just over a month later, on March 12, Clarke and two of his subordinates were forced to surrender. Clarke was later deemed by the Union to be the notorious Sue Mundy, and he was hung as a common criminal just three days later on March 15—before a military tribunal could even hear his case.

Maintaining his fiction to the end, editor Prentice wrote that Union forces had still failed to capture the real Sue Mundy.

- *Robert E. Lee's troops nicknamed him "The King of Spades" because he often had them "dig in." This strategy was a success at the Battle of Cold Harbor. His troops also affectionately called him the "Old Man" and "Bobby Lee."*

THE PROFOUND EFFECT OF *UNCLE TOM'S CABIN*

★ ★ ★ ★

*A first-time novelist dramatized the
problem of slavery for all to see.*

When Harriet Beecher Stowe was introduced to President Abraham Lincoln, as the story goes, he said, "So, you're the little woman who wrote the book that started this great war." There's no question that few elements fueled the flames of hate across the country as much as *Uncle Tom's Cabin* did. Stowe's story of Tom, a saintly black slave, and the difficult life he and his fellow slaves must endure, earned either praise or condemnation. Abolitionists across the North thought it was brilliant and oh, so true. Southern critics, however, complained that it was completely inaccurate in how it portrayed plantation life.

Borrowing from Real Life

Stowe was a dedicated abolitionist who was more concerned about illustrating the evils of slavery than creating an accurate view of life on the plantation. Although she lived in Cincinnati, Ohio, for 18 years, just across the river from the slave state of Kentucky, she had little actual experience with Southern plantations. The information in most of her book was taken either from abolitionist literature or her own imagination. Stowe was researching a series of articles she intended to write when she heard about a slave woman who escaped from her masters in Kentucky across a frozen Ohio River. She immediately realized that she could use such a scene in a book. One of the most exciting parts of *Uncle Tom's Cabin* features Eliza, the slave heroine, escaping across the ice.

A Publishing Sensation

Uncle Tom's Cabin first appeared in 1851, serialized in the abolitionist newspaper *National Era*. Its popularity there led to the book's publication as a complete work the next year. It was an instant success, selling 10,000 copies in the first week and more than 300,000 by the end of its first year. *Uncle Tom's Cabin* had even greater popularity in Britain, where more than one million copies sold within a year. Stowe exposed the general public to an issue that most knew very little about. But the book didn't simply educate its readers—it also provoked heated debates in state and federal legislatures.

Interestingly, given today's negative meaning of the term *Uncle Tom*, the character in Stowe's book demonstrated strength and traits that were quite heroic. In one instance, when ordered to whip a sickly female slave, Tom refuses and suffers the lash himself. He is ultimately killed by his wicked master, Simon Legree, because he will not betray two runaway slaves. When Legree tries to have the information beaten out of him, Tom goes to his death without revealing a thing.

Not Controversial Enough?

As shocking as a lot of people found *Uncle Tom's Cabin,* many—particularly radical abolitionists—didn't think the book went far enough in denouncing slavery. Others, usually those who lived in the South, condemned the book as grossly exaggerated. One of Stowe's admirers was William Lloyd Garrison, the editor of an abolitionist newspaper called *The Liberator.* "I estimate the value of antislavery writing by the abuse it brings," he wrote to tell her. "Now all the defenders of slavery have let me alone and are abusing you."

★　★　★　★

- *Jefferson Davis met Zachary Taylor's daughter, Sarah Knox Taylor, while in the service during the Black Hawk War. The couple wed in 1835, but on a visit to Louisiana both contracted malaria. Sarah died three months later. It would be ten years before Davis would remarry, this time to the socially prominent Varina Howell.*

(Continued from p. 21)

1861

January 9
Mississippi secedes from the Union.

January 10
Florida secedes from the Union.

January 11
Alabama secedes from the Union.

January 19
Georgia secedes from the Union.

January 26
Louisiana secedes from the Union.

January 29
Kansas is admitted to the Union as a free state. It is the 34th state.

February 1
Texas secedes from the Union.

February 8
The seven seceded states adopt a constitution and set up a provisional Confederate government.

February 18
Jefferson Davis is inaugurated President of the Confederate States of America.

March 4
Abraham Lincoln is inaugurated as the 16th President of the United States.

The Confederacy adopts its first flag and raises it over its capitol in Montgomery, Alabama.

March 11
The Confederate Congress adopts a permanent constitution to replace the temporary one it adopted a month earlier.

April 12
Confederates open fire on Fort Sumter. Union forces there surrender the next day.

April 15
Lincoln asks for 75,000 militia soldiers to serve for three months.

April 17
Virginia secedes from the Union.

April 20
Robert E. Lee resigns his commission in the U.S. Army.

May 3
Lincoln calls for another 42,000 volunteers—this time for three years—and 18,000 sailors.

May 6
Arkansas secedes from the Union.

May 7
The Tennessee legislature votes to secede from the Union. The decision is confirmed by popular vote on June 8.

May 13
The U.S. Naval Academy reopens in Newport, Rhode Island, after being moved from Annapolis, Maryland.

May 20
North Carolina secedes from the Union.

The Confederate Congress votes to move the capital to Richmond, Virginia.

May 31
The U.S. Postal Service ceases service to the South.

(Continued on p. 122)

LIKE DOMINOES FALLING ON THE RIVER

★ ★ ★ ★

Forts Henry and Donelson, guarding strategic rivers
in Confederate territory, held the key to success
for an ailing federal army.

Cigar-chomping Union General Ulysses S. Grant was courageous and aggressive, but in 1862 he needed a second chance to prove his leadership. He had left the army back in 1854 only to go on to a succession of failed business ventures.

At the same time, the Union as a whole needed a second chance—an opportunity to prove that it could turn its industrial superiority and the numerical advantage of its soldiers into significant battle-field victories. So far, after almost a year of war, the Federals had not proven themselves to be a fine fighting machine.

Action in the West

In February 1862, the highly strategic Confederate Forts Henry and Donelson in northwestern Tennessee provided both Grant and the Union military the opportunities they were looking for.

Fort Henry sat on the Tennessee River. Though the river offered an ideal invasion route into the South, Union generals were unsure about attacking the haphazardly defended fort. Not Grant, though. He and Commodore Andrew H. Foote proposed a joint land-water assault on Henry, which was finally approved by their superiors.

A Naval Operation

Army and navy were intended to attack together, but when cold, wet, and muddy conditions delayed Grant, Foote started without him. On February 6, his force of ironclads and wooden gunboats began shelling the fort heavily. Confederate General Lloyd Tilghman and his soldiers fiercely fought back as long as they could, but Tilghman finally surrendered to Foote just before Grant's mud-caked troops arrived on the scene. It soon became evident that, amazingly, there had only been about 100 soldiers in this rebel force—Tilghman had ordered the bulk of his troops to Fort Donelson 12 miles east, while he stayed behind to defend Henry.

Onto the Next Stop

Fort Donelson was next on Grant's list. A military prize, it lay on the Cumberland River leading directly into Nashville, an industrial center and Confederate state capital. What's more, Donelson's commanding officer was General John Floyd, a former U.S. secretary of war who was wanted by the federal authorities for allegedly having transferred arms to the South.

Grant and Foote attacked on February 13 and soon had Fort Donelson in a choke hold, squeezed by land troops on three sides and floating artillery on the fourth. Somehow, two days later, the rebels broke out of one side and drove the Union forces back a mile—but the Union pushed back and forced the Confederates back into the fort.

That night, General Floyd and General Gideon J. Pillow passed command of Donelson to General Simon Boliver Buckner and fled, taking some troops with them. Ironically, Buckner was a friend of Grant who had loaned him money during his "down-and-out" period in the 1850s. No one knows if that act of friendship was on his mind when he sent Grant a request for terms of surrender.

Unconditional Surrender

Grant may not have realized that Buckner was now in command of the fort, but if he did, sentiment apparently had no effect on him. His response was, "No terms except unconditional and immediate surrender can be accepted."

Capturing Henry and Donelson was a rewarding victory for the Federals. They took control of most of Kentucky and Tennessee, used the Tennessee and Cumberland rivers as supply lines, and made Nashville a supply center for the Union army in the West.

THE ANGEL OF THE BATTLEFIELD

★ ★ ★ ★

One of the war's bravest, most influential figures was an ardent feminist who started off as a teacher and a patent clerk.

We never know the extent of what we can do until we're caught in a crisis, and sometimes that crisis brings out the best in us. Nowhere is this truer than in the life of Clarissa H. Barton—better known as Clara Barton. Her story proves that men didn't face the dangers of battle and hardships of the field alone. Barton was one of the greatest heroes of the Civil War. Her fearless work for the wounded earned her the nickname "Angel of the Battlefield."

A Beginning in Medicine

Clara Barton quit a teaching career after she discovered she couldn't earn the same pay men did. She was the first woman ever hired by the U.S. Patent Office in Washington, D.C., but although they hired her as a "clerk," they later dropped her title to "copyist" and paid her a mere 10 cents for every 100 words she copied. The Civil War allowed her true talents to come to the fore. In her free time, Barton had begun tending to wounded soldiers in the hospital. She quickly recognized the Army Medical Department's inability to care properly for so many casualties. At the time of the First Battle of Bull Run, the Union army had practically nothing in terms of a hospital corps. Taking on the daunting task herself, Barton placed an ad in a Massachusetts newspaper for donations of medical supplies. Ultimately, she founded an organization to collect and distribute provisions for wounded soldiers.

Cutting through official red tape, Barton won permission from the War Department to go out into the field and help the wounded.

She began personally delivering critical supplies to battlefields where they were most needed. In August 1862, Barton witnessed firsthand the chaos, inefficiency, and unsanitary nature of military medical care during combat. At the Second Battle of Bull Run, for example, she came upon hundreds of federal wounded, dumped on a hillside where they'd lain in the summer sun without water for two days. The aftermath of the Battle of Cedar Mountain and the Union field hospital in Fredericksburg, Virginia, were even worse. These experiences strengthened Barton's resolve to help, which in turn led her to some of the grimmest, most deadly battle-fields of the war.

Braving the Battle

The worst of these must have been Antietam, where on September 17, 1862—during the war's bloodiest single day of fighting—23,000 combatants were killed, wounded, or missing. The night before, she knew a major battle drew near. Stuck at the end of the Army of the Potomac's long supply trail, she drove her wagons full of medical supplies all night to get to the battlefield. Arriving at midday, she was greeted by horrific slaughter. Dead and dying soldiers lay in heaps, while frantic doctors were reduced to binding wounds with cornhusks. Like an answered prayer, Clara Barton arrived with an entire wagonload of bandages. She dove into the fray, the only woman on the field, and indeed, the work was harrowing. At one point a soldier begged her to cut a bullet from his cheek. She hesitated, as she had no surgical instruments and was not a doctor. But the young man pleaded with her. She ended up cutting the bullet out with a pocketknife! As she cradled another wounded soldier in her arms to give him water, a bullet zipped past her, tearing the sleeve of her dress and killing the man she was helping. Rather than relent, she set upon creating a makeshift field hospital in a barn. When a surgeon she was assisting was suddenly killed, Barton took his place at the operating table. After the sun set, the doctors had no lanterns. Barton saved the day again by seeking out lanterns and bringing several herself. She worked all through the night until she collapsed and was carried exhausted off the field.

Barton's own words describing the moment when the bullet that killed her charge nearly ended her own life best sums up her stoic and determined state of mind: "A ball had passed between my body and the right arm which supported him, cutting through the sleeve and passing through his chest from shoulder to shoulder. There was no more to be done for him and I left him to his rest. I have never mended that hole in my sleeve. I wonder if a soldier ever does mend a bullet hole in his coat?" For the duration of this long, tumultuous war, she paused in her labors only to recuperate from incapacitating illnesses, including typhoid fever.

Receiving Recognition

Clara Barton continued her service at Fredericksburg, where she worked beside Walt Whitman, as well as at Hilton Head, Petersburg, Richmond, and the siege of Fort Wagner. By this time, Union leadership had recognized her value, and Union General Benjamin Butler named her "Lady in Charge" of field hospitals for his Army of the James.

At the end of the war, she helped identify some of the 13,000 unknown Union dead at the notorious Confederate prison camp at Andersonville. Establishing the Office of Correspondence, Barton helped families learn the fate of nearly 30,000 soldiers missing in action. To put this number in perspective, the U.S. military today lists only 10,000 MIAs from Vietnam and Korea combined.

Barton remained busy as a lecturer and activist after the war, campaigning for women's suffrage. Four years after the war's end, she traveled to Europe for a much-needed and long-overdue sabbatical. Ironically, she arrived just in time for the Franco-Prussian War of 1870–1871. Signing on as a member of the International Red Cross, she was instrumental in getting the organization to broaden its focus from merely caring for the war-wounded to providing disaster relief. On her return home, Barton performed her most lasting act on behalf of suffering peoples everywhere—she founded the American Red Cross. In a sense, whenever we turn on the television today and see the Red Cross providing assistance in natural disasters, we are looking at Clara Barton's shining monument.

YOU CAN'T COMPROMISE FOREVER

★ ★ ★ ★

Since the founding of the country, proslavery and antislavery forces looked for common ground until they could find it no longer.

When the founders of the United States adopted the Constitution and established the nation, they had already started to compromise on the issue of slavery. Although the Constitution put a limit on the slave trade and decreed that the importation of slaves must end 20 years later, it also allowed slaveholders to chase and recapture fugitive slaves in any state of the Union, and it counted a slave as three-fifths of a person for purposes of representation in the House of Representatives. This was just the first in a long line of compromises.

The Missouri Compromise

North and South never really stopped encountering friction over the issue of slavery. By 1820, slavery had effectively been abolished in the Northern states. Congress was evenly split between 11 free and 11 slave states when citizens of the Missouri Territory, a slaveholding area, petitioned for statehood. Admitting Missouri as a slave state would tip the carefully balanced scale in favor of the South, and that was an unacceptable situation for Northern legislators. Still, the United States was expanding, pioneers were moving westward, and no one wanted to stop admitting new states. A compromise was reached, and the issue was resolved when Maine also petitioned to enter the Union, but as a free state—Congress was able to maintain its balance with 12 slave and 12 free states. But what became known as the Compromise of 1820 or, more popularly, the Missouri Compromise, contained more issues than simply the admittance of Missouri and

Maine. Slavery was barred from the rest of the Louisiana Territory north of the 36° 30' line, which was the southern border of Missouri. This legislation allowed Congress to settle into a period of relative peace.

Bleeding Kansas

The Missouri Compromise was still in effect when the territories of Kansas and Nebraska were established. Kansas was due west of Missouri, north of the 36° 30' line and, therefore, off-limits to slavery. But there were several interested parties who wanted to make the territory safe for slaveholders. In 1854, Congress passed the Kansas-Nebraska Act, which put an end to the restrictions of the Missouri Compromise. The citizens of the Kansas and Nebraska territories, as well as those of any future territories, would be able to decide for themselves whether or not they wanted to allow slaves within their borders.

That meant the fate of slavery in Kansas would be left to popular vote. However, it was a territory ripe for settling, which meant new settlers were coming in all the time. Both proslavery and antislavery factions rushed their supporters into Kansas to affect the vote. When elections were finally held in 1855, thousands of residents from the slave state Missouri crossed into Kansas to vote illegally. The legislature they elected was in favor of slavery. Not everyone, however, was content with that election. Later that year, free-soil Kansans held their own convention and adopted a constitution that abolished slavery.

The Sack of Lawrence

In May 1856, 800 proslavers, many of them from Missouri, attacked and damaged much of the antislavery stronghold of Lawrence, Kansas. One man was killed. A few days later, the fanatical abolitionist John Brown led four of his sons in an attack on a small settlement of proslavers at Pottawatomie Creek, Kansas, killing five. It would be another five years, several bloody clashes, and nearly 200 more deaths before Kansas was admitted to the Union as a free state. But the Union it joined on January 29, 1861, was about to fight for its very existence.

ON THE HIT PARADE

★ ★ ★ ★

The feelings of civilians and soldiers in the North and South were captured in song. Lyrics of famous songs were sometimes altered to reflect what was going on at the time.

Music has the ability to evoke a time or place more than just about anything. If filmmakers want to remind an audience of the '60s, they can use popular rock or soul songs of the time, just as the '20s can be invoked by playing ragtime. The Civil War era has its recognizable melodies, as well.

Northern Note-Worthies

Perhaps the most famous song to come out of the Civil War was written not by a soldier or a famous songwriter, but by a dedicated social activist named Julia Ward Howe. An ardent abolitionist living in Boston, Howe had attended a public review of infantry marching off to battle at the beginning of the conflict. With them, she sang what was becoming a very popular song of the time, "John Brown's Body," written by Vermont soldier Thomas Bishop. While many—including Howe—believed that "John Brown's Body" was a stirring tribute to the martyred abolitionist of Harpers Ferry, the song was actually a good-natured ribbing of Bishop's commanding officer, who also shared that common name. "John Brown's body lies a mouldering in the grave!" the song joyously declared.

Regardless of who the subject of the song was and how it was interpreted, the lyrics were somewhat macabre, perhaps too dark for the civilian public, and one of Howe's companions suggested that she try to compose some new lyrics for the popular tune. Always up to a challenge, Howe quickly developed lyrics whose power and potency are unquestionable: "The Battle Hymn of the Republic." Her words were published on the front page of *The Atlantic Monthly* and became an overnight sensation, spreading across the North like wildfire.

Southern Ditties

On the other side of the Mason-Dixon Line, lots of people were singing the regional anthem "Dixie," which, ironically enough, is generally attributed to a man from the Union state of Ohio named Daniel Decatur Emmett. The song, whose famous opening line declares, "I wish I was in the land of cotton," reflects the mood of the South in the years leading up to the Civil War. With pressure increasing from the Northern abolitionists and the impending inauguration of Abraham Lincoln, the South felt that its very way of life was under attack.

Emmett's first drafts of the song attempted to portray slavery in a positive light, eschewing the harsh and brutal aspects of the peculiar institution in an effort to counteract the waves of abolitionist literature coming from the North. During the war, soldiers often modified the lyrics to speak directly of current events. A Confederate version boasted: "Northern flags in South wind flutter / Send them back your fierce defiance! / Stamp upon the cursed alliance!" Union soldiers, on the other hand, sang the song with a mind for reclaiming what belonged to the United States: "Hurrah! Hurrah! The Stars and Stripes forever! / Hurrah! Hurrah! Our Union shall not sever!"

Bitter Ballads

While music could be a great tool for rallying support for each side's cause, it also reflected the bitterness and sorrow that the Civil War brought to the United States. Confederate Major James Randolph's "O I'm a Good Old Rebel" is a post-war lament and vicious condemnation of the victorious Union. "I can't take up my musket / and fight them now no more," the song spits, "but I ain't going to love them / now that is sartin sure."

Stephen Foster, the illustrious songwriter responsible for "Oh, Susannah," "My Old Kentucky Home," "Beautiful Dreamer," "Camptown Races," and "Old Folks at Home," composed a haunting ballad that echoed the cries of many Americans during those years: "Was My Brother in the Battle?" "He was ever brave and valiant, and I know he never fled / Was his name among the wounded or numbered with the dead?" Foster captured the terrible reality of the war, and the deep sorrow embedded in the lyrics is still palpable today.

Common Ground

Despite the differences between the soldiers of the North and South, they had still grown up in the same country, and their similarities led them to cherish a number of the same songs. "Lorena" was a song that wasn't partisan—it didn't take sides or taunt the opponent. In fact, it didn't make any kind of ideological pronouncements at all. It merely tugged at the heartstrings of all those who missed the ones they loved and the homes they left behind. The war itself is only mentioned fleetingly, as the impediment to the singer's love for his woman: "A duty, stern and pressing, broke / The tie which linked my soul with thee." In the end, it is clear that the stress of war has disillusioned the singer and that he can only hope to be rejoined with his beloved Lorena in the peace and purity of heaven. This stirring song swept through the ranks of both armies, a rare bit of common ground between two warring forces.

"Find out where your enemy is. Get at him as soon as you can, and strike him as hard as you can. And keep moving on!"
Ulysses S. Grant's philosophy of war

"John Brown's zeal in the cause of freedom was infinitely superior to mine. Mine was as the taper light; his was as the burning sun. I could live for the slave; John Brown could die for him."
Frederick Douglass

Fast Facts

- *After Jefferson Davis's death, his last home, Beauvoir, in Biloxi, Mississippi, became a home for Confederate veterans and their wives or widows. It has since become the Jefferson Davis Home and Presidential Library, and it suffered heavy damage from Hurricane Katrina.*

- *Northern Democrats who wanted to end hostilities with the South were called "Copperheads" by Republicans, a nickname that may have derived from their comparison to the venomous American snake of the same name. They wore copper Liberty-head pennies as identifying badges.*

- *The* thumbstall *was a buckskin thumb cover used to stop the vent during the loading of a cannon. It prevented air from entering and igniting material that would then prematurely ignite the cartridge.*

- *Students at the University of Mississippi left en masse in 1861 to join the University Grays or the Lamar Rifles. The university may be better known by its nickname, Ole Miss, which was the antebellum term for the mistress of a Southern plantation.*

- *The Battle of Shiloh is also known as the battle of Pittsburgh Landing, Tennessee. Confederate Generals Joseph E. Johnston and P.G.T. Beauregard launched a surprise attack against General Grant and nearly defeated him. Fought in April 1862, it was the bloodiest battle in American history up to that time. It was the Confederates' last stand to prevent a Union invasion of Mississippi.*

- *The* kepi *was a shortened version of the familiar forage cap. It was not as popular because it didn't provide protection from the sun and rain.*

THE MAKING OF WEST VIRGINIA

★ ★ ★ ★

The Union wasn't the only entity to split during the Civil War. The state of Virginia broke into two pieces, as well.

When the war started, there was just one Virginia. In the hearts of many residents, however, the state was already divided. The eastern and southern parts were more aristocratic, with grand plantations in the countryside and wealthy cities near the Atlantic coast. The northwestern part was mountain country. As early as 1829, northwesterners complained that their counties didn't benefit from their taxes as much as eastern counties did. In 1830, a newspaper in the northwestern city of Wheeling said the area should separate from the rest of the state "peaceably if we can, forcibly if we must."

A Reason to Split

The Civil War sparked the separation. The Virginia legislature voted to join the Confederacy, but residents of two dozen northwestern counties objected. They started their own governing body, which they called the Restored Government of Virginia.

The U.S. Constitution stipulates that states can't be formed from already existing states without approval of that state's legislature. But Virginia had seceded from the Union, so the new Restored Government of Virginia claimed to be the legitimate legislature and voted to separate from the rest of the state. Congress agreed. President Lincoln was reluctant to approve such an irrevocable change during wartime, but in the end, he signed on. West Virginia officially became the 35th state on June 20, 1863.

The name West Virginia makes sense, but it wasn't a given when the northwestern leaders debated seceding from the state. Other proposed names were Allegheny, New Virginia, Augusta, and Kanawha. Imagine John Denver singing, "Kanawha, mountain mama..."

AFTER THE
WAR WAS OVER...

★ ★ ★ ★

*Life didn't end when the Civil War was over. A number of
soldiers from both sides went on to find fame—or infamy—in
other pursuits after the war.*

Lived to Tell

Some young veterans turned their war experience into literary
careers. General Lew Wallace, for instance, saw action under
General Grant at the Battle of Shiloh. After serving on the military
commission that tried the Lincoln assassination conspirators, he
gained worldwide acclaim for penning the novel *Ben-Hur.*

Ambrose Bierce began the war as a battlefield cartographer, serving bravely under fire until he was sidelined with a head wound at
Kennesaw Mountain. Today, he's best known for penning the short
story "An Occurrence at Owl Creek Bridge."

Missourian Mark Twain served in a Confederate militia under his
real name of Samuel Langhorne Clemens for a few uneventful
weeks before heading west and beginning his literary career.

Wild Subjects

Some notables gained their notoriety after the war in the Ameri-
can Wild West. Chief among them was George Armstrong
Custer, who proved himself at Antietam, Brandy
Station, and Gettysburg. Unfortunately, his mili-
tary career had a less than heroic end at
Little Big Horn in 1876.

James "Wild Bill" Hickok was a
Nebraska constable when the war
began, and he served as a scout for
the Union. His skills with a gun and a

rather nonchalant disposition toward killing would eventually catch up with him during a poker game in Deadwood in the Dakota Territory.

Another Union scout was William Cody, who began the war in the employ of the Pony Express. Afterward, his prowess as a buffalo hunter working for the railroad earned him a name, a reputation, and a subsequent career as the showman "Buffalo Bill." His "Wild West Show" helped establish many myths of the West.

Among the infamous Confederate guerrilla fighters known as Quantrill's Raiders were Frank and Jesse James. After the war they continued some of their guerrilla exploits, robbing banks, stage-coaches, and trains.

And Last But Not Least...

Erroneously credited with inventing baseball, Captain Abner Doubleday does have one legitimate claim to fame. He fired the first return shot of the war at Fort Sumter.

- *Lieutenant Jacob Parrott, a member of Andrews's Raiders, journeyed nearly 200 miles into enemy territory to capture a railroad train in an attempt to destroy the bridges and tracks between Chattanooga and Atlanta. Parrott was captured and whipped more than 100 times on his bare back in an effort to extract information from him. His role in the undercover operation netted him the first Congressional Medal of Honor ever awarded.*

- *When two or more pieces of field artillery moved frequently and rapidly along a battle line, they were called a "flying battery."*

- *Among his many idiosyncrasies, Lieutenant General Thomas J. "Stonewall" Jackson refused to use pepper on his food, saying it gave him pains in his left leg.*

THE NEWS IS WHAT THE PRESIDENT SAYS IT IS

★ ★ ★ ★

*When it comes to Lincoln's repression of
newspapers, rumors battle with the truth.*

Politicians often cite the actions of their historical forebears to
justify their own indiscretions. Abraham Lincoln, for example, is
said to have suppressed civil rights during the Civil War, so he
occasionally gets referenced when a modern politician wants to do
the same thing. Today's official might say, "Lincoln suppressed
newspapers during the Civil War, so I should be able to meddle
with a few civil liberties, too." But did Lincoln really work to
curtail freedom of the press? It's not quite so clear cut.

Freedom of the Press?

A handful of cases are frequently cited to portray Lincoln as
opposed to a free press. In June 1863, the editor of the *Chicago
Times* wrote inflammatory antiwar articles that attacked the efforts
of Lincoln and the Republicans. Union General Ambrose Burnside, who was in command of the Department of the Ohio at the
time, was alarmed at what he considered the *Times*'s "repeated
expression of disloyal and incendiary sentiments." The general had
the editor arrested and the paper shut down. Although Lincoln
had suspended habeas corpus in areas where he feared physical
unrest, he was troubled by Burnside's actions and consulted his
Cabinet for a response. They agreed that the editor's arrest had
been improper, so Lincoln freed him and allowed the *Chicago
Times* to return to press. When people asked Lincoln why he
hadn't supported the closure of the newspaper that had been so
critical of him, he wrote that those with such a question did "not
fully comprehend the dangers of abridging the liberties of the
people." That doesn't sound like something a hater of the press
would write!

Lies Instead of News

The President wasn't completely above shutting down a printing press if he thought it was necessary. On May 18, 1864, the *New York World* and the *Journal and Commerce* each published a forged presidential proclamation calling for a new draft of 400,000 troops. Once these papers were on the street, the administration wasted no time in going after them. Lincoln himself ordered General John A. Dix to arrest the publishers and editors and to seize their presses. When further investigation determined that the journalists had been taken in by the forgery themselves and had never intended to convey false information, the journalists were released and allowed to resume publication.

In his telegram to Dix releasing the journalists, Secretary of War Edwin Stanton wrote of the President, "He directs me to say that while, in his opinion, the editors, proprietors, and publishers of The World and Journal of Commerce are responsible for what appears in their papers injurious to the public service, and have no right to shield themselves behind a plea of ignorance or want of criminal intent, yet he is not disposed to visit them with vindictive punishment."

The People Have Spoken

Official action from the government wasn't the only sort of suppression that affected newspapers. In March 1863, the 2nd Ohio Cavalry was camped outside of Columbus, Ohio. After the local newspaper, *The Crisis,* printed antiarmy stories—including the wish that no member of the 2nd Ohio return from the war alive— the soldiers ransacked its offices. *The Crisis* continued publication, however. The next year, its editor was indicted by a federal grand jury and arrested for conspiracy. He died in November before he could go on trial.

Although Lincoln wasn't afraid to take action when he felt it necessary, he was keenly aware of the danger in restricting civil rights and did so only after careful consideration. Those wishing to use him as a role model for their actions against free speech should perhaps take a closer look.

SO THEY SAID

"General, if you put every [Union soldier] now on the other side of the Potomac on that field to approach me over the same line, I will kill them all before they reach my line."

General James Longstreet's vow to Robert E. Lee as countless federal assaults were beaten back by Longstreet's force at Fredericksburg

"By some strange operation of magic I seem to have become the power of the land."

George McClellan, shortly after he assumed command of Union forces around Washington in 1861

"Will you pardon me for asking what the horses of your army have done since the battle of Antietam that fatigues anything?"

Abraham Lincoln, to General George McClellan, who had excused his lack of action in the fall of 1862 due to tired horses; McClellan was removed from command shortly thereafter

★ ★ ★ ★

"At early dawn, darkened by the threatening rain, Armistead, Garnett, Kemper and your Soldier held a heart-to-heart powwow. All three sent regards to you, and Old Lewis pulled a ring from his little finger and making me take it, said, 'Give this little token, George, please, to her of the sunset eyes, with my love, and tell her the "old man" says since he could not be the lucky dog he's mighty glad that you are.'"

Confederate General George Pickett to his fiancée on the day of Pickett's Charge

WHAT CALIBER WERE BEECHER'S BIBLES?

★ ★ ★ ★

Although his moral light faded in later years, Henry Ward Beecher continues to be remembered for abolitionist work and his power in the pulpit.

Henry Ward Beecher became one of the best-known and most influential men in America during the mid-1800s. His family's legacy, his oratorical skills as a preacher, and his moral authority as a moderate abolitionist brought him fame and large audiences. He was so famous that at one point his name was borrowed for rifles used to fight the forces of slavery in Kansas. But his legacy became somewhat compromised by positions he took in post-war politics and by a love affair that went public toward the end of his life.

Beecher's Beginnings

Born in Litchfield, Connecticut, Henry was the son of Lyman Beecher, a prominent religious leader. The elder Beecher later headed Lane Seminary in Cincinnati, which exposed Henry to activity at a key stop on the Underground Railroad. His sister, Harriet Beecher Stowe, penned the famous antislavery novel *Uncle Tom's Cabin.* Henry was critical of slavery and actively spread the message of emancipation. He attended Amherst College and Lane Seminary to prepare for a life in the church. By 1837, Beecher had joined the ministry, gotten married, and started preaching at a small Presbyterian church in Lawrenceburg, Indiana.

A Preacher's Life

Beecher quickly advanced within his profession, moving to a larger church in Indianapolis and then on to New York. He also earned a reputation on the speakers' circuit. In Brooklyn, Beecher served Plymouth Church and delivered a series of speeches entitled "Lectures to Young Men" that gained great popularity. His message both from his pulpit and while on tour was keeping moral values, with emphasis on the sins to be avoided. Each week, hundreds of young men came to hear him. By the end of the 1850s, Beecher's church regularly filled to capacity. He also learned to use the growing press, writing books and regular newspaper columns.

Political Pursuits

Beecher's efforts to emancipate slaves went beyond the moral message from his rostrum and into the political arena. He was an early backer of the Republicans and an ardent supporter of abolitionism. As the sectional conflict heightened and as abolitionists and proslavery transients flooded into Bloody Kansas to stack the vote on slavery, Beecher raised money to send 25 guns and just as many Bibles in with abolitionist immigrants. These guns, and soon any others used in the conflict, became known as "Beecher's Bibles," an ironic reference to a unique form of moral persuasion.

Soon after Congressman Preston Brooks of South Carolina clubbed abolitionist Senator Charles Sumner of Massachusetts in the Capitol, Beecher joined the controversy and painted Sumner as a martyr in the fight to rid the country of slavery. In similar fashion, he branded Brooks a villain, comparing his physical assault on Sumner to attacking a blind man, and sarcastically noting the Southern "chivalry of the man Brooks." He publicly wondered if Brooks might also enter "the sleeping room of a woman" to "bludgeon" her to death.

Taking Up the Union Cause

Once the actual war broke out, Beecher took the side of the Union, supported Lincoln, and traveled to England to persuade British audiences and the government not to side with the Confederacy. On more than one occasion he held slave auctions at his church to

purchase the freedom of slaves. After introducing one chattel for sale, he asked, "May she read liberty in your eyes? Shall she go free? Let the plates be passed and we will see." Those in the congregation wept and donated to the cause.

Though he and Lincoln did not see eye to eye throughout the war, Beecher gained greater respect for the President after he issued the Emancipation Proclamation. Lincoln recalled Beecher's efforts in England and asked him to deliver a commemorative address at Fort Sumter after the war's end.

Postwar Positions

During Reconstruction, Beecher did not always agree with the reigning Radical Republicans in terms of suppressing the South and the civil rights of freed slaves. He opposed federal protection of blacks and wanted instead to persuade Southern public opinion to move in favor of equal treatment of former slaves. Also, though many public figures saw the appointment as an abomination, Beecher supported Confederate General Robert E. Lee's selection as president of Washington College in Lexington, Virginia, asking, "When war ceased, and he laid down his arms...who could have been more modest, more manly, more true to his own word and honor than he was?" Beecher felt political practicality should replace radicalism and that the Christian approach was to accept Southerners as brothers. This position brought him great criticism from Northerners and Republicans alike.

A Legacy Tarnished

Beecher joined other religious movements in the latter half of the century and took moderate positions on temperance, women's rights, and evolution. His final days, however, are remembered for something else altogether. Beecher's national reputation as a civic leader and moral authority began to fade after Theodore Tilton, a radical writer and editor and friend of Beecher, accused the preacher of having an affair with his wife, Elizabeth. Elizabeth Tilton confessed to the affair and recanted several times, and a church trial in 1874 and a civil suit in 1875 made it a giant media event, well catalogued in *The New York Times* and other urban newspapers. Beecher's church twice exonerated him, and the civil trial ended in a hung jury, but his reputation was sullied. Henry Ward Beecher died in 1887 at age 73 of a cerebral hemorrhage. More than 40,000 mourners came to pay their respects as he lay in state.

HELPING CHILDREN TO "SEE THE TRUTH"

★ ★ ★ ★

The power of the written word is nothing new, so it's not surprising that both the North and South used publications to try to influence children.

In any war, winning the hearts and minds of those on the home front is often as important as winning battles in the heat of the conflict. During the Civil War, written propaganda was widely used on both sides to achieve this aim. And the propaganda was aimed not only at adults but at children, as well.

Northern Influence

In the North, with its industrial centers as resources, countless magazines and books containing factual and fictional war tales were aimed directly at children. One of the most popular Northern children's magazines of the day, *The Little Corporal,* used a banner across the cover to proclaim: "Fighting against wrong and for the good, the true and the beautiful." This magazine told stories of how children could help their Republic through love of God and country. It also offered toys and games with a military theme so children could feel as if they were part of the war effort.

Older children who enjoyed reading had their choice of limitless titles and "dime novels." Adventure books with such titles as *The Spy of Atlanta, Vicksburg Spy,* and *War Trails* spun yarns of brave Northern heroes who gave their lives to defeat what was portrayed as a Godless South and its treacherous soldiers.

Teaching children to support the war even entered the educational system, as can be seen in a simple ABC book of the time: "*A* is for America, land of the free, *B* is a battle our soldiers did see." This primer sought to influence students and was illustrated with engravings of dead and dying Confederate soldiers. Other books taught the alphabet using letter examples such as *A* for "Abolitionist" and *B* for "Brother with a skin of somewhat darker hue."

The glorification of children in combat also began at this time, leading to a new literary style called the "dead drummer boy poem." Dramatic poems that glorified the lost lives of innocent boys became immensely popular and are still emotionally gripping today. Northern writers were even accused of encouraging young boys to run away from home to join up under a false ideal of war.

Southern Views

The South also produced literature for its youth, but due to the shortage of ink, paper, and printing facilities, the number of books was limited, and the writings focused mostly on religion and learning. In fact, of all the children's books published in the South during the war, three-quarters were schoolbooks. The textbooks worked to create a sense of Southern nationalism in the next generation of Confederates and included such books as *The Dixie Primer, The Confederate Spelling Book,* and *A New Southern Grammar.*

Southern children had their literary heroes as well, but they were limited. Protagonists were usually faceless and nameless men and boys or the great generals of the South. In contrast to the Northern themes of heroism and winning for the glory of God, family, and country, however, the stories printed in the South leaned more toward teaching young people how to deal with the horrors of war. Southern children's magazines showed the young that they should accept loss and death as part of the greater good. "We are fighting... to drive wicked invaders from our land," one source told Southern kids. Stories such as "The Young Confederate Soldier" and "Story of a Refugee" implanted images of horrid treatment of brave Confederate soldiers and civilians at the hands of Yankees.

Educators and social scientists continue to debate the effectiveness of such children's propaganda. While most agree with the importance of involving children in an ongoing conflict such as the Civil War, some have speculated that the information and attitudes presented on both sides may have laid the groundwork for belief systems that permeate the North and the South to this day.

CAPTURED AT SEA

★ ★ ★ ★

Already embroiled in a devastating Civil War, the United States almost went to war with the entire British Empire over four men at sea.

Toward the end of 1861, Jefferson Davis hoped to gain some aid from Britain and France to help the South break the Union blockade that was slowly cutting off his shipping lanes. Accomplishing this would require convincing those two countries to recognize the Confederate States of America as a nation. The South had little chance of building a fleet capable of breaking the blockade, but both European nations had large fleets at the ready for such a task. Factors that shored up Confederate chances of convincing these countries to intercede were the facts that the French and British were major consumers of Southern cotton, and that France had its imperial eye on Mexico, which bordered Confederate Texas. Thus, the mills and banking industry of Britain and the pro-expansion political forces in France favored intervention in the American conflict, but sentiment among the public did not. In Britain, especially, the fact that the South's economy was based on slavery was not popular.

Southern Ambassadors

Davis chose former U.S. Senators James Mason and John Slidell as emissaries to those countries to negotiate recognition. The diplomats were smuggled out of Charleston by a blockade runner on October 12 and sailed to Havana, where they transferred to a British mail steamer, the *Trent*. The *Trent* left Havana on November 7 and was intercepted at sea by a U.S. vessel, the *San Jacinto*, the next day. In violation of international law, the *San Jacinto* fired warning shots across the bow of the *Trent* and forced its captain to hand over

Mason, Slidell, and their two secretaries. Because Britain was not at war with the United States, seizing these men was a violation of the same laws that Britain had violated to start the War of 1812. In short, Captain Charles Wilkes of the *San Jacinto* had just committed an act of war against Britain.

Armed and Ready

When the *San Jacinto* reached port with its prisoners, its captain was treated like a hero by the Union press and public. Initially, the official American response was also favorable, with Congress sending its official thanks to Wilkes. President Lincoln, a lawyer, quickly saw the legal problem he faced, however. On the flip side, when the *Trent* reached port with word of Wilkes's actions, the British public and government were outraged. And Britain was not alone—France was also up in arms over the incident and indicated that if Britain joined the American conflict, France would quickly follow.

Lincoln was presented with a demand for the release of the four men, and British troops were sent to Canada, from where they could attack southward if need be. Plans were drawn up detailing how many British ships would be needed to destroy the American navy, and weapons and equipment were stockpiled for the coming war against the United States. The debates in Britain became heated, with conservative newspapers, businesspeople, and politicians wanting war, while major figures ranging from Charles Darwin to Albert, the Prince Consort, argued for peace.

In late December, Lincoln decided that he needed to keep to "one war at a time." He ordered that a formal note of "apology" be sent to the British, disavowing the illegal actions of Captain Wilkes, and he then released Mason, Slidell, and their secretaries. Thousands of British troops arrived off the coast of America, only to find they weren't going to fight after all.

Mason and Slidell resumed their journeys to Britain and France, respectively. The Confederates had finally reached Europe, but Britain and France remained neutral.

THE GREAT DISSENTER OFFERS ADVICE

★ ★ ★ ★

Future Supreme Court Justice Oliver Wendell Holmes, Jr., never shied away from voicing his opinion. According to one tale, that even meant barking orders at the President.

Oliver Wendell Holmes, Jr., is primarily known as one of the most influential justices of the U.S. Supreme Court. Like many men of his generation, however, he was also a veteran of the Civil War. A native of Boston and a proponent of abolishing slavery, Holmes joined the Union army as a private before graduating from Harvard. After his graduation in 1861, he was commissioned as a 2nd lieutenant in the 20th Massachusetts Infantry.

Under Fire

Holmes became well acquainted with the hazards of battle. Of the 2,000 Union regiments that served during the war, the 20th Massachusetts was among the top five in casualty rates. Holmes himself was wounded three times during the first two years of the war, at the battles of Balls Bluff, Antietam, and Fredericksburg, and he saw many comrades killed or wounded in some of the bloodiest altercations of the war.

Too Close for Comfort

In July 1864, a relatively small force of Confederate soldiers under General Jubal Early penetrated into Union territory toward the national capital. By the afternoon of July 11, some 10,000 rebels were at the very walls of Fort Stevens, part of the formidable ring of fortifications that surrounded Washington, D.C. Military and civil leaders alike panicked, and reinforcements were rushed up to the lines. Curious to survey the situation, the President himself was present.

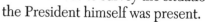

Holmes, by then a lieutenant colonel, was part of the regiment guarding Fort Stevens.

Useful Advice

By the next morning, Early knew an attack was hopeless, and he ordered his troops to retreat under cover of sharpshooter fire. According to lore, Lieutenant Colonel Holmes was present on the ramparts, keeping tabs on the action as Confederate bullets whizzed by. Suddenly, he spotted an exceptionally tall man in dark civilian garb standing up on the parapet, where he could clearly be seen by the attackers.

Without taking the time to identify the figure, Holmes yelled, "Get down, you damn fool!" Much to his surprise, the man he had chastened was Abraham Lincoln. The President, as the story goes, cheerfully complied with the order.

An Eloquent Career

Despite the directness required that day, Holmes later became known for his eloquence. He would write that the war was one of the most meaningful episodes of his life. "We have shared the incommunicable experience of war. We have felt, we still feel, the passion of life to its top," he wrote. "In our youths, our hearts were touched with fire."

After the war, Holmes returned to Harvard to study law and went on to a distinguished career as a jurist. In 1902, President Theodore Roosevelt named him a justice of the U.S. Supreme Court, a position Holmes held for 30 years until age 90. While on the Court, he gained quite a reputation from his forceful dissenting opinions. But no matter what else he accomplished, Holmes will always be known for the storied day the Great Dissenter met the Great Emancipator.

- *Throughout the North and South, ringing church bells were used to alert the general public to gather for significant news.*

- *The "Tennessee" or "Virginia quickstep" (depending upon where they were campaigning) was the name Union troops fighting in the South gave to diarrhea.*

- *A division is a military unit composed of three brigades led by a major general. A brigade was an organized military unit generally made up of two or more regiments and led by a brigadier general.*

- *Some Confederate volunteers wore homespun attire dyed a yellowish-brown using, among other things, walnut shells. Their uniform color led to their nickname of Butternuts.*

- Chain-shot *was an artillery shot consisting of two iron plates that were connected by a bolt, with nine or more iron balls between them.*

- Hardtack, *a 3-inch square and 1½-inch thick piece of bread shaped like a cracker, was a staple for soldiers on both sides. Nine or ten squares of hardtack constituted a ration.*

- Lamp posts *is the name gunners affectionately bestowed on particularly big shells, usually those weighing one hundred pounds or more.*

- *During the March to the Sea and the Carolinas Campaign, the name "bummers" was given to Sherman's Union Army of Georgia, who were authorized to live off the land. The term may have derived from the German* bummler, *which means* loafer *or* waster.

- *The* wooden mule *was a punishment in which a soldier was forced to sit for hours on a narrow fence rail that was set high enough so that his feet didn't touch the ground.*

FIRE ON THE WATERS

★ ★ ★ ★

The battle for the Mississippi River was a
make-or-break effort for both North and South.

After Winfield Scott's blockade of Confederate ports went into
effect in 1861, the only unfettered trade route
left open to the Confederacy came
through Mexico. To reach the South's
mills and armies, that route had to cross
the Mississippi River. If the Union could take
control of the Mississippi, it would cut
the Confederacy in two, and the
South's trade with the rest of the
world would effectively be over.

Taking Charge in New Orleans

One end of the Mississippi, New Orleans, swiftly fell to the Union
navy, but to control the waters further north, river navies would be
necessary, and both sides began in earnest. With shipbuilding
centers in St. Louis, Louisville, and Cincinnati, the Union had a
definite edge, and soon a fleet of ironclads, gunboats, and transports were fighting their way south toward Vicksburg. On July 1,
1862, two pincers closed in on that river city, but the Union didn't
control the water just yet.

Confederate Resistance

The South fought back, building makeshift warships in local boat-
yards. When the powerful Confederate ironclad *Arkansas,* under
construction at Memphis, was moved to the headwaters of the
Yazoo River just above Vicksburg for completion, Admiral David
Glasgow Farragut sent the Union ironclad *Carondelet,* the gunboat *Tyler,* and the ram *Queen of the West* up the Yazoo to find her
in mid-July. He discovered the *Arkansas* was far stronger than
he'd expected. The Confederate ironclad badly damaged the

Carondelet and chased the other two boats away, and then it approached Vicksburg without warning. No Union vessel had steam up, so the *Arkansas* chugged past, exchanging fire with 20 Union ships, devastating 3 of them and disabling the ram *Lancaster*. But the *Arkansas* was damaged as well, losing an eighth of its crew. In a dramatic moment following the clash, as the ship sailed alongside the Vicksburg waterfront, cheering spectators saw how badly it had been damaged and fell silent.

Farragut ordered the *Essex* and the *Queen of the West* to attack the *Arkansas* at its moorings. The *Essex* ran aground, and for ten minutes the two ships blasted away at one another, their heavy armor protecting them from fatal damage. Losing power, the *Essex* floated away downstream. The *Queen of the West* rammed the *Arkansas* but did no great damage, leaving the *Arkansas* a still-potent threat.

Further Down the River

Downstream at Baton Rouge, Confederate General John C. Breckinridge attacked the Union troops who, with the aid of the *Essex* and two gunboats, were holding the city. The Confederates had counted on the *Arkansas* coming to help them, but it had not arrived.

Unbeknownst to Breckinridge, the *Arkansas,* which had not been fully repaired, had broken down just north of Baton Rouge. Seeing her smoke, the *Essex* sailed to investigate. Under intense fire from the *Essex,* the *Arkansas* ran aground and, set afire by her crew, exploded and sank.

Switching Sides

The *Arkansas* had died nobly, but the game was not yet over. Southerners were still shipping supplies from Louisiana, so in February 1863, Admiral David Dixon Porter sent the *Queen of the West* down to blockade the Red River. Unfortunately, the ram came under fire from shore batteries, was hit and, ultimately, captured by the Confederates. While the Southerners repaired the *Queen,* Porter, unaware of what had happened, sent the new ironclad *Indianola* down to join it. When the *Indianola*'s skipper, George Brown, saw the *Queen* coming toward him in the company of the rebel ram *Webb* and two Confederate gunboats, he tried to flee up the Mississippi, but the rebels caught the *Indianola* and drove it ashore.

Psych!

Admiral Porter, realizing that the *Indianola* was in enemy hands but not knowing its condition, plotted to delay any potential salvage the Confederates might have planned. Using an abandoned flatboat, he built a dummy ironclad and set it adrift. With smokepots in her "smokestacks," she looked like the South's worst nightmare. When the crews attempting to salvage the *Indianola* saw this formidable monster coming, they panicked, burned the *Indianola,* and fled. Union forces reached the *Indianola* in enough time, however, that they put the fire out and reclaimed the ironclad without too much damage.

The Mississippi finally came under complete Union control a few months later. On July 4, 1863, after dozens of river and land battles, Vicksburg finally surrendered. As Lincoln declared, "The Father of Waters once more goes unvexed to the sea."

"They couldn't hit an elephant at this distance."
Union General John Sedgwick, just moments before being shot dead by a Confederate sniper at Spotsylvania

"My religious belief teaches me to feel as safe in battle as in bed. God has fixed the time for my death. I do not concern myself about that, but to always be ready, no matter when it may overtake me."
Stonewall Jackson

REBUILDING AFTER IT WAS ALL OVER

★ ★ ★ ★

When the Civil War ended in 1865, the South was in shambles. Some 258,000 Southerners—including 50,000 civilians—had been slain in the four-year conflict, and another 100,000 or so had been wounded. (That compares with 360,000 dead and 275,000 wounded in the Northern forces). The surviving Confederate troops marched home through a devastated landscape past burned farms, shattered towns, and abandoned counties. What industry that had been established before the war was obliterated—infrastructure such as roads, bridges, and railways had been demolished, and anything like a normal economy was nonexistent.

For governing purposes, the U.S. government divided the 11 states of the former Confederacy into 5 large military zones, each under the control of a U.S. Army general. Approximately 200,000 Union troops were deployed to the South to enforce the will of the federal government. The "Yankee rule" the Southerners had fought to prevent had arrived, but in a manner that went far beyond their worst fears.

Putting Back the Pieces

As early as 1863, leaders in the North began to discuss how to "reconstruct" the South, including how to change its political and social institutions. Lincoln and his closest generals had favored a plan for Reconstruction that would have helped mend the rifts of the war. Had the President survived, the country might have been put back together in a more painless manner, but much of the clemency Lincoln desired died with him. Many of the measures Congress ultimately imposed under Reconstruction were intended as revenge and did little to help the country's healing process.

Andrew Johnson, the Southerner who followed Lincoln as President, did not have the popularity or political force to see Lincoln's plan through to completion. His attempts at a relatively lenient "Restoration," rather than the harsh "Reconstruction" that was actually carried out, led to his impeachment.

Some Constitutional measures—such as the 13th, 14th, and 15th Amendments, which guaranteed social, political, and legal rights to the freed blacks—were designed to ensure civil rights and social justice. White Southerners seethed. One of the least popular institutions forced upon the former Confederacy was the Freedmen's Bureau, an agency established by Lincoln as part of the War Department in 1865 that helped newly freed slaves obtain their own land, become self-sufficient, and wield political power. The bureau quickly became rife with corruption and inefficiency.

Migrating South

During the period of Reconstruction, thousands of Northern civilians flooded into the devastated South. Some were opportunists, unscrupulous adventurers, and con artists seeking personal gain and political offices. Everyone who came from the North was dubbed a *carpetbagger* by Southerners, after a popular form of cheap luggage that many of them carried. Despite the widespread use of this derogatory term, however, many of these transplants were not self-seeking vagabonds at all—they emigrated to the South with the intent of rebuilding industry, restoring infrastructure, and educating blacks.

Some Southern politicians, including a number of former Confederate soldiers, joined the Northern-based Republican Party during this period and advocated working within the parameters of Reconstruction. Such men were widely hated by others in the South, and most were branded as unprincipled *scalawags* by those committed to resisting Union rule. Again, like the Northern carpetbaggers, some leeway has to be given: Certainly there were scoundrels active in Southern politics at this time, but some participants were sincere individuals who recognized that cooperating with the federal government was the quickest and most effective way to ensure the rapid withdrawal of federal troops and the return of some measure of autonomy to their states.

The Rise of Hate

These events and sentiments made Reconstruction a difficult and painful time for the South and nurtured long-term animosities. Many white Southerners resented the ability of newly enfranchised black voters to put hated Republican politicians in power. They formed organizations supporting white supremacy—secret societies opposed to blacks, the Republican Party, and the federal government. Most notable among these was the Ku Klux Klan (KKK), whose members were sworn to secrecy and hid their identities behind white robes and hooded masks.

Terrorism is not a recent phenomenon. Criminal paramilitary organizations such as the KKK conducted increasingly violent and horrifying terrorist activities against U.S. citizens and their government throughout the Reconstruction period and beyond. Some former Confederate soldiers carried on the war as "night riders," which had started as patrols of white men deputized specifically to look for runaway slaves, enforce slave curfews, and squash any possible black uprisings. One of the founding members of the KKK was former Confederate General Nathan Bedford Forrest, who served as the organization's first Grand Wizard.

Local Klan organizations, or "klaverns," touted the flaming cross as their symbol and were especially active during election campaigns, using intimidation, violence, rape, and murder to help sway votes and prevent Republican political victories in their states. Those who were often targeted included local Republican leaders—white or black—and blacks who no longer conformed to antebellum standards of conduct.

In areas under Republican control, authorities were hard-pressed to quell the violence and were loath to deploy their mostly black state militias against the KKK and other organizations for fear of provoking a full-blown race war. In areas under Democratic control, the authorities themselves were frequently members of the Klan or sympathizers. Even when local law enforcement authorities did take action, Klan members often sat on juries or judges' benches, ensuring little or no justice would be done.

Slowly Healing

By the early 1870s, most Americans—Northern and Southern alike—agreed that the KKK was out of control. Even Forrest publicly renounced its activities. In 1871, the Republican-led Congress authorized President Ulysses S. Grant to use federal troops to restore order in areas deemed the least under control. The troops had the power to arrest suspects and hold them indefinitely without trial.

By 1872, the Ku Klux Klan had been defeated, and it ceased to exist as an organization until it was revived more than four decades later in 1915. In the 1870s, Southerners opposed to the rule of the federal government ultimately regained influence over their towns, counties, and states through political and economic means. They then used that power to corrupt and undermine many of the changes the federal government had made. It would be another century before the rights won for blacks during the war would come to fruition.

Reconstruction lasted 12 years. Although the states that had seceded were readmitted to the Union by early 1870, violence, civil unrest, and military occupation continued until 1877. All of this contributed to a long-term bitterness that has survived far beyond the lives of those who fought in that bloodiest of American conflicts.

- *It took a minimum of ten days for a letter to travel from San Antonio to Washington. This was not an era of instantaneous communications, which greatly affected a commander's ability to control his troops and sharply limited his options.*

BEATEN ON THE SENATE FLOOR

★ ★ ★ ★

*After Massachusetts Senator Charles Sumner's speech
got personal, a South Carolina representative took
matters into his own hands—literally.*

Raw emotion and angry exchanges can often come to dominate a
political debate, and at times it can be downright dangerous. In
the tension-filled years that led up to the secession of the Southern states, the U.S. Senate was a frequent setting for passionate,
and often bitter, oratory in which the adversaries were North
versus South, slaves states versus free.

An Acrid Address

It can be argued that no speech in the history of the Senate has
been more provocative than the address made by Massachusetts
Senator Charles Sumner on May 19 and 20, 1856. For two days,
the fervent abolitionist delivered his blistering "Crime Against
Kansas" speech. It was an attack on proslavery forces in the
Kansas territory and beyond that was loaded with personal invec-
tive directed toward the supporters of that peculiar institution.
Sumner made a number of personal insults against senators who
advocated slavery, calling them imbeciles and immoral. He referred to Illinois Senator Stephen Douglas, one of his political
enemies on the slavery question, as a nameless animal unfit to be
an American senator.

Sumner also specifically singled out South Carolina Senator
Andrew Butler for scorn. Butler was ill at the time and therefore
not present in the Senate chamber to hear the address himself.
Sumner identified Butler as a prominent example of hypocrisy on
the slavery question and repeatedly disparaged South Carolina as a
state whose contributions to the Union were so historically

insignificant that it would be immediately overshadowed by the admission of a new territory such as Kansas. He also made a number of pointed personal attacks against Butler, the most graphic of which was his repeated suggestion that Butler kept a "harlot, Slavery."

A Personal Attack

The fallout from this incendiary speech was far more than merely political. The response from Butler's camp came two days later when Preston Brooks, a member of the House of Representatives from South Carolina and the nephew of Senator Butler, offered his reply. He had heard the Sumner speech from the Senate gallery and, incensed by its tone, was determined to avenge the honor of both his uncle and his state.

Brooks entered the Senate chamber during a recess. Seeing Sumner sitting at his desk, Brooks began to denounce the senator for the insults he'd made two days earlier. Before Sumner could reply, Brooks suddenly struck him with his hollow, metal-tipped cane, delivering a series of vicious blows to Sumner's head and body that left the senator battered and semiconscious. When his cane broke after 30 blows, Brooks walked away from the crippled Sumner and returned to his business in the House of Representatives. In many contemporary reports of the attack, Southern senators present in the chamber were said to have laughed as Sumner was beaten. It took three years for Sumner to fully recover from the injuries he received.

Although a motion to expel Brooks from the House of Representatives for dishonorable conduct was defeated when representatives from the South refused to support it, the House did vote to censure him. He resigned from office, but his South Carolina district elected him right back into Congress. Brooks became a hero in the South, a symbol of a man prepared to defend principle and honor when challenged. Sumner became a heroic figure in the North, where he was characterized as both a victim of Southern brutality and an example of how proslavery forces attempted to suppress free speech.

WHAT KIND OF WEAPON IS THAT?

★ ★ ★ ★

How did Johnny Reb and Billy Yank fight a modern war? With new-fangled weapons! Inventors from North and South struggled to create new devices that could fill the bill.

The Civil War is commonly known as the "first modern war" because of the introduction of so many "firsts." For instance, great measures were taken to improve the conditions for soldiers on both sides, including innovations such as the use of railroads and ships to move soldiers, supplies, and the wounded from one place to another; food preservation methods such as canned goods; and improved medical procedures. Inventors from the Union and the Confederacy also tirelessly worked to create weapons that would give their troops the advantage on the battlefield. They successfully introduced ironclad ships, submarines, and land and sea mines. The need to provide maximum firepower, however, resulted in a collection of weapons that were innovative—perhaps too innovative.

Rapid Fire in the North

The Agar "Coffee Mill" gun, invented by Northerner Wilson Agar, was used ineffectively by both sides during the war. It was called the "Coffee Mill" because its top-mounted hopper and crank closely resembled a coffee grinder. It percolated much more than a morning beverage, however. The gun fired either a loose-powder .58-caliber Minie-type ball or a paper round through its single barrel at a rate of about 120 rounds per minute—it could fire at a faster rate, but that tended to overheat the barrel. The gun had a range of about 1,000 yards. The ammunition was loaded into steel containers and fed by gravity through the hopper into a crank-driven revolving chamber. Lincoln purchased 12 Agar guns in November 1861, followed by another 50 the next month.

Southern-Style Firepower

Ingenuity was not limited to Northern inventors. Some of the most creative designs were developed in the South. Unfortunately, the designs proved to be less than efficient on the battlefield.

On April 22, 1862, several men stood near Newton's Bridge outside of Athens, Georgia, to test an invention of John Gilleland, who was a carpenter prior to the war. The newly forged cannon—a double-barreled six-pounder gun—was rolled into position. The barrels were aligned with a three-degree divergence to fire shells at a slight angle from each other. Lying on the ground next to the gun were pairs of shells attached to each other by a chain. If the gun worked, the two shells would propel the chain to cut down anything in its path. Gilleland stepped up and loaded a shell in each barrel, leaving a portion of the chain draped between the muzzles. But when he fired both barrels, the shells didn't fire simultaneously. Instead, the first traveled erratically while the other followed behind it. Subsequent tests ended with the same result. When the gun was sent to the Confederate government for evaluation, it was returned to be reconfigured so that instead of shells connected by a chain, each barrel was loaded with a canister. The gun eventually saw action on August 2, 1864, when Northern forces approached Athens. It successfully drove away Union troops and now stands outside Athens City Hall.

Rapid Fire That Worked

One successful Confederate invention was the Williams rapid-fire gun, created by Captain R. S. Williams. A breech-loaded artillery piece, it had a four-foot-long barrel. This weapon differed from other artillery in that it was hand-cranked and capable of firing up to 20 rounds per minute with a maximum range of 2,000 yards. The Williams rapid-fire gun proved to be very effective in its first action on May 31, 1862, at the Battle of Seven Pines. Although it was discovered that rapid fire caused the breech to expand and fail to lock, the gun was used in both the Eastern and Western Theaters throughout the war. "We had heard artillery before," one Union officer observed, "but we had never heard anything that made such a horrible noise as the shot from these breechloaders."

LIFE IN THE CAMPS

★ ★ ★ ★

*Army life was not all it was cracked up to be. Soldiers
certainly experienced their share of adventure and drama,
but daily life was often quite the opposite.*

What was the difference between Confederate and Union soldiers? When it came down to it, not much. Although their view-
points and goals may have been wildly different, they were, in
essence, mostly cut from the same cloth. With 38 percent of
Union generals and 35 percent of Confederate generals having
graduated from West Point, it stands to reason that many of these
officers had been classmates and close friends. Since they had
trained together, it's no surprise that many of them ran their
armies in similar ways. Whether Northern or Southern, most
participants agreed on a single sentiment: The majority of a Civil
War soldier's life was very tedious. "Soldiering is 99 percent boredom and 1 percent sheer terror," wrote one soldier to his wife.

Daily Doldrums

When not campaigning, soldiers settled into camps that were temporary in warm weather and long-term in winter. For North and
South both, an average day in camp began when reveille was
blown at 5:00 A.M. in the summer and 6:00 A.M. in the winter.
There was little difference in the condition of the troops who
answered the call on one side of the fight or the other. "Some wore
one shoe," observed Union correspondent George Townsend,
"and others appeared shivering in their linen. They stood ludi-
crously in rank, and a succession of short, dry coughs ran up and
down the line."

Following roll call, soldiers ate breakfast, which was usually followed by the first of several one- to two-hour drill sessions. "The
first thing in the morning is drill," said one soldier. "Then drill,
then drill again. Then drill, drill, a little more drill. Then drill,
and lastly drill." The type of drills depended on the type of soldier.

A squad of infantry would drill with each other, practicing marching, parading, and moving together. Cavalry would perform sword drills, either on horseback or on foot. Anything a soldier needed to do was subject to a drill. Everybody practiced loading and readying their firearms. One activity that didn't get a lot of drill time, surprisingly, was actually firing the weapons. There wasn't a lot of extra ammunition, and the military brass wanted to use it on targets that mattered.

Between drills, a soldier would perform necessary chores around the camp, such as picking up waste, digging latrines, or standing on guard duty. When on his own, a soldier engaged in a variety of activities to keep busy, including playing games such as chess and baseball, reading, and writing letters to loved ones at home. Much less wholesome (and far more popular) was the trio of gambling, whiskey, and women. "If there is any place on God's fair earth where wickedness 'stalketh abroad in daylight,'" one Confederate wrote to his family, "it is in the army." A new recruit also wrote about the activity of camp: "There is some of the onerest [*sic*] men here that I ever saw, and the most swearing and card playing and fitin [fighting] and drunkenness that I ever saw at any place."

Eat Up

As addictive as such self-indulgences were to a soldier, nothing was more important than food, which was plentiful for both sides in the opening months of the war. "We have better meat hear [*sic*] than you have in St. James," one Confederate soldier wrote to his sister. "We have Ice Water & Coffee three times a day." If the army didn't serve what the soldier liked, he either asked his family to send it or, when he had money, bought it from one of the sutlers who followed the armies and set up businesses near the camps.

Troops were formed into four to eight messes, and the men were expected to share in the food preparation. Some soldiers cooked while others cleaned up or went foraging for any foodstuffs available within the camp or from neighboring civilians. They cleared out nearby areas, so the longer the troops were in camp, the further they had to travel for firewood and other necessities.

While on the march, however, food was not as plentiful because of the logistical difficulty of carrying all the supplies an army would need. While camping, food supplies were far more abundant, though as the war progressed, the Confederates weren't able to find the amount and quality of food necessary to sustain the energies of an army.

In Sickness and in Snow

Due to a lack of sanitary conditions, the longer the armies camped, the more susceptible soldiers were to disease, which could bring down even the heartiest of them. "Camp streets and spaces between tents [were] littered with refuse, food and other rubbish," one Union soldier noted, "sometimes in an offensive state of decomposition; slops deposited in pits within the camp limits or thrown out broadcast; heaps of manure and offal close to the camp." Such filthy living bred disease, which in turn resulted in many deaths.

Armies sometimes remained camped for six months or more, and the problems of boredom and disease were particularly intense during the winter. Ingenuity was necessary at this time to make both work and play bearable. To get out of their tents, soldiers built cabins with chimneys when wood was available. If there was little or no building material during the winter, they still needed fires to keep themselves warm, so they built chimneys in the openings of their tents.

Both Union and Confederate soldiers found ways to entertain and amuse themselves and each other throughout the winter. Music played an important part in camp life, whether it was singing songs around the campfire or even formal orchestral concerts. To break up the boredom, snow fights between regiments or even brigades would break out at a moment's notice. For those less inclined to participate in the usual debauchery of gambling, whiskey, and women, religious revivals could also be found.

Life in camp was a trial for all soldiers no matter their rank, but those battle-free days or months were far preferable to time spent marching or fighting.

BREAKFAST AT SHILOH

★ ★ ★ ★

The Union soldiers turned the tide in the brutal Battle of Shiloh when the Confederates eyed their breakfast.

In April 1862, President Lincoln's grand plan of splitting the Confederacy in two by controlling the Mississippi River was nearing reality. The battle-hardened armies of Union generals Ulysses S. Grant and Don Carlos Buell were marching unopposed toward the city of Corinth, Mississippi, where the South's rail lines converged. If Grant and Buell took Corinth, not only would the Confederacy be cut in two along the western rivers, but Southern rail transportation would be crippled, as well.

In a Holding Pattern

Grant's army rolled into the town of Pittsburg Landing, Tennessee, north of Corinth on the west bank of the Tennessee River, on April 6. He planned to wait until Buell's force joined him there and then to march together into Corinth. But Grant, and his subordinate General William Tecumseh Sherman, made a critical tactical error. They set up camp with their backs to the wide and deep river.

Confederate General Albert Sidney Johnston recognized an opportunity. He took 44,000 of his troops who were guarding Corinth and marched them right up to the edge of the Union camp. At dawn, the rebels sprang upon the unsuspecting bluecoats, completely surprising the Union soldiers and driving them quickly to the bank of the river.

Hmm, That Smells Like Breakfast!

Once the enemy was on the run, however, the hungry Confederates' stomachs betrayed them. The federal soldiers had been making breakfast when the battle started, and they'd left the food behind in the rush of the battle. Some of the rebels slowed their attack to gobble down a meal.

This gave Grant's army a chance to pull themselves together. Hundreds of them made a stand in a sunken road known as "The Hornet's Nest." The Union defense was bolstered further when General Johnston was mortally wounded. A bullet—possibly from one of his own soldiers—had torn through an artery in his leg.

Fighting Back

Union forces clearly lost the battle that day, but they weren't crushed. Grant acknowledged the defeat but was quick with a comeback—"Whip 'em tomorrow, though." Not long after that conversation, Buell arrived. On April 7, 1862, the combined Union armies retook the ground lost the previous day. In two days of fighting, Shiloh had become the bloodiest battle of the war so far, with more than 23,000 combined casualties.

"In my tent last night, after a fatiguing day's service, I remembered that I failed to send a contribution for our colored Sunday school. Enclosed you will find a check for that object, which please acknowledge at your earliest convenience and oblige yours faithfully."
General Stonewall Jackson, in a letter to his pastor after the First Battle of Bull Run

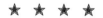

"The next time we met was at Appomattox, and the first thing that General Grant said to me when we stepped inside, placing his hand in mine was, 'Pete, let us have another game of brag, to recall the days that were so pleasant.' Great God! I thought to myself, how my heart swells out to such magnanimous touch of humanity. Why do men fight who were born to be brothers?"
General James Longstreet on General Grant

Fast Facts

- *The tune for Elvis Presley's song "Love Me Tender" was based on a popular Civil War ballad about a maiden, "Aura Lee." Music for the 1861 song was written by George R. Poulton, with lyrics by W. W. Fosdick.*

- *General David E. Twiggs was the longest-serving U.S. Army officer to join the Confederate army, having fought during the War of 1812. Twiggs, a distinguished veteran of the Mexican War, became commander of the Department of Texas in 1857. Although he was strongly sympathetic to the Southern cause, he requested instructions from Washington about the disposition of his command if Texas seceded. When he did not receive any orders, Twiggs formally turned over every fort and outpost in the Department of Texas, along with 2,000 soldiers and most of the equipment and all of the U.S. Army funds in his possession, to Colonel Ben McCulloch, commander of Confederate troops in Texas. After Twiggs was dismissed from Union service, he joined the Confederate army as a major general.*

- *The fall of Atlanta in 1864 had significant political ramifications: It boosted Northern morale and was seen as a "turning point" for the reelection of President Lincoln. McClellan was running against Lincoln on a peace platform that called for a truce with the Confederates.*

- *Traveller, perhaps the best-known horse of the war, was Robert E. Lee's favorite mount. Other mounts of his were named Richmond, Brown-Roan, Lucy Long, and Ajax.*

- *Rutherford B. Hayes, the 19th president, was almost 40 and had no prior military experience when he enlisted as a major in the 23rd Regiment of the Ohio Volunteer Infantry. Hayes was severely wounded at the Battle of South Mountain and eventually rose to the rank of brevet major general.*

A LICENSE TO PRINT MONEY

★ ★ ★ ★

*Faced with shortages of metal for coins, the Union decided that
paper money was the way to keep the economy going.*

When the war began, the Union economy was far more robust and
resilient than that of the Confederates, but that wasn't saying
much. The shock of secession had severely affected the North.
American citizens were hoarding gold and silver coins, the dominant currency of the day. For its part, the government was faced
with a ballooning payroll packed with soldiers and other war
expenditures. Bold action had to be taken to prevent bankruptcy.
The U.S. government decided that the way to alleviate this pressure would be to introduce paper currency, which would allow it
to have more control over the money supply.

Potential Paper Problems

There hadn't been a paper currency in the United States since
colonial times, when the weak and easily faked "Continentals"
were used to fund the Revolution. Furthermore, paper money has
to be carefully regulated, because if too much of it is printed and
put into use, it can cause inflation. If the inflation is bad enough,
the paper money itself can become worthless. The Confederate
economy fell into this trap, and the cost of goods skyrocketed. The
Union was determined to avoid such a calamity, so the Treasury
made a strong—and ultimately successful—effort to limit the
amount of paper bills it would print.

The Color of Money

The first paper note to be issued for wide circulation in the North
was the Demand Note. It got its name because it was redeemable
for its worth in gold "on demand." This note was only issued for
one year before it was replaced by another, the Legal Tender
Note. The new notes were known as *fiat money*, which means that
they weren't backed by anything other than the government's

word. Naturally, these were not nearly as popular as the Demand Notes had been.

The design of these first paper notes was carefully considered to reduce the chance that they could easily be counterfeited. The familiar green color of American money was chosen for the first time during the Civil War. Photography was still in its early stages and could only create images in black, so the green color ensured that some clever person with a primitive camera couldn't create a convincing copy.

Although there was some green ink on the front of Demand Notes, the back was printed entirely in green, and the notes became known as *greenbacks*. The patterns and designs on these notes were quite complicated. The greenback side displayed the value in large text on top of a field of smaller numbers. Alexander Hamilton was on the front of the five-dollar bill, and Abraham Lincoln was on the ten. The twenty featured a female representation of Liberty. The skilled engravers of Northern mints and print houses had created very fine and ornately constructed bills that would prove very difficult to replicate. When the Legal Tender Notes were released the following year, they had similar, but distinct, designs.

- *In 1862, British Chancellor of the Exchequer William E. Gladstone predicted that secession would be successful: "There is no doubt that Jefferson Davis and other leaders of the South have made an army; they are making, it appears, a navy; and they have made what is more than either—they have made a nation. . . . We may anticipate with certainty the success of the Southern States so far as regards their separation from the North."*

- *Abraham Lincoln's second secretary of war, Edwin M. Stanton, is believed to have originated Lincoln's nickname, "The Original Gorilla," although General McClellan adopted it and used it frequently in his correspondence with his wife.*

GREAT CIVIL WAR BOOKS

★ ★ ★ ★

What are some other favorite Civil War books? Here's a list of a few—both fiction and nonfiction—in no particular order.

Fiction

Gone With the Wind
(1936)—Atlanta's Margaret
Mitchell only wrote one book
in her entire life—good thing
that book was the best seller
Gone With the Wind. Winning a Pulitzer Prize in 1937, the epic
novel tells the story of Scarlett O'Hara and her romances during
the Civil War. Mitchell didn't quite get everything right in the first
draft, however. She originally wanted Scarlett's first name to be
Pansy!

The Killer Angels (1974)—Michael Shaara penned this stirring
story of the Battle of Gettysburg, earning himself a Pulitzer Prize.
Shaara describes the event through the eyes of Union soldiers and
generals, including General John Buford and Colonel Joshua
Lawrence Chamberlain, as well as Confederate leaders such as
generals James Longstreet and Robert E. Lee. Although it is a
work of fiction, many history professors use this in college history
classes. The book was also the basis for the 1993 film *Gettysburg.*

The Last Full Measure (1998)—Jeff Shaara picks up where his
father left off, dramatizing the Confederate retreat after Gettysburg and the events through to the end of the war as seen by
several key players in the conflict. This book rounds out a trilogy
that includes Michael Shaara's *The Killer Angels* and Jeff Shaara's
1996 prequel, *Gods and Generals.*

Little Women (1868)—Louisa May Alcott's classic story tells of
the lives of the March family and its four daughters—Meg, Jo,

Beth, and Amy—during and after the Civil War. This story has been turned into countless movies, a musical, and even an opera. Alcott penned two sequels, *Little Men* and *Jo's Boys*.

The Red Badge of Courage (1895)—Written by Stephen Crane, this longtime best seller tells the story of young Union soldier Henry Fleming and his personal experiences around the time of the Battle of Chancellorsville. *The Red Badge of Courage* has become an indispensable work of literature for classrooms across the United States.

John Brown's Body (1928)—A narrative poem of epic proportions, this book was written by Stephen Vincent Benet and won the Pulitzer Prize in 1929. Benet covers the entire expanse of the war, from Harpers Ferry to Generals Grant and Lee at Appomattox Court House.

North and South (1982)—The first of a three-novel series by John Jakes, *North and South* relates the friendship of two young men—South Carolinian Orry Main and Pennsylvanian George Hazard—who meet on the way to West Point. When the Civil War splits the friends, the story follows the complex consequences through the rest of the trilogy, which includes *Love and War* and *Heaven and Hell*. The books became enormous hits as three TV miniseries in the 1980s and '90s.

March (2005)—Another look at Louisa May Alcott's March family, this book focuses on the absent father, gone to the war. Geraldine Brooks takes *Little Women* as a starting point to imagine what Meg, Jo, Beth, and Amy's father experienced as a Union chaplain. *March* is the fourth Pulitzer Prize winner on this list, snagging the award in 2006.

Nonfiction

Battle Cry of Freedom (1988)—Many regard *Battle Cry of Freedom*, written by noted historian James McPherson, as the finest single-volume work on the Civil War. As a professor of American history at Princeton University, McPherson brought life and vision to the American struggle from 1850 to Reconstruction.

Many colleges and universities with classes focusing on the war use this book. And yes, it's another Pulitzer Prize winner.

The Civil War: A Narrative (1974)—Author Shelby Foote spent 20 years researching and writing this seminal series on the War Between the States. The 3,000-page, three-volume set was written entirely by hand with an old-fashioned dipped-ink pen. Foote's knowledge led to prominent appearances on Ken Burns's PBS series, *The Civil War.*

Chancellorsville (1996)—Historian Stephen W. Sears penned hundreds of pages on what many consider to be the greatest of Robert E. Lee's victories. But Sears takes a path less chosen, giving much of the credit for Lee's success to luck. Sears is also the author of *Landscape Turned Red: The Battle of Antietam* and *To the Gates of Richmond: The Peninsula Campaign.*

A Stillness at Appomattox (1953)—Aiming to explain the strategies and battles of General Ulysses S. Grant beginning in 1864 until the end of the war in 1865, this well-written book earned author Bruce Catton a Pulitzer Prize in 1954. It is the third in a three-volume series about the Army of the Potomac. The first two are entitled *Mr. Lincoln's Army* and *Glory Road.*

Lincoln at Gettysburg: The Words that Remade America (1992)—The Gettysburg Address is possibly the most famous speech ever given in America, and author Garry Wills takes an in-depth look at it piece by piece, examining Lincoln's influences in writing it and his intentions in delivering it. Wills helps readers gain a new appreciation and understanding of these few but immortal words.

The Life of Johnny Reb: The Common Soldier of the Confederacy (1943)—Bell Irvin Wiley wrote this book and its companion, 1952's *The Life of Billy Yank: The Common Soldier of the Union,* to present the experience of the regular trooper down among the rest of the rank and file. Through contemporary letters and diaries, Wiley portrays what everyday army life was like for all those people whose names we'll never know.

DRAFT RIOTS ROCK NEW YORK CITY

★ ★ ★ ★

Angry draftees demonstrated just how much they didn't want to join the army.

Throughout its early history, the United States had always survived with volunteer militias and armies. There had never been a draft to call men to war. By 1863, however, it was becoming clear that not enough men were joining the Union army. President Lincoln signed a conscription bill into law. It assigned each Congressional district a particular number of soldiers to recruit, and all men ages 20 to 45 were eligible, although various exemptions were available.

Not So Simple

All this seems easy enough, but there were a few problems. Although a number of parts of the nation had witnessed opposition to the draft, New York City seemed particularly unwelcoming. The legislation had set the city's recruitment target at 26,000. In early July 1863, however, the Battle of Gettysburg had just ended, and gruesome descriptions of combat and long lists of casualties appeared in New York papers, making the idea of war completely unappealing. In addition, one of the many loopholes in the draft legislation allowed able-bodied men who were chosen to serve to buy their way out of the obligation by paying $300 to the government. Or these same men could also find a replacement to serve in their place. This obviously meant that rich people didn't have to fight if they didn't want to fight. Further, because many poor whites in New York found themselves competing for jobs against black laborers, they certainly didn't want to fight a war that had the freedom of slaves as its root. Toss in the fact that Lincoln was a Republican who was strongly disliked by New York Democratic leaders, and the stage was set in the city for some serious antidraft protests.

On Sunday, July 12, 1863, New York newspapers printed the names of those who had been drafted the day before. The next morning, groups of people gathered to protest, peaceably at first. Soon, however, the crowds started attacking people or places that symbolized the draft, such as police and the office of the Provost Marshall, where the draftees' names had been drawn. The targets of the violence continued to expand and ultimately included anything at all related to the draft, the Republican party, or wealth.

City Gone Wild

Crowds attacked jewelry stores, homes of business leaders, and the offices of the *New York Tribune,* a Republican newspaper. The armory at Second Avenue and 21st Street was burned to the ground.

Perhaps worst of all, the rioters began turning on black residents of the city. They looted the Colored Orphan Asylum, destroyed the homes of blacks as well as those of whites who tried to protect them, and lynched several blacks. By the end of the first day, it was clear that the draft was merely the spark igniting a race riot.

As the second day of rioting began, city officials hotly debated how to quell the violence. One proposal was for the city to pay the federal government $2.5 million to cover the $300 fee to release each drafted New Yorker from his military obligation. But that didn't help. Even when the government announced that the draft would be delayed by a month, the rioters continued to wreck the city. Police proved ineffective in quashing the violence, as did troops from the National Guard. Not until soldiers fresh from the battlefields of Gettysburg marched into New York to keep the peace did the city begin to settle down.

At the end of five days of rioting, more than 70 people had been killed, and property damage totaled $1.5 million. Yet it still wasn't enough to stop the draft, which resumed in August with 10,000 federal troops stationed throughout the city. By then, however, New York Governor Horatio Seymour had convinced the federal government to reduce New York City's quota to 12,000 men. This time, the Democratic city leaders oversaw the lottery, which eased the anxiety in the working class about the draft's fairness.

SAILING FROM SLAVERY TO FREEDOM

★ ★ ★ ★

*In the early hours of a spring morning, Robert Smalls
became a fugitive slave—and a national hero.*

Robert Smalls was born into slavery in 1839 in Beaufort, South
Carolina, where he lived until he moved with his owner to
Charleston at age 12. There his owner allowed Smalls to hire
himself out, with all but one dollar of his wages going to the
owner. When he turned 18, Smalls renegotiated with his owner to
pay the owner $15 per month and keep the rest of what he earned.
He married Hannah Jones, who was owned by a different slave-
holder. The next year, Hannah Smalls gave birth to a daughter,
Elizabeth. Robert Smalls quickly made arrangements to buy
Hannah and Elizabeth from their owner for $800. He had saved
$700 toward that purpose when the Civil War broke out.

Smalls held several jobs prior to the war, and through them he
accumulated a variety of skills. Many of these skills were related to
sailing, and in 1861, Smalls was hired as a sailor on the *Planter,* a
cotton steamer, for $16 a month. After the war began, the *Planter*
came under control of the Confederate government. It served
General Roswell Ripley, commander of the Second Military District of South Carolina. Smalls's superiors again recognized his
skills: Although his status as a slave kept him from gaining the
official title, for all intents and purposes, Smalls was made the
Planter's pilot.

An Early-Morning Excursion

With that position, Smalls was given details of the signals and pass
codes necessary for a vessel to navigate the heavily fortified
Charleston harbor. This information came in very handy in the
early hours of May 13, 1862. Smalls, then a 23-year-old illiterate
slave, did something astonishing: He commandeered the *Planter.*

The day before, the ship had been loaded with armaments to transport to forts where they were needed. While the white Confederate crew was all ashore, leaving the remaining crew of eight slaves aboard, Smalls took the ship and went to pick up their families. He then sailed toward the Union fleet blockading Charleston Harbor, giving the appropriate pass codes as he navigated past Confederate ships. He had carefully watched and studied the *Planter's* captain, and this early morning he wore the captain's hat and coat, mimicking his voice and movements as best he could to avoid suspicion from others in the Confederate fleet. As Smalls and his crew approached the nearest blockading ship, the USS *Onward,* they were aware that their Confederate steamer looked suspect. Smalls raised the white flag of surrender, and as the *Planter* drew near the Union vessel, the nattily dressed slave doffed his cap, shouting, "Good morning, sir! I have brought you some of the old United States' guns, sir!"

A New Life

For the capture of the *Planter,* President Lincoln awarded Smalls and his associates $1,500 in prize money. The Union press made Smalls a hero, and newspapers across the North regaled his bravery, citing his actions as an argument against racial stereotypes. In one *New York Daily Tribune* editorial, the author wrote, "Is he not also a man—and is he not fit for freedom, since he made such a hazardous dash to gain it?... Perhaps [blacks are inferior to whites] but they seem to possess good material for improvement. Few white men have a better record than Robert Smalls."

In August 1862, Smalls and Mansfield French, a missionary, traveled to Washington, D.C., to meet with the President. Their request: to ask the Union army to recruit 5,000 black soldiers to fight in the war. That request was granted, and black soldiers and all-black units were enrolled in the military for the first time in U.S. history.

Smalls remained active throughout the war. On April 7, 1863, he piloted the ironclad ship *Keokuk* during an attack on Fort Sumter. The ship was struck 19 times and sank the following morning. On

December 1, 1863, Smalls became the first black captain of a U.S. vessel and was honored for his bravery under fire.

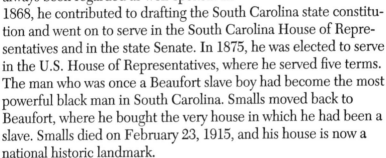

Going Home

After the war, Smalls entered the world of politics. Tutors had taught him to read and write, and he had always been regarded as well-spoken. In 1868, he contributed to drafting the South Carolina state constitution and went on to serve in the South Carolina House of Representatives and in the state Senate. In 1875, he was elected to serve in the U.S. House of Representatives, where he served five terms. The man who was once a Beaufort slave boy had become the most powerful black man in South Carolina. Smalls moved back to Beaufort, where he bought the very house in which he had been a slave. Smalls died on February 23, 1915, and his house is now a national historic landmark.

★ ★ ★ ★

- *Embalmers charged families of fighting men according to the deceased's rank. An enlisted soldier cost $25 and an officer cost $50. Later in the war the prices increased to $30 and $80 respectively.*

- Chicken guts *was a Confederate slang term for an officer's gold braiding.*

- *The 1st Minnesota Union regiment suffered the largest percentage of casualties in any one battle, 82 percent at Gettysburg.*

- *Many parts of the South harbored grudges long after the war was over. Most residents of Vicksburg, Mississippi, refused to celebrate the Fourth of July until 1945, near the end of World War II, because of the city's surrender to General Grant on July 4, 1863, following a 47-day siege.*

(Continued from p. 67)

1861

July 4
President Lincoln reiterates his intention to keep the Union together and calls for another 400,000 volunteers.

July 21
The First Battle of Bull Run is fought. Union forces are surprised by the resistance they meet.

July 25
The Crittenden Resolution, defining the purpose of the war as the preservation of the Union rather than the abolition of slavery, passes Congress.

August 5
In order to aid the war effort, Lincoln signs the first national income tax.

August 30
General John C. Frémont proclaims martial law and issues an unauthorized emancipation proclamation in Missouri.

September 11
Lincoln orders Frémont to rescind his order of emancipation.

September 12
The federal government orders the arrest of alleged disloyal members of the Maryland legislature.

October 12
The first Union ironclad, the USS *St. Louis,* is launched at Carondelet, Missouri.

October 21
The Battle of Ball's Bluff in Virginia is a disaster for Union troops.

October 24
The transcontinental telegraph is completed.

People in western Virginia vote to form a new state.

November 1
George B. McClellan is named General-in-Chief of Union troops.

November 6
Jefferson Davis is elected to a six-year term as Confederate president.

November 8
Confederate commissioners James M. Mason and John Slidell are seized from the British mail steamer *Trent* by the Union navy.

November 30
Great Britain officially protests the seizure of Mason and Slidell and demands an apology.

December 2
The first Union prisoners arrive at Salisbury Prison in North Carolina.

December 4
John Breckinridge of Kentucky, former U.S. vice president, is expelled from the U.S. Senate after joining the Confederate army.

December 20
Fighting at Dranesville, Virginia, results in the first Union land victory east of the Alleghenies.

December 27
The U.S. government agrees to release Mason and Slidell and issues an unapologetic statement to the British government.

(Continued on p. 163)

THE DOWNSIDE TO COLLECTING COINS

★ ★ ★ ★

Faced with a frustrating coin shortage, a New York barkeep took matters into his own hands.

By the second year of the war, Northern merchants were finding it more and more difficult to make change for their customers. Americans, set on edge by the war and worried that financial catastrophe was just around the corner, started to hang onto their coins. At that time, coins were cast from actual gold and silver—commodities that would remain valuable even if the government that had stamped its name on the coins were to crumble. This paranoia led to a coin shortage, which made everyday life difficult for those who couldn't amass their own stockpiles. The machinery of the American economy threatened to grind to a halt.

Lindenmueller Coins

In 1863, frustrated with the lack of coins, New York bartender Gustavus Lindenmueller took matters into his own hands. In order to make change for his patrons, he literally made change—about one million cents' worth—and began to distribute it. The coins were simple, featuring his bearded face on the front and a frothy mug of ale on the back. The large volume of coins Lindenmueller dumped into circulation in the city made them popular with a public equally annoyed by the lack of coins. Many businesses accepted them, despite the facts that they had absolutely no true value and that there was no indication they would be honored if ever put to the test. Streetcars began to accept them, for instance, because exact change made traveling easier than using cumbersome paper money.

Filling a Void

Lindenmueller coins were just one of several tokens privately created in the war's early years. It's believed nearly 25 million such tokens were minted across the North. They filled a void that the government had not been able to account for and reflected American ingenuity and patriotism. Many were adorned with spirited slogans and pro-Union sentiments. It may seem strange that so many people and even companies accepted these dubious tokens and private currencies, but in the midst of the Civil War, they had little choice. As long as everyone agreed to treat the tokens as though they had real worth, the needs of daily life could be met.

Put to the Test

The situation could not remain like this forever. The Third Avenue Railroad served the city of New York with streetcar service, and rather than go bankrupt due to the lack of coins for train fare, they decided to play along with the Lindenmueller tokens, accepting them from riders in lieu of actual U.S. currency. Lindenmueller had given them out as change instead of real U.S. coins, so the railroad apparently assumed that, as a reputable and honorable tavern keeper, he would honor them himself. When the company presented him with a large number of his tokens in an attempt to redeem them for actual money, however, Lindenmueller laughed in their faces. Although he was happy to give them out, he had no intention of accepting them himself—at least not in bulk. Because the railroad had participated in the scheme willingly, and because Lindenmueller had never made explicit promises to honor the coins, there was absolutely nothing the railroad could do. Problems such as this finally stirred the government to take action against these illegal currencies.

Two-Cents Worth

The U.S. Congress undertook a two-pronged attack on the Civil War tokens, rendering them both unnecessary and illegal. Anyone caught using or creating such currency would be subject to the same treatment as counterfeiters or forgers—a significant fine and possibly five years in jail. Congress also decided to beat those tokenmakers at their own game by introducing the two-cent coin. In many ways, it was modeled after the very tokens it was created to eliminate. But it also added a new feature that had never before appeared on U.S currency, a motto that stuck: "In God We Trust."

THE SLOW SLIDE OF GENERAL ROSECRANS

★ ★ ★ ★

Every Civil War general had his ups and downs, but few started so high and ended so low as William S. Rosecrans.

Union General William S. Rosecrans came from a family of patriots. His great-grandfather on his mother's side, Stephen Hopkins, was the governor of the Rhode Island colony and a signer of the Declaration of Independence. His father, Crandell Rosecrans, had fought against the British in the War of 1812 and was an aide to General William Henry Harrison. It was only natural that young William Starke Rosecrans would follow in the family tradition and seek to attend West Point.

Rosecrans graduated fifth in the West Point class of 1842. While at the academy, he once came to the defense of a young Ulysses S. Grant, who was a year behind "Old Rosy," as he came to be called. Rosecrans saved Grant from being hazed by older students. After graduation, Rosecrans went on to a career in army engineering, but he left the service in 1854 to seek more success in civilian life as an architect and civil engineer. His new venture was quite successful—Rosecrans created a number of inventions and made profitable mining discoveries.

When the Civil War broke out, Rosecrans joined the staff of General George McClellan, who was commanding Ohio's state forces at the time. Rosecrans took command of the 23rd Ohio Volunteer Infantry and soon earned a general's appointment. His talent at battle planning led to a victory over the Confederates at Rich Mountain, Virginia, but, as he was still on McClellan's staff, most of the credit and glory for the victory went to the superior officer. McClellan rode this success to eventual command of the entire U.S. Army. Rosecrans, on the other hand, felt cheated and requested a transfer to the West.

In the West, he engineered even more Union successes, initially at the Battle of Corinth, Mississippi, and later at Stones River and Tullahoma in Tennessee. Yet despite these successes, his relationships with his superior officers continued to decline. General Grant was unhappy that he hadn't pursued the Confederates after the victory at Corinth and believed that Rosecrans took too long to commit to battle in other engagements.

Rosecrans's command fully broke down at the Battle of Chickamauga. His army had been skirmishing with Braxton Bragg's forces with neither getting the upper hand. At one point, Rosecrans mistakenly believed he had a hole in his line and ordered one of his subordinates to fill it. Although it was clear that rearranging the troops would create a hole rather than fill one, General Thomas Wood followed the order. The Confederates took advantage of the opportunity and pushed the Union army from the field. This finally provided Grant with a reason to fire Rosecrans from his command. Rosecrans was given meaningless jobs in Missouri thereafter, and he concluded a promising Civil War career in shameful disappointment.

Regardless of this, Rosecrans enjoyed a respected career in public service after the war. He was appointed minister to Mexico and then elected to Congress from California. President Grover Cleveland made him register of the Treasury in 1885, a post he held until his retirement in 1893. He died five years later.

"I have not permitted myself, gentlemen, to conclude that I am the best man in the country; but I am reminded in this connection of a story of an old Dutch farmer, who remarked to a companion once that it was not best to swap horses when crossing a stream."
Abraham Lincoln, during the presidential campaign of 1864

Fast Facts

- Colonel was the highest rank Robert E. Lee achieved in the U.S. Army. When he joined the Confederate service, he entered as a major general and made his way up to commander in chief of the Army of Northern Virginia.

- The Civil War was the first U.S. conflict in which soldiers were issued canned rations. Troops were given milk, beef, and vegetables. Union soldiers nicknamed canned beef from the Chicago meat-packing plants "embalmed beef." They made a concoction they called "milk toast" by combining hardtack with condensed milk.

- Buglers had to learn 25 general calls and 24 skirmisher calls in the infantry alone.

- Although the U.S. postmaster discontinued the exchange of mail between the North and the South, a few private companies such as the American Express Letter Company were allowed to transport mail between the two regions for several more months.

- Irish immigrant Patrick Gilmore composed the popular song "When Johnny Comes Marching Home" in 1863. It was enjoyed by both Northerners and Southerners.

- Abatis were defensive fortifications made of logs with tips sharpened into pointed spikes and formed into rows directed toward the enemy. They have been used in battles since Roman times.

- Bleedings, dosages of opium or quinine, and application of mustard plasters were some of the treatments for pneumonia and bronchitis.

AN OASIS OF UNION CONTROL

★ ★ ★ ★

Despite being fired upon even before Fort Sumter,
Florida's Fort Pickens never fell to the Confederates.

Tradition holds that the first shots of the Civil War were fired on
April 12, 1861, by Southern artillery batteries attacking Fort
Sumter in the harbor of Charleston, South Carolina. Tradition is a
bit off the mark, however. Hostilities actually erupted a full three
months earlier, 500 miles to the southwest, and involved a fort the
Union never lost to the Confederacy.

On January 8, 1861, a band of Confederate sympathizers made a
midnight raid on Fort Barrancas, one of several U.S. military
redoubts around Florida's Pensacola Bay that also included Fort
Pickens, Fort McRee, and the Navy Yard. The band's attempt to
capture Fort Barrancas was ultimately thwarted by the troops
stationed there.

A Successful Redeployment

Despite the raiders' initial failure, Lieutenant Adam J. Slemmer,
commander of the Union forces in the area, had apprehensions
about his troop's ability to withstand a determined Confederate
attack. To remedy the situation, he proceeded to spike the cannons, destroy more than ten tons of gunpowder stored at Fort
McRee, and move his garrison of 80 troops just across Pensacola
Pass to Fort Pickens, on the western end of Santa Rosa Island.
Fort Pickens was an older, larger, somewhat dilapidated fortification that hadn't been occupied since the Mexican War. Despite the
fort's shortcomings, Slemmer still believed it would be a more
defensible location. He was right. Although Fort Pickens came
under attack and continued to face Confederate threats, the
fortress remained a Union stronghold until the conclusion of the
Civil War.

THE COMFORTING IDEA OF THE LOST CAUSE

★ ★ ★ ★

After the war, many Southerners turned to a much-needed belief system to make sense of their experience.

As the Civil War ended, large parts of the South were left desolated. In order to cope with the difficulties of the war's aftermath, many Southerners needed to feel that, despite its outcome, the struggle had been worthwhile. As a way to fill that need, the concept of "The Lost Cause" was born. Arising after the war, this is a view of the antebellum South that romanticizes plantation life and whitewashes the evils of slavery. From this point of view, the Confederate cause was just and necessary.

Origins of the Idea

The term *Lost Cause* first appeared in 1866, just one year after the end of the war, in Edward Pollard's *The Lost Cause: A New Southern History of the War of the Confederates.* At the heart of the idea of the Lost Cause is an idealized image of the prewar South. The vision of the Lost Cause has been so successful that its point of view continues to color our current understanding of antebellum Southern life. Visions of a magnolia-lined driveway opening onto the porch of a towering Georgian mansion; a delicate Southern lady fanning herself on the porch; the happy, smiling slave serving her genteel mistress a glass of sweet tea—all of these images fit into the typical Lost Cause revisionist scenario. *Gone With the Wind,* the 1939 movie adaptation of Margaret Mitchell's novel, is probably the most enduring and well-known example of the Lost Cause tradition.

The Perfection of Plantation Life

For those who were left to rebuild their shattered lives and culture, imagining the peace and prosperity of plantation life was a comforting distraction from the reality of post-war defeat, destruction, and occupation of the South. This culture of the plantation was as close as America has come to having an aristocratic class—in fact, many of those who made up the functional ruling class of early America were Southerners. Before the Civil War, Virginia was home to more presidents and military leaders than any other state. Four of the first five presidents—George Washington, Thomas Jefferson, James Madison, and James Monroe—were Virginians.

Foremost among these Virginians was Jefferson, whose philosophy of agricultural life defined the Southern worldview and provided the romanticized version of the region after the war. Jeffersonian notions of freedom—that is, the freedom to own and work the land—took root in the South, but new economic forces were gaining strength in the North. Part of the Northern industrial makeover included the concept of freedom more and more being tied to the right to work for wages. Industrialization and the factory-wage system were seen as a threat to the Southern way of life. As some historians see it, the impersonal industrial might of the North threatened Southern culture even before the first gunshots were fired.

A Vital Idea

The image of the happy slave was crucial to this concept of Southern civilization. Plantation life rested on several assumptions about the ethics of slavery. It was not viewed as a necessary evil but instead as beneficial to the black race. Looking back at the peculiar institution, proponents of the Lost Cause believed that blacks were inherently suited to slavery, which next led to the assumption that blacks had been happy with their enslavement and desired to be loyal to their white masters. In keeping with this theory, Southern masters saw themselves as kind and compassionate to their docile servants, certainly more so than Northern factory bosses could be. Southern slaveowners wanted to believe themselves to be like fathers to their chattel, but factory bosses could never share that kind of paternalistic relationship with their employees, black or white.

In support of this view, Jefferson Davis wrote a post-war memoir in which he glowingly expounded on slavery in the South: "Their servile instincts rendered them contented with their lot, and their patient toil blessed the land of their abode with unmeasured riches. Their strong local and personal attachment secured faithful service.... Never was there happier dependence of labor and capital on each other. The tempter came, like the serpent of Eden, and decoyed them with the magic word of 'freedom.'"

"Mr. Lincoln's War"

Even though a sanitized version of slavery is a large part of this worldview, the Lost Cause concept does not accept that slavery caused the war. Davis also wrote in his memoir that slavery "was in no wise the cause of the conflict, but only an incident." According to Davis, the Civil War was merely the Southern defense of the homeland against the "tremendous and sweeping usurpation" and "the unlimited, despotic power" of the federal government. It is little wonder, then, why so many Southerners referred to the conflict not as the Civil War, but as "The War of Northern Aggression" or, more pointedly, as "Mr. Lincoln's War."

The war itself, however, played a great role in defining how the Lost Cause came to be understood. Besides casting the North as antagonistic, the believers in the Lost Cause largely focused on Southern heroism. Many Southerners saw the perfect embodiment of bravery, honor, and manliness in the figure of General Robert E. Lee. Even the fact that the South lost didn't weaken the legitimacy of the Southern cause. Edward Pollard, who gave the concept its name, noted that although the South lost on the battlefield, it would ultimately win the "war of ideas." And unfortunately, Pollard was right to some degree, at least until the Civil Rights movement (often called the "Second Reconstruction") rooted out the last residue of state-sponsored white supremacy.

Keepers of the Cause

After the war ended, various organizations such as the United Confederate Veterans (later Sons of Confederate Veterans), the United Daughters of the Confederacy, and the Southern Historical Society made sure that history wouldn't be written entirely by the victors. Many of these organizations lobbied local, state, and national governments for money to build Confederate monuments, and their efforts were quite successful.

Through movies, the idea of the Lost Cause has shaped the American memory of the Civil War. Two phenomenally successful films—*The Birth of a Nation* in 1915 and *Gone With the Wind* in 1939—bore the marks of Lost Cause revisionism: white superiority, glorification of plantation life, and the infantilization and demonization of blacks. The success of these two movies wasn't just limited to the South—it was nationwide, which is a testament to the widespread acceptance of the Lost Cause narrative. Indeed, after seeing *The Birth of a Nation* at a special White House screening, President Woodrow Wilson is reported to have remarked: "It is like writing history with lightning, and my only regret is that it is all so terribly true." In a way, it could be argued that it wasn't the Northern victory but the Lost Cause that unified the nation after the war.

- *Robert E. Lee's estate was confiscated at the beginning of the war and used as a burial ground for Union soldiers. It was returned to the family in 1882 but later sold back to the federal government, becoming Arlington National Cemetery.*

- *Union General Lew Wallace was removed from field duty for a few years after his forces arrived too late to help in the first day of fighting at the Battle of Shiloh. He later acquitted himself at the Battle of Monocacy by delaying a Confederate advance in Virginia and preventing the capture of Washington, D.C. He went on to win fame as the author of* Ben Hur.

JEB STUART RIDES

★ ★ ★ ★

The success and leadership qualities of this Confederate cavalry commander place him among some of the finest leaders of Civil War history.

Confederate Calvary General James Ewell Brown "Jeb" Stuart was one of the most charismatic and daring leaders on either side of the war. A Virginian, Stuart possessed an impeccable military pedigree that included graduation from West Point, a U.S. Army commission as a cavalry officer, and marriage to the daughter of renowned cavalry officer Colonel Philip Cooke. Before the war, Stuart played a key role in the capture of John Brown and his rebels at Harpers Ferry in 1859. He seemed destined for both honor and high rank in the American military.

Leading a Local Crew

When Virginia seceded in 1861, Stuart resigned his commission in the U.S. Army and took command of a state cavalry unit as its colonel. As a local commander leading local troops who rode their own mounts over their own countryside, Stuart possessed significant advantages in cavalry warfare. The Virginia riders knew the subtleties of their home terrain and were aware of how their horses would perform under the pressure of combat. This familiarity with their geography often meant the difference between military success and failure. Knowledge of the safest places to cross creeks and rivers, where to find watering holes and forage spots for their mounts, and the best hiding places in the densely forested Virginia hills were each critically important to Stuart's success. It also often provided security from Union ambushes.

Long List of Achievements

The list of engagements in which Stuart and his Virginians were prominent in Confederate battle movements is remarkable. Stuart's unit, referenced in various battle reports as the "Black Horse

Cavalry," provided support to the main Confederate army at the First Battle of Bull Run in July 1861, and as a result, Stuart was promoted to general. Stuart built an impressive and flamboyant reputation for himself, even going so far as to wear an ostrich plume in his hat. His rebel horse soldiers followed their dashing leader enthusiastically.

Stuart achieved enduring fame in 1862's Peninsula Campaign in northern Virginia, as Union forces led by General George McClellan sought to advance on Richmond. Directed by General Robert E. Lee to find the right flank of the Union army, Stuart boldly took a brigade of cavalry around the entire 80,000-strong Union force, allowing him personally to provide his reconnaissance to Lee at Richmond. Stuart replicated this feat in August 1862 during the Second Bull Run campaign, taking 1,500 soldiers around the rear of Union General John Pope's army to attack his supply line and a Union gunboat.

The Black Horse Cavalry executed a third surprise penetration of Union defenses after Antietam on September 17, 1862, sweeping around the much larger and robust Northern forces. Covering 80 miles in just 27 hours, Stuart's Virginians wreaked havoc on Union positions and supply depots with their hit-and-run tactics. Other key successes included prominent roles in the crucial Confederate defense of Fredericksburg in December 1862 and at the Battle of Chancellorsville in April 1863. Ultimately promoted to the rank of major general, Stuart possessed talent and an ability to lead that placed him alongside Jackson and Lee in the pantheon of great Confederate commanders.

His Final Battle

Like Jackson, however, Stuart did not survive the war. In May 1864, General Philip Sheridan was given orders to destroy Stuart's cavalry. Sheridan's force took on the Confederate horse soldiers at the Battle of Yellow Tavern. Although it had worked to his advantage so far, Stuart's plumed hat proved too effective a target, and the general was shot and killed. Lee was particularly saddened by the death. "He never brought me a piece of false information," General Lee said in tribute.

NOT FROM THESE PARTS

★ ★ ★ ★

*A handful of officers who fought for the North were not
actually American. They came from foreign lands to
lend their expertise to the Union cause.*

For years, armchair generals have criticized President Abraham
Lincoln for the large number of foreign-born officers he commissioned to serve in the army during the Civil War. The complaints
often center around accusations that the nearly four dozen officers
were little more than roguish, flamboyant mercenaries. In reality,
the foreign-born generals behaved no better or no worse than
many American-born Union generals. Many, in fact, proved to be
excellent leaders.

It's often been suggested that Lincoln commissioned officers from
other countries in order to cater to immigrant voting blocks, but in
fact, the President's concerns were probably much more centered
on the war itself. After all, although foreign-born officers might be
politically helpful, they could also be far more effective in raising
regiments from their home countries than any officers born on
American soil ever could.

The Fighting Irish

The Irish served the Union well throughout the Civil War at various levels of command. One good example is Thomas Meagher,
also known as "Meagher of the Sword," an Irish revolutionary who
served with the Union in hopes of gaining American support for
Irish independence from Great Britain. Meagher arrived in the
United States in 1852 and became an American citizen. When the
Civil War began, he initially served the Union as a major in the
"Fighting 69th" New York Infantry Regiment, and then in September 1861 he formed the 4,000-strong Irish Brigade. He resigned as brigadier general in 1863 after army officials refused to
allow him to return to New York to raise reinforcements for the
hard-fighting unit, which had been reduced to a mere 500 troops.

It wasn't long before Meagher's commission was reinstated, however, and he was transferred to the Western Theater of operations where, following the war, he became the territorial governor of Montana.

Another Irish general was Michael Corcoran, a former constable who served as the commander of the 69th New York in the years before the war. Another Irish nationalist, he gained notoriety in 1860 when he refused to parade his troops past the visiting Prince of Wales. He was relieved from duty. His punishment didn't last long, however, and Corcoran was reinstated when the war began. He led his troops at the First Battle of Bull Run, where he was wounded and taken prisoner. While held by the Confederates, Corcoran was offered parole on the condition that he not fight for the Union after his release. He refused to make such a promise—an act that drew praise from Lincoln, among others—and he returned to the Union army in August 1862. Corcoran was promoted to general, and he raised a unit of Irish immigrants that became known as the Corcoran Legion. He was later named commander of the 1st Division of the U.S. 7th Corps. Corcoran was killed on December 22, 1863, when his skull was fractured during a riding accident near Washington.

Aid from Deutschland

Many Germans also came to the Union's aid during the war, including officers such as Franz Sigel, Alexander Schimmelfennig, Louis Blenker, and Felix Constantin Alexander Johann Nepomuk, prince of the German state of Salm-Salm. August von Willich was another such fellow, a former Prussian army officer who had resigned his commission in the Prussian military and participated in the 1848–1849 procommunist uprisings in Germany. Emigrating to the United States after the failure of that movement, Willich became a radical editor, activist, and organizer. When the Civil War began, he helped recruit German immigrants into the Union cause and served as a lieutenant in the 9th Ohio Infantry Regiment.

Willich rose steadily through the ranks to become a brigadier general and led troops in some of the bloodiest battles of the war—including Shiloh, Chickamauga, and Chattanooga. During his career, he was both captured and severely wounded. In recognition of his service, he received a brevet promotion to major general in October 1865.

Others Pitch In

Less common in the U.S. Army were Swedish officers, such as Charles John Stolbrand, a veteran soldier who had fought against the Prussian invasion of Denmark during the Schleswig-Holstein Campaign of 1848–1850. He later immigrated to the United States and, when the Civil War broke out, raised an artillery company and served as its commander. Word of Stolbrand's abilities spread, and he was eventually put in command of a full artillery brigade of 1,000 troops. General William Tecumseh Sherman recommended to Lincoln that Stolbrand be promoted to general, and the President followed his advice in February 1865. Stolbrand led three Illinois infantry regiments in the U.S. 17th Corps until the end of the war. After the war, he relocated to South Carolina and served in various capacities in the state and federal governments until his death in 1894. He is buried at Arlington National Cemetery.

Russians, too, were fairly unique in the Union forces. Ivan Vasilyevich Turchaninov, who was more commonly known as John Basil Turchin, was a graduate of the Russian Imperial Military School and a veteran of the Crimean War when he joined the U.S. Army in 1861. He soon rose to colonel in command of the 19th Illinois and later was given command of a brigade in the 3rd Division of the Army of the Ohio. Turchaninov earned quite a bit of infamy in the South for the sacking of Athens, Alabama, a seat of insurrection against Union troops, in 1862. Although Turchaninov was court-martialed for this offense, Lincoln realized the need for strong measures against the South and set aside that ruling. Not content to stop there, Lincoln promoted Turchaninov to general and returned him to the field.

SO THEY SAID

★ ★ ★ ★

"The whole army is burning with an insatiable desire to wreak violence upon South Carolina. I almost tremble for her fate."

William Tecumseh Sherman, as he prepared to march his army into South Carolina following his March to the Sea

"I hope to live long enough to see my surviving comrades march side by side with the Union veterans along Pennsylvania Avenue, and then I will die happy."

Former Confederate General James Longstreet in 1902

"I am short a cheek-bone and an ear, but am able to whip all hell yet."

Union General John M. Corse, making a peculiar boast after sustaining a head wound at the Battle of Allatoona in 1864

"The battle is over, and although we did not succeed in pushing the enemy out of their strong position, I am sure they have not any thing to boast about. They have lost at least as many in killed and wounded as we have. We have taken more prisoners from them than they have from us. If that is not the case, why did they lay still all to-day and see our army going to the rear? An army that has gained a great victory follows it up while the enemy is badly crippled; but Meade, their commander, knows he has had as much as he gave, at least, if not more. As yet I have not heard a word from my brother Morris since the first day's fight."

Confederate Private Louis Leon, Company B, 53rd Regiment North Carolina, on the aftermath of the Battle of Gettysburg

THE FOX OF HARPERS FERRY

★ ★ ★ ★

A Southern colonel fighting for the Union uses
his heritage against the rebels.

The federal troops garrisoned at Harpers Ferry in September 1862 were grimly hunkered down, surrounded by eight regiments of Confederates under General Lafayette McLaws. Southern artillery had been lobbing shells into town most of the day, and morale was low. Garrison commander Colonel Dixon S. Miles stood useless, stunned by fear and indecision. When some Union regimental commanders began discussing mutiny, Colonel Benjamin Franklin "Grimes" Davis of the 8th New York Cavalry knew he had to act.

Born in Alabama and raised in Mississippi, Davis was a rare Mississippian who stayed with the U.S. Army when the conflict erupted. It apparently never occurred to him to break his oath to the Union.

Getting Out

At Harpers Ferry, Davis went to Colonel Miles and informed him that he and his troops would not be captured in Harpers Ferry because they were breaking out. Miles objected vehemently, but in the end, he reluctantly agreed to let them go.

After dark, Davis organized his 8th New York Cavalry, the 12th Illinois Cavalry, and smaller units of Maryland and Rhode Island horse troops into two columns. They planned to go through Confederate lines with two locals who knew the area. At 9:00 P.M., moving as quietly as cavalry could, they crossed the pontoon bridge over the Potomac and turned west. Davis didn't know that General McLaws had withdrawn seven of his eight regiments to defend Crampton's Gap from Union attack, so he was astonished to find the roads unguarded. In the wee hours near Sharpsburg, his troopers slipped quietly past groups of retreating, disorganized, Confederate soldiers.

A Little Subterfuge

Just before dawn, they came upon a Confederate wagon train. Davis was unwilling to plunge his tired force into a fight and had an idea of how to avoid it. Going to the lead wagon, he informed the wagon master in his best back-home Mississippi accent that Union cavalry were on the road ahead and that the train needed to detour—down a road that would take them north into Pennsylvania. The Illinois cavalry so smoothly ran off the rebel escort following the train that the wagon drivers suspected nothing until the sun came up.

"What outfit you with?" asked a driver suspiciously.

"The 8th New York," a trooper replied.

"The hell you say."

It was too late to resist. Davis's horse soldiers had the situation well in hand. At 9:00 A.M., they reached Greencastle, Pennsylvania, and Davis took stock of what he'd captured. It was General Longstreet's reserve ammunition train: more than 40 mule-drawn wagons and 200 prisoners. The citizens of Greencastle turned out with food and drink, delighted finally to hear good news about their cavalry instead of the usual exploits of General Jeb Stuart and his Confederates.

Meanwhile, Back at Harpers Ferry

By this time, the remaining Yankees at Harpers Ferry, pounded by 50 Confederate guns, had surrendered to a shabbily attired Stonewall Jackson. One observing Union soldier said, "Boys, he is not much for looks, but if he had been in command of us we would not have been caught in this trap."

This was the Union's biggest surrender of the war: 70 cannons, 13,000 rifles and muskets, and 12,500 soldiers. Colonel Miles himself barely lived to see it. He was killed by a shell after he laid down his arms. The only sour note for Confederates was that the cavalry had escaped. There would be no fresh mounts for Jeb Stuart.

Colonel Davis would soldier on valiantly until he was killed the following summer in the largest cavalry action of the war, the Battle of Brandy Station, which occurred just before Gettysburg.

SUNBONNET HEROINE OF THE CONFEDERACY

★ ★ ★ ★

Emma Sansom never achieved much notoriety, but she risked her life to aid her fellow Southerners.

Confederate General Nathan Bedford Forrest was one of the most celebrated officers on either side of the Civil War. A successful prewar slave trader, Forrest was nicknamed "The Wizard of the Saddle" for his leadership and tactical brilliance. The general used his cavalry as effective raiders in a series of engagements throughout the war. His troops followed him because he never shied away from the action.

Chasing the Feds

In May 1863, Forrest led his cavalry across northern Alabama in hot pursuit of Union Colonel Abel D. Streight. Near Gadsden, Streight had crossed Black Creek on the only bridge spanning the water for miles and then burned it behind him. When Forrest reached Black Creek, he struggled to find a secure place to cross it where his soldiers and their horses would be sheltered from possible Union snipers.

The Sansom farm was in the path of Forrest's cavalry. As Forrest examined possible places to ford the creek, 16-year-old Emma Sansom volunteered to lead the general to a place where she had previously taken her family's cattle safely across.

Into the Action

Emma offered to saddle her own horse, but given the close proximity of the Union units, Forrest feared that time was too short and helped Emma onto the back of his own saddle to ride behind him. As reported at the time by the *Jacksonville*

(Alabama) *Republican,* "With no maiden coyness, but actuated only by the heroic impulse to serve her country, she at once consented. Her mother, however, overhearing the suggestion, and sensitively alive to her daughter's safety and honor, interposed the objection. 'Sir, my child cannot thus accompany a stranger.' 'Madam,' respectfully urged the far-famed chieftain, 'my name is Forrest, and I will be responsible for this young lady's safety.' 'Oh,' rejoined the good woman, 'if you are Gen. Forrest she can go with you!'"

As Emma directed the Confederates to the crossing, Union snipers opened fire. She is said to have taken off her sunbonnet and waved it defiantly at the Union soldiers across the creek. The Confederates crossed to the opposite bank, and Forrest returned Emma safely to her farm as promised.

Preserving Her Memory

Emma Sansom's simple act of volunteering local knowledge to Forrest was a dangerous one. If she had been captured, Emma and her family could have faced execution by Union forces for lending aid to their enemy. The Black Creek incident itself might have been lost to history but for the commendation written by Forrest as his unit continued to move at high speed through Alabama. In a note from his "Headquarters in the Saddle," Forrest noted both Sansom's bravery and her assistance to the Confederate cause.

After the war, a monument to Sansom's heroism was erected in Gadsden. Sansom later married and moved to Texas, where a historical marker at the courthouse of Upshur County honors her as the "Sunbonnet Heroine of the Confederacy."

- *One of the South's best tacticians and fighters, Nathan Bedford Forrest enlisted in the army as a private and left as a general. Prior to that he was a wealthy businessperson, plantation owner, and slave trader.*

THE EXPLOSION OF THE *SULTANA*

★ ★ ★ ★

A mysterious ship explosion took the lives of hundreds on board, including many Union soldiers on their way back home after the South had surrendered.

It should have been a voyage of joy for many of the Union soldiers on the steamship *Sultana.* On April 27, 1865, the war was over, and they had finally been released from Andersonville and other prison camps. They were hungry and fatigued, and they simply wanted to go home. Passing the time on the two-day voyage north up the Mississippi, they played cards, slept, and told stories of the war recently concluded. They didn't know that, although the war was over, their ordeal was not.

Heavy Load

The *Sultana* had only been in service for two years. A side-wheel steamboat of 1,700 tons, it was overcrowded as it left the port of Memphis at around midnight on its way to Cairo, Illinois. At least 2,300 people crowded the decks, far more than the boat's capacity of at least 400. In addition to its soldiers, refugees, and civilians, the boat had also taken on more than 1,500 horses, cows, pigs, and other animals.

Boiling Point

Nate Wintringer, the *Sultana's* chief engineer, had been dealing with a leak in the ship's boiler since the start of the voyage in Vicksburg, Mississippi. Wintringer and his crew were doing the best they could to patch the boiler with plugs and iron straps. He knew the boiler needed major

work, but his experience told him the machine would hold out until they reached their final destination.

At about 2:00 A.M., as the ship was passing Paddy's Old Hen and Chickens islands just north of Memphis, a huge explosion shook the vessel. Passengers scrambled to escape the flaming wreckage, but the disaster claimed about 1,700 lives—because the precise number of passengers is unknown, so is the number who died, but it was more than died on the *Titanic*. Many of the hundreds who did make it off later died from the wounds they had sustained. Only one woman escaped: Anna Annis. Her husband—Union Lieutenant Harvey Annis—her child, and her sister all perished in the tragedy.

Conspiracy Theory

An official inquiry blamed the explosion on the leaking boiler, although leaking equipment such as that was not known to explode. Theories abounded that it was a guerrilla attack, which would not have been unheard of at the time. Confederate sympathizers continued to harass Union ships and troops, even after the official surrender had been signed. In fact, just before the *Sultana* sailed, a communications ship named the *Greyhound* had been sabotaged when explosives were placed in the coal bunkers.

The belief that the explosion was not an accident was given new life in 1888 when William Streetor, formerly a Union prison clerk, claimed that Robert Lowden, a known Confederate operative, had destroyed the *Sultana*. Streetor said that Lowden had told him how he smuggled a bomb disguised as a lump of coal onto the ship and placed it in the coal pile. When that bomb was shoveled into the furnace, the theory goes, the ship exploded.

Sunken Treasure

Following the explosion, the charred hulk of the ship would remain in the Mississippi mud. When the river was low, bones, skulls, and personal articles could be seen on the ship. Some of the items would occasionally wash to shore to be grabbed by morbid souvenir hunters. A rumor also surfaced that $18,000 in gold was on the ship, launching a number of dives, but no such find was ever discovered.

Fast Facts

- Horses were essential to the war. At the beginning of the hostilities, the North had more than 4.4 million horses, and the South had more than 1.7 million.

- Lincoln's friend Colonel Elmer Ellsworth, 24, was the first Union officer to die in the Civil War. The day after Virginia seceded, Ellsworth marched his troops into Alexandria, Virginia, to secure the city. While they were there, Ellsworth removed a large Confederate flag from the roof of a hotel. As he came down the hotel's stairs, the innkeeper shot him through the heart.

- Ulysses S. Grant graduated from West Point and served in the Mexican War at a lower rank than Lee did. But Grant left the Army in 1854 as a captain after he became dissatisfied with his prospects for promotion to general. He tried and failed at farming and real estate, and by the time the Civil War started, he was working as a clerk in his father's leather shop in Galena, Illinois. When President Abraham Lincoln put out a call for 75,000 volunteers, Grant helped to recruit a company and accompanied it to Springfield, Illinois, where he accepted a position from Illinois Governor Richard Yates to recruit and train volunteers.

- During battles, drums were used to signal the infantry to load and fire. They were also sometimes used to signal maneuvers. In the artillery and cavalry, buglers performed a similar role to infantry drummers.

- Major Martin R. Delany, commissioned a major in 1865, was the first black line field officer in the U.S. Army. Prior to the war, he had advocated black separatism, but he later changed his mind and decided to devote himself to the emancipation of slaves.

GOING DOWN TO MEXICO

★ ★ ★ ★

*Defeated and unwilling to face their shattered lives in the South,
a number of Confederates crossed the border to create
a new life in Mexico ... at least for a moment.*

After the Confederacy collapsed in the spring of 1865, some of its leaders, refusing to surrender to the Yankees or return to their now-ruined plantations, fled the country to begin new lives in Mexico. Their attempt to recreate the Confederate lifestyle south of the Rio Grande began with Confederate diplomat Matthew Fontaine Maury. He was a man of many talents, also having a background as an ocean explorer and the inventor of an early torpedo. Maury sought help from a close friend of his: Emperor Maximilian I.

The Situation in Mexico

Maximilian, an Austrian archduke, was struggling to hold on to his position in Mexico after France's Emperor Napoleon III placed him in power as part of a short-lived stab at expanding French ambitions into North America. Poorly informed about the actual political situation in Mexico, Maximilian had accepted the crown in 1864 under the mistaken belief that the Mexican people had chosen him to be their emperor. In fact, only a conservative faction of Mexicans supported Maximilian and his French benefactors, while the liberal armies of the ousted Zapotec president Benito Juarez were actively fighting back to topple the new monarchy.

Into this situation came Maury, who had been overseas when peace between the warring states had been declared and the Confederacy dissolved. Instead of returning to his defeated homeland, he went to Maximilian with an idea that the emperor quite liked. Together, they could build support for Maximilian's government by inviting Confederate settlers to come and settle plots of land. The widely admired Southerner spread word among defeated Confederates that 500,000 acres were available for the taking at bargain rates in the Mexican kingdom—and tax-free the first year.

Agrarian Heaven

Among the Confederate exiles who answered the call was General Sterling "Old Pap" Price, who at the end of the war found himself in Texas at the head of a beaten army, having failed to take Missouri for the South. He and General Joseph Shelby led their troops and their families across the border to the new colony. Protected by Maximilian's French army, the former Confederates started new lives and farms. In the colony of Carlotta, named for the emperor's wife, Price set himself up in a bamboo house. The combination of sun, cheap labor, and fertile soil seemed to promise agrarian heaven.

But it couldn't last. Now that the American Civil War was over, the United States was able to pay more attention to the activity across its border. The federal government turned up the heat on the French presence in North America, which it viewed as an intrusion under the Monroe Doctrine. With 80,000 American troops, General Phil Sheridan rushed to the border to rattle his saber and run guns to Juarez's rebel army. The French decided a Mexican colony wasn't worth all the trouble or the resources, so they withdrew, leaving Maximilian to face whatever fate the Mexicans had for him.

Back to Reality

When, in 1867, a Mexican firing squad put Maximilian against a wall, the exiled Confederates again found themselves without a country, or, in this case, a benefactor. The reinstalled government of President Juarez lowered the boom on their land rights, and the new colony was gone. Dixie colonists, including Price and his followers, fled back to the United States to face Reconstruction. "Old Pap" died later that year under U.S. rule in Missouri. Maury held out a bit longer, returning to Virginia the following year. He stepped back into American public life with a professorship at the Virginia Military Institute.

THE COMING OF THE IRONCLADS

★ ★ ★ ★

Fighting at sea was nothing new, but Civil War battleships were decidedly different than any that had been used before.

In 1860, the United States had hundreds of merchant ships to protect. Surprisingly, the U.S. Navy was pitifully small. Between them, Britain and France had 93 screw ships-of-the-line, the battleships of the day, so named because of their screw propeller. The United States had none, its largest ships being 13 frigates and sloops.

The U.S. Navy suddenly found itself assigned to blockade the 3,350-mile Confederate coast. The Confederate navy, which had to be built from scratch from converted merchant ships and a few captured warships, had to keep the sea lanes open. To break a determined blockade of heavily armed ships, the Confederacy needed armored vessels to stand up to Union cannons, while the Union, realizing that Southern ports and rivers could only be penetrated by ships that could resist fire from Confederate forts, needed the same thing. Overnight the naval arms race went into high gear.

Dueling Ships

The first American ironclads were commissioned and deployed on the western rivers, notably the Mississippi. On October 12, 1861, the first Union ironclads—shallow-draft, humpback armored gunboats designed by Samuel Pook and built by James Eads of St. Louis—were launched. Initially there were seven of these slow but tough "Pook Turtles," as they were called, which included the USS *St. Louis* and the USS *Carondelet.* Later, improved ironclads such as the *Benton* and *Essex* gave the Union flotillas a war-winning edge.

The Confederates countered with their own ironclads such as the *Tennessee* and the ram *Manassas*. The *Manassas* was the Confederacy's first ironclad, outfitted with iron plating in 1861. It couldn't do much except smash into other ships—but it performed that task very well, indeed. Backed by gunboats and stern-wheelers, the rebel ironclads contested every mile of the rivers, but after the Union captured New Orleans, it was only a matter of time before it controlled the Mississippi and cut the Confederacy off from Texas. The *Manassas* itself didn't survive David Farragut's Mississippi assault that led up to the capture of New Orleans.

Being superior to the Confederate states in ironworks, shipyards, cannon foundries, skilled mechanics, and money, the Union had major advantages in ship design and began building several types of armored vessels. Broadside ironclads were large ships. One such broadside ironclad, *New Ironsides,* was commissioned in August 1862. It could navigate under sail or steam at seven nautical miles per hour. Its vital spaces had 4½ inches of iron armor and carried 20 guns. *New Ironsides* fought at Charleston and Fort Fisher, survived a torpedo explosion, and was still operating when the war ended.

The South Takes the Lead in the East

When it comes to ironclads in the Civil War, the marquee event, of course, is the first battle of naval ironclads between the USS *Monitor* and the CSS *Virginia*. Somewhat surprisingly, the Confederates won the race to get ironclads into service in the Eastern Theater, but that distinction was only significant for a single day.

When Southern troops captured the Gosport Naval Yard in Norfolk, Virginia, on April 21, 1861, they found the sunken, partly burned hull of the frigate USS *Merrimack*. Stripping it down to the deck, they built a sloping casemate box on top of the deck armored with iron plates and installed new guns, creating a potential nightmare for the Union. On March 8, 1862, the ironclad— renamed the CSS *Virginia*—sailed into Hampton Roads, Virginia, and sank the Union frigates *Congress* and *Cumberland*. The naval blockade was broken, but the Confederate navy had little time to celebrate, because late that night the *Monitor* arrived.

Uncharted Waters

In the fall of 1861, engineer and inventor John Ericsson went to the U.S. Navy and told them that he could build a supership in 100 days. The result was the *Monitor*, which had a deck so low to the water that it would be a tough target to hit. With two smooth-bore cannons, however, it would be able to dish it out.

The *Monitor* was completed in less than four months and sent immediately to Hampton Roads. When the two ironclads faced off on March 9, the result was anticlimactic. Both ships could barely be harmed. They fired at each other, but damage was limited to a few dents on each ship, and the battle ended in a stalemate. The first duel of iron warships was over, and despite its lackluster results, new technology had captured the imagination of the world.

The *Monitor* inspired a raft of imitators of similar design, which were also called *monitors*. There was quite a range of monitors, including the *Miantonomah*, which was big enough to sail across the Atlantic. Shallow-draft monitors were commissioned in 1864 and 1865, designed to operate on shallow bays and rivers such as the James. Many of these were later converted to sweep Confederate mines or attack with spar torpedoes, though by 1865 there were few Confederate ships left to hit.

The Confederacy built its ironclads to local specifications, hammered together, as one Southerner put it, "out of junk." The ram *Albemarle* was built in a cornfield and armored with scrap iron salvaged by her captain, yet she managed to sink or cripple several Union ships before being torpedoed by a Northern launch in the Roanoke River. Some rebel ironclads were never finished, and others died in gallant battle or were cornered and sunk in rivers and ports as the Union closed off their avenues of escape.

The war ended in April 1865, but ironclads sailed on. In 1866, Austria and Italy fought at the Battle of Lissa with ironclads. The strong armored hulls of the broadsiders and the revolving turrets of the monitors were soon incorporated into a new generation of naval vessels that would one day be called battleships.

LINCOLN AND THE BLUE MASS

★ ★ ★ ★

In the 19th century, the cures for many common ailments were often worse than the sicknesses.

Lincoln was known for the composure, patience, and calmness he displayed while under the stress of the presidency. But in earlier years, the gangly prairie lawyer was known to suffer from bouts of anxiety, depression, tremors, insomnia—and to make others suffer from his outbursts of rage.

During an 1858 debate, Lincoln became so infuriated that "his voice thrilled and his whole frame shook." He grabbed a man by the collar and shook the poor fellow "until his teeth chattered."

Why was his personality so different in the period prior to his becoming president? A recent study by the University of Chicago Medical Center may have the answer.

Blue Mass for a Blue Mood

According to the study, Lincoln had been using a common medication for depression known as "blue mass." Taken as a syrup or in pill form, blue mass was used for a number of ailments, such as birthing pains, constipation, parasitic infestations, toothache, and tuberculosis. Although it differed from pharmacist to pharmacist, the concoction could include chalk, sugar, honey, licorice root, rosewater, rose petals—even mercury. A daily dosage of blue mass would have likely contained somewhere between 100 and 9,000 times more mercury than modern medicine would find acceptable

Symptoms of mercury poisoning can include severe mood swings and aggression. Lincoln stopped taking the medicine in 1861, a few months after his inauguration, noting that it made him "cross." His mood swings disappeared after that.

WHAT THE SOLDIERS USED FOR FIGHTING

★ ★ ★ ★

In what's often called "the first modern war," technical advances in weaponry broke the mold, doing what weapons had never done before.

The technological leaps made in weaponry during the Civil War had both a positive effect on the evolution of combat capability and devastating consequences for tens of thousands of soldiers in the midst of battle. Among the weapons that were in widespread use were powerful, long-range, high-trajectory cannons; hollow cannonballs that exploded into searing iron fragments and tiny, lethal iron balls; and grooved-barrel rifles that provided deadly accuracy up to 300 yards. Larger numbers of soldiers at greater distances and in a wider variety of landscapes could now be slain more quickly and more efficiently than during any war in human history up to that point.

Understanding the weapons used, why they were used, and what specific capabilities they had allows for a deeper insight into the war and the people who fought it. Realizing the strength and limitations of widely used machinery brings insight into military strategy. For example, there were two types of muskets, rifles, and artillery pieces used:

- Smoothbore: the inside of the barrel is smooth; bullets or shells fit loosely into the barrel, which limits their range and accuracy.

- Rifled: the inside of the barrel is grooved; bullets or shells fit snugly in the barrel, which, when fired, puts a spin on them and increases their range and accuracy.

The use of either type of barrel required different approaches to battle. Soldiers using them had to take into account their distance from the enemy, angles from which to attack, and how to deal with the landscape.

Cannons

Cannons formed formidable walls of both defense and offense, holding enemy lines at bay for hours, sometimes days. Six classes of cannons dominated the Civil War:

Smoothbore:

- Napoleon—considered the "workhorse" of the artillery

    Long, bronze, with front-loading barrel; Confederate version straight at the mouth; Union version bulge at the mouth

    Excellent maneuverability

    Very effective for both long-range dueling and firing canister (encased shots intended for close-range fire) at onrushing infantry

    Could shoot 1,600 yards

- Howitzer

    Short, bronze, front-loading barrel

    Required less gunpowder

    High trajectory

    Used more frequently by Confederates

    Could shoot 1,300 yards

Rifled:

- Parrott—patented in 1861 by Robert Parrott, superintendent of West Point foundry

    Long, slim, cast- and wrought-iron front-loading barrel with reinforced iron band around breech

Interior cooled

Accurate at long distances, but somewhat less effective at short range

Could shoot 2,800 yards

- Ordnance

    Long, slender, wrought-iron front-loading barrel

    Accurate at long distances, but relatively ineffective at short range

    Could shoot 2,100 yards

- Whitworth—manufactured in England

    Long, slender, iron, breech-loading (loaded in back) barrel

    Accurate at long distances, but relatively ineffective at short range

    Could shoot 2,500 yards

- James

    Long, bronze, front-loading barrel

    Could shoot 1,700 yards, shortest distance of all rifled artillery

Cannonballs

Beyond the sheer force and weight (anywhere from 9 to 20 pounds) of the average cannonball—the "solid shot"—several different types of cannonballs were developed to increase deadliness and short-range accuracy. These included:

- Canister

    Tin cylinder filled with 27–50 balls of iron

    Effective at less than 400 yards

    Double canister effective at less than 150 yards

- Spherical Case Shot

    Hollow iron projectile filled with iron balls and surrounded by powder; set off by a fuse, and tiny balls explode and spread through the air like bullets

    Effective at more than 500 yards

- Shell

    Hollow iron projectile filled with powder and set off by a fuse—spreads jagged iron fragments

    Effective at more than 1,300 yards

Muskets and Rifles

The guns used were either muskets or rifles, and they remain the weapons most commonly associated with the Civil War. Most people think of blue-coated soldiers marching with tall, pointed bayonets against their shoulders toward a fierce battleground, hiding behind rocks and trees when arduously reloading, and resorting to swordplay with their blades when the guns couldn't be reloaded fast enough. Yet how does that common notion stack up to reality?

- Muskets

    Various models of smoothbore muskets used by most Union and Confederate soldiers at war's outset—even when more rifled barrels that could increase their range and accuracy became available

    Spherical ball bullets

    Bayonet blades attached with a socket by many because of slow reload time—up to only about three shots per minute using gunpowder or paper cartridges

    Unreliable aim

    Effectiveness: good up to 50 yards, poor between 50 and 100 yards, ineffective at more than 100 yards

- Springfield Rifles

    Named "Springfield" because many were manufactured in Springfield, Massachusetts

    Three basic types: models 1855, 1861, and 1863

    Most popular rifle during the war, with a total of almost 1.5 million manufactured

    Soldiers able to load, aim, and fire these weapons three times per minute

    Conical bullet on top of a short hollowed-out shaft; expands to fit snugly against barrel once ignited

    Effectiveness: excellent up to 100 yards, good at 100 to 300 yards, poor at 300 to 500 yards, ineffective at more than 500 yards

- Enfield Rifles

    British rifles manufactured at the Royal Small Arms Factory at Enfield, England

    More than 900,000 imported by Northern and Southern quartermasters during the course of the war; thousands privately purchased for whole regiments

    Same bullet structure as Springfield rifles—conical on top of a short hollowed-out shaft that expands to fit snugly against barrel once ignited

    Effectiveness: excellent up to 100 yards, good at 100 to 300 yards, poor at 300 to 500 yards, ineffective at more than 500 yards

Weapons technology moved quickly during the middle of the 19th century, and many times the weapons outpaced the generals' strategies. It would take several more years before military leaders understood how to respond to advanced weapons in the hands of the enemy.

Fast Facts

- *Confederate General Joseph E. Johnston moved his troops from Winchester to Manassas via the Manassas Gap Railroad for the First Battle of Bull Run on July 18, 1861. It marked the first time in military history a railroad was used to mobilize troops for a strategic advantage.*

- *During the Civil War, the westernmost region represented by a delegate to the Confederate Congress was the Territory of Arizona.*

- *After the birth of their first child, Lincoln's pet name for his wife was "Mother." She sometimes called him "Father" in turn, though more often "Mr. Lincoln."*

- Carpetbagger: *a term for the horde of Northern politicians and unscrupulous financial adventurers who came to the South after the Civil War with a satchel of money to exploit newly enfranchised freedmen. The satchel was made of carpet, hence the term.*

- *Although the first national draft law allowed men to hire a substitute or to purchase an exemption for $300, it also stimulated volunteering.*

- *More Civil War battles were fought in Virginia than in any other state.*

- *The* Times *of London began referring to the C.S.A. as "the new nationality" in late 1862.*

- *General Philip Kearney's favorite mount was Moscow, a white horse, but because the big horse made an inviting target, the general switched to a bay named Decatur, and then to Bayard, whose color was light brown.*

THAT DEVIL FORREST

★ ★ ★ ★

A master tactician and a ruthless leader, Nathan Bedford Forrest saw his influence last long after the war ended.

The essence of Confederate General Nathan Bedford Forrest's military strategy was to "get there first with the most men." It sounds elementary enough, but Forrest, who fought against many better-educated generals during the Civil War, won nearly all of his battles. It's said that during the war he came under fire 179 times and captured 31,000 prisoners.

Rising from the Ranks

Unlike many famous Civil War generals, Forrest wasn't a product of West Point. His education came from his own experience. His father died when Forrest was a teenager in northern Mississippi, so he left school to support his mother and eight siblings. Initially, he worked his family's farm, but he soon expanded into trading cotton, livestock, real estate, and slaves. By 1860, he ran a highly successful business and was the owner of a 3,000-acre plantation in Memphis, Tennessee.

At the outbreak of war, he enlisted in the Confederate army as a private, but he soon received permission to raise his own cavalry unit. Spending his own money, he outfitted a cavalry battalion of 600 and earned the rank of lieutenant colonel. Shortly thereafter, his exploits as a cavalry leader became the stuff of legend.

A Ruthless Reputation

A number of notorious tales surround Forrest. He had a reputation throughout most of the war for being tough and ruthless. This may be summed up in one of the most famous quotes attributed to him: "War means fighting, and fighting means killing."

One of Forrest's earliest exploits that started to build his reputation is his cavalry regiment's escape from besieged Fort Donelson in Tennessee. Ulysses Grant's army had won the day, and Confederate commanders were getting ready to surrender the fort to him the next morning. Forrest would have none of it, declaring, "I did not come here for the purpose of surrendering my command." A few officers planned to slip away, Forrest among them. He announced to his troops: "Boys, these people are talking about surrendering, and I am going out of this place before they do or bust hell wide open." His unit disappeared into the night.

While covering the Confederate retreat from the Battle of Shiloh two months later, Forrest was wounded. He was far ahead of his troops when he got shot, but he grabbed a Union soldier and used him as a shield to make his escape back to Confederate lines.

Raiding Behind Enemy Lines

When he recovered, Forrest was promoted to brigadier general and began a series of successful cavalry raids against Union supply lines. In one memorable raid into Tennessee in 1863, his regiment of fewer than 1,000 attacked a Union garrison twice that size at Murfreesboro. His horse soldiers trounced the 2,000 bluecoats there and captured all survivors, including Union commanding officer General Thomas T. Crittenden.

In an attempt to disrupt General Sherman's campaign on Atlanta, Forrest and his unit went behind enemy lines to attack a Union supply depot at Johnsonville, Tennessee. The Union forces were caught by surprise, and Forrest was able to destroy a gunboat fleet and several million dollars' worth of Union supplies. Sherman wrote to Grant, "That devil Forrest was down about Johnsonville and was making havoc about the gun-boats and transfers." Still, it had no effect on his maneuvers in Georgia. Years later in his memoirs, Sherman had to admit a grudging respect, calling the incident "a feat of arms which, I confess, excited my admiration."

The Fort Pillow Massacre

Forrest cemented his reputation as a ruthless general at Fort Pillow, Tennessee, in April 1864. He led a successful attack against the fort and offered fair treatment to the defenders if they surrendered. When Union commanders refused, Forrest's army brutally overran the fort and its defenders, reportedly shooting many men—primarily black soldiers—as they attempted to surrender. Forrest denied these accusations, but he later said, "The river was dyed with the blood of the slaughtered for 200 yards." The incident, which came to be known as the Fort Pillow Massacre, became a rallying cry for black Union soldiers.

This made Forrest a bit of a target himself, leading Sherman to wish that the army would "go out and follow Forrest to the death, if it cost 10,000 lives and breaks the Treasury." Four times Union generals sent forces out specifically to defeat Forrest; each time they failed. The second of these attempts led to the Battle of Brice's Crossroads in Mississippi, where Forrest's troops routed a federal force that was twice their size. He was finally beaten in the spring of 1865 and forced to surrender in Gainesville, Alabama, that May. This was after both General Lee and General Johnston had surrendered their own forces at Appomattox Court House and Durham Station.

A Lasting Legacy

After the war, Forrest returned to planting cotton and speculating on railroads. He certainly didn't abandon his Confederate ideals, though. Forrest, known as the Wizard of the Saddle during the war, became the first Grand Wizard of the Ku Klux Klan in 1867. The Klan formed to terrorize blacks, Northerners, and Republicans. Forrest died on October 29, 1877, at the age of 56.

★ ★ ★ ★

"We were lavish of blood in those days, and it was thought to be a great thing to charge a battery of artillery or an earthwork lined with infantry."
Confederate Major General D.H. Hill, on the Seven Days Battles, June–July 1862

THE EMANCIPATION PROCLAMATION: FREEING THE SLAVES?

★ ★ ★ ★

In late 1862, Lincoln needed to make a bold move to redefine the war and the reasons for fighting it. But not all slaves received their freedom as a result of the Emancipation Proclamation. Who was free, and who remained in servitude?

Five days after the bloody Battle of Antietam in September 1862, President Abraham Lincoln issued a preliminary Emancipation Proclamation to his Cabinet. Scheduled to go into effect on January 1, 1863, the document was intended to apply only to states that were still in rebellion against the federal government on that date. In those states, any and all slaves would be freed from their masters for all time.

The Fine Print

Lincoln's plan caught everyone's attention, but it was not greeted with universal approval. The proclamation referred only to states (or parts of states) in rebellion, so slaves in the border states—Maryland, Kentucky, Missouri, and Delaware—or parts of Confederate states that were  under Union occupation would remain in bondage. Radical Republicans who wanted to see an end to all slavery were angry, believing Lincoln had not gone far enough. Editorials in foreign and antigovernment domestic presses lambasted the President, pointing out that Lincoln had freed slaves only in areas where the federal government was no longer recognized nor accepted— where his authority had been rejected and the order would be ignored.

In Defense of Lincoln

In limiting the scope of emancipation, Lincoln believed he was acting within his constitutional powers to seize enemy resources—in this case, the enemy's slaves. He also remained within his powers by not acting against slavery in territory that remained loyal to the United States. The President recognized that he had to wait for legislation from Congress to end the practice of slavery in the Union itself.

It's All PR

Even though it freed no slaves immediately, the Emancipation Proclamation was a brilliant public relations move. With one stroke of his pen, Lincoln turned the war into one of liberation for the slaves, and he helped doom Confederate hopes for foreign recognition. No European country would dare to enter the war on the side defending enslavement. In addition, the possibility of slaves abandoning their owners and undermining what was left of the Southern economy was extremely appealing. The final January 1863 Emancipation Proclamation expanded on this idea by authorizing the government to enlist black soldiers and sailors. "In giving freedom to the slave, we assure freedom to the free," Lincoln declared. "We must disenthrall ourselves, and then we shall save our country."

- The London Spectator *denounced the Emancipation Proclamation as a hypocritical sham: "The government liberates the enemy's slaves as it would the enemy's cattle, simply to weaken them in the . . . conflict. . . . The principle is not that a human being cannot justly own another, but that he cannot own him unless he is loyal to the United States."*

- *Early in the war, the Union armies were led by politically appointed generals who lacked experience—probably a key factor that contributed to prolonging of the war.*

(Continued from p. 122)

1862

February

Julia Ward Howe's "The Battle Hymn of the Republic" appears in the February issue of *The Atlantic Monthly*.

February 13–16

Union troops under Ulysses S. Grant force the surrender of 15,000 Confederates at Fort Donelson, Tennessee.

February 22

Jefferson Davis is inaugurated as President of the Confederacy.

March 8–9

The CSS *Virginia* sinks two Union warships near Hampton Roads, Virginia, and fights the USS *Monitor* to a draw in the first naval engagement between ironclad ships.

March 18

Judah P. Benjamin, the Confederate secretary of war, is transferred to the post of secretary of state by Jefferson Davis.

April 6–7

The Union army triumphs in the Battle of Shiloh in Tennessee.

April 16

Slavery is abolished in the District of Columbia. Slaveholders are compensated up to $300 for each emancipated slave.

President Davis approves the conscription of every white male between the ages of 18 and 35 for three years of military service. This is the first national military draft to be instituted in the United States.

April 28

After Captain David G. Farragut's Union fleet overcomes the defenses of New Orleans, the city surrenders.

May 3

Confederate troops evacuate Yorktown in Virginia, leaving it for General George B. McClellan's Army of the Potomac.

May 8

Confederates defeat U.S. troops at the Battle of McDowell, Virginia, as part of General Stonewall Jackson's Shenandoah Valley Campaign.

May 13

Robert Smalls, a slave, pilots the CSS *Planter* to the Union blockading fleet off Charleston, South Carolina.

May 31–June 1

During the inconclusive Battle of Fair Oaks in Virginia, Confederate General Joseph E. Johnston is wounded, forcing him to give up his command. He is replaced by Robert E. Lee.

June 9

Jackson's Shenandoah Valley Campaign comes to an end with the Battle of Port Republic, Virginia. After the Union loss, Lincoln orders troops to withdraw.

June 27

After fierce, bloody fighting, Lee's Confederates take the upper hand at the Battle of Gaines' Mill, Virginia. McClellan withdraws from his failed Peninsula Campaign.

(Continued on p. 210)

ESCAPE OF THE JOURNALISTS

★ ★ ★ ★

Condemned for reporting for a "bastion of Northern propaganda,"
two New York Tribune *reporters survived a harrowing*
escape from a Confederate prison camp.

Most of the POWs held within the walls of Civil War prison camps
were soldiers captured on the battlefield. However, on May 3,
1863, reporters Albert Richardson and Junius Browne of the *New
York Tribune* and Richard Colburn of the New York *World*
became the first reporters to be captured during the conflict. A
year and a half later, Richardson and Browne would stage one of
the most thrilling and harrowing escapes of the war.

A Wrong Turn

The three men were attempting to join up with General Grant and
his troops near Vicksburg, Mississippi, when they decided to take
a shortcut to reach the front lines as quickly as possible. Unfortunately, it's hard to remain inconspicuous when you're riding a
barge down the Mississippi River, and sure enough, they were
spotted by the Confederates. The reporters' hopes of scooping
their fellow correspondents on Grant's activities vanished when
the rebels took to the river after them. All three were captured
and imprisoned in the local jail.

Northern Rag

Richardson and Browne were warned by other prisoners that the
Tribune was not respected in the South. "Tell them you are correspondents of some less-obnoxious journal," they were advised.
Indeed, a casual conversation with some Confederate officers
confirmed that any reporter from the *Tribune* was likely to be
hanged. Despite this, the two reporters decided to tell the truth.
At first, all three reporters were promised release and given food

and clothes by some of their Southern newspaper counterparts. However, when Colburn was freed, the two *Tribune* reporters were told that, because their newspaper was regarded as a bastion of Northern propaganda, they would be imprisoned for the remainder of the war. They were immediately transferred to Libby Prison in Richmond.

Southern Hospitality

Richardson and Browne would see the insides of seven prisons over the next 20 months, eventually ending up in Salisbury, North Carolina, where they met Confederate Lieutenant John Welborn, a member of the secretive fraternal organization Sons of America. This order believed that it was its duty to try to return as many Northern prisoners to their homes as possible, and Welborn risked his life to do just that. The Southern lieutenant helped the reporters secure assignments in the prison hospital, where they were able to obtain passes that allowed them travel outside the walls without supervision. On December 18, 1864, Richardson and Browne informed a guard that they were picking up some desperately needed medical supplies and walked out of the prison. This began an adventure that found the pair escaping from Southern patrols, living with local slaves, and joining up with Confederate deserters and federal sympathizers.

Free at Last

Nearly one month and 340 miles later, the ragged group of more than a dozen that had collected around the pair staggered into a Union camp near Knoxville, Tennessee. They had successfully run away from the dogs used to capture escaped prisoners and navigated the dangerous swamps and unforgiving mountains. They had come up against and escaped bushwhackers, the "vicious, passionate, bloodthirsty" men who captured escaped prisoners and slaves and would just as soon kill them as take them back alive. "I walked within the lines that divided freedom, enlightenment, loyalty from slavery, bigotry, treachery," Richardson wrote upon his arrival in the North. "Out of the jaws of death, out of the mouth of hell."

MAKING IT UP AS THEY WENT ALONG

★ ★ ★ ★

Rapid progression through the ranks wasn't uncommon, but one officer had three upper-level ranks created just for him.

At the beginning of the war, the U.S. Navy had a limited rank structure, which made promotions difficult. The highest rank one could attain was captain. If officers were in command of more than one vessel, they might also be accorded the title "commodore," but their actual rank was still no higher than captain.

Expanding the Ranks

The Civil War forced the Navy to expand. The service increased its strength from about 9,000 officers and enlisted sailors to 24,000 by the end of 1861, which meant that the Navy needed to expand its rank structure. In July 1862, Congress created the official rank of commodore to be the equivalent of an Army brigadier general and authorized the Navy to promote 18 officers to the position. One of those selected was David G. Farragut, but in terms of receiving promotions, he was only just beginning.

In 1862, Farragut captured New Orleans and opened the Mississippi for Union traffic up to Vicksburg. In recognition, Congress authorized his promotion to rear admiral, equal to an Army major general, the first time in U.S. history that such a rank had been bestowed.

As Farragut led his squadron under fire against Mobile, Alabama, in August 1864, he uttered the now-famous phrase: "Damn the torpedoes, full speed ahead!" Four months later, Congress took the same attitude, authorizing the rank of vice admiral, equal to an Army lieutenant general, to promote Farragut again.

Despite failing health, Farragut remained on active duty. In 1866, after the fighting had ended, he was made a full admiral, equal to an Army full general and the highest one could go in the military.

Fast Facts

- According to a well-known story, Confederate Lieutenant George Dixon was saved from a Yankee minié ball by a $20 gold piece in his trouser pocket at the 1862 Battle of Shiloh. The coin stopped the ball from entering his leg and possibly saved his life. That coin had been given to him by his sweetheart as a good luck charm. Dixon had the bullet-bent gold piece engraved and thereafter always carried it on his person. Dixon went on to serve with the crew of the submarine H. L. Hunley. When the Hunley was raised in 2000, an archaeologist was preparing to lift Dixon's skeleton from the sub when she found a warped gleaming gold piece engraved "Shiloh. April 6th, 1862. My life Preserver. G.E.D."

- The cost of the war to the Union, not including pensions and interest, as finally tabulated 14 years after hostilities ceased, was more than $6.1 billion.

- "Young Lions" were the Southern cadets at four major military colleges during the Civil War—Georgia Military Institute, South Carolina Military Academy (Columbia's Arsenal campus and the Citadel in Charleston), University of Alabama, and Virginia Military Institute.

- Gettysburg National Military Park has approximately 1,328 monuments, markers, and memorials.

- The only Confederate officer executed for war crimes was the commander of the infamous Andersonville Prison, Major Henry Wirz.

- Two Confederate governors fought at Shiloh: Tennessee governor Isham G. Harris was an aide to Confederate commander Albert Sidney Johnston, and Kentucky governor George W. Johnson was killed on the second day of battle.

UP, UP, AND AWAY

★ ★ ★ ★

*As the war continued, the armies were desperately in
need of military innovation. One man helped them look
to the skies for possible answers.*

Only eight days after the Confederate assault on Fort Sumter and
the beginning of fighting in the Civil War, a strange object
appeared in the sky above Unionville, South Carolina. Within
minutes, the apparition began to descend, and its sole occupant
was captured near the town and jailed on the suspicion of being a
Union spy.

The man who fell from the sky was Thaddeus
Lowe, a balloonist from Cincinnati, Ohio. He
had been on one of several practice runs he'd
been making lately that he hoped would eventually lead to an attempt to cross the Atlantic
Ocean by balloon. On this excursion, he set a
distance record for traveling 900 miles from Cincinnati in nine hours. But with war now underway, he
was also suddenly a prisoner. Once the South Carolina authorities determined that Lowe presented no
threat to them, they released him and allowed him to return north
by train.

An Idea Is Launched

Once he arrived back in Cincinnati, Lowe got together with an
influential supporter who also happened to be the editor of the
Cincinnati Daily Commercial, Murat Halstead. Lowe wanted
Halstead's help in approaching the government with a lofty idea:
using balloons to observe the position and movements of enemy
troops. Utilizing balloons in warfare was certainly not a new concept by any means—observation balloons had been used by the
French for military reconnaissance during the Battle of Fleurus in
1794. Observers in balloons could rise above the landscape and

gather valuable information to share with commanders on the ground. With this in mind, Halstead contacted Secretary of the Treasury Salmon Chase, who arranged a meeting between Lowe and President Lincoln.

Upward Bound

The balloon *Enterprise* was launched on the first of several flights from the Columbian Armory in Washington, D.C., on June 18, 1861. For one launch, telegraph equipment was set up between the balloon and the ground, and Lowe telegraphed to Lincoln the very first message sent from a balloon. The demonstration was a success. Within months, the President called for the creation of a Balloon Corps and placed it under the Bureau of Topographical Engineers. It was to be manned by civilians under Lowe's direct supervision. Lincoln also authorized funds to purchase equipment and hire personnel. Lowe used that funding to construct five observation balloons of varying sizes, the smaller ones intended to accommodate inclement weather.

Lowe finished constructing his first military balloon, made from the "best India silk," on August 28, with an initial test run scheduled for September 24 outside of Arlington, Virginia. As he reached approximately 1,000 feet on that test flight, Lowe telegraphed the position of Confederate troops near Falls Church, Virginia, to his assistants below. Coordinates were then passed to the artillery, which began firing on the Confederates' position. It was the first time in history that artillery successfully hit an enemy target the gunners couldn't see.

Not All Smooth Sailing

Lowe was not without his detractors and competitors, however. Contrary to Lowe's wishes, John Wise of Pennsylvania and John La Mountain of New York, both experienced aeronauts, were considered by the Bureau of Topographical Engineers and the War Department to serve as vendors of balloons and, more annoyingly for Lowe, his assistants. In the end, however, Lowe's wishes prevailed due to the intervention of General George McClellan. Lowe and his balloonists joined the general's Virginia Peninsula

Campaign to participate in the federal advance on Richmond. During that campaign, Lowe made hundreds of trips to survey Confederate positions.

In addition to his flights over land, Lowe also experimented with flights tethered to a boat. In these instances, a barge was converted into an "aircraft carrier" by replacing its deck with a wooden platform from which several flights were launched. One of the launched flights carried a balloon piloted by Lowe for approximately 13 miles at a height of about 1,000 feet.

Diminishing Returns

After roughly four months of surveying Confederate positions, Lowe contracted malaria, which caused the activities of the Balloon Corps to be suspended. When his health was restored, Lowe provided reconnaissance during the Fredericksburg and the Chancellorsville campaigns, but a disagreement with his supervisor over funding eventually led to his resignation from the Balloon Corps. He was replaced by two of his assistants, brothers James and Ezra Allen. They also ran into conflicts with military authorities, and the corps was finally disbanded in August 1863.

The experiment with the Balloon Corps ended with mixed results. On one hand, Lowe's observations certainly helped the Federals during the Peninsula Campaign. Using the balloons, he discovered that the Confederates had abandoned Yorktown, and his observations during the Battle of Fair Oaks played an important role in the Union victory.

On the other hand, there had been some problems with the quality and interpretation of some of Lowe's reports. McClellan's approach to battle was already turtle-like, but Lowe's ambiguous sightings of enemy troops only heightened the general's anxiety. Ultimately, the sightings contributed to McClellan's decision to shift his army from a position of offense to a defensive posture around Harrison's Landing, Virginia. While Generals Ambrose Burnside and Joseph Hooker requested Lowe's assistance, they placed little value on his observations. That lack of trust contributed to the end of the Balloon Corps.

Experiments in the Southern Skies

Once the Federals revealed their balloon project, the Confederate government began examining the merits of the concept. In early 1862, Captain John Randolph Bryan was directed to build an observation balloon. Northern balloons had been inflated with gas. The Confederates, however, did not have the ability to produce gas in the field, so their balloon was filled with hot air. Bryan's initial flight went very well, but on his second trip, someone got tangled in the balloon's tether. When the tether was cut to free the person, the balloon moved away in free flight. Thinking it was a Union balloon, Confederate troops used it for target practice before Bryan safely brought it in for a landing.

A second Confederate balloon was constructed, but this time it was filled with gas in Richmond and carried to the field tethered to a locomotive. It was then picked up by a tugboat, but the balloon ran aground and was captured by Union troops. A third Confederate balloon was ripped from its mooring by high wind and also fell into the hands of the enemy. This was enough to make the Confederates end their balloon experimentation.

Ultimately, the idea of observation balloons was uncomfortable to both Union and Confederate commanders. Each side abandoned its respective program because neither side grasped the worth of the information relayed from the pilots. The real value of flight in military operations would not be recognized for several more decades.

- *American achievements with aerial reconnaissance balloons inspired the Prussian army to send Count Ferdinand von Zeppelin to learn what he could about this kind of warfare.*

- *The first sitting U.S. member of Congress to be captured during a battle was Alfred Ely of New York. He had ridden out to witness the First Battle of Bull Run in northern Virginia and was captured and held in Libby Prison for six months.*

ART FOR ARTISTS' SAKE

★ ★ ★ ★

During the war, many artists traveled with the troops, hoping to capture the grandeur and agony of battle for the rest of the nation.

Northerners

Winslow Homer. Ultimately becoming one of America's most famous painters, Winslow Homer first made a name for himself by creating Civil War illustrations and sketches for magazines such as *Harper's Weekly.* Although Homer was fairly green when the war began, *Harper's* sent the aspiring artist to the front lines to capture the action for readers in the North. Armed with a letter of reference from the editor, he was able to move around in the war zone with little difficulty. In fact, Homer was one of several people granted "Special Artist" status who was allowed to sketch, draw, and paint the unfolding war. These artists were given almost total access to Northern troops and battles, though this often created tension between the desire for journalistic integrity and the army's desire to protect its image. Mingling with the rank and file of the Army of the Potomac, Homer rendered the group's training and preparations for battle with a keen eye. He sketched the 6th Pennsylvania Cavalry regiment—the only cavalry soldiers to carry long lances—portraying them with a stark drama that inspired awe as well as pride. His simple woodcut illustrations in *Harper's* became extremely popular, since they were often the only documentary footage of the war that most readers would encounter. Ultimately, Homer's sketches played a large part in shaping the public's perception of the Civil War.

Augustus Saint-Gauden. The large Augustus Saint-Gauden monument to the 54th Massachusetts regiment is one of the most enduring and prominent displays of Civil War art, having loomed over Boston Common for more than 100 years.

Saint-Gauden's bronze, bas-relief memorial depicts the company's white commander, Colonel Robert Gould Shaw, and his black troops. This regiment took many casualties in its attack on Fort Wagner, South Carolina, losing more than 270 of its number, including Shaw. Though that assault was not successful, the sculpture serves as a vivid reminder of the company's bravery and the contributions that black troops made to the Union war effort.

Edward Lamson Henry. While Southern artists played up the nobility and grandeur of the Confederate cause, many Northern artists went a different direction, focusing instead on the destruction and devastation being meted out by Union forces. Edward Lamson Henry's paintings portrayed the horrors of war and how they affected civilians as well as combatants. Henry traveled extensively with Union forces, and in 1864 he witnessed a vast Virginia estate being dismantled by Northern troops. In 1869, he put some of the images he'd seen on canvas in his painting *Old Westover Mansion,* depicting the once glorious home in ruins, its façade pocked with damage.

Southerners

Frank Vizetelly. The *Illustrated London News* sent Frank Vizetelly to America to cover the war. Vizetelly hadn't intended to focus on one side over the other, but after he accurately portrayed the Union's defeat at the First Battle of Bull Run, Union General George McClellan had him barred from the front. Unable to continue his work in the North, Vizetelly trekked south to the Confederacy and became one of the few journalistic artists to produce sketches from the Southern perspective. His work is an invaluable resource to historians and provides insight into the actions and experiences of Confederate soldiers during the conflict.

Conrad Wise Chapman. The son of distinguished American artist John Gadsby Chapman, Conrad Wise Chapman received his artistic training in Rome, but when the Civil War broke out, he returned home to join the Confederate army. After being wounded in the head, Chapman was transferred to Charleston to recover. While there, he was commissioned by General P.G.T.

Beauregard to create a series of paintings depicting the siege operations of the city.

John Ross Key. A former Confederate soldier and resident of Charleston, John Ross Key portrayed the beginning of the war with his vivid and stunning portrayal of the attack on Fort Sumter. Instead of the typically dreary battle scene one might expect, the sweeping, panoramic view of Charlestown's waterfront is a vibrant, luminous depiction of the attack, bathed in rich sunshine and the deep blue hues of the sky and ocean. Key was a grandson of Francis Scott Key, who wrote "The Star-Spangled Banner."

William D. Washington. The Confederate artist William D. Washington took up residency in Richmond, Virginia, during the war. His 1864 memorial painting, *The Burial of Latane,* commemorated the death of Captain William Latane, the only soldier to be killed in Jeb Stuart's daring 1862 cavalry ride around the forces of Union General McClellan. The painting became a fixture in Southern homes for years after the war as a symbol of the Confederacy's heavy losses.

Louis Mathieu Didier Guillaume. Based in Richmond, Virginia, but originally from France, Louis Mathieu Didier Guillaume immortalized the final moment of the Civil War with his painting of Lee's surrender to Grant at Appomattox Court House on April 9, 1865.

"We cannot afford to be idle, and though weaker than our opponents in men and military equipments, must endeavor to harass, if we cannot destroy them."
General Robert E. Lee to President Jefferson Davis, Sept. 3, 1862

"No tongue can tell, no mind conceive, no pen portray the horrible sights I witnessed this morning."
Captain John Taggert, 9th Pennsylvania Reserves, on Antietam

PAYING FOR THE WAR

★ ★ ★ ★

Bullets cost money. Bandages cost money. Horses cost money. No matter which side you're on, war costs money. How did the Union and the Confederacy pay for their Civil War?

The Union:

Had the advantage of an established Treasury Department. A national apparatus was in place for raising and spending money, but even so, a recent depression had resulted in lower tariffs on foreign goods, which in turn dropped Northern revenues by nearly 30 percent. Meanwhile, the federal budget suffered from four years of deficit spending between 1858 and 1861. The South's secession caused a new panic in the North, making the war even less affordable.

Had a secretary of the Treasury with no prior experience in finance. Secretary of the Treasury Salmon P. Chase had been a lawyer, the governor of Ohio, and a U.S. senator. But even without banking or finance knowledge, Chase kept the North solvent by offering short-term bank loans at 7.3 percent. Chase also developed the now-common practice of selling bonds to the public, with some as small as $50. Banks also bought long-term bonds at a rate of 6 percent, bringing the government more than $1 billion between the two sales. The North actually financed more than 66 percent of the war this way.

Had a solid tax base to draw from. In August 1861, the North had the dubious distinction of enacting the first federal income tax in U.S. history. Up until that time, the developing war had depended on receiving its financing from the lowered tariffs for foreign goods. Once the income tax was in place, however, the Union received more than 20 percent of its war funding from the new source of revenue. The subsequent Internal Revenue Act of

1862 covered everything from liquor and tobacco to professional licenses and inheritances.

Relied on actual gold to back up the bonds that were sold. When early Northern failures on the battlefields led to another financial panic, gold supplies dropped to dangerous levels by the end of 1861. Without gold, the United States couldn't pay for supplies—it couldn't even pay its own army. The result was an innovative bill that introduced the concept of "legal tender," or paper money backed by U.S. reserve gold. The Legal Tender Act became law in February 1862 and created the "greenback."

Enacted the National Banking Act in February 1863. This legislation federalized banks of a certain stature, allowing them to issue the "greenback" as legal U.S. currency. The measure also allowed hundreds of banks to do away with their own proprietary banknotes. State banks issuing their own notes were eventually driven to federal compliance by 1865 and were forced to pay a 10 percent tax on all paper issued.

The Confederacy:

Did not have much available capital with which to begin a war. Most of the South's wealth was represented by land and slaves, which made up 30 percent of the area's financial assets. However, the South held only 12 percent of the currency in circulation and just over 20 percent in bank holdings. Many Southern cotton plantations were heavily indebted to Northern bankers and merchants. When the Confederate Congress tried to force debt payment in exchange for Confederate bonds in May 1861, Southern debtors surrendered a mere 5 percent of what they owed.

Lacked tax savvy. The Confederate States of America, being a new governmental machine, did not have an active Treasury Department and had no economic devices such as taxation and collection. In fact, when the South tried to enact a direct property tax at the state level, only one state actually collected it.

Had a false sense of security. The South would eventually print more than $1.5 billion in paper currency, to be redeemed in gold within two years of the war's end—so strong was the South's faith in being victorious. In many cases, states, cities, and some businesses generated their own "money" by actually printing it themselves, without having anything to back it. Talk about inflation! The art and craft of counterfeiting quickly added to the depreciation of the Southern economy.

Issued bonds that no one could afford to buy. The Confederate Congress issued $100 million of Confederate bonds in 1861 at 8 percent interest. The trouble was, even those Southerners who had extra money to invest had to think twice, especially when the inflation rate soared to 12 percent per month by the end of 1861, which meant that the bonds were actually losing money.

Saw pricing controls go through the roof. The cost of living in the South became too great for many families. For example, the price of common salt—used by many farms and homes to preserve meat—increased from $2 per bag to more than $60 per bag by the end of 1862.

Had fiscal responsibilities that did not end when Lee surrendered to Grant in April 1865. According to a 1947 national news magazine article, Southern states were still paying out more than $3 million in pensions to veterans and their surviving dependents—more than 82 years after the end of the Civil War!

- *The Union began the war with huge advantages due to its extensive industrial development, while the South lagged far behind because its economy produced mostly raw materials. Railroads were used to transport troops and supplies, and the North possessed about 22,000 miles of rails to the South's roughly 9,000. Near the end of the war, the South's lines were mostly destroyed, leaving the Confederacy totally unable to supply its troops or feed its population centers.*

THE CLASH OF
THE IRONCLADS

★ ★ ★ ★

Although anticlimactic, this fight—the first between ironclad
battleships—revolutionized modern warship design.

Confederate Secretary of the Navy Stephen Mallory had a major
challenge from the first day of his appointment: His navy had no
ships. What Mallory did have, however, was the Gosport Navy
Yard at Norfolk, Virginia, which contained the best and largest dry
dock on American soil.

While the North had been building standard wooden warships,
Mallory found himself fascinated with drawings of an ironclad ship
presented to him by a young former U.S. Navy officer named John
Mercer Brooke. Brooke assured Mallory that iron plating
mounted at an angle over a wooden backing would protect it from
gunfire.

Then Mallory realized that he did indeed have a ship—the recovered hull of the USS *Merrimack,* a steam frigate that had earlier
been burned to the waterline. He ordered Brooke and a local
shipbuilder named John Luke Porter to build Brooke's ironclad
using the hulk of the *Merrimack.* The ironclad, rechristened the
CSS *Virginia,* would be armed with six large smoothbore cannons
and four rifled cannons. Porter reluctantly agreed to help. He, too,
had presented his idea for an ironclad to the U.S. Navy several
years earlier, but at the time, the Navy considered ironclad ships a
folly and rejected his idea. Now the ironclad was being champi-
oned enthusiastically, but Porter was getting no credit for it.

The Race Is On

When Union spies got word of the planned Confederate ironclad,
officials in Washington, D.C., created a committee to develop
their own ironclad design. Lincoln approved a radical design for

an ironclad ship that would ride low in the water. The warship, named the *Monitor,* would be armed with just two 11-inch cannons mounted in a revolving turret, earning it the nickname "cheese box on a raft" by detractors.

Both sides raced to finish their ironclads. The *Monitor* was finished before the *Virginia* in late January 1862, but it took several weeks until the ship was ready for combat. When it was all set, it headed south from Brooklyn, New York, on March 6 in search of the *Virginia.* The *Virginia* moved out on March 8, and Captain Franklin Buchanan quickly launched an attack on the federal wooden fleet blockading Chesapeake Bay.

In a fight of metal against wood, there was virtually no contest. The *Virginia* smashed the Union ships to pieces. One wooden ship sank, another went up in flames, and three more ran aground. The *Virginia* withdrew at the end of the day, but later that evening, the *Monitor* arrived on the scene. The crew lay in wait for the return of the *Virginia.*

The Big Showdown

The appearance of the *Monitor* surprised the Confederates—they had heard that the warship was under construction, but their spies had failed to keep them informed when it started making its way south down the coast. Shortly before 9:00 A.M., the two ships clumsily began to circle each other. The circling continued for the next four hours.

Shot after shot was fired one against the other, sometimes at a range of just a few yards. Each ship dented the other, and the *Monitor* even succeeded in jamming some of the *Virginia's* gun ports and cracking its new armor plating in spots, but neither could land a conclusive blow. Eventually, leery of running aground himself, Captain Buchanan pulled the *Virginia* away from the battle. Neither ship had sunk the other—the fight was a draw.

SO THEY SAID

"With this honor devolves upon you also a corresponding responsibility. As the country herein trusts you, so under God it will sustain you."

Abraham Lincoln, conferring the army's highest rank of lieutenant general upon Ulysses S. Grant

"So the case stands, and under all the passion of the parties and the cries of battle lie the two chief moving causes of the struggle. Union means so many millions a year lost to the South; secession means the loss of the same millions to the North. The love of money is the root of this, as of many other evils. The quarrel between the North and South is, as it stands, solely a fiscal quarrel."

Charles Dickens

"There are those damn black-hatted fellows again. T'aint no militia, it's the Army of the Potomac."

Confederate soldier, July 1, 1863

"Forced marches, wakeful bivouacs, retreat, retreat. O, it was pitiful! The events of the past weeks are incredible. Disaster, pitiable, humiliating, contemptable!"

Union Lieutenant Colonel Wilder Dwight, 2nd Massachusetts, with Pope's army

"In firing his gun, John Brown has merely told what time of day it is. It is high noon."

William Lloyd Garrison

WHAT COULD HAVE BEEN

★ ★ ★ ★

After years spent teaching the leaders of the Civil War, General Charles Ferguson Smith became a hero in his own right.

Union General William Tecumseh Sherman was a protégé and friend of Ulysses Grant, but there was another officer who Sherman respected even more. "Had C. F. Smith lived," Sherman stated, "Grant would have disappeared to history after Donelson."

Charles Ferguson Smith entered West Point in 1820 at 14, graduating in 1825 the 19th of 37 cadets. Smith returned to West Point as an assistant instructor of infantry tactics in 1829, ultimately rising to commandant of cadets. He held that position while Grant, Sherman, and various other Civil War figures were cadets.

His Short Civil War Career

Smith left that post in 1842 and, a few years later, made a name for himself in the Mexican War. He won three brevet promotions, rising to the rank of lieutenant colonel. When the Civil War started, he was promoted to brigadier general of volunteers. He was transferred to Grant's Army of the Mississippi in January 1862 and made a division commander during the campaign against Forts Henry and Donaldson. When the Confederates attempted to break through Union lines outside of Fort Donaldson, he led a counterattack that sealed the fate of the rebels. When Confederate General Simon Buckner—another former student—requested surrender terms, Smith advised Grant to accept no less than unconditional surrender. Grant agreed and was forever after known as Unconditional Surrender Grant. Smith was promoted to major general. "I owe my success at Donaldson emphatically to him," Grant wrote.

A short time later, however, Smith jumped into a rowboat and fell and scraped his leg. The wound became infected and killed him on April 25, 1862. To hear Sherman tell it, Smith was arguably Grant's superior. Had he lived, could he have replaced Grant and the public career we know today?

CONFEDERATE RIOTING IN BALTIMORE

★ ★ ★ ★

Federal troops heading to Washington, D.C., were met by hostile civilians in Baltimore. At the end of the altercation, 17 were dead.

On April 14, 1861, two days after the cannons fired on Fort Sumter, Abraham Lincoln called for 75,000 volunteer troops. Some of these would be assigned to defend Washington, D.C.—the federal army numbered only 13,000 at the time, with most of the soldiers stationed out West. Almost all that stood between the Capitol and the Confederates were clerks, quartermasters, and engineers.

The 6th Steps Up

First to respond to the President's call was the 6th Massachusetts. The new troops marched through Boston in long frock coats and tall caps while the city erupted with cheers. As they passed through other towns on their way south to Washington, they were met with waving handkerchiefs, fireworks, and marching bands.

The Mason-Dixon Line—traditionally the dividing line between North and South—is the boundary between Pennsylvania, a free state, and Maryland, a slave state. Crossing that boundary, the soldiers started to notice a difference in how they were treated. By the time the 6th arrived in Baltimore, all enthusiasm had stopped. Instead, unsmiling locals greeted their train as it chugged to a stop at the President Street Station. The soldiers had a second train to catch at Camden Street Station, a mile away. Meeting that connecting train would be a battle the troops had not bargained for.

Hostile Hellos

Military planners had underestimated the hostility awaiting the troops in Maryland. About the time the 6th had boarded the train in Boston, Virginia had announced its secession in protest of Lincoln's proclamation. By the time they arrived in the Old Line

State, rumors were flying that Maryland's state government would stop the advance of the Yankees to the nation's capital.

Connections between the two Baltimore stations were usually made by hooking train cars to horses and carting them from one station to the other. Seven military companies made the journey safely, but after livid Baltimore residents barricaded the roads, the remaining 260 volunteers were forced to get out and walk to the connection. Rocks, bricks, cobblestones, knives, and fists flew at the 6th as they marched and were escorted by Baltimore Mayor George William Brown, who was trying to keep the peace in his city.

Under Attack

In his official report, Colonel Edward Jones of the 6th Massachusetts recalled that the remaining troops "were furiously attacked by a shower of missiles, which came faster as they advanced." He reported that the volunteers picked up their pace, which seemed only to make the mob angrier. Jones reported pistol shots being fired at the volunteers, killing one soldier. Although he wrote that at this point soldiers were ordered to stop and fire into the crowd to protect themselves, it is certain that some of the soldiers had already started shooting. Several in the mob were hit, and the troops again picked up their pace and continued toward the station. Mayor Brown, still marching with the Massachusetts volunteers, tried to calm the situation between them and the people of Baltimore, but as Jones wrote, "The mayor's patience was soon exhausted." Brown took a soldier's gun and fired on a citizen himself, as did a Baltimore police officer.

The soldiers who made it to the second train left behind their marching band, as well as five slain soldiers and at least a dozen dead Marylanders. Baltimore had now become a crisis. Lincoln was determined to keep the route clear for troops to pass through to Washington and even more determined to save Maryland for the Union, so he suspended the writ of habeas corpus and declared martial law. A number of citizens were jailed for inciting a riot, and even Mayor Brown and other state and city officials ultimately found themselves behind bars.

Fast Facts

- Adelbert Ames was the last surviving full-rank Civil War general. He died in Florida in 1933 at age 97.

- When short of artillery, Southern defenders often resorted to the use of Quaker guns, which were logs cut to resemble cannons and painted black on the firing end. To aid in this deception, the logs were sometimes mounted on real gun carriages. This defensive strategy often misled the Union into thinking that Confederate positions were more strongly armed than they actually were.

- General Sherman himself estimated the damage inflicted on Georgia during his 90-day March to the Sea to be more than $100 million, with $80 million of that "simply waste and destruction."

- When Ulysses Grant asked Julia Dent's father permission for her hand in marriage, her father offered her younger sister, Ellen, instead. Ulysses and Julia were married anyway on August 22, 1848.

- For the first time in a large-scale war, troops were deployed en masse via the railroads.

- Most of Stonewall Jackson is buried at Virginia Military Institute in Lexington, Virginia, but his arm is buried near where it was amputated after the Battle of Chancellorsville.

- In June 1864, the longest pontoon bridge in military history—2,100 feet—was constructed near Windmill Point on the James River in nine hours by 450 federal engineers. It consisted of 101 wooden pontoons that carried a roadbed 11 feet wide. There was even a removable section to allow vessels on the water to pass through the bridge.

PONTOONING THE RIVERS

★ ★ ★ ★

*A European military tactic helped keep
troops dry in soggy situations.*

Throughout the history of warfare, rivers have been enormous obstacles for advancing armies, but they have also played a part as vital supply lines and as a source of freshwater. Northern and Southern armies needed to be able to cross these waterways quickly, to use them for their own defense, and sometimes even to hold them in battle. In order to perform all these tasks, they turned to advances made by their military counterparts in Europe, who had devised a sort of floating, temporary bridge—a pontoon system—that addressed these problems.

Before pontoon technology came along, armies had to build bridges over rivers from timber that was available on the scene. If there was no timber to be found, they couldn't cross. Also, if the enemy happened to be in the area, trying to build a bridge could be extremely dangerous, as well. The task could take days, and without the possibility of cover, the construction crew would be easy targets for enemy fire. With the new pontoon boats, however, it took mere hours and far less labor. Now armies could build bridges quickly, have some soldiers available to give covering fire if necessary, and pull the pontoon boats out and move on to another location when they were finished.

 The French army had developed a pontooning system that consisted of flat-bottomed wooden boats, vessels that could easily be transported on land and quickly dropped into place in a river. American armies advanced this idea, creating self-contained boats movable by railway to the river locations where they were needed. Engineers in the United States improved the system further by borrowing from the Russian army, which had begun to build their pontoon boats out of lightweight canvas, making them even easier to transport.

Containing ropes, oars, boat hooks, and anchors, the pontoon boats were lowered into the water and anchored in a row. Engineers would then lay planks across them until the river had been bridged. Hay or soil was spread on top of the planks to protect and strengthen the bridge. Army engineers became very adept at this process, at one point spanning Virginia's James River with a 2,200-foot bridge in a little more than five hours. This was usually done after troops had secured both banks of the river, but there were some situations, such as at the Battle of Fredericksburg, in which engineers had to construct a pontoon bridge under fire.

The pontoon bridges were primarily built in groupings, so if one was destroyed or damaged, there were still other avenues by which to cross the river. Often the enemy would do its best to take down the structure, sending heavy floating objects downstream with the intent of smashing up the lightweight boats. Engineers devised a defense against this by adding a series of chained logs as a protective barrier. If these logs didn't stop the heavy objects, sentries armed with a small boat and grappling hooks were placed along the riverbank to fend off the improvised torpedoes. Pontoon bridges were primarily used by the North during the Civil War. Perhaps because Union soldiers advanced into Southern territory more often than Confederates ventured into the North, they had a greater need to find new ways across rivers.

"General Sickles, this is in some respects higher ground than that to the rear, but there is still higher in front of you, and if you keep on advancing you will find constantly higher ground all the way to the mountains."
Union General George Meade, commanding the Army of the Potomac, to General Dan Sickles at the Battle of Gettysburg, July 2, 1863

MR. LINCOLN, WHO'S IN YOUR CABINET?

★ ★ ★ ★

If you judge people by the company they keep, you have to judge a president by the Cabinet he chooses.

Ideally, Abraham Lincoln intended to fill his Cabinet with the best individuals to help him save the Union. Unfortunately, his Cabinet in reality ended up being a mix of people with vision and appointees rewarded for political favors.

Secretary of State
William Seward *(1861–1865)*

Born: 1801   Died: 1872

Previous Positions and Accomplishments: U.S. Senator (New York); Governor of New York

One of only two secretaries to serve through Lincoln's entire presidency, Seward was instrumental in handling the *Trent* Affair and convincing the British to withhold official recognition of the Confederacy. One of the victims attacked in the Lincoln assassination conspiracy, Seward survived and went on to negotiate the purchase of Alaska from Russia in 1867.

Secretary of the Navy
Gideon Welles *(1861–1865)*

Born: 1802   Died: 1878

Previous Positions and Accomplishments: Member of the Connecticut General Assembly

Welles also remained through all of Lincoln's administration. He was a favorite of the president, earning the nickname "Father

Neptune." Under Welles's watch, the Navy experienced massive expansion and developed the power to enforce the blockade of Southern ports.

Secretary of War

Simon Cameron *(1861–1862)*

Born: 1799   Died: 1889

Previous Positions and Accomplishments: Journalist; State Adjutant General (Pennsylvania); U.S. Senator (Pennsylvania)

Cameron, who was in the Cabinet for barely more than a year, left the War Department filled with scandal. Nominated for president in 1860, he stepped aside and shifted his support to Lincoln. His Cabinet post was a reward for his loyalty, but he was quickly accused of bribery, favoritism, and war profiteering. Lincoln made him the ambassador to Russia in 1862, and jokes followed that he'd been sent to Siberia for his dirty dealings.

Edwin M. Stanton *(1862–1865)*

Born: 1814   Died: 1869

Previous Positions and Accomplishments: Lawyer; Attorney General

In 1859, Stanton made his mark in legal circles by being the first American lawyer to use the insanity defense for a client. He was known for speaking his mind. One concerned constituent wrote a letter to Lincoln about Stanton: "His foolish aspirations for the presidency will ruin you and our country." Stanton never became president. After Lincoln's death, he oversaw the trials and executions of the Lincoln conspirators.

Secretary of the Treasury

Salmon P. Chase *(1861–1864)*

Born: 1808   Died: 1873

Previous Positions and Accomplishments: U.S. Senator (Ohio); Governor of Ohio

The first U.S. national paper currency was created and put into use during Chase's tenure in office. Although he was accused of leaking his disagreements with Lincoln to Congress and to the press, Lincoln had enough respect for Chase's talents that he appointed him Chief Justice of the Supreme Court in 1864. Chase's portrait appeared on the $10,000 bill.

William Fessenden *(1864–1865)*

Born: 1806   Died: 1869

Previous Positions and Accomplishments: U.S. Senator (Maine); U.S. Representative (Maine)

A vocal opponent of slavery before the war, Fessenden chaired the Senate Finance Committee, which led to his selection to head the Treasury. Facing an immediate need for cash to fund the war effort as he took office, he arranged short-term loans to create cash flow. Returning to the Senate after serving in the Treasury, Fessenden voted against the impeachment of Andrew Johnson.

Hugh McCulloch *(1865)*

Born: 1808   Died: 1895

Previous Positions and Accomplishments: President of the State Bank of Indiana; Comptroller of the Currency

Described as a gloomy man and economic pessimist, McCulloch served as secretary of the Treasury under three presidents: Lincoln, Andrew Johnson, and Chester A. Arthur. Appointed to the post in March 1865, he primarily addressed the economic demands of Reconstruction.

Attorney General

Edward Bates *(1861–1864)*

Born: 1793   Died: 1869

Previous Positions and Accomplishments: U.S. Representative (Missouri)

Bates was known for his constant friction with Lincoln, which included an ongoing clash over Bates's support for the idea that freed slaves should be deported to Africa. A former slave owner, Bates opposed mandatory emancipation.

James Speed *(1864–1865)*

Born: 1812   Died: 1887

Previous Positions and Accomplishments: State Senator (Kentucky)

A zealous abolitionist, Speed called slavery "the greatest national sin." He was the brother of Lincoln's longtime friend Joshua Speed. During his time as attorney general, he defended before the Supreme Court the administration's suspension of habeas corpus and use of military trials for civilians.

Postmaster General

Horatio King *(1861)*

Born: 1811   Died: 1897

Previous Positions and Accomplishments: Journalist; Assistant Postmaster General

King was a holdover from the Buchanan administration, serving a little more than two weeks under Lincoln before retiring. Prior to Lincoln's inauguration, he was the first federal official to say publicly in 1861 that a state had no right to secede from the union.

Montgomery Blair *(1861–1864)*

Born: 1813   Died: 1883

Previous Positions and Accomplishments: Attorney; Mayor of St. Louis

A successful federal attorney who had worked for Lincoln during the campaign of 1860, Blair was the primary (and at one time only) Cabinet member to support fighting to keep Fort Sumter. He was removed from the Cabinet during the 1864 election as a sacrifice to appease Radical Republicans and ensure Lincoln's reelection.

William Dennison *(1864–1865)*

Born: 1815   Died: 1882

Previous Positions and Accomplishments: Governor of Ohio

Appointed as a reward for his loyal service to the Republican party, Dennison served as postmaster general for only six months before Lincoln was assassinated at Ford's Theatre. He continued in his post under President Johnson but ultimately left over a policy disagreement.

Secretary of the Interior

Caleb Smith *(1861–1862)*

Born: 1808   Died: 1864

Previous Positions and Accomplishments: Attorney; U.S. Representative (Indiana)

Smith was another political appointee, and he wasn't terribly interested in the post. He turned many of his responsibilities over to his assistant secretary and then resigned at the end of 1862 because of ill health.

John Usher *(1863–1865)*

Born: 1816   Died: 1889

Previous Positions and Accomplishments: Attorney; State Attorney General (Indiana); Assistant Secretary of the Interior

Usher was the assistant secretary who handled much of Caleb Smith's actual workload as secretary of the interior. Once he got the secretary's job himself, there wasn't a lot of difference in his responsibilities. Usher was described as a pleasant and unobtrusive man who worked for more humanitarian treatment of Native Americans, whose welfare fell under the duties of the Department of the Interior.

Fast Facts

- *General McClellan carried a portable printing press into the field to produce notices.*

- *When his native state of Virginia seceded from the Union, Robert E. Lee declined an offer to command Union forces. Although he disliked secession and slavery, he felt duty bound to stand with Virginia. "Duty is the most sublime word in our language," he said. "Do your duty in all things. You cannot do more. You should never wish to do less."*

- *Sapper was the special name given to an engineer who specialized in digging fortifications. Sappers would dig zig-zag trenches toward the enemy fortifications, then they would dig holes under them and fill them with explosives.*

- *In April 1861, blacks in Boston demanded the right to serve in the army.*

- *The Shenandoah Valley town of Winchester, Virginia, was the site of several major Civil War battles. It changed hands 70 times over the course of the war.*

- *The four border states were Delaware, Kentucky, Maryland, and Missouri. These slave states were so named because of their geographical position on the border between Union and Confederate states and because of their large factions with divided loyalties. When West Virginia entered the Union, it did so as a slave state.*

- *At the end of the Civil War, a migration of Confederates to Brazil began with the total number of immigrants estimated in the thousands. They settled primarily in the southern Atlantic coastal region of the country, and some of their descendants live there still.*

THE "BATTLE" OF NEW ORLEANS

★ ★ ★ ★

No shots were fired nor blood shed on the soil of New Orleans in the ultimate lightning-fast takeover.

The Confederates never imagined losing New Orleans. They believed its defense was impenetrable. On the Mississippi 70 miles south of the city, two brick forts, Jackson and St. Philip, were armed with 126 large guns that would surely sink any invasion fleet. "Nothing afloat could pass the forts," one New Orleans citizen proclaimed. "Nothing that walked could get through our swamps."

That thinking hit a brick wall in April 1862. Led by Captain David G. Farragut, a Union squadron of 24 wooden vessels and 19 mortar schooners broke the heavy chain defense cables that had been stretched across the river near the forts and immediately blitzed and bombarded the forts. The shocked Confederates defended the forts valiantly, even using tugboats to push flaming fire-rafts in the direction of the Yankee ships. This created a huge fireworks display but couldn't stop the Union fleet from sweeping past.

The Element of Surprise

The attack so thoroughly shocked Confederate General Mansfield Lovell, that he evacuated his 3,000 troops from the city. Though the mayor refused to surrender and mobs of citizens took to the streets, New Orleans fell easily on April 29 when marines entered the city to raise the American flag. Not one shot was fired.

Were the Confederates overconfident? Complacent? Historians will forever debate the circumstances that surrounded the "Battle" of New Orleans. But what's incontrovertible is that the loss of geographically crucial New Orleans—the seceded states' most populous city and busiest port—proved to be a major blow to the Confederacy.

THE ODDNESS OF STONEWALL JACKSON

★ ★ ★ ★

Despite his reputation as a great warrior for the South, Stonewall Jackson was one of the Confederacy's quirkiest heroes.

Thomas J. Jackson had far more than his fair share of oddities and strange habits. From a young age, he was plagued by numerous illnesses—many of which were likely psychosomatic. He was a tremendous hypochondriac who complained of failing vision, poor hearing, stomach pains, and constant aching in his joints, muscles, and nerves. Many of these maladies may have been the result of his insatiable curiosity. In researching medicine and anatomy in an attempt to diagnose himself, he would convince himself that he suffered from the conditions he was reading about.

Once Jackson was finished diagnosing himself, he decided to set up his own treatment. After consulting numerous doctors—many of whom were outright quacks—he subjected himself to dozens of unnecessary and highly questionable treatments, such as ingesting or inhaling concoctions of silver nitrate and glycerin, convinced that they were having a positive effect on his health. Once a problem "cleared up," he wasted no time in dreaming up new and even more improbable sicknesses he might be experiencing. His constant exploration of medicines and therapies led him to many popular fads of the time, such as hydropathy. Proponents of hydropathy extolled the virtues of swimming in mineral waters or hot springs, claiming that the natural essence of the water healed all illnesses. Jackson jumped in with both feet and would often incorporate soothing baths into his daily exercise.

Exercising to a Fault

Ahead of his time in some ways, Jackson had a devotion to exercise that was considered strange by his contemporaries. He embraced calisthenics and regular exercise decades before most Americans would see them as a part of a healthy and fit lifestyle. Jackson, to the bemusement of other pedestrians and onlookers, could often be seen engaging in brisk walks. He would hold his long cane aloft, batting away tree branches or other obstacles that might get in his way. Moving quickly with an exceptionally long stride, he wasn't quite running, exactly, but his loping and hopping down various roads and paths might be considered a precursor to modern jogging.

A Man of Deep Faith

Stonewall was also a very religious man, holding fast to his beliefs with a fervor and intensity that raised eyebrows even in a time of great piety. Many viewed him as a fanatic. He believed in the literal interpretation of the Bible and held it as the true letter of the law. He usually refused to work and disrupt his rest on Sundays, in observance of the Sabbath, making an exception only during the war. Religion often clouded his wartime judgment: He promoted observant Protestants over capable—but less pious—military men and believed that he and his cause would be protected by the divine.

Ridiculed by Students

Jackson's eccentricities were a bit of a hindrance in the early part of his career. As a professor at Virginia Military Institute, he was not a beloved teacher—in fact, his students gave him the nickname "Tom Fool." At one point, an alumni campaign attempted to have him removed from his position. The issue was dismissed by his superiors in 1856, however, and he remained at VMI until the outbreak of the war.

Jackson's wartime success quickly set aside concern over his peculiarities, but they continued to be noticed. Once, several soldiers noticed him raising his arm straight up into the air and occasionally lifting his leg slightly off the ground. When they asked what signal he meant to give them with that display, he informed them that one of his arms and one of his legs were each heavier than the other arm and leg, and in order to help his blood flow properly to and from his extremities, he had to raise his limbs in this fashion.

TOO SOON TO TELL

★ ★ ★ ★

During the fall of 1864, two opposing generals fell victim to complacency and wrongly assumed their victories.

At dawn on October 19, 1864, a Confederate force of 21,000 led by General Jubal Early launched a surprise attack against Union General Phil Sheridan's Army of the Shenandoah. Early had developed what he considered a masterful plan of attack, taking advantage of a weak spot on the 32,000-strong Union army's left flank as the soldiers camped along Cedar Creek, Virginia. "Like a resistless sea driven by the tempest," a Confederate officer later recalled, "poured a steady stream of gray-jackets over the works and into the Union camp."

A month earlier, Sheridan's troops had routed Early's army outside of Winchester, Virginia. There, the Southerners fled in disorder and disarray through the city streets. A second Union victory, three days later at Fisher's Hill, had seemed to leave Early's Army of the Valley destroyed. Sheridan was no longer concerned with his opposition.

Early's Avengers

On that morning of October 19, however, the Confederates sought revenge against the army that had disgraced them. Attacking before Union troops were awake from their night's sleep, the rebels roused the startled Federals. Small bands of Union soldiers managed to fire a volley or two into the advancing enemy, but they were soon engulfed by the Confederate tide. Sheridan had spent the night away from his army, so there was no one capable of organizing the Union force. "Large numbers were captured," wrote Confederate General John Gordon. "Many hundreds were shot down as they attempted to escape.... Across the open fields they swarmed in utter disorganization, heedless of their officers' commands—heedless of all things save getting to the rear." Finally, only small pockets of Union resistance were all that separated Early from total victory. His subordinates encouraged him to complete the route, but Early refused, satisfied that the Union troops posed no further threat to him.

Whoops!

Early made the same unfortunate supposition Sheridan had suffered from back in Winchester, believing he had done all that was necessary. Although Sheridan had been away from the camp when the attack began, he was returning to his troops that morning after a meeting in Washington. Hearing the boom of cannon fire from the direction of his encampment, he galloped to the field at once. Coming across his fleeing troops, he stopped them and ordered them to form a line of battle. Encouraged by their leader, the Union soldiers rallied and struck the Confederate line, causing it to crumble. Sheridan's cavalry soon drove the enemy from the field. This time they were finished: The Confederates never posed a threat in the Shenandoah Valley again.

- *The northern-most military action involving the Confederate army is considered to be the Battle of Salineville, which occurred on July 26, 1863, near Salineville, Ohio, during Morgan's Raid. A Confederate raid further north in St. Albans, Vermont, was an unofficial action.*

- *Stephen A. Douglas became the first presidential candidate in history to undertake a nationwide speaking tour when he campaigned in the 1860 election.*

- *After Union General Philip Kearney rode into enemy lines and was killed in 1862 at the Battle of Chantilly, General Robert E. Lee returned his body to federal forces under a flag of truce. Originally buried at Trinity Churchyard in New York, his remains were exhumed and reinterred at Arlington National Cemetery, where the statue in his honor is one of only two equestrian statues there.*

A GENERAL ORDER

★ ★ ★ ★

*Can you put these commandeers of the Army
of the Potomac in the order they served?*

The Army of the Potomac was the primary Union army in the
Eastern Theater and is often (if incorrectly) considered the focus
of the Northern effort in the Civil War. President Lincoln had a
difficult time finding someone who he thought was an effective
commander, so a succession of generals was placed in charge.
Match these generals with the dates they served as that army's
commanding officer. Here are two hints: At the beginning of the
war, this fighting force was called the Army of Northeastern Virginia. One of these generals, although often associated with the
Army of the Potomac, never actually served as its commander.

General Ambrose Burnside   May 27, 1861–July 25, 1861

General Ulysses S. Grant   July 27, 1861–November 7, 1862

General Joseph Hooker   November 7, 1862–January 26, 1863

General George McClellan   January 26, 1863–June 28, 1863

General Irvin McDowell   June 28, 1863–June 28, 1865

General George Meade   Never served as commander

Answers: 1. General Irvin McDowell, May 27, 1861–July 25, 1861 (the army was still called the Army of Northeastern Virginia at this time.); 2. General George McClellan, July 27, 1861–November 9, 1862; 3. General Ambrose Burnside, November 9, 1862–January 26, 1863; 4. General Joseph Hooker, January 26, 1863–June 28, 1863; 5. General George Meade, June 28, 1863–June 28, 1865; 6. General Grant, who was General-in-Charge of all Union armies, traveled with the Army of the Potomac in 1864 and 1865 and maintained his own headquarters with it, but General Meade formally continued to hold command.

A STEP TOO FAR

★ ★ ★ ★

*The Union occupation of New Orleans turned ugly
when the city's women started their own resistance.*

When Union General Benjamin Butler and Captain David Farragut captured New Orleans in late April 1862, federal troops
occupied the city under Butler's command as military governor.
The New Orleans citizenry was not happy with this turn of events,
to say the least.

Women Let Their Feelings Be Known

Butler took a draconian approach to governing
the city. New Orleans residents despised the
federal occupation and Butler's tactics, but
the men—particularly those who had fought
against the Union—couldn't openly express
their disdain for Butler and his soldiers without
facing drastic punishment. But in the chivalrous
mood of the era, women sometimes had more flexibil-
ity. If fathers, husbands, and brothers couldn't express their feelings, wives, sisters, and daughters could.

When Union soldiers passed on the streets, the usually genteel
Southern ladies contemptuously crossed streets to shun them,
issued insulting remarks, and gathered their skirts as if walking
through mud. Some Union troops suggested that the women
wanted to lure federals into an unpleasant exchange that might rally
local men to retaliate. At one point, in response to a group of ladies
on a balcony who had turned their backs to him, General Butler
said, "Those women evidently know which end of them looks best."

The Last Straw

The situation had gone too far when one woman in the French
Quarter dumped the contents of a chamber pot onto Captain
Farragut's head. Butler took action beyond snide remarks. On

May 15, 1862, he issued General Order 28, which declared: "When any female shall by word, gesture, or movement insult or show contempt for any officer or soldier of the United States she shall be regarded and held liable to be treated as a woman of the town plying her avocation." In other words, he authorized his soldiers to treat rude women as nothing more than prostitutes.

For the most part, as one might imagine, the insults ceased. Women who continued to be aggressive were sent to Ship Island on the Gulf Coast. This included one lady who laughed loudly when a Union soldier's funeral procession passed. The response from locals and Southern newspapers, however, highlighted the fact that Butler had already been despised for his harsh rule of the city. Empowering his soldiers to treat disrespectful women as prostitutes struck at Southern womanhood and angered those beyond Louisiana's borders. He was soon dubbed "Beast Butler." Jefferson Davis branded Butler and his lot "outlaws" and promised to hang the general if he were captured. The *Daily Mississippian* offered a reward for Butler's head, and others joined the cause. "I will be good for $5,000," one reader submitted. "Let the money go to the family of the party who succeeds in the undertaking, if he should forfeit his life in so doing."

Butler's tenure in New Orleans remained controversial, and not surprisingly, his regard among the populace never improved. President Lincoln, of course, was faced with the challenge of bringing New Orleans and its residents back into the Union. Before the year was out, he had relieved Butler of his command of the city. General Order 28, however, was not rescinded.

"America has no north, no south, no east, no west. The sun rises over the hills and sets over the mountains, the compass just points up and down, and we can laugh now at the absurd notion of there being a north and a south. We are one and undivided."

Sam Watkins, 1st Tennessee

CONFEDERATE RAIDERS

★ ★ ★ ★

Following in the tradition of Revolutionary War guerrilla
tactics, several Confederates raided Union towns with
sneak attacks, resulting in some of the
worst atrocities of the Civil War.

Hit-and-run attacks on bigger armies have figured into American warfare since the colonists fought the redcoats. In fact, during the Revolution, South Carolina's Francis Marion, known as the "Swamp Fox," bedeviled the British to become one of the new republic's first heroes. It was only natural that the outgunned Confederacy drew from this tradition, sponsoring reckless warriors who considered even rebel law to be too much authority. Here are a few of them.

William Quantrill

Quantrill, an Ohio schoolteacher in a bow tie and slouch hat, saw opportunities in Kansas thievery. In 1858, he entered into the state's quickening bloodshed and joined the proslavery Bushwackers. His gang burned the crops of "free-soilers" and set fire to homes, fueling the conflict in the years prior to Fort Sumter. Those who had known Quantrill from his Ohio days would have been surprised, for at that time he had been an outspoken abolitionist. But while he was working as an Army teamster the year before he arrived in Kansas, he befriended Southern sympathizers who sold him on their cause. These new views didn't stop Quantrill from pretending to be an abolitionist if it suited his schemes, however. One of his ploys was to help slaves escape and then turn them in for the reward money.

By the time the conflict between the states became an all-out war, Quantrill's gang of desperados included the likes of "Bloody Bill" Anderson, a bearded killer who carried the scalps of the Union soldiers he killed and sent illiterate letters to *The New York Times* threatening his enemies with death. Also along for the ride were Frank and Jesse James, for whom Quantrill's raids were on-the-job training for future careers as celebrity Wild West bandits.

The most notorious act credited to Quantrill was the destruction of Lawrence, Kansas, in the predawn hours of August 21, 1863. With 450 raiders, he laid siege to the town. Deaf to pleas of mercy, Quantrill drew his six-shooters and bellowed: "Kill! Kill! Lawrence must be cleansed, and the only way to cleanse it is to kill!" While outlaws set fire to downtown Lawrence, others dragged 183 men and boys into the town center to kill them in front of wives, mothers, and daughters. It was one of the worst atrocities of the Civil War.

If Quantrill hadn't been a primary target of the Union army before Lawrence, he certainly was afterward. He was chased from Kansas, escaping first to Texas, then to Missouri. In 1865, his gang resumed its banditry in Kentucky. On May 10, 1865, Quantrill was ambushed there by Union soldiers. A short time later, he died of his wounds.

John Hunt Morgan

A Confederate raider of somewhat less infamy was the bearded, Alabama-born, Kentucky-raised John Hunt Morgan. He'd been expelled from Kentucky's Transylvania University for fighting with a fraternity brother. After fighting in the Mexican War in 1847, he returned to Kentucky to start a hemp factory, organize a militia, and get married. When the Civil War came, he joined the faction of Kentuckians fighting against the North.

Morgan fought in the 1862 Battle of Shiloh with the 2nd Kentucky Cavalry. His hit-and-run attacks on Union supply lines gained him and his raiders acclaim from Southerners as the heirs to the "Swamp Fox" tradition of guerilla attacks. But in the North, his reputation darkened with the revelation that his partisans had slain the helpless Northern General Robert McCook as he was lying wounded in an ambulance in August 1862.

Morgan, who rose to the rank of brigadier general, staged his most famous raid into Indiana and Ohio in July 1863. Violating General Bragg's direct orders, Morgan and his band of raiders crossed the Ohio River from Kentucky in a reckless effort to create havoc in the North. The entire raid covered more than 1,000 miles. Morgan didn't cause the trouble he'd intended, however, thanks in part to dogged pursuit by a Union armada of soldiers and gunboats. With escape routes blocked, nearly all of Morgan's troops were captured. Of the roughly 2,400 troops that started with him, only about 400 evaded Union forces. Taken prisoner himself, Morgan engineered a prison break from Ohio State Penitentiary a few months later. He returned to the Confederate service only to be ambushed and killed at Greeneville, Tennessee, on September 4, 1864.

John Mosby

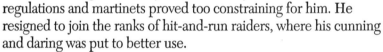

Frail, 125-pound John Mosby was another man too hot-tempered not to be tossed from school, where he shot a classmate in 1853. He studied for the bar in jail, and when freed he became a lawyer. At the coming of the war, Mosby joined the elite 1st Virginia Cavalry, whose military regulations and martinets proved too constraining for him. He resigned to join the ranks of hit-and-run raiders, where his cunning and daring was put to better use.

In the spring of 1862, Virginia authorities placed Mosby in command of a group of partisan rangers. For the next three years, the "Gray Ghost" freely roamed, raided, and controlled a region of Virginia that became known as "Mosby's Confederacy." In March 1863, he broke into Union General Edwin Stoughton's headquarters in Fairfax Court House, Virginia, and captured the sleeping general in his bed. When Lincoln heard the raiders had nabbed the general, more than 30 prisoners, and 58 horses, he expressed his dismay. "Well, I'm sorry for that. I can make new brigadier generals, but I can't make horses."

After the war, Mosby disbanded his rangers, fled the scene, and returned to practicing law. A few years later, the Dixie hero dismayed his admirers when he not only became a Republican but also managed Ulysses Grant's presidential campaign in Virginia—believing the candidate's reconstruction policies were the best for the South. He later served in the administrations of Rutherford B. Hayes, William McKinley, and Theodore Roosevelt.

ACCORDING TO ROBERT E. LEE

"I shall carry with me to the grave the most grateful recollections of your kind consideration, & your name & fame will always be dear to me. Save in the defense of my native State, I never desire again to draw my sword."
To General Winfield Scott

"I can anticipate no greater calamity for the country than a dissolution of the Union. It would be an accumulation of all the evils we complain of, and I am willing to sacrifice everything but honor for its preservation."

"With all my devotion to the Union, and the feeling of loyalty and duty of an American citizen, I have not been able to make up my mind to raise my hand against my relative, my children, my home. I have, therefore, resigned my commission in the Army."
To his sister, Anne Marshall, in 1861

"I am now considered such a monster, that I hesitate to darken with my shadow, the doors of those I love, lest I should bring upon them misfortune."
On his public image shortly after his surrender at Appomattox Court House

★ ★ ★ ★

"It is well that war is so terrible—we should grow too fond of it."

SHHH! IT'S A
SECRET SOCIETY

★ ★ ★ ★

*Though documentation proves this secret organization
to preserve the Southern cause did indeed exist, many
mysteries remain about the Knights of the Golden Circle.*

The Knights of the Golden Circle was a pro-South organization
that operated out of the Deep South, the border states, the Midwest, and even parts of the North both before and during the Civil
War. Much of its history is unknown due to its underground
nature, but it is known that this secret society, bound by pass-
words, rituals, and handshakes, intended to preserve Southern
culture and states' rights. Its precise origin, membership, and
purpose are documented in a handful of primary sources, including the club's handbook, an exposé published in 1861, and a
wartime government report that revealed the K.G.C. to be a
serious threat to the federal government and its effort to quash the
rebellion and maintain the Union.

Some historians trace the organization of the Knights of the
Golden Circle back to the 1830s, though the name did not surface
publicly until 1855. According to a report by the U.S. government
in 1864, the organization included as many as 500,000 members in
the North alone and had "castles," or local chapters, spread across
the country. Members included everyone from notable politicians
to the rank and file, all prepared to rise up against federal coercion
as they saw their rights to slavery slipping away.

What's in a Name?

The group's name referred to a geographic "Golden Circle" that
surrounded the Deep South. Its boundaries were the border states
on the north, America's western territories, Mexico, Central America, and even Cuba. Southern leaders and organization members
hoped to gain control of these lands to create a strong, agrarian

economy dependent on slavery and plantations. This would either balance the numbers of slave states to free states in the federal government or provide a distinct nation that could separate from the Union. The proslavery leader John C. Calhoun of South Carolina was the group's intellectual mentor, although the K.G.C. didn't likely achieve great numbers before his death in 1850. The 1864 government report cited that members initially used *nuohlac, Calhoun* spelled backward, as a password.

Adding Fuel to the Fire

Once the Civil War began, the K.G.C. became a concern for both state and federal governments. The most obvious public figure associated with the K.G.C. was Dr. George Bickley, an eccentric pamphleteer of questionable character. He is credited with organizing the first castle of the Knights of the Golden Circle in his hometown of Cincinnati. He also sent an open letter to the Kentucky legislature declaring that his organization had 8,000 members in the state, with representatives in every county. The legislature called for a committee to investigate the organization, which had begun to menace that state's effort to remain neutral by importing arms and ammunition for the secession cause. Federal officers arrested Bickley in New Albany, Indiana, in 1863 with a copy of the society's *Rules, Regulations, and Principles of the K.G.C.* and other regalia on his person. He was held in the Ohio state prison until late 1865. Bickley died two years later, never having been formally charged with a crime.

Methods and Tactics

The underground group used subversive tactics to thwart the Lincoln administration's effort once the war began. A telegram between a Union colonel and Secretary of War Edwin Stanton states how the "Holy Brotherhood" sought to encourage Union soldiers to desert and to paint the conflict as a war in favor of abolition. Some of the government's more questionable wartime tactics, such as the suspension of habeas corpus and the quelling of some aspects of a free press, were rallying points in the Midwest, and they were issues that surely connected northern dissidents such as Copperheads with the Knights in spirit if not in reality. When antiwar sentiment and Peace Democrats influenced populations in Indiana, a U.S. court subpoenaed witnesses for a grand jury to learn more about the organization. The grand jury claimed the secret organization had recruited 15,000 members in Indiana alone and indicted 60 people in August 1862. The Union army attempted to infiltrate the organization and expose its subversive operations by sending new recruits back home to join the K.G.C.

Political Ties

Nationally known political leaders were also allegedly tied to the group. The 1861 exposé referred to a certain "Mr. V—of Ohio" as one of the few reliable members among prominent Northern politicians. It would likely have been assumed that this referred to leading Copperhead and Ohio Representative Clement Vallandigham, who decried abolition before the war and criticized Republicans in Congress and the administration. Union officers arrested Vallandigham, and a military court exiled him to the South. Another possible member was John C. Breckenridge, vice president under James Buchanan and a presidential candidate in 1860. Even former President Franklin Pierce was accused of having an affiliation with the organization.

Assassination Conspiracy

Some also believe that the K.G.C. had a hand in the assassination of Abraham Lincoln. The contemporary exposé stated, "Some one of them is to distinguish himself for—if he can, that is—the assassination of the 'Abolition' President." According to a later anonymous account, Lincoln's assassin, John Wilkes Booth, took the oath of the society in a Baltimore castle in the fall of 1860.

The organization had several counterparts during the war, including the Knights of the Golden Square, the Union Relief Society, the Order of American Knights, and the Order of the Sons of Liberty, to name a few.

THE BATTLE OF
THE CRATER

★ ★ ★ ★

While the Union army was ultimately victorious in its
Siege of Petersburg, it suffered a number of losses as well.

General Grant was having a hard time finding success. In the early summer of 1864, his attempt to outflank General Lee's Army of Northern Virginia and reach Richmond, Virginia, in the Overland Campaign had failed. In an effort to improve the Union army's situation, Grant led the Army of the Potomac across the James River to try instead to capture Petersburg and destroy the railroads that tied Richmond to the rest of the Confederacy. Lee had set up a successful defense of Petersburg, and after a number of failed Union assaults on the Confederate line in the middle of June, both armies settled in for a long siege.

An Explosive Idea

Union Lieutenant Colonel Henry Pleasants, whose previous line of work had been as a mining engineer, requested permission to construct a tunnel under the Confederate line. His idea was to plant explosives beneath the Southern army and blow up a section of their entrenchments. The idea was taken to General Ambrose Burnside, commander of the 9th Army Corps, who passed it on to General George Meade, in charge of operations.

Construction on the tunnel began on June 25 and was completed almost a month later. The final tunnel was 511 feet long, and it ended 20 feet below a Confederate battery. Four additional days after the tunnel's completion were needed to plant the 8,000 pounds of gunpowder within the tunnel.

The plan called for the Union army to attack the Confederate line after the explosion. Burnside chose a division of black infantry to lead the assault, but Meade overrode his decision. Although he'd approved the plan, Meade had little faith in its success from the beginning. If black soldiers led a failed attack, Meade was concerned that he'd be criticized for sacrificing them callously and unnecessarily.

Lacking the Proper Follow Up

On July 30, after a first attempt in which the fuse went out, a second try was more successful. Four tons of gunpowder exploded at 4:44 A.M., creating a crater 150 to 200 feet long, 60 feet wide, and 30 feet deep, and leaving the Southerners shocked and confused. Shortly after the detonation, instead of running around the crater, Union troops attacked by charging right into it. Unfortunately, they quickly found themselves trapped in the crevasse—easy targets for the Confederates, who fired upon the helpless soldiers.

All told, the Union suffered 5,300 casualties compared to the Confederate body count of just over 1,000. Grant and Meade had had hopes of breaking the siege, capturing Petersburg, and then marching into Richmond. Instead, the Union had presided over a disaster and failed to take Lee's army. The siege of Petersburg lasted for another nine long months.

"Gen. Grant habitually wears an expression as if he had determined to drive his head through a brick wall and was about to do it."
A Union soldier

"I leaned down from the saddle, rammed the muzzle of the carbine into the stomach of my man and pulled the trigger. He tried to get his bayonet up to meet me; but he was too slow, for the carbine blew a hole as big as my arm clear through him."
Adjutant William W. Blackford, 1st Virginia Cavalry, at the First Battle of Bull Run

(Continued from p. 163)

1862

July 1
Lincoln issues a call for 300,000 volunteers to the Union cause.

July 12
Lincoln signs the bill creating the Congressional Medal of Honor.

July 16
Congress authorizes the rank of rear admiral. David Farragut is promoted to it.

August 2
Surgeon Jonathan Letterman of the Union Army of the Potomac establishes the Army's first ambulance corps.

August 9
Stonewall Jackson defeats General Nathaniel Banks at the Battle of Cedar Mountain, Virginia.

August 29–30
Miscalculations by General Pope at the Second Battle of Bull Run bring about another major defeat for the Union army.

September 4
Lee's army crosses the Potomac River to begin its invasion of Maryland.

September 13
Union troops find three cigars wrapped in a copy of General Lee's invasion plans, which are passed along to McClellan.

September 15
The Union garrison of Harpers Ferry, Virginia, surrenders to Stonewall Jackson.

September 17
In the bloodiest day of the war, Union and Confederate armies fight to a draw at the Battle of Antietam, Maryland.

September 22
Lincoln issues his preliminary Emancipation Proclamation.

September 24
Lincoln suspends the writ of habeas corpus for anyone who helps the enemy.

September 27
The first black Union regiment is mustered into service in New Orleans.

October 26
More than a month after Lee's retreat from Antietam, McClellan takes his army back into Virginia.

November 4
Democrats make gains in congressional elections, but Republicans maintain a majority in the House of Representatives.

November 7
McClellan is replaced by Ambrose Burnside as commander of the Army of the Potomac.

December 13
Burnside leads his troops in the ill-fated Battle of Fredericksburg, Virginia, where Union forces lose more than 12,000.

December 31–January 2, 1863
The Union army defeats Confederate forces at the Battle of Stones River, Tennessee.

(Continued on p. 254)

CALIFORNIA DIVIDED AGAINST ITSELF

★ ★ ★ ★

Although admitted into the Union as a free state,
California spent the next few years looking for its
identity in the heated battle over slavery.

Because most of the Civil War was concentrated in the eastern portion of the United States, it is often forgotten that at the outbreak of the conflict, California had been a state for more than a decade. It had been admitted into the Union as a free state, but California had spent much of its time as a state searching its place in the slavery debate. The fact that the state elected an abolitionist and a slave owner as its first two senators didn't help matters.

A Strange Proposition

Shortly after becoming a state in 1850, California was presented with an unusual offer. The California Assembly received a petition signed by more than 1,200 South Carolinians requesting that they be allowed to immigrate to the Golden State with their slaves. They argued that the full potential of the rich California soil could only be reached if slaves were used to till the land. The California Assembly denied the request, but many slave owners moved west anyway.

This migration of slave holders and slaves soon became an issue that could not be ignored. In 1852, the state assembly passed a controversial fugitive slave law. Although California was a free state, this law required that if slaves escaped from their masters within California, they had to be returned to their masters. In 1855, the state legislature failed to renew the law, allowing it to lapse.

California continued to wrestle with the treatment of nonwhites, passing more laws that removed the rights of free blacks and other minorities. "Black and mulatto persons are rendered incompetent as witnesses to give evidence against white persons," one law read. Another piece of legislation outlawed mixed marriages, an act that would not be repealed until 1948.

A Land Without Laws

During this period of California's history, San Francisco was considered the cultural center of the state. The state's southern portion was considered by many to be almost lawless. Law enforcement was inadequate at best in that area, and escaped criminals used the region to hide out and launch attacks on travelers and ranchers. The region also became a safe zone from prosecution where slave owners and military deserters could live their lives as they wished.

Slavery sympathizers continued to make inroads into the free state's political system, especially in southern California. The California territory had debated the idea of creating two separate states even before its admittance to the Union, although the idea had not come from the desire to create a slave state. Instead, it was a protest against unequal taxation and the lack of law enforcement and infrastructure in the southern region. But slave owners and their political cronies identified this as a perfect opportunity to turn the turmoil to their advantage.

Laws of Division

Bills were introduced almost every year during the 1850s asking for the state to be split in two around the town of San Luis Obispo. Over and over again, the proposals were defeated until a referendum finally passed during the administration of Governor John B. Weller in 1859. Although the legality of the referendum was openly questioned, the people voted to split California into two distinct units, and all that was needed to put it into effect was the approval of the U.S. Congress. Congress, however, was tied up with a small problem of its own—keeping the entire nation together. The issue of some squabbling ranchers and gold seekers was not as important as the possible secession of the South and the dissolution of the Union. Congress let the movement to divide California die as it moved on to other items on the agenda.

MR. DAVIS, WHO'S IN YOUR CABINET?

★ ★ ★ ★

In devising a new structure for his government, Jefferson Davis borrowed heavily from U.S. tradition.

The organization of the Confederacy's executive branch mirrored that of the United States, so the departments in Davis's Cabinet were the same as those in Lincoln's. The Southern Cabinet was plagued with clashes of ideals, beliefs, and egos, especially in the important secretarial positions of State and War, which had nine secretaries between them.

Secretary of State

Robert Toombs *(1861)*

Born: 1810   Died: 1885

Previous Positions and Accomplishments: U.S. Representative (Georgia); U.S. Senator (Georgia)

An aspiring Confederate presidential hopeful, Toombs begrudgingly accepted a Cabinet position after Davis was elected but stayed less than two months before stepping down to serve as a general in the army. He did not distinguish himself in that position and resigned from the army in 1863.

Robert Mercer Taliaferro Hunter *(1861–1862)*

Born: 1809   Died: 1887

Previous Positions and Accomplishments: U.S. Speaker of the House; U.S Senator (Virginia)

At age 30, Hunter had been the youngest person to hold the position of U.S. Speaker of the House up to that time. He left the position of Confederate secretary of state to move to the

Confederate Senate, where he could take a more active political role. Toward the end of the war, Hunter was part of a commission to bring about a peaceful end to the hostilities, even meeting with Lincoln to discuss reconstruction following Lee's surrender.

Judah P. Benjamin *(1862–1865)*

Born: 1811   Died: 1884

Previous Positions and Accomplishments: U.S. Senator (Louisiana); Confederate Attorney General; Confederate Secretary of War

As secretary of state, Benjamin worked to secure Britain as an ally for the floundering Confederacy but was unsuccessful. He also advocated freedom for slaves who took up arms to protect the Confederacy, a position that initially was widely opposed but eventually put into practice too late to make a difference in the war's result.

Secretary of War

Leroy Pope Walker *(1861)*

Born: 1817   Died: 1884

Previous Positions and Accomplishments: Attorney; Speaker of the House (Alabama)

Before the war, Walker served as a commissioner from Alabama to convince Tennessee to secede. As secretary of war, Walker had a reputation as a hard worker, but his lack of administrative experience ultimately undermined the war effort. He resigned after only seven months to join the army as a general.

Judah P. Benjamin *(1861–1862)*

Born: 1811   Died: 1884

Previous Positions and Accomplishments: U.S. Senator (Louisiana); Confederate Attorney General

During his tenure, Benjamin became the public face for military failures and was ultimately forced to resign. He accepted criticism for losses that were actually due to insufficient numbers of troops. President Davis rewarded him for his loyalty by making him secretary of state.

George W. Randolph *(1862)*

Born: 1818   Died: 1867

Previous Positions and Accomplishments: Attorney

Grandson of Thomas Jefferson, Randolph served in the Confederate Cabinet for less than eight months. He worked to organize the War Department but bristled at the micromanagement of Jefferson Davis, who had served as U.S. secretary of war during the Franklin Pierce administration. Randolph resigned, hoping to join the fight on the field, but his health wasn't strong enough for that.

James Seddon *(1862–1865)*

Born: 1815   Died: 1880

Previous Positions and Accomplishments: Attorney; U.S. Representative (Virginia)

Seddon served in this post longer than anyone. One of Davis's closest advisors, he was greatly concerned with the welfare of the army. At one point, he went so far as to break Confederate law by trading cotton to the enemy in order to secure food for the troops. As the war progressed, Seddon became a scapegoat for the South's continuing defeats at the hands of the North, which led to his resignation.

John C. Breckinridge *(1865)*

Born: 1821   Died: 1875

Previous Positions and Accomplishments: Vice President of the United States; U.S. Presidential Candidate; U.S. Representative (Kentucky); U.S. Senator (Kentucky); Confederate General

Under James Buchanan, 35-year-old Breckinridge served as the youngest vice president in U.S. history. He represented Kentucky in the Senate, remaining in that office as other Southern states seceded. Once Kentucky ended its neutrality and declared itself for the Union, Breckinridge resigned from the Senate and took a commission as a general in the Confederate army. He served as secretary of war for the final two months of the fighting.

Secretary of the Treasury

Christopher Memminger *(1861–1864)*

Born: 1803   Died: 1888

Previous Positions and Accomplishments: Attorney; State Representative (South Carolina)

Memminger entered college at age 12 and graduated at 16. His involvement in drafting the Confederate Constitution and his experience as chair of the South Carolina House Committee on Finance made him an ideal choice for Treasury. However, inflation and a failing Confederate economy led to a vote of no confidence by the Confederate House, and Memminger resigned in 1864.

George Trenholm *(1864–1865)*

Born: 1807   Died: 1876

Previous Positions and Accomplishments: Prominent Cotton Merchant

One of the wealthiest men in the South, Trenholm used his fortune to keep the struggling Confederacy afloat through loans and the purchasing of warships and blockade runners. After fleeing Richmond with the Confederate government but before the government dissolved completely, Trenholm resigned his position. Shipwreck hunter E. Lee Spence, in his book *Treasures of the Confederate Coast: The "Real Rhett Butler" & Other Revelations,* made the claim that Trenholm was the inspiration for the character of Rhett Butler in the book *Gone With the Wind.*

John H. Reagan *(1865)*

Born: 1818   Died: 1905

Previous Positions and Accomplishments: Confederate Postmaster General; U.S. Representative (Texas); State Judge (Texas)

When Trenholm resigned his post, Jefferson Davis appointed the Confederate Postmaster General to replace him. Reagan held the title of secretary of the Treasury for about two weeks before the Confederate government was no more.

Secretary of the Navy
Stephen Mallory *(1861–1865)*

Born: c. 1813   Died: 1873

Previous Positions and Accomplishments: U.S. Senator (Florida)

Before the war, Mallory was the chair of the Senate Committee on Naval Affairs, which made him very useful to the Confederacy. His knowledge of Union naval strengths made him an obvious choice for this post. Mallory was also an anglophile who spoke in a British accent when the mood suited him.

Postmaster General
John H. Reagan *(1861–1865)*

Born: 1818   Died: 1905

Previous Positions and Accomplishments: U.S. Representative (Texas); State Judge (Texas)

When the U.S. Postal Office stopped delivery to the seceded states, the Confederacy had to build a new postal system from almost nothing. Reagan established his new system in record time, patterning the Southern mail structure after the U.S. system. It also helped that he lured many of the heads of the U.S. Post Office to the Confederacy, bringing with them their plans and equipment.

Attorney General
Judah P. Benjamin *(1861)*

Born: 1811   Died: 1884

Previous Positions and Accomplishments: U.S. Senator (Louisiana)

Davis said that he appointed Benjamin because of a brilliant legal mind as well as "the lucidity of his intellect, his systematic habits, and capacity for labor." Because of his abilities and his loyalty to Davis, Benjamin would also serve in two more Cabinet positions.

Thomas Bragg *(1861–1862)*

Born: 1810   Died: 1872

Previous Positions and Accomplishments: U.S. Senator (North Carolina); Governor of North Carolina

Often overshadowed by the exploits of his brother, Confederate General Braxton Bragg, Thomas Bragg sought to protect the rights of civilians in the Confederacy. He resigned this post to return to his home state of North Carolina to defend Confederate policy, which was under attack from peace activists there.

Thomas Watts *(1862–1863)*

Born: 1819   Died: 1892

Previous Positions and Accomplishments: State Representative (Alabama); State Senator (Alabama)

As attorney general, Watts wrote more than 100 opinions on Confederate law and worked to establish a Confederate Supreme Court, although he was unsuccessful. He left the position to run for and win election as governor of Alabama in 1863.

George Davis *(1864–1865)*

Born: 1820   Died: 1896

Previous Positions and Accomplishments: Attorney; Confederate Senator (North Carolina)

Taking office late in the war, Davis was a strong advocate of a powerful federal government, the opposite position of many Southern states when they seceded in the first place. After the fall of the Confederacy, Davis was caught trying to flee the country from Key West.

Fast Facts

- A Confederate spy used a horological torpedo (which was essentially a time bomb) hidden in a box of candles and detonated with a clockwork mechanism to destroy a Union ammunition barge loaded at Grant's headquarters in City Point, Virginia, on August 9, 1864.

- The North had 100,000 factories to the South's 20,000.

- Battle Above the Clouds was the poetic-sounding name given to the 1863 Tennessee Battle of Lookout Mountain. It was one of the battles that helped end the Confederate siege of Union troops at Chattanooga.

- Colonel Paul Joseph Revere of the 20th Massachusetts, grandson of Revolutionary War hero Paul Revere, was mortally wounded at Gettysburg, Pennsylvania.

- Twice as many soldiers died from disease as they did from battle. Common diseases were dysentery, smallpox, measles, malaria, typhoid, and pneumonia.

- Buck and gag was a common corporal punishment of noncommissioned officers and enlisted troops in both armies. The offending soldier's hands and feet were bound. The knees were then drawn up between the arms, and a rod was inserted over the arms and under the knees. Finally, a stick was inserted in the soldier's mouth.

- At the close of the war in 1865, the national debt was $2.7 billion, an increase of 4,100 percent.

- Agreeing with Abraham Lincoln that Tennessee was crucial, Confederate General Braxton Bragg called the state "the shield of the South."

A WEEK'S WORTH OF FIGHTING

★ ★ ★ ★

General McClellan's timidness cost the Union
a quick victory in the Seven Days' Battle.

Union leaders believed that the capture of the Confederate capital of Richmond, Virginia, would lead to a quick end to the war, so they made the city an early strategic target. By the middle of June 1862, Union General George McClellan's army had marched within four miles of the prize. He had 70,000 troops under his command, with another 30,000 commanded by General Fitz John Porter nearby. Richmond seemed doomed.

But McClellan's counterpart on the Confederate side, General Robert E. Lee, knew McClellan well. They had served together during the Mexican War. He understood that McClellan was cautious, tedious, and slow to act. Lee figured that, if he was clever, he could use his 60,000-strong army, together with Stonewall Jackson's 17,000 soldiers currently in the Shenandoah Valley, to drive the Yankees away and keep the capital safe.

A Brilliant Tactician

When Lee discovered that Porter's army was separated from McClellan's main force, he decided to face it first. This was an age-old military tactic—divide and conquer. He swung his own troops toward Porter and also ordered Jackson to leave the Shenandoah Valley and attack Porter at Mechanicsville. Together Lee and Jackson battered Porter's smaller force and pushed it back in a series of battles at Gaines' Mill, Glendale, and Malvern Hill.

Going after Porter forced Lee to leave Richmond only lightly defended. If McClellan had known this and acted boldly, his army could have easily rolled into the city. But Lee recognized that McClellan was probably too timid to take such an initiative, and the city remained out of enemy hands.

The Union Backs Away

Porter's troops fought well, and the Union army was much better equipped than the Confederates. The Union technically won many of the engagements that came to be known as the Seven Days' Battle, but Lee was able to anticipate McClellan's tactical weakness. Panicked at the unexpected appearance of Jackson from the Shenandoah Valley, McClellan never took advantage of his victories but instead kept ordering retreats. Even though his forces succeeded in the individual battles, they lost ground each step of the way. Finally, McClellan's army ended up on the banks of James River, far from Richmond but under the protection of Union gunboats.

What had been expected to be a successful campaign to capture the Confederate capital—and maybe end the war—resulted in a demoralized Union army.

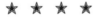

"At what point shall we expect the approach of danger? By what means shall we fortify against it? Shall we expect some transatlantic military giant, to step the Ocean, and crush us at a blow? Never! All the armies of Europe, Asia and Africa combined, with all the treasure of the earth (our own excepted) in their military chest; with a Buonaparte [*sic*] for a commander, could not by force, take a drink from the Ohio, or make a track on the Blue Ridge, in a trial of a thousand years.

"At what point then is the approach of danger to be expected? I answer, if it ever reach us, it must spring up amongst us. It cannot come from abroad. If destruction be our lot, we must ourselves be its author and finisher. As a nation of freemen, we must live through all time, or die by suicide."

Abraham Lincoln, 1838

ORATOR, AUTHOR, ABOLITIONIST—AND SLAVE

★ ★ ★ ★

One of the most influential American writers and lecturers of the 19th century was a man who was not sure what day he had been born and had to change his name to keep from being returned to slavery.

Frederick Augustus Washington Bailey, who later became internationally renowned as Frederick Douglass, was born the son of a black slave mother and an unknown white father in Maryland. Although he once thought his date of birth lay somewhere in February 1818, he was never certain of the year, and his calculations later in life led him to believe he had been born in 1816.

Escape from His Shackles

Trained as a shipwright (and having secretly learned how to read), young Frederick Bailey made a daring escape to freedom in 1838 and eventually ended up in Massachusetts. He took the name Douglass to reduce his chances of being identified as an escaped slave and returned to his master in Maryland. Soon after, he met abolitionist William Lloyd Garrison, who hired him to lecture for his Anti-Slavery Society. Like his new friend and mentor, Douglass attacked the institution of slavery in the most vehement terms: "I assert most unhesitatingly that the religion of the South is a mere covering for the most horrid crimes—a justifier of the most appalling barbarity, a sanctifier of the most hateful frauds, and a dark shelter under which the darkest, foulest, grossest, and most infernal deeds of slaveholders find the strongest protection."

Achieving Success

Douglass achieved national prominence with the 1845 publication of his first book, *Narrative of the Life of Frederick Douglass, an American Slave*. Immediately fearing arrest and reenslavement, he went to Great Britain for two years, traveling throughout England, Ireland, and Scotland. He gave human rights lectures in many locales, mostly Protestant churches, and became a very popular figure. Befriending Irish Nationalist Daniel O'Connell and feeling treated not "as a color, but as a man," these were important years for Douglass. As a testament to his influence in the British Isles, there remains to this day a colorful mural dedicated to him in Belfast. During the time he was in Britain, friends purchased his freedom from his Maryland owner, and he was able to return triumphantly to New England. Soon after, Douglass launched the abolitionist newspaper *North Star*, which in 1851 merged with the *Liberty Party Paper* and officially became *Frederick Douglass's Paper*.

Becoming a Man of Influence

As might be expected, the fiery Douglass exerted some of his greatest influence on the struggle against slavery during the war, urging abolition no longer simply on moral grounds but as a means of taking a critical strategic asset from the rebellious South. He also campaigned for the federal government to allow blacks to serve as soldiers. In both of these efforts, he was ultimately successful.

President Lincoln respected Douglass's opinions on emancipation, and the two conferred on a number of occasions. Douglass repeatedly urged the President to proclaim that the emancipation of slaves was the supreme purpose of the war, but Lincoln was frank in explaining that he couldn't do that until it would actually benefit the war effort. Looking for an opportunity, he finally found one after a Confederate advance into the North was stopped at Antietam, and Lincoln announced the Emancipation Proclamation. That new policy went into effect on New Year's Day, 1863, to tremendous celebration by Douglass and other abolitionists.

Bringing Black Troops to the Fight

As a great orator and respected member of the black community, Douglass also recruited regiments of U.S. Colored Troops. "Fly to arms," he urged, "and smite with death the power that would bury the government and your liberty in the same hopeless grave." These regiments included the famous 54th Massachusetts, in which two of his sons served, and the 55th Massachusetts. Douglass was disappointed however, with how poorly these units were treated and with the fact that they were paid less than their white counterparts, so he continued to work tirelessly on their behalf.

Public Service

After the war, Douglass did not cease his activism but in fact added the duties of a public official. Throughout the years, he served as U.S. marshal to the District of Columbia, recorder of deeds for the District of Columbia, U.S. minister to Haiti, and chargé d'affaires to Saint Domingue. He published two more books and several essays. After marrying Helen Pitts in 1884—she was a white feminist 20 years his junior, which caused quite the scandal at the time—Douglass also aligned himself with feminist causes and spent his later days traveling extensively throughout Europe. He finally retired to his home in Washington, D.C., where he died at age 77—or 79, depending on how you count it.

"In thinking of America, I sometimes find myself admiring her bright blue sky, her grand old woods, her fertile fields, her beautiful rivers, her mighty lakes, and star-crowned mountains. But my rapture is soon checked—my joy is soon turned to mourning. When I remember that all is cursed with the infernal spirit of slaveholding robbery and wrong, when I remember that with the waters of her noblest rivers the tears of my brethren are borne to the ocean, disregarded and forgotten, and that her most fertile fields drink daily of the warm blood of my outraged sisters, I am filled with unutterable loathing."
Frederick Douglass, The Life and Times of Frederick Douglass

"Verily, the work does not end with the abolition of slavery, but only begins."
Frederick Douglass

BEHIND SOUTHERN LINES

★ ★ ★ ★

Some Southerners were antislavery, while others just wanted to be left alone. There were many reasons for supporting the Union in the South, and many people went to great lengths to follow their beliefs.

When the Southern states seceded from the Union in 1860 and 1861, it wasn't exactly a unanimous decision. Plenty of citizens throughout the South opposed secession and weren't particularly inclined to don the grey fatigues of a Confederate soldier. Large groups of nonslaveholding citizens felt that they and their home-lands had been hijacked for the benefit of wealthy plantation owners looking to secure their own right to keep slaves—and to keep making money.

Nickajack

Upon Abraham Lincoln's election, Alabama's governor gathered a convention of elected delegates in an attempt to protest by leaving the Union. It quickly became apparent to the representatives of northern Alabama that the state's slaveholding southern half was trying to dominate the vote. The northern delegates wanted the decision to be made by popular vote, while the southern delegates, whose number was increased by the slaves they "represented," wanted the issue kept within the convention. Secessionists couldn't muster a two-thirds majority, but its simple majority of 61–39 was enough to pull out of the Union. Disgruntled northern Alabamans discussed seceding from Alabama itself. Along with parts of Tennessee, they intended to form an independent state called Nickajack that would exist as a neutral entity within the South.

Events soon caught up with the state, however, and after Fort Sumter was attacked and Lincoln began mustering troops to respond to the Southern provocation with force, the people of Alabama clung together, and the idea of forming Nickajack all but disappeared. Though there was no formal separation, the people of northern Alabama still refused to embrace the Confederacy, and many fled north to join the Union army.

Republic of Winston

For Christopher Sheats and his neighbors in Winston County, Alabama, however, the story did not end when the shooting started. Sheats had been the Winston County representative to the secession convention, and his stubborn refusal to go along with the state's plan to leave the Union got him thrown in jail in 1861. The people of Winston County were enraged, and more than 3,000 of them gathered at a local tavern to officially wash their hands of the whole thing. Their demand was simple: that both the Union and Confederacy leave them alone. It was there in Looney's Tavern that the idea of an independent, neutral Republic of Winston was born.

The county never did actually secede, but when the population of the "Republic of Winston" tried to maintain its sovereignty, the withering Confederate army exploited them through violence and coercion. Food, supplies, and even men were hauled away to support the Southern cause against their will. These incidents, while difficult for the people of Winston, never completely broke them, and their remote location deep in the hills of rural Alabama made it impossible for the Confederacy to exert complete control over the area. Today, this tumultuous time in the history of Winston County is memorialized with a statue of a solider, like any other you'd see all over the United States, except one half is dressed in Union blues, and the other in Confederate grey. The plaque reads, in part, "Johnny Reb and Billy Yank, disillusioned by the realities of war, shared dual destinies as pragmatic Americans in a reunited nation."

Red Strings

Other Southerners took a more subtle approach to subverting Confederate interests in their areas. Small bands of Union supporters and pacifist Quakers in the slavery-free foothills of Virginia and North Carolina developed a covert organization to undermine the Confederacy from within. Their secrecy was so total that most members did not know who their compatriots were—they could only identify each other by a display of red strings on their clothing. Their cautious and meticulous attention to covering their tracks made the Red Strings nearly invisible in the South. Confederate officials, attempting to disrupt these rebels' efforts to harbor deserters and aid escaping slaves, were flummoxed and unable to root out the subversives. The Red Strings are said to have numbered 10,000 strong.

One Red String, Byron Scott of Kentucky, was swept up into Southern State's Guard and used his proximity to vital military information to become a spy. He would gather intelligence on Confederate plans and strategies and pass it on to the Union. Within the Confederate army, Scott personally obstructed the pursuit of several Southern draft dodgers, directing the posse that had been formed to capture them away from their actual location, allowing the resisters to escape.

Much of the anti-Confederate sentiment in the South drew from a vast reservoir of poor and disaffected citizens who saw the war as a rich man's folly. The popularity of organizations such as the Red Strings proves that the lines of battle were not always clearly drawn.

"The duty of its citizens, then, appears to me too plain to admit of doubt. All should unite in honest efforts to obliterate the effects of the war and to restore the blessing of peace. They should remain, if possible, in the country; promote harmony and good feeling, qualify themselves to vote and elect to the State and general legislatures wise and patriotic men, who will devote their abilities to the interests of the country and the healing of all dissensions. I have invariably recommended this course since the cessation of hostilities, and have endeavored to practice it myself."
Robert E. Lee, letter to former Confederate governor of Virginia, John Letcher

FIREPOWER AND PROGRESS

★ ★ ★ ★

Throughout the Civil War, armies struggled
to keep up with military technology.

Providing a rapidly growing army with sufficient arms to conduct a war was the primary responsibility of the Federal Ordinance Department in the spring and summer of 1861. The regular Army's stockpile of arms was insufficient to meet the needs of thousands of volunteer troops, especially after state militias on both sides of the Mason-Dixon Line had raided government arsenals and taken whatever rifles and cannons they could find.

Colonel Henry Knox Craig was appointed head of the Ordnance Department in 1851, and he used his position to fight any attempt to modernize the arms used by the regular Army. It took the intervention of sitting U.S. Secretary of War Jefferson Davis to convince Craig to begin ordering .58 caliber rifles in place of .69 caliber smoothbore muskets. The .58 caliber rifle was a big step forward, providing much more accuracy at longer distances.

To Breech or Not to Breech

Colonel James Ripley, a 67-year-old veteran and West Point graduate, replaced Craig when war broke out in April 1861. One of Ripley's first acts was to perform an inventory of federal arsenals, in which he discovered that many had been all but emptied by state forces. Through a combination of government manufacture and private sources and overseas purchases, Ripley was able to rebuild the federal stockpile and provide much-needed rifles and artillery to the armies forming across the Union. This helped restore order to a department that had been ineffective in its preparation for war. Ripley also worked to standardize ammunition and weapons, making resupply in the field more efficient.

Like his predecessor in the office, however, Ripley was resistant to change, especially when it came to technological advances in warfare. For instance, he rejected the purchase of breech-loading carbines for the infantry, as well as of weapons that used magazines able to fire multiple rounds before reloading. More interested in saving ammunition than in saving lives, Ripley believed that it was more efficient for infantry soldiers to load single bullets one at a time down the muzzle and to take careful aim before firing. This wasted less ammunition but also lowered firepower in battle. Breech loaders, he further reasoned, were not as accurate and were more expensive. They required more maintenance and were heavier than muzzle loaders, as well.

President Lincoln was interested in testing and supporting new weapons, such as the Henry Rifle, but Ripley refused to test or purchase this gun. The Henry had a 15-round magazine that enabled the user to fire several rounds per minute. The Ordnance Department purchased only about 1,700 Henry Rifles during the war, but state governments and regimental commanders bought more than 10,000.

Had to Let Him Go

After several disagreements with Lincoln and Secretary of War Edwin Stanton, Ripley was finally replaced in September 1863. It was said that "instead of seeking out better designs, [Ripley] applied his ingenuity, which was considerable, to fighting them off." He was replaced by Brigadier General George Ramsay, who was willing to purchase new technology but later had his own feud with Stanton. He was relieved of his post in September 1864.

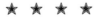

- *Georgia Governor Joe Brown directed his troops to carry pikes—wooden poles with long knives mounted at the end—instead of rifles. His rationale was that pikes "never fail to fire and never waste a single load." Of course, they are not nearly as effective at long distances as rifles, either. Brown changed his mind about the weapons when he was reminded that relatives of pike-carrying soldiers killed in battle would most likely refuse to vote for him again.*

Fast Facts

- *Captain Abner Doubleday, popularly, if incorrectly, credited with the creation of the game of baseball, is reputed to have aimed the first Union gun fired in defense of Fort Sumter after the Confederate attack on it, which began the Civil War.*

- *Cheavaux-de-frise were most common in Confederate fortifications. These barriers were defensive structures of timbers fitted with long stakes pointed outward and positioned in front of earthworks.*

- *A crew of eight used hand cranks to power the Confederate H. L. Hunley submarine.*

- *Many amputated arms and legs from the Civil War were sent to medical colleges for teaching purposes.*

- *Kady Brownell, a soldier's daughter and wife of a 6th Rhode Island Infantryman, followed her husband into battle and fought side by side with him at the First Battle of Bull Run. She tended the wounded, and when the regiment's standard bearer was hit, she picked it up and carried it into combat. She accompanied her husband on Burnside's victorious campaign in Newbern, North Carolina, and carried the regiment's colors once more. When her husband was wounded and discharged, she returned to Rhode Island with him. Little is known of the many working class women who, like Kady, went to war.*

- *The United States spent $1,103 per veteran for compensation and pension in 1860.*

- *By the time of Lincoln's inauguration, seven states had announced their secession from the Union—South Carolina, Mississippi, Florida, Alabama, Georgia, Louisiana, and Texas—in that order.*

THEY CALLED THEM COPPERHEADS

★ ★ ★ ★

*Not everyone in the North fully supported Lincoln and
the war. Out of this opposition grew a new group
called the Peace Democrats, or "Copperheads."*

As with any conflict, the Civil War saw its share of dissent, especially in the North. The most well-known of these antiwar groups
was the Peace Democrats, also called "Copperheads." The Peace
Democrats emerged mostly among urban Catholic immigrants
and civilians living in the Midwestern states of Ohio, Indiana, and
Illinois. They were neither supporters of the Confederacy nor of
secession, but they strongly opposed Lincoln and the Republicans.
They argued that the war had reached a stalemate and was achieving nothing but bloodshed. They wanted the U.S. government to
enter into negotiations with the Confederacy and find some sort of
compromise to end the conflict. This put them into obvious conflict with the President and his party.

It's not clear how they received the name "Copperheads." On one
side, the name reflected the general opinion people had of them—
that they were a slithery, poisonous lot who lurked in the shadows
waiting to strike. More positively, others thought that they may
have been named for the copper pennies—which featured a bust
of Liberty—they wore on their lapels. Whatever its origin, the
name stuck, and Copperheads wore the label with pride.

Peaceful (and Not So Peaceful) Protests

In the beginning, many Copperheads were content to oppose the
war with spoken words or by writing letters to newspapers and
public officials. Most Copperheads were public figures—elected
politicians, even—and professed their beliefs openly, giving
speeches and holding rallies. Copperhead ideas could be openly
read in many newspapers, such as the *Chicago Tribune* or New

York's *Metropolitan Record*. The editors of these papers filled their pages with scathing and intensely bitter screeds against Lincoln and incitements to Northern men to dodge the draft. Some more radical Peace Democrats even encouraged Northern soldiers to desert, mailing them civilian clothes, train tickets, and instructions on how to flee the Army. Those who engaged in nefarious and criminal plots were not so public and kept their involvement secret, of course, and only a few organized attempts at rebellion were undertaken.

Racial Undertones

Many Copperheads considered themselves religious people working toward a nation at peace, but the movement was not without its racial prejudices. While placing most of the blame for the current state of affairs squarely at the feet of President Lincoln and his administration, many Peace Democrats also faulted abolitionists, whom they said had hijacked the country and sparked the Civil War. They accused abolitionists of promoting a new way of life that would embrace free blacks, something Copperheads believed most of the nation did not want. The Copperheads had no problem using existing prejudices in the North to fan the flame of their cause.

Riotous Repercussions

Occasionally, their anger toward the government and the war brought them dangerously close to aiding and abetting the enemy. Some newspaper editors were even so bold as to demand Lincoln's murder. The President eventually suspended the writ of habeas corpus and imprisoned about 15,000 citizens for what his administration called "traitorous activities." One of the most notable of these arrests was that of former Ohio Representative Clement Vallandigham, who was jailed after he publicly denounced the President's policies.

In response to the arrests, Copperheads held a meeting in 1863 that was attended by 40,000 people sympathetic to their cause. They condemned the suspension of their civil rights and stated that advancing the war further would "subvert the Constitution and the

Government." Lincoln replied by asking, "Must I shoot a simple-minded soldier boy who deserts, while I must not touch a hair of the wily agitator who induces him to desert?"

The anger among opponents of the war continued, and in July 1863, it erupted into protests and riots across the North, the most spectacular of which took place in New York City. Rioters there against the draft yelled racial slurs, attacked and lynched free blacks, and burned the Colored Orphan Asylum as well as mixed-race brothels and saloons. The homes of several prominent Republicans were destroyed, as was a Brooks Brothers shop that made Union army uniforms.

A Movement Ended

These riots and the accompanying violence hurt the peace movement and turned public opinion against the Peace Democrats. Vallandigham escaped to Canada, where in 1864 he campaigned in absentia for the governorship of Ohio, eventually losing by more than 100,000 votes to the Republican candidate. His fellow Copperhead candidates fared no better in the fall elections, and the movement essentially died.

- *Upon returning from scouting the enemy at the Battle of Chancellorsville with some of his officers, Stonewall Jackson was accidentally fired upon by his own troops. The 18th North Carolina Infantry Regiment was responsible for the "friendly fire" incident. Jackson was struck by three .57 caliber bullets. He was taken to a field hospital near the battlefield, where his left arm was amputated. He later contracted pneumonia. Jackson was moved to a field hospital at the Chandler Home near Guiney's Station, where he lingered for eight days before dying.*

- *Stonewall Jackson's horse Little Sorrel is stuffed and on display at the VMI Museum in Lexington, Virginia.*

LINCOLN'S BATTLEFIELD VISITS

★ ★ ★ ★

Throughout the war, President Lincoln frequently visited combat sites—before, after, or sometimes even during battle.

It's well-known that Lincoln was a hands-on commander-in-chief. Sometimes he wanted a firsthand view of how the war was coming along, so he'd journey from Washington to the field of battle itself.

Lincoln visited several battlefields throughout the war. He was on site at Fredericksburg, Virginia, about six months before the start of the 1862 Fredericksburg Campaign. Just two weeks after the 1862 Battle of Antietam, he traveled to nearby Sharpsburg, Maryland, where he posed for a famous series of photographs with General George McClellan. Lincoln didn't shy away from visiting battles in progress, either, as evidenced by his 1864 tour of Fort Stevens near Washington, D.C., during a Confederate attack.

The soldiers felt that a presidential visit was a significant occasion, and given the time and opportunity, the troop commanders would often put on a show. "Those who have never seen a grand review of well-drilled troops in the field have never seen one of the finest and most inspiring sights the eyes of man can behold," wrote Harry M. Kieffer, a drummer boy whose Virginia camp received a visit from Lincoln, his wife, and their son Tad on April 9, 1863.

Most of Lincoln's battlefield visits focused on conferring with commanders and boosting troop morale. But his most famous came several months after the battle. The President went to Pennsylvania to dedicate a cemetery for more than 3,500 Northern soldiers, to honor the dead and give hope to the living. Referring to the battleground, he said, "The brave men, living and dead, who struggled here, have hallowed it, far above our poor power to add or detract." The words are remembered today as part of the Gettysburg Address.

THE THORN IN LINCOLN'S SIDE

★ ★ ★ ★

Although he was known as a "Peace Democrat," there was nothing peaceful about Clement Vallandigham's harsh, highly inflammatory words.

Ohio politician Clement Vallandigham was antiemancipation, antiwar, and anti-Lincoln, and he routinely advertised those feelings with the force of a verbal shotgun blast. In 1863, after being defeated for reelection to the House of Representatives, he decried "the violation of freedom of the mails, of the private house, of the press and of speech...which have made this country one of the worst despotisms on earth." He further claimed that the war had brought only "defeat, debt, taxation, sepulchers." The former member of Congress called for an end to the war and for the North's immediate withdrawal from the seceded states.

Jailed for Treason

This gadfly annoying the Lincoln administration went too far a few months later. At a rally in Mount Vernon, Ohio, Vallandigham criticized the war as a "wicked, cruel, and unnecessary" conflict that was being fought "for the freedom of the blacks and the enslavement of the whites." Those would be his last public words for a while, because General Ambrose Burnside, Commander of the Department of the Ohio at the time, arrested him for treason, tried him in a military court, and threw him into a Cincinnati prison for what was intended to be the duration of the war.

Burnside's action put Lincoln in an uncomfortable political position, however. National Democrats denounced the proceedings and blamed them on the President, who they claimed wanted nothing more than to jail his foes. Meanwhile, even some fellow Republicans questioned the basic idea of a military court trying a civilian for treason. Could a citizen making an antiwar speech be considered treasonous—even during wartime? Lincoln tried to rid himself of the issue by taking Vallandigham out of jail and banishing him to live in the Confederacy.

The problem with that plan was that the Confederacy had no use for a loose cannon like Vallandigham, either. Though he was sympathetic to the South, having been born into a Virginia family, Vallandigham kept telling Southerners things they didn't want to hear, such as, "Abandon the idea of independence and return to the Union."

On to Canada

With the new environs not working out, the rabble-rouser moved to Windsor, Canada, from where he ran for governor of Ohio in absentia. His main campaign theme was what he called the "failure" of the Union's war effort, but that issue soon lost its firepower after major Northern battlefield triumphs at Gettysburg, Vicksburg, and elsewhere. Vallandigham lost his electoral bid by a wide margin.

Putting on a disguise, Vallandigham reentered the United States in 1864. President Lincoln was aware of the ruse but publicly ignored him—even while he privately had him watched closely. This scrutiny didn't temper Vallandigham's politics. At the 1864 Democratic National Convention in Chicago, he wrote a presidential campaign plank that continued sniping at the war and demanded a "cessation of hostilities" at all costs. Unfortunately for Vallandigham and the Democrats, more and more people in the North rejected this defeatist view of the conflict, seeing a Union victory as imminent.

In an instance of grandiose, tragic irony after the war, the Peace Democrat fired a real shot, and it killed him. As a lawyer cleverly trying to make a point about the innocence of his client, Vallandigham held a supposedly unloaded gun to his head and pulled the trigger. A bullet remaining in the chamber ended the controversial man's life at age 50.

EXECUTED FOR WAR CRIMES

★ ★ ★ ★

*Was the commander of Andersonville Prison a butcher or just
an officer trying to do his job under terrible circumstances?*

After the Civil War, only one Confederate was executed for
war crimes. Captain Henry Wirz had been the officer in
charge of the notorious Andersonville Prison in Georgia,
where 13,000 Union prisoners died in just over a year
in 1864 and 1865. He was held responsible for this
and hanged on November 10, 1865. Unfortunately, whether or not the responsibility for
these deaths actually fell upon Wirz and whether
it was in his power to have prevented them in the first place may
never be known.

Wirz was a Swiss-born resident of Louisiana when the Civil War
started. He served as a military prison official in Alabama before
being named as the officer in charge of prisons in Richmond,
Virginia. When Andersonville Prison opened in 1864, Wirz was
assigned to be its commander. Conditions in the prison camp were
overcrowded and unsanitary, which led to the prisoners' deaths
under Wirz's watch.

What to Do with the Prisoners

Prior to 1863, very few prisoners of war were held for extended
periods by either the North or the South because of regular prisoner exchanges. The exchange system broke down in the summer
of 1863, however, because Southerners refused to consider black
Union soldiers to be bona fide prisoners of war. Later in the war,
the rebels asked to resume the exchanges because they needed the
prisoners held in the North back to shore up their front lines, but
Union leaders thought it more prudent to keep those prisoners out
of combat. Consequently, prison populations swelled. By July 1864,
Andersonville housed 36,000 prisoners on just 26 acres. Shelter was
at a minimum, and barely any food or water were available—by this

time, the South as a whole had meager resources, and the health and well-being of Union prisoners was not a top priority.

Held Responsible

When the war ended, Wirz was arrested as a war criminal and jailed at the Old Capital Prison in Washington, D.C. He argued that he cared for the prisoners as well as he could under the circumstances he was given at Andersonville, and others sided with him on that. A member of the Andersonville medical staff, Dr. W.J.W. Kerr, published a defense of Wirz after the war and quoted from a letter Wirz wrote to Confederate leaders asking for better provisions for the prisoners in his charge: "With the means at my disposal, it is utterly impossible to take proper care of the prisoners. As long as 30,000 men are confined in one inclosure [*sic*] the proper policing and cleansing are impossible.... I hope your official report will make such an impression on the authorities at Richmond that they will issue the necessary orders to enable us to get what we badly need."

However, 160 witnesses, mostly former prisoners held at Andersonville, testified against him. He was found guilty and hanged on November 10, 1865, as four companies of Union soldiers chanted, "Wirz—remember—Andersonville."

"It's all a damned mess! And our two armies ain't nothing but howling mobs!"
A captured Confederate private, on the Battle of the Wilderness

"We were in the very maelstrom of the battle. Men were falling every moment. The horrible noise was incessant and almost deafening. Except that my mind was absorbed in my duties, I do not know how I could have endured the strain."
Lieutenant Frederick L. Hitchcock, 132nd Pennsylvania, at Bloody Lane at Antietam, September 17, 1862

Fast Facts

- *In the states loyal to the Union, 777,000 men were drafted and classified as fit for military service.*

- *The USS* Onondaga, *a double-turreted iron monitor, participated in action against Confederate installations on the James River. At the end of the war, it was sold to France, where it defended the coasts until 1903.*

- *The Civil War was the last major conflict in which most regiments had their own military bands to inspire them in combat. During the Civil War, the federal government paid the expenses of volunteer regiments, but Congress determined that the cost of maintaining the bands in many of these regiments was too high. In 1862, Congress passed a law that provided for one band to every four regiments. The law only applied to bands in the volunteer service and not the regular Army. There were also field musicians and militia bands that were controlled by individual states, so there was no lack of music on either side.*

- *Grant's Tomb was completed in New York City in 1897. It stands 159 feet tall and is the largest tomb in North America.*

- *President Lincoln and his family escaped the heat of the White House from June through November and resided at the Soldier's Home about three miles away. Because of its location on the third highest area in Washington, it enjoyed cooler air.*

- *By 1864, the Henry Repeating Rifle was selling for $35, and the famous Whitworth, with telescopic sight, could sell as high as $1,250.*

- *According to* Hardee's Tactics, *a soldier should take 180 steps per minute.*

THE WORST DAY
OF THE WAR

★ ★ ★ ★

*This confrontation on Union soil became
the most ruthless battle of them all.*

On September 17, 1862, the United States experienced the bloodiest and perhaps even the most un*civil* battle of the Civil War.
Occurring around Antietam Creek in the border state of Maryland, the battle put armed combatants just yards from one
another. No one was safe: Even a Union general was shot three
times from three different directions. One Northern soldier
described the scene at Antietam as "full of the hiss of bullets and
the hurtle of grape-shot. The mental strain was so great that I
saw... the singular effect mentioned... in the life of Goethe on a
similar occasion—the whole landscape for an instant turned
slightly red."

By the end of a single day of battle, the dead and the dying littered
the landscape. The North and the South lost a combined total of
23,000 dead, wounded, or missing. That casualty figure exceeded
the number the United States and its allies would suffer on D-Day
at Normandy Beach more than 80 years later. According to one
Northern soldier, you could walk on top of dead Confederates in
the road without ever touching the ground. The Northern forces
lost even more troops.

What made Antietam so horrifically intense? While many books
have been written about the causes, large and small, one pivotal
reason stands out—the uncompromising, unyielding, singlemind-
edness each side brought to the battle.

Newly empowered after victories at Richmond and the Second
Battle of Bull Run, the Southern army—led by General Robert E.
Lee—invaded Maryland as a first step toward trying to seize Har-

risburg and Pittsburgh in Pennsylvania. Lee believed that bringing the war to the North would demoralize its population and that Southern victories there would convince European governments to recognize the Confederacy as a separate nation.

The North was also determined—but in this case desperation was one of the driving factors. After the Union had suffered a string of battlefield losses, it was essential to Northern morale to prevent the humiliation of another defeat. On the political side, President Lincoln wanted to announce the emancipation of slaves in the South, but he felt he couldn't do it without the support of a battle-field victory. So Lincoln's order to the cautious Union General George McClellan was clear: "Destroy the rebel army, if possible."

McClellan believed he had the advantage in facing down Lee. One of the Confederate general's staff had used a copy of Lee's Special Order 191 to wrap around three cigars and left it behind in a field. The lost orders, which detailed the hows and wheres of Lee's strategy to invade the North, found their way to McClellan.

Lee found out from a civilian that McClellan had gained this Confederate intelligence, so he made contingency plans. He intended to concentrate his army in a wide arc around Sharpsburg, along Antie-tam Creek, just miles from the Potomac River. The only danger was that his soldiers could end up in the river if they didn't prevail.

McClellan attacked the Confederate left flank at dawn on September 17. The battle began with almost maniacal violence. By mid-morning, fighting had shifted to the Sunken Road, a farm lane controlled by the Confederates and worn down from wagon traf-fic. Eventually, a mistaken order for retreat on the Confederate left flank opened a gap that allowed Union forces onto the road. They poured fire down the Confederate line, inevitably hitting anyone trapped in the depressed lane.

By midday, the fighting had moved to the far right as several thousand Union troops tried to take a stone bridge across Antie-tam Creek. Remarkably, only several hundred Georgians who had dug into a hillside held them at bay until one particularly determined Union regiment suddenly stormed across and forced the Confederates into retreat.

By late afternoon, it seemed Union forces were on the verge of finishing off Lee's battle-weary army. They paid scant attention to a distant cloud of dust that soon emerged as a blue-clad column moving toward their flank. Suddenly a 3,000-musket volley erupted into the Northern ranks, and the Federals discovered that the unfamiliar column was a Confederate division, many of its members wearing federal overcoats they had recently captured in anticipation of winter.

Understandably alarmed by the attack, the Union troops rushed for the safety of their rear lines, allowing Lee's army to flee back across the Potomac to escape. McClellan feared that the new Confederate reinforcements were just the first of many and held back. Despite insistent pleas from Washington—and a more than 20,000-soldier superiority in troops—McClellan chose not to follow Lee across the river into Virginia.

Even with the bloody losses on both sides, Antietam became a strategic victory for the North and one of the most pivotal battles of the Civil War. It ended the South's first invasion of the North. It kept Britain and France from aiding the Confederacy by offering diplomatic recognition. And it gave Lincoln the opportunity to announce his Emancipation Proclamation, which went into effect a few months later on January 1, 1863. Unfortunately for McClellan, it also convinced the President that his general was incapable of leading his army to victory. Lincoln relieved the overly cautious, indecisive McClellan of his tenuous command once and for all.

★ ★ ★ ★

- *Thirty-six horses were needed to pull the six guns of a standard field battery, three pairs in tandem per gun.*

CONFEDERATE CASH

★ ★ ★ ★

*Printing nearly $1.7 billion in Confederate money
during the Civil War wasn't as easy as it seemed.*

When the Confederacy declared its independence from the Union in
1861, the fledgling government knew it had to establish the institutions that all functioning and legitimate governments must have.
Within its first two months, the Confederacy introduced its first run
of currency—a big gamble, riding on whether or not its independence would be successful and whether the money would actually be
worth anything in the long run. This decision ultimately devastated
the South, flooding it with useless, valueless currency. But there were
still more problems ahead before matters got to that point.

Lack of Skill

Perhaps the first indication that the South should have held off on
printing its own currency was the fact that the currency had to be
printed in the North. The agriculturally based economy of the
South had previously had no need for skilled industrial tradespeo-
ple available to engrave and print money. In the first year of the
war, the Confederate government contracted the National Bank
Note Company of New York to produce one million dollars in
paper currency and transport it secretly across the battle lines.

When the mint in New Orleans discovered that the South lacked
sufficient metals to produce its own coinage, mint officials again
reached out, this time to a Philadelphian, Robert Lovett, Jr. The
Northern minter decided against trying to create and smuggle
thousands of pounds of enemy coins into the Confederacy, and he
quickly abandoned the project. As a result, the South was never
able to establish its own coinage. Over time, the South took control of printing its own paper currency, but its quality would never
match the Northern product. In fact, Southern currency had
several crucial shortcomings that would plague the Confederacy
throughout the war.

Please Sign Here

One of the more troubling features of Southern banknotes was the official signatures they bore. Each note had the signatures of the Confederate registrar and treasurer, which were placed there to thwart counterfeiters. Unfortunately, Confederate printers couldn't figure out how to turn the signatures into printer's dies. This meant that each official had to sign the millions of notes by hand—an impossible task. Ultimately, the job fell to hundreds of clerks who copied the signatures with varying degrees of success, making them useless as a tool for identifying counterfeit money.

The Picture Tells the Tale

Confederate currency also displayed scenes of idyllic Southern life and honored the men and women who devoted themselves to the cause. One of the more striking pieces of currency was the $100 bill, which displayed images epitomizing the secessionist South's view of itself. The main subject of the bill was Lucy Pickens, South Carolina's first lady and an ardent supporter of secession. Many saw her as the quintessential Southern belle, representing the beauty and gentility of the South. Her image was countered by another portrait, that of George Randolph, Confederate secretary of war and a grandson of Thomas Jefferson. With these two images, the $100 bill conveyed the nobility of the South, its strength and willingness to fight, and its connection to America's founders.

Worthless Wealth

Backed by the rebellious spirit that fueled the war effort, Confederate money was initially a hot property. Over time, however, the unrestrained printing of money and a lack of oversight that allowed individual states and banks to develop their own notes resulted in mass confusion and hyperinflation. During the five years of the war, nearly $1.7 billion in Confederate currency was printed, far more than the Confederate economy was really worth. Outside of the South, the only place where these bills were desired was the Union, where curious Northerners purchased them as souvenirs—$2,000 worth of Confederate money could be bought for 50 U.S. cents.

GIVING THANKS IN A TIME OF WAR

★ ★ ★ ★

We may think of Thanksgiving as celebrating pilgrims, parades, football, shopping sales, and eating until we're fit to burst. But Thanksgiving wasn't a national holiday until Lincoln made it one.

Harvest festivals have been held in North America since the 17th century to celebrate the year's bounty. After the founding of the nation, George Washington and other presidents every so often declared periods of national "thanksgiving." The holiday was more popular in some states than others—in 1858 the governors of 25 states and two territories proclaimed various days of thanksgiving.

Wartime Thanksgiving

After the war's onset, Sarah Josepha Hale, editor of the influential *Godey's Lady's Book* monthly magazine, appealed to President Lincoln to declare a national holiday of thanksgiving. Lincoln, seeing a chance to boost war morale, complied and on October 3, 1863, declared the final Thursday of November a national Thanksgiving Day.

In his speech, he reminded Americans of the country's industriousness and abundant bounties and asked Americans to praise God accordingly. "In the midst of a civil war of unequalled magnitude and severity, . . . peace has been preserved with all nations, order has been maintained," Lincoln said in his proclamation. "I do therefore invite my fellow citizens in every part of the United States . . . to set apart and observe . . . a day of Thanksgiving and Praise to our beneficent Father who dwelleth in the Heavens."

And since that proclamation, Thanksgiving has been celebrated annually in the United States. The official date of Thanksgiving has shifted somewhat over the course of time, though never by much. In 1941, Congress decided that Thanksgiving would be celebrated as it is today—on the fourth Thursday in November.

THE TUNE'S FAMILIAR

★ ★ ★ ★

Which of these songs were not popular during the Civil War? Answers are below.

"Alexander's Ragtime Band"

"Aura Lee"

"Barbara Allen"

"The Battle Cry of Freedom"

"The Battle Hymn of the Republic"

"The Bonnie Blue Flag"

"Boogie Woogie Bugle Boy"

"The Caisson Song"

"Dixie"

"The Drummer Boy of Shiloh"

"God Save the South"

"Goober Peas"

"I'll Be Home for Christmas"

"It's a Long Way to Tipperary"

"John Brown's Body"

"Just Before the Battle, Mother"

"Lorena"

"Maryland, My Maryland!"

"Oh, Susanna"

"The Stars and Stripes Forever"

"Tenting on the Old Camp-ground"

"Tramp, Tramp, Tramp"

"The Vacant Chair"

"Was My Brother in the Battle?"

"When Johnny Comes Marching Home"

"Yankee Doodle"

THE CONFEDERACY'S PRESIDENT

★ ★ ★ ★

Jefferson Davis had a dashing and distinguished career as a leader in both the United States and the Confederate States.

In the years leading up to the Civil War, Jefferson Davis had one of the best résumés in Washington, D.C., with a long and illustrious career in and out of government. But the decisions he made as war approached made him one of the most controversial figures in U.S. history. Was he a hero or a villain? That depends on the observer's point of view.

Early Life

Born in Kentucky in 1808, Davis trained at West Point and served in the Army for seven years after he graduated. He distinguished himself in the military—one early assignment was to escort the captured Native American chief Black Hawk to prison. The chief reportedly appreciated the kind treatment Davis showed him. The Army also brought Davis more than he might have expected. While in the service, he met his first wife, Sarah Knox Taylor, the daughter of his commanding officer, Zachary Taylor, a future president of the United States. He retired from active duty to wed her, but shortly after the wedding both Davises came down with malaria, and Sarah died only three months into the marriage. Davis spent most of the next decade growing cotton on his Mississippi plantation, but when he reentered public life, he seemed to have renewed energy.

A Political Career

In 1844, he won a seat in Congress, and the next year he married 18-year-old Varina Howell. Davis didn't stay in the House of Representatives long, however, resigning his seat to rejoin the Army for the Mexican War. After being wounded in 1847, he was appointed as a senator from Mississippi, and he served in that post until 1851, when he resigned to run for Mississippi governor. He lost that race, but President Franklin Pierce made the Mississippian his secretary of war, and Davis remained in that post throughout Pierce's term. Washington life agreed with Davis, and after the Pierce administration, he returned to the Senate.

Though an ardent supporter of states' rights, Davis opposed secession. On July 4, 1858, Senator Davis delivered an antisecessionist speech aboard a ship near Boston. He reiterated his support for preserving the Union again that autumn, but he was preparing for how the South might have to react if an "abolition president" were to be elected in 1860.

Leaving the Union

After South Carolina split its ties with Washington, Davis finally succumbed to pressure from his constituents and colleagues, and in January 1861 he announced Mississippi's secession, subsequently resigning from the Senate himself. The following month in Alabama, delegates from the states that had so far seceded met to write a provisional Constitution and organize a government. They named Davis provisional president of the Confederate States of America—he would be popularly elected later that year. Yet still Davis tried in vain to appoint a peace commission to travel to Washington to negotiate a way of avoiding war. That effort came to nothing when Confederates fired on Fort Sumter. Jefferson Davis and his family moved to the new Confederate capital of Richmond, Virginia, on May 29. These early days of the war with their success in battle looked as if they might lead to victory, or at least a victorious stalemate and international recognition for the South.

A Micromanager

That optimism didn't last, however. Although Davis had a strong military background, he faced a torrent of criticism for his handling of the war. Defying what he'd learned as a cadet at West Point and during his seven years of military service, Davis insisted on defending all Southern territory with nearly equal strength.

This failed strategy diluted the South's already limited resources and made it vulnerable to strategic thrusts by the Union army, which dominated the Western Theater, capturing New Orleans and, later, Atlanta. Davis twice gave Lee permission to invade the North even though the Confederate military faced heavy pressure in the West. Yet, despite his confidence in Lee, he refused to appoint him General-in-Chief of the army until almost the very last minute, on January 31, 1865.

As the war turned sour for the South, those closest to Davis saw him gradually change from a confident, poised leader to a stubborn chief executive, increasingly withdrawn when leadership and guidance were desperately needed. "He did not know the arts of the politician and would not practice them if understood," said Varina Davis.

The End Is Nigh

As the South was falling, Davis and his government escaped Richmond, but he was caught in May 1865 at Irwinville, Georgia, and subsequently jailed at Fort Monroe, Virginia, to wait for trial on charges of treason against the United States. In 1867, however, in the spirit of reconciliation, prominent citizens of Northern and Southern states, led by abolitionist and *New York Tribune* editor Horace Greeley, bailed him out of jail.

In 1869, federal prosecutors dropped the charge of treason against him. He lived the rest of his days in freedom, traveling to Canada, Cuba, and Europe, though his American citizenship, stripped when he was indicted for treason, was never restored in his lifetime. Still popular in the South, Davis was even elected to the U.S. Senate in 1875, but the new 14th Amendment of the Constitution barred him from federal office for having served in the Confederacy.

At Jefferson Davis's 1889 funeral—one of the largest ever held in the South—supporters ran a continuous march, day and night, from New Orleans, where he died, to Richmond, Virginia, where he lies buried. Davis once again became an American citizen 89 years later, when Congress restored his citizenship (on the heels of similar action to posthumously forgive Robert E. Lee) in legislation signed by President Jimmy Carter, a Southerner himself.

Fast Facts

- Confederate General Thomas Carmichael Hindman wore rose-colored kid gloves and shirts with frilled fronts. A prominent player in the secession of Arkansas, he was assassinated in Helena, Arkansas, in 1868. The motive and killer were never identified.

- Grant first rode into battle on the back of his horse Rondy. During the war he also rode Fox, Jack, Jeff Davis, and Kangaroo, but Cincinnati, presented to him in 1864, was his favorite.

- The Treasury Department's fledgling Office of Internal Revenue was charged with raising as much money as possible for the war effort and instituted stamp taxes on documents and goods sold by proprietors. Few stamps remain as artifacts today because, to prevent reuse, they were to be positioned so that they would be destroyed when a package or document was opened.

- The first four ironclad ships, part of an intended Union armada of seven, were built in 100 days by St. Louis contractor James B. Eads.

- Mathew Brady's Civil War negatives were acquired by photographic supply company E & HT Anthony as payment for his debt. These negatives, known as the Civil War Photographs Collection, were acquired by the Library of Congress in 1943.

- In April 2004, the remains of the crew of the submarine H. L. Hunley were buried with full military honors in Charleston's Magnolia Cemetery in what was called "the last Confederate funeral."

- The term redan was used for a small fortification with an open entrance, usually having two parapets.

THE NAVAL ACADEMY MOVES NORTH

★ ★ ★ ★

With unrest in the border state of Maryland, the powers that be thought it wise to move the U.S. Naval Academy out of Annapolis and away from possible Confederate influence.

The U.S. Naval Academy in Annapolis, Maryland, had only existed for 15 years when the Civil War began. Seafarers had traditionally learned all they needed to know while onboard a ship, and this is how the first U.S. naval officers trained, as well. But in 1845, the Navy introduced a formal academic training program. An obsolete army post in Annapolis, Maryland, Fort Severn, was chosen by Secretary of the Navy George Bancroft and converted into a campus. The first classes of the U.S. Naval Academy (then called the Naval School) commenced on October 10, 1845, with a student body of 50 and a staff of 7.

Unsafe Surroundings

By 1861, the nation was in turmoil. Maryland was a slave state with strong secessionist tendencies—crowds in Baltimore had even fired on U.S. troops. The danger of having the academy's entire corps of midshipmen captured or even killed was a risk no one was willing to take. On April 21, 1861, U.S. Army troops landed to secure the Naval Academy, and four days later Captain George S. Blake took the faculty and midshipmen aboard the frigate *Constitution* and sailed away. On May 13, the academy reconvened at Newport, Rhode Island, where it remained throughout the war. Meanwhile, in Annapolis, the academy campus was transformed into an army hospital.

In 1865, the Academy returned to Annapolis, but a vestige remained in Newport, where the U.S. Naval War College opened in 1884.

THE DIARIES OF MARY CHESNUT

★ ★ ★ ★

*A privileged Southern woman offered her views on war and
slavery (and touched on women's rights while she was at it).*

The daughter of a U.S. senator and governor of South Carolina, and
the wife of another senator from South Carolina, Mary Boykin Miller
Chesnut lived a life of privilege and wealth. Educated and well-read,
she left behind her war diary, one of the most fascinating primary
sources from the time. When her husband, James Chesnut, resigned
from the Senate to join the Confederate cause, Mary took pen to
paper and documented her experiences in a series of diaries that are
still read and honored more than a century after her death.

Scribbling Mania

"The scribbling mania is strong upon me," she wrote. That mania led
to her writing several volumes of diaries that would shed light on the
Southern home front during the war. Chesnut tried to aid the war
effort by volunteering in hospitals like other women in the community, but she fainted and "deemed it wise to do my hospital work
from the outside." But in writing about her brief time at the hospitals, she allows modern readers a glimpse into the lives of Southern
women. "I cannot bear young girls to go to hospitals," she wrote,
explaining how women were subjected to the leers and inappropriate
comments of the soldiers, a situation that disgusted her.

In fact, Chesnut devoted much of her writing to the behavior and
customs of Southern women. She was open about her feelings in
her diaries, often penning scathing entries on women in her social
circles and giving them nasty nicknames such as "Lucy Long-
tongue." The diarist was also appalled by the behavior of war
widows who openly flirted. "As soon as she began whining about
her dead beaux I knew she was after another one. She wouldn't
lose any time."

No Subject Spared

Chesnut didn't reserve her poison pen just for her Southern comrades. When fleeing from invading Union troops, she turned her weapon toward a Northern woman who offered hospitality: "She does not brush her teeth—the first evidence of civilization and lives amidst dirt in a way that would shame the poorest overseer's wife."

Though Chesnut had stated with Southern pride that she was never afraid of her slaves, her position changed after her cousin was smothered to death by her own servants. Although Chesnut wrote about slavery and her opposition to it, it is not in the way modern readers might expect. Raised with slavery as a common part of her life, her issue with the institution was not its human indignity but rather the practice of Southern men using their female slaves as sex objects, which she believed cheapened the men by giving them easy access to sex. Unfortunately, Chesnut neglected to record any thoughts she may have had about how this affected the slave women.

Early Women's Lib

It could be said that Mary Chesnut struck some early blows for women's rights with her writing, especially when she addressed the social standing of women who took a more nontraditional route with their lives. "South Carolina as a rule does not think it necessary for women to have any existence outside of their pantries or nurseries," Chesnut, who couldn't have children, wrote. "If they have not children, let them nurse the walls."

After the war, Mary and James Chesnut returned to their plantation, which they discovered had been ransacked by Northern forces. In order to survive, Chesnut sold eggs and butter, but she never forgot her writing. As her husband resurrected his law practice, she sold some stories to local newspapers for nominal sums and wrote three novels. She also turned her eye to her diaries, editing them after the fact into a coherent story line. They were first published in 1905, almost 20 years after her death. The diaries would continue to be reedited until 1981, when what is now considered the definitive version was released as *Mary Chesnut's Civil War* and awarded the Pulitzer Prize.

(Continued from p. 210)

1863

January 1
Lincoln's Emancipation Proclamation goes into effect.

January 20
General Burnside sends his army upriver from Fredericksburg in search of a place to cross the Rappahannock. Heavy rainfall ensures this action will soon be known as the "Mud March."

January 23
General Burnside orders the exhausted Army of the Potomac out of the mud, and it returns to its original position.

January 25
General Joseph Hooker replaces Burnside as commander of the Army of the Potomac.

February 24
Congress establishes the Arizona Territory, separating it from the New Mexico Territory.

March 2
Edward Stanly resigns as military governor of North Carolina in protest of the Emancipation Proclamation.

March 3
Lincoln signs the Enrollment Act, calling for the conscription of men between 20 and 45.

March 9
John S. Mosby's Confederate irregulars capture Union General Edwin H. Stoughton in his bed at Fairfax Court House, Virginia.

March 25
Secretary of War Edwin Stanton awards the first Medals of Honor to the six members of Andrews's Raiders who were not killed or captured by the enemy.

April 2
A bread riot breaks out in Richmond, Virginia.

April 4
President Lincoln, with a group that includes his wife, Mary, and his son Tad, leaves Washington to meet with General Hooker and his army at Falmouth, Virginia, near Fredericksburg.

April 16
Admiral Porter's ships successfully steam south past the Confederate batteries at Vicksburg, Mississippi.

April 19
Lincoln again visits the Army of the Potomac in Virginia, this time with Secretary of War Stanton and General-in-Chief Halleck.

April 21
Colonel Abel D. Streight, his Union cavalry riding mules, launches a raid into Alabama and Georgia.

April 28
Hooker's Army of the Potomac crosses the Rappahannock River in an attempt to circle behind Lee's Army of Northern Virginia.

April 30
Grant's troops begin crossing the Mississippi River south of Grand Gulf, Mississippi.

(Continued on p. 284)

THE FIRST UNION "MARTYR"

★ ★ ★ ★

*The Union lost a popular figure, and Abraham Lincoln
lost a friend in the first high-profile death of the war.*

Elmer Ephraim Ellsworth took an unlikely path to
gaining popular recognition shortly before the Civil
War. As head of the Chicago-based U.S. Zouave
Cadets, he toured the country performing precise
close-order military drills. Zouaves were French
soldiers in North Africa who wore colorful
uniforms consisting of baggy pants, vests, and
billed caps, fezzes, or turbans.

At the time, this drill team was as close to the military as Ellsworth
could reasonably expect to get. He'd always wanted to go to West
Point, but he didn't have the education or the political connections
necessary to gain admittance. Instead of a military career, he
settled on studying law. After a tour with the Zouave cadets in
1860, he took a job as a clerk in the law office of Abraham Lincoln.
Lincoln was fond of Ellsworth, and the young man took part in
Lincoln's presidential campaign. When Lincoln moved to Washington, Ellsworth went with him.

Ready to Fight

As the war broke out in 1861, Ellsworth saw his chance to make
something of himself in the military and traveled to New York City
to recruit troops from the New York Fire Department. These
became the 11th New York Volunteers, but they were also known
as the Fire Zouaves, and Ellsworth quickly returned with them to
Washington. In May 1861, the 11th New York received orders to
cross the Potomac to enter Alexandria, Virginia. Ellsworth wrote a
letter to his parents, saying: "It may be my lot to be injured in
some manner. Whatever may happen, cherish the consolation that
I was engaged in the performance of a sacred duty."

A Colonel Down

Colonel Ellsworth marched the 11th into town. In the seemingly peaceful setting, he took a small squad of Zouaves into a hotel, the Marshall House, from which a large Confederate flag was flying. It was said that the flag could be seen across the river in Washington, and it may even have been visible by Lincoln himself from the White House. Ellsworth went with some troops to the roof and removed the flag. He was bringing it down the stairs when the hotel proprietor, James Jackson, appeared, carrying a shotgun. As Ellsworth descended the stairs with his arms filled by the large flag, Jackson aimed at him. One of Ellsworth's escorts, a private named Francis Brownell, tried to deflect the gun, but Jackson fired, fatally wounding Ellsworth. Brownell retaliated by shooting Jackson, killing him instantly.

Ellsworth and Jackson were each proclaimed to be martyrs by their respective sides. Lincoln was particularly weighed down by the news and had Ellsworth lie in state in the East Room of the White House. The Commander in Chief wept and wrote a letter to Ellsworth's parents: "In the untimely loss of your noble son, our affliction here, is scarcely less than your own. So much of promised usefulness to one's country, and of bright hopes for one's self and friends, have rarely been so suddenly dashed, as in his fall."

- *Of the 75,000 residents of the District of Columbia in 1860, 14,000 were black, and 3,000 were slaves.*

- *Dred Scott was the slave who sued to gain his freedom before the Supreme Court. The case started in 1846 and was decided against him in the Supreme Court in 1857. After the Court decided against Scott, his former master's son purchased Scott and his wife and set them free.*

- *Confederate General Wade Hampton of South Carolina owned more than 3,000 slaves on his huge Southern plantation.*

THE BATTLE OF THE BANDS

★ ★ ★ ★

*A melancholy "Home Sweet Home" sustained both Northern
and Southern armies before the Battle of Stones River.*

A bitter war doesn't usually inspire its combatants to break into
song, but that's exactly what happened on the haunting night of
December 30, 1862. With Union and Confederate forces bedding
down yards from each other in Tennessee, military bands on each
side began battling in song. The North played "Yankee Doodle"
and "Hail Columbia," and the South responded with "Dixie" and
"The Bonnie Blue Flag." In a bittersweet moment, both sides
drifted into "Home Sweet Home," and they were joined by tens of
thousands of soldiers singing along. For one brief period in the
lonely holiday season, soldiers whose only goals were to kill each
other and survive shared a song of empathy and comfort. But the
chorus would die before dawn.

The Respite Over, the Fighting Begins

The next morning, the music was replaced by gunshots, screams,
and groans as the Battle of Stones River began. One of the most
brutal battles of the Civil War, it resulted in 24,000 casualties,
almost one third of the battle's total forces.

Both sides were desperate for a win, particularly the Union, whose
General William Rosecrans was ordered by the President to drive
Confederate General Braxton Bragg out of Tennessee. The South
struck first, pushing Union forces back three miles. Neither army
attacked on January 1, but Bragg took the offensive again the next
day. Northern artillery fought back, and a bloodied Rosecrans
refused to yield. His forces thoroughly demolished advancing gray
columns, and Bragg eventually had to retreat 25 miles south.

This news temporarily allowed Lincoln to silence war critics. He
told Rosecrans, "You gave us a hard-earned victory, which, had there
been a defeat instead, the nation could hardly have lived over."

THE BOUNTY JUMPERS

★ ★ ★ ★

When the North and South started offering bounties to encourage civilians to enlist, a new breed of con artist arose to get while the gettin' was good.

While patriotism can be a very persuasive tool in the recruitment of soldiers, the governments involved in the Civil War quickly discovered that they needed something a bit more tangible to convince new recruits to don uniforms and fight for their respective causes. To sweeten the pot, both the North and South offered a bounty to soldiers who signed up. In fact, the North increased cash bonuses as the need for fresh fighters grew. What began as less than $100 soon became quite lucrative for the average person. In 1864, a soldier wrote home: "I receive for re-enlisting nearly eight hundred dollars which I shall devote to straightening things at home."

A New Kind of Scam

Considering the average pay for Northern infantry privates was $13 a month, such a large bounty was very enticing. But these bonuses also attracted a new group of con artists, called bounty jumpers, who would register for the armed forces, pocket their bounties, and then never appear for duty. They'd often use false names and addresses so they could move on to another community or state and repeat the offense. One bounty jumper enlisted 32 different times before he was caught and sentenced to four years in prison.

Bidding Wars

The amounts of money in play rose as the army had a more and more difficult time recruiting new soldiers. While the draft was in place, communities were required to send a certain number of recruits to war. If a community didn't want to send their own residents, they could simply find other people to send to the army in their place. Districts would collect cash (which would be in addition to any bounties the army itself was offering) and engage in bidding wars, while soldiers and bounty jumpers moved from area to area in search of the best offer. When President Lincoln called for 500,000 more recruits in 1864, bounties skyrocketed. It was not uncommon during these recruitment drives to see offers as high as $1,000.

On to the Con

Eventually the method of paying bounties changed in order to fight the jumpers. Instead of a huge lump sum, the bonuses were paid in installments during service or came in the form of a deposit upon enlisting, with the remainder paid when and if the soldier survived the war. Even with this change in payment, it is estimated that the North spent between $500 million and $700 million on bounties alone.

- *Hardtack was usually very hard and difficult to chew for many because of their bad teeth. It was often infested with insects such as maggots and boll weevils. Soldiers made a dish they called* skillygalee *or* cush, *by mixing hardtack crumbs with water and frying it with animal fats.*

- *James A. Garfield entered the army as a colonel in 1861 and was promoted to major general after the Battle of Chicka-mauga. He eventually made it all the way up to Commander in Chief when he was elected president in 1881, but his tenure was cut short when he was assassinated four months after taking office.*

- *According to the prison exchange agreement of July 1862, 60 privates could be exchanged for 1 general. Grant ended prisoner exchanges in 1863 because Southerners were violating the agreement by returning to duty.*

SO THEY SAID

★ ★ ★ ★

"Little did I conceive the greatness of the defeat, the magnitude of the disasters which it had entailed upon the United States or the interval that would elapse before another army set out from the banks of the Potomac onward to Richmond."
William Howard Russell on the First Battle of Bull Run

"Lee's army will be your objective point. Wherever Lee goes, there you will go also."
General Ulysses S. Grant to General George Meade, commander of the Army of the Potomac

"Our march yesterday was terribly severe. The sun was like a furnace, and the dust thick and suffocating. Many a poor fellow marched his last day yesterday. Several men fell dead on the road. Our boys have all come through so far, accepting the hardships as a matter of course, and remaining cheerful and obedient I assure you I feel proud of them."
Union Colonel Rufus R. Dawes

"With malice toward none, with charity for all, with firmness in the right as God gives us to see the right, let us strive on to finish the work we are in, to bind up the nation's wounds, to care for him who shall have borne the battle and for his widow and his orphan, to do all which may achieve and cherish a just and lasting peace among ourselves and with all nations."
Abraham Lincoln, Second Inaugural Address, 1865

PROUD CHEROKEE SOLDIERS OF THE CONFEDERACY

★ ★ ★ ★

The white chief of a Cherokee tribe in North Carolina led a band
of Native American soldiers in support of the Southern cause.

While Union forces enlisted foreign immigrants to their ranks in
numbers far greater than the Confederacy, the Southern cause was
taken up by an unlikely band of soldiers from a nation within the
United States: the Cherokee. Some of these Native American fighters followed the command of William Holland Thomas, the only
white man ever to be named chief of a Cherokee tribe. Though they
played a minor role in the Confederate army, the Cherokee soldiers
were a strong and loyal force who served with honor.

An Unlikely Chief

While clerking at a North Carolina trading post as a teenager,
Thomas met the Cherokee chief Yonaguska, who helped him learn
the native language. This developed into an unusually close relationship with the Cherokee. When the trading post was forced to
close in 1820, Thomas studied law and began to represent his
Cherokee friends as legal counsel. Thomas was fascinated with
and drawn to the Cherokee, and Yonaguska welcomed his curiosity and interest to the point of adopting him as his own son. In
response, Thomas became a tireless advocate for the Cherokee
cause, regularly dealing with government officials to secure their
assets and standing as well as raising money to purchase vast tracts
of land on which the Cherokee could live without fear. His work
was so appreciated that before Yonaguska died in 1839, he named
Thomas his successor as chief. Though such a thing had been
unheard of, Thomas had gained the trust of the Cherokee, and
they were pleased to accept his ascent to the position.

An Unlikely Band of Soldiers

With the coming of the Civil War, Thomas and a band of Cherokee warriors offered their service to the Confederacy. Thomas
would eventually command a force of 2,000, which included 400
Cherokee. The decision by the Native Americans to join the Confederacy may seem odd at first glance: They'd been battling North
Carolinians for decades, and there was certainly no love lost
between the two. But the Cherokee decision came about because
of their devotion to one man, Thomas, and their hatred of another,
Union General-in-Chief Winfield Scott.

It was under Scott that many Cherokee marched on "The Trail of
Tears," which forced them to leave their homelands in the southeastern United States for Oklahoma and resulted in roughly 4,000 deaths
along the way. Although these North Carolina Cherokee had long
been separated from their cousins, they still hated Scott for treating
their nation so terribly. Cherokee anger often led them to take brash
actions during Civil War battles, sometimes even scalping Union
soldiers—a practice Confederate officers quickly forbade. For most
of the war, Thomas and his legion chased marauders, outlaws, spies,
and Confederate deserters in North Carolina and Tennessee.

A Last-Ditch Effort

When the war was virtually over, Thomas and his Cherokee soldiers
attempted a risky plan they hoped would turn things around. In May
1865, after Lee had already surrendered, Thomas tried to bluff a
larger Union force on his home turf of Waynesville, North Carolina,
building large decoy campfires to give the illusion of a larger force
and inciting his Cherokee troops to fill the night air with hideously
chilling war whoops and screams. He then chose to confront the
Union officers with an entourage of 20 soldiers to ask for their surrender. Unfortunately for Thomas, the Union troops weren't intimi-
dated, and they made it clear to Thomas that his efforts were
foolhardy at best. The conventional wisdom was that fighting was
over, and the war-weary officers weren't looking to risk their lives for
no apparent purpose. Thomas finally agreed to surrender as the
reality of the situation sank in. The Thomas Legion was no longer.

NO HOOPSKIRTS, PLEASE

★ ★ ★ ★

*An unusual woman with a passion for health care
emerged as both a "dragon" and an "angel."*

Anyone who thinks that women's lives during
the Civil War revolved around nothing more
than tea and crinolines—or thinks that life
ends at 50—should discover Dorothea Dix.
A tireless crusader for humane treatment of
the mentally ill before the war, at age 59 in
1861 she'd written five books, founded 32 mental hospitals, and visited Western Europe, Russia, and
Turkey. At war's outbreak, she obtained the post of superintendent
of women nurses for the Union army—up until then, men had
primarily served as army nurses. Dix's many responsibilities
included nurse recruitment, organizing first aid stations, purchasing supplies, and helping establish training facilities and field
hospitals. She performed this work without pay for the duration of
the war.

Female nurses were a brand new concept, and U.S. military officials
remained skeptical about the ability of women to serve effectively.
As a result, Dix—a rather severe woman herself—established rules
for hiring and conduct that are quite amusing by modern standards. To dissuade the "wrong" kinds of ladies from rushing to her
cause, she announced she would hire only plain-looking women
over the age of 30. The imposed dress code allowed only black or
brown dresses, no bows, no jewelry, no curls...and certainly no
hoopskirts! This code helped to exclude young women Dix saw as
flighty or marriage minded from the ranks. Though she may have
gone a bit overboard, she did recruit more than 3,000 women,
including Louisa May Alcott.

Dorothea Dix was greatly admired for her work, and she succeeded in giving her multitude of nurses a high reputation. The

train she was riding was once stopped by Confederate troops but was allowed to proceed when a Southern officer recognized Dix and remembered her work with the mentally ill. On the flip side of the coin, however, she became equally known in some circles for her prickliness. Daughter of a fire-and-brimstone preacher, Dix often quarreled with hospital bureaucracy and took male doctors to task for habits such as guzzling liquor on the job and dribbling tobacco juice on the patients. After losing arguments with military administration, she'd often ignore their deeply embedded protocols. Although soldiers called her an "angel of mercy," her detractors called her "Dragon Dix."

Inexplicably—and indeed, sadly—Dorothea Dix considered this Civil War chapter in her career to be a failure. She did not force the acceptance of—and establish lasting rules for—female nurses as she'd intended. Still, she tirelessly worked for human health causes and soldiers' rights well beyond the war's end, helping families track down missing soldiers and assisting wounded veterans in getting their pensions—as well as continuing her crusade for the mentally ill—for another 20 years. Her own words sum up her life: "In a world where there is so much to be done, I felt strongly impressed that there must be something for me to do."

- *Annie Etheridge was a vivandiere and battlefield nurse who was awarded the Kearney Cross for her service to the Union troops.*

- *Civilian Sally Tompkins ran one of the South's most successful hospitals and was the only woman given a commission in the Confederate army.*

- *Called "white gold," cotton was considered by Confederate leaders to be its best weapon for use as a diplomatic bargaining tool with European governments. Cotton supplies from Egypt, India, and Brazil, however, soon replaced cotton from the South in foreign markets.*

Fast Facts

- *New York, the North's largest city in 1860, had a population exceeding 800,000.*

- *In the election of 1860, Lincoln, who had pledged to preserve the Union whatever the cost, received only 40 percent of the popular vote but the majority of the electoral votes. He was not even on the ballot in nine Southern states.*

- *At the First Battle of Bull Run in July 1861, a reported 76 newspaper correspondents (26 from the South, 50 from the North) were present.*

- *In 1856, Albert Sidney Johnston led U.S. forces against the Mormons in the Utah war when the administration of President James Buchanan deemed them in rebellion against the United States. Ironically, Johnston died at Shiloh on April 6, 1862—the 32nd anniversary of the founding of the Mormon church—commanding his own force in rebellion against the United States.*

- *General Daniel Sickles had a miniature coffin made for his amputated leg and donated it to the Army Medical Museum. For years afterward, he delighted in taking friends there to "visit" his leg. It now resides in the National Museum of Health and Medicine.*

- *As president of the United States, Abraham Lincoln's annual salary was $25,000.*

- *Hiram Berdan, a wealthy New York inventor and top rifle shot, proposed recruiting the country's best shots and arming them with the most reliable rifles. The troops, known as Berdan's Sharpshooters, would serve as snipers, scouts, and skirmishers.*

CIVIL WAR–ISMS

★ ★ ★ ★

As in any war, people who spend an excessive amount of time together—training, marching, attacking—are bound to develop their own nicknames and slang. The common words and phrases listed below weren't typically used in letters home but were used regularly among the soldiers themselves.

- Arkansas toothpick: a knife

- Barrel shirt: a barrel worn by thieves for punishment

- Blizzard: a volley of musket fire

- Bowlegs: a cavalry soldier

- Boys of the sod: an affectionate name for the Irish

- Bragg's bodyguard: lice

- Bull pit: a confinement area for those under arrest

- Bumblebee: the sound of flying minie balls

- Bummers: soldiers sent out to forage for food or other supplies from the land

- Butternut: the yellow-brown uniforms of Confederates, or a rebel soldier

- Cashier: to dishonorably dismiss from the military

- Chicken guts: the gold braid on an officer's uniform

- Copperhead: a Northerner with Southern sympathies

- Cracker line: the line for transportation of food supplies

- Croaker: a pessimist
- Deadbeat: a person exempt from fighting
- Desecrated vegetables: dehydrated vegetables shaped into yellowish squares
- Dog robber: the soldier designated as cook
- Doughboy: an infantry soldier
- Embalmed beef: official-issue canned beef
- Forty dead men: a full cartridge box, which usually consisted of forty cartridges
- French leave: absent without leave
- Fresh fish: raw recruits
- Grab a root: to eat a potato
- Grape shot: artillery ammunition using nine iron balls encased between two iron plates
- Graybacks: lice, or a derogatory term for a Confederate soldier or Confederate dollar
- Greenbacks: money
- Hayfoot/strawfoot: commands used to teach raw recruits the difference between left and right
- Hornets: bullets
- Hospital rat: someone who fakes illness
- Housewife: a small sewing kit for soldiers
- Iron rations: a combination of hardtack, a chunk of salt pork, and coffee
- Jonah: one who continually has bad luck
- Lucifers: matches

- Mugger: a prisoner who preys on other prisoners
- Muggins: a scoundrel
- Mule: meat of dubious quality
- Paleface: a new recruit
- Paper collar soldier: a person from the Northeast
- Pepperbox: a multishot pistol
- Pig sticker: bayonet
- Play old soldier: to fake illness
- Powder monkey: the person who carries shells and gunpowder from the magazine to the gun
- Pumpkin rinds: a lieutenant's gold bars
- Quaker gun: a tree trunk made to look like a cannon
- Quick step, flux: diarrhea
- Salt horse: salted or pickled meat
- Seeing the elephant: to experience combat
- Sheet iron crackers: hardtack
- Sherman's neckties: bent railroad rails after being heated in fire then wrapped around trees to make them useless
- Sherman's sentinels: chimneys left standing in the army's wake after the house was burned down
- Sunday soldiers, parlor soldiers: insults for soldiers who were of little merit
- Sutlers: vendors who followed the armies and sold goods to them that were not provided by the government
- Tumbled over: to be killed in action
- Web feet: a cavalry term for the infantry

WHAT TO DO WITH THE PRISONERS?

★ ★ ★ ★

Prisoners of war were sometimes more trouble than they were worth. Many weren't even kept imprisoned until near the end of the conflict.

Early in the war, the North and the South readily exchanged prisoners through a formal system that gave a value to each captured soldier. A private would be traded for a private, two privates traded for one noncomissioned officer, four privates for one lieutenant, and so forth, all the way up to sixty privates traded for one general.

Developing Problems

This exchange program was strained from the beginning. The North argued that such an agreement could be seen as recognition of the Confederacy's sovereignty, and the South looked on it as an opportunity to force exactly that by holding prisoners as collateral. However, the lack of prison space in the early days of the war proved to be more important than either of these issues, and both sides accepted the situation as best they could.

Racial Issues

By December 1862, the Union had released 247,000 soldiers, and the South had traded 16,000. Because most of the fighting took place on Southern soil, Union forces found it less trouble to trade or release captured enemy soldiers than to ship them North to prison. But the Confederacy refused to exchange captured black soldiers, telling the North that any such prisoners would instead be sold into slavery. This caused the system to collapse. The Union refused to continue the exchanges and retaliated further when Lincoln declared that for every black soldier sold into slavery, a Confederate soldier would be forced into hard labor. He also announced that for every execution of a Union soldier, one imprisoned Southern soldier would be killed.

Holding Hostages

In order for the South to save their own soldiers but continue using the prisoners they held as bargaining tools, the Confederates began to use captive black soldiers as hostages. They would be placed, for instance, in construction crews in dangerous areas on the front line. Eventually the North followed suit, forcing Southern POWs into similar perilous situations.

As the war raged on, the use of hostages became more grim. Henry White, a captured Union chaplain, recalled in a letter that 50 of his fellow prisoners, all officers, had been gathered up in what they thought was to be a release. They later discovered that the prisoners were to be placed in Charleston, South Carolina, a major battlefront. "The object was to compel our men not to shell the city," he wrote. The plan fell apart when the Union decided to attack as they normally would anyway, and the prisoners in question were eventually exchanged.

In all, the use of hostages literally played out the adage of "an eye for an eye." One side would often have the captured ranks pick a number of "volunteers" to be placed in dangerous areas or even executed as retaliation for a previous offense by the enemy. This act would more often than not then be mirrored by the other side in an attempt to keep a type of wartime balance.

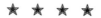

"The valley was filled with an impenetrable smoke and nothing could be seen but the fire belching from the guns. Loud above all was the exultant, fiendlike yell of the Confederate soldiers."

Private Thomas Southwick, 5th New York, at Gaines's Mill, June 27, 1862

THE SIEGE AGAINST VICKSBURG

★ ★ ★ ★

The civilians of this city on the Mississippi, caught between two armies, dug into the hills to survive.

Before the war, Vicksburg was a major trading center on the Mississippi River, which had been a sort of superhighway of goods traveling north and south. Union generals realized that control of Vicksburg would give them control of the Mississippi, and that would allow them to transport their troops deep into the South with ease. Controlling Vicksburg would also split the Confederacy in two, cutting Arkansas and Texas off from the rest of the Southern states.

Vicksburg was securely in Confederate hands in early 1863. Southern guns in the fort on the bluffs above the river could lob shells at any oncoming Union ships. The Yazoo River, a snag-filled tributary of the Mississippi that ended in impenetrable swamps, guarded the northern edge of the city. To the east of the city was solid Confederate territory. With the Mississippi River on the west, the only undefended path into the city was from the south. But surely Northerners wouldn't attack from the south.

Plan of Attack

General Ulysses S. Grant decided that the southern route would be ideal. Across the river, he marched his army south to the town of Hard Times, Louisiana, about 30 miles below Vicksburg. There, Admiral David Porter, whose Union gunboats had snuck past the Confederate guns, shuttled Grant's troops east across the Mississippi.

The surprise from the south worked. Grant marched his troops north toward Vicksburg, defeating a few scattered Confederate units along the way. Confederate General John C. Pemberton, in charge of the defense of Vicksburg, recognized the threat and tried to slow the flow of bluecoats. He made a stand on May 16 at Champion's Hill and the next day at Big Black River, but his outnumbered soldiers were no match for the Union force, so Pemberton ordered everyone back to Vicksburg.

Mounting a Defense

Pemberton could have given up the defense of Vicksburg then and fled east to safer territory with his army, but he decided to stay and fight. Even with Grant approaching from the south, the general had a strong defensive position. In addition to the bluffs facing the river, a vast network of trenches provided excellent cover. Pemberton established his defenses and waited.

Grant appeared to hold the upper hand. Knowing he had cut the rebels off from resupply, he could afford to wait it out. Perhaps he assumed that his opponents realized that as well and wouldn't have any fight in them. Anxious to take the city, he sent waves of troops straight into the Confederate forts and trenches. The Southern soldiers had dug in, however, and they easily repelled the attacks.

Digging In

Grant backed off and decided on another tactic: a siege. He dug his own trenches and gun pits and pointed all his cannons at the city. Then he rained shells onto Vicksburg and its defenses. Grant didn't just fire a few in from time to time—he bombed Vicksburg continuously.

A blockading army laying seige to a city causes war to spill over into the civilian world. Before this time, the war was the business of soldiers, but with the seige, the residents of Vicksburg were trapped. The Union army surrounded the city, bombing it and hoping to starve out the Confederates and citizenry alike.

To the Caves

The citizens of Vicksburg had only one choice to escape the bombardment—

move underground. They took advantage of the rolling hills and dug caves into the bluffs and hillsides. Unsure of how long they'd have to stay there, many civilians moved their furniture into the new living quarters.

Food was a problem, of course, and it eventually ran out. People began searching for new sources and began cooking mules, rats, and even family pets.

A Difficult Surrender

Finally, on the Fourth of July—day 47 of the siege and the day after General Lee was defeated at Gettysburg—Pemberton surrendered. His 30,000 remaining soldiers poured out of the city, giving up 172 cannons. But it was a costly victory—Grant's army suffered 10,000 casualties.

The highest price, however, was paid by the civilians. When they finally crawled out of their caves, they found Vicksburg a pile of rubble. The shelling had destroyed everything. It was a sad end to a terrible siege. The defeat was so traumatic to the town, in fact, that it would not celebrate Independence Day again for 82 years.

"As soon as our troops took possession of the city, guards were established along the whole line of parapet, from the river above to the river below. The prisoners were allowed to occupy their old camps behind the entrenchments. No restraint was put upon them, except by their own commanders. They were rationed about as our own men, and from our supplies. The men of the two armies fraternized as if they had been fighting for the same cause. When they passed out of the works they had so long and so gallantly defended, between the lines of their late antagonists, not a cheer went up, not a remark was made that would give pain. I believe there was a feeling of sadness among the Union soldiers at seeing the dejection of their late antagonists."

Ulysses S. Grant, on the surrender of Vicksburg

WAVE THE FLAG

★ ★ ★ ★

*It took the Confederacy the entire war before it settled
on a flag everyone could agree on—therefore,
the colors never officially flew.*

"Receive, then, from your mothers and
sisters, from those whose affections
greet you, these colors woven by our
feeble but reliant hands; and when this
bright flag shall float before you on the
battlefield, let it not only inspire you with
brave and patriotic ambition of a soldier aspir-
ing to his own and his country's honor and glory, but also may it
be a sign that cherished ones appeal to you to save them from a
fanatical and heartless foe."

These were the words Idelea Collens proclaimed as she presented
a flag to a Louisiana regiment. As Collens stated, flags typically
served two purposes in battle: to display pride in state and country
for those in battle and to act as a beacon around which the members of a regiment would form and fight. Therefore, it was important to both Union and Confederate soldiers that much care was
taken in the design of their flags.

Throughout the Civil War, Union regiments carried at least two
flags: a national flag, or colors, and regimental colors. Many rebel
regiments also carried the national colors and a battle flag, although no single battle flag design was adopted by the Confederacy during the war.

First Flags

Soon after the Confederacy was born, a congressional committee
was formed to choose a design for a national flag. The first design
proposed was what they called "The Stars and Stripes," so named
because it was very similar to the U.S. flag, with 13 red and white

horizontal stripes and a blue field in the upper left corner with 13 stars. It was quickly rejected by Confederate Congress delegates as being too similar to the Yankees' flag.

Their second choice was called the "Stars and Bars" and featured two thick red horizontal stripes separated by a thick white horizontal stripe, with seven stars on a blue background in the upper left corner. This design was a compromise between those delegates who wanted a unique design and those who wanted to keep the Union's national colors.

The Stars and Bars, however, created confusion at the First Battle of Bull Run—without any wind to waft the flag, its colors made it look too similar to the Union flag. Along with the fact that the colors of the Union and Confederate uniforms were also so similar, the Stars and Bars made it difficult for soldiers to tell if other troops were friend or foe. As a result, some rebels fired on friendly troops. Following the battle, the Southern commanders began designing a new flag.

A Battle Flag Is Born

The Beauregard battle flag was adopted on October 1, 1861, by the Confederate Army of the Potomac (which later changed its name to the Army of Northern Virginia). This design is familiar to people today—a St. Andrew's Cross on a field of red, with 13 stars aligned across the blue cross. Instead of a rectangle, however, the Beauregard battle flag was a square. The Stars and Bars remained the national colors, yet many Confederate citizens and politicians identified with the battle flag and demanded that it replace the unpopular Stars and Bars as the national flag.

Not every Confederate regiment adopted the Beauregard battle flag, especially in the western theater. Many flags had a similar design, but others were unique to a particular regiment. The Confederate Navy adopted a rectangular form of the Beauregard battle flag in 1863, the "Confederate Navy Jack," and this is the flag that today is often mistakenly believed to have been the national flag of the Confederate States of America.

I Surrender

Throughout all of this, many continued to seek a flag that could take the place of the Stars and Bars. A third national flag, the "Stainless Banner," was adopted on May 1, 1863. Its design featured a rectangular white background—intended to signify the purity of the Confederate cause—with the Beauregard battle flag in the upper left corner. One of its initial displays was over the coffin of General Stonewall Jackson. Criticism of the new design poured into Richmond soon after it was adopted. Some said its dimensions created the impression of a long tablecloth; others thought it looked like a flag of surrender. The flag was also too long to float properly in the wind.

Too Little, Too Late

In response to these criticisms, yet another new flag design was sought. Major Arthur Rogers, gravely wounded during the Battle of Chancellorsville in May 1863, proposed that a shorter version of the Stainless Banner be adopted with a thick vertical red stripe running along the right side. As the fortunes of the Confederacy slipped away, its Congress took time to debate the design until finally adopting it on March 4, 1865. Ironically, it took the Confederacy its entire lifetime before it finally adopted a flag that met the approval of the nation. General Lee surrendered his Army of Northern Virginia a little more than a month after the new flag was adopted. As a result, it never flew over the Confederate capitol or any of its armies.

- *The Confederate flag that troops carried into battle had 13 stars, representing the 11 secession states and the governments of Kentucky and Missouri.*

- *The last city to stop the official practice of flying the Confederate flag was Columbia, South Carolina, which removed it in the year 2000.*

WORTH A THOUSAND WORDS

★ ★ ★ ★

Civil War photographers blazed a new trail to provide a visual record of the war and paved the way for photojournalists today.

In today's digital world, the current crop of photographers has a fairly easy time pursuing their craft, compared to even ten years ago. It would be quite a task for most of today's photographers to endure the extreme demands placed upon the legendary Mathew Brady and his peers nearly a century and a half ago as they laid the groundwork for photojournalism. The technical ability of photography during the Civil War was in no way up to the task of documenting the actual fighting—photographers could really only hope to record the aftermath of the battles, with the dead lying where they fell or lined in rows for a hasty burial. For all that, the images with which we are familiar today are still extremely powerful and continue to have an immediacy that no advanced technology can surpass. Given the conditions in which these photographers worked, their accomplishments are little short of miraculous.

Road Blocks

One of the primary obstacles photographers had to face was transporting themselves and their equipment. The "film" of the day was glass plate negatives, some measuring a mammoth 11×17 inches. Simply moving these "wet plates" from one locale to another was arduous, given the coarse terrain and the less-than-smooth ride afforded by a horse-drawn wagon. A day spent capturing images could be lost forever simply by taking a spill. Moreover, the process itself—both in taking pictures and holding onto them— was slow. The time necessary for an exposure could run anywhere from 5 to 20 seconds, which tended to preclude asking combatants to "Hold it! This is for *Leslie's!*" In fact, the challenge of a prolonged exposure time largely eliminated the possibility of taking pictures of animals in the field as well.

Timing Is Everything

A typical "shoot" would go something like this: A photography team, two people at a minimum, would rush to a battlefield once word arrived of a major engagement. Speed was of the essence, as everyone wanted to scoop the competition. Arrival at the battlefield would have to be timed just so. If they were too late, the armies may have already cleared the battlefield of the dead and, therefore, any compelling subject matter—all that would be left was an empty field. If they arrived too soon, however, they risked life and limb by being caught up in the battle itself, not to mention the chance of being captured by the combatants. Indeed, one of photographer Alexander Gardner's associates was briefly detained by lingering Confederate troops after they left Gettysburg. Gaining permission and cooperation was necessary not only to access the site but also to get a handle on what had happened and where. Ghoulish tourists and souvenir hunters were another hazard, frequently picking the landscapes, and the casualties, clean of anything of value.

The photographers would typically scout for compelling subject matter, each with their own signature style. Mathew Brady was partial to including landmarks and vistas in his work, while his former employee Gardner seemed to focus exclusively on lifeless combatants. It must be remembered that adding to the challenge of working smoothly in the field was the unavoidable stench of decaying bodies, both human and equine. Burial parties would naturally concentrate on retrieving fallen comrades, so dead horses and mules were typically given last priority in refuse removal. That the photographers could stand to be in this environment for as long as was necessary to do their work speaks volumes about their dedication.

Strike a Pose

Though most of the striking battlefield images known to us today record soldiers at their place of death, study of the photos more than a century later has revealed that not every photographer was intent on simply documenting what he found. One photo historian has revealed demonstrable evidence that Gardner and his assistants were not above "improving" upon warfare's aesthetic qualities by physically moving and "posing" corpses into more inspiring arrangements, sometimes transporting the decaying remains great distances. There, a dropped weapon might be added for poignancy.

Once a commercially viable scene was selected, the team was ready to begin its work. Wet plate photography, universally employed throughout the Civil War, meant the arduous task of applying a syrupy concoction (known as *collodion* and made from an egg white derivative) to a spotless piece of glass on location. Next, chemicals were applied in complete darkness to render the sticky coating photosensitive. The tacky plate was now considered "film" and had to be placed into a film holder and rushed out into the camera, which presumably had already been set into position by a team member. Once an image had been recorded, an assistant would rush the film container to the darkroom wagon for development, mindful of the need to begin processing before the plate dried. With enough team members to assure a smooth, practiced routine, the entire process could be done in as little as ten minutes per exposure.

★ ★ ★ ★

- *Battlefield photographers were, above all, entrepreneurs. They labored over generating the most salable product. To meet public demand, this meant providing images in the preferred format of the day—"stereo-view." To achieve this effect, three-dimensional images were captured with dual-lens cameras. Direct precursors to Viewmasters of more recent vintage, a handheld viewer provided the illusion of depth to the beholder. Many households of the time owned one, thereby affording gawkers the chance to experience violent death in the comfort of their own homes. Updated reissues of these stereo-view images became widely available in the 1960s, the war's centennial decade.*

Fast Facts

- Grapeshot *is loosely packed metal slugs in a canvas bag. It can also be improvised from chain links, shards of glass, or rocks. When fired, the balls spread out from the muzzle at high velocity, giving an effect similar to a shotgun.*

- *General George B. McClellan didn't find out that President Lincoln had decided to remove him from the command of the Army of the Potomac until he read about it in a day-old newspaper.*

- *Under the best conditions, the roar of artillery during battle could be heard for more than ten miles.*

- *William Tecumseh Sherman sent, via telegram, the most famous Christmas gift of the Civil War. On December 22, 1864, he wrote Lincoln, "I beg to present you as a Christmas gift, the city of Savannah, with 100 and 50 guns and plenty of ammunition, also about 25,000 bales of cotton."*

- *The only father-son winners of the Congressional Medal of Honor are Arthur MacArthur, Jr., who at age 18 in 1863 planted the flag on Missionary Ridge during the Battle of Chattanooga, and his son Douglas MacArthur, who earned his medal during World War II.*

- *Although Jefferson Davis had no official Cabinet, he had 14 heads of executive departments serving under him.*

- *Samuel Ely Parker, a member of the Seneca nation, was Ulysses Grant's military secretary from 1864 to 1869. He was present at Lee's surrender in 1865 at Appomattox Court House, and he took down the terms of surrender that Grant dictated. When Grant became president in 1869, he named Parker commissioner of Indian affairs.*

TOPPING OFF THE CAPITOL

★ ★ ★ ★

As the Civil War raged on, the uncompleted dome on the U.S. Capitol became a symbol of a country fighting to remain united.

The U.S. Capitol in Washington, D.C., was originally topped with a short copper dome. A new, more majestic dome was approved in 1855 with an estimated cost of $100,000. That price tag rose exponentially over the next decade, rising to a final total of $1,047,291.

Starting, Stopping, and Starting Again

Work began in 1856 and mostly continued smoothly. That changed with the Civil War, however. One month after war broke out, construction ceased. Congress decided that the funds should be used for the war rather than the Capitol. The building was even used as a temporary barracks for troops stationed in Washington, D.C., to protect the city.

The order to stop construction left the contractor, James, Fowler, Kirtland and Company, with 1.3 million pounds of iron onsite. Worried about keeping their business afloat, they decided to continue with the dome construction on their own.

At this point, the line between reality and myth becomes blurred. Some sources suggest that Lincoln used the contractor's decision to his advantage, while others claim that it was always his intention to finish the dome for the sake of the country. According to Lincoln biographer Carl Sandberg, the President said, "If people see the Capitol going on, it is a sign we intend the Union shall go on."

As the exterior of the dome neared completion on December 2, 1863, crowds gathered on Pennsylvania Avenue to watch. After the years and months of construction and a war that was tearing the country apart, the great dome over the Capitol at last appeared to be finished. One can only imagine the emotion felt when the 19.5-foot-tall statue of Freedom was hoisted atop the immense dome.

KEEPING AN EYE ON THINGS

★ ★ ★ ★

The Union relied on many spies—both male and female—to remain informed of the Confederacy's actions and strategies.

The Spy Onstage

Pauline Cushman was born in the bayou of New Orleans in 1833. Her family eventually moved to Grand Rapids, Michigan, but that wasn't big enough for the ambitious Cushman. As a young woman, she headed to the East Coast for a successful theatrical career.

In 1863, Cushman was in Louisville, Kentucky. Although a Union town, Louisville had a fair share of Confederate supporters. One day, Cushman was dared by Southern officers to offer a toast to Jefferson Davis during a play. She agreed, tipping off the local Federals. When the toast came, so did the marshals, and audience members who'd cheered were arrested. Cushman's life as a Union spy had begun.

A beautiful woman, Cushman had high cheekbones and a dark Creole complexion. Regardless, she often fooled unknowing Southerners by donning a false mustache and posing as a man. Later in 1863, she was sent deep into a Confederate camp near Shelbyville, Tennessee. But before she could complete her mission, Cushman was captured and brought to General Braxton Bragg. A quick trial found her guilty of spying, and she was sentenced to hang. Quickly advancing Union soldiers, however, soon drove the Confederates from Shelbyville, and Cushman was saved.

Fame ended Cushman's spying days. Still, she received the honorary title of "major" and continued performing, sometimes in shows by P. T. Barnum, billing herself as "Miss Major Cushman." When she died in 1893, she was buried with full military honors.

A Light and Bright Life

In 1861, 19-year-old Spencer Kellogg Brown joined the U.S. Navy, serving on the *Essex*. He bravely volunteered to infiltrate the shores near Forts Henry and Donelson on the Tennessee and the Cumberland rivers to seek intelligence. Caught after several days, Brown convinced his captor to release him so he could join the Confederates. He actually did join for a brief time in Louisiana, only to escape and bring his findings personally to General Grant.

In 1862, Brown was dispatched to attack a ferry supplying Confederates at Fort Hudson in Georgia. Although the mission was successful, Brown was captured as a spy and tried in Richmond. Found guilty, he was hanged in 1863. His last words were reported to be, "Did you ever pass through a tunnel under a mountain? My passage, my death is dark, but beyond all is light and bright."

The Unassuming Spy

Not much is known about Mrs. E. H. Baker, a Chicago-based member of the Pinkerton Agency. What is known is that she single-handedly saved the Union navy that patrolled Virginia's James River.

In November 1861, Baker, posing as a bored and apolitical woman on an extended visit, called on some old Richmond friends. Baker made herself at home and discovered that these friends had a young son who was a captain in the Confederate army.

At a party on the shore of the James River, Mrs. Baker witnessed the South's secret weapon—a submarine. The demonstration included the attachment and detonation of an explosive charge to an old scow. Union ships traveling the river would be the next targets.

Baker soon became "homesick" and was sent off with a fond farewell. When she arrived in Washington, she delivered a complete accounting, including sketches, of the entire submarine demonstration. With plans relayed to the Union commander of the James River flotilla, the Confederate plot was foiled on its first attempt. Air lines into the submarine were closed off, leaving the Confederate sailors inside to suffocate.

Although she made a valuable contribution to the Union war effort, Mrs. Baker returned to the Pinkerton Agency and disappeared into anonymity.

(Continued from p. 254)

1863

May 1
The Confederacy adopts the Stainless Banner as its official flag.

May 1–3
Lee defeats Hooker at the Battle of Chancellorsville, Virginia.

May 10
Stonewall Jackson, wounded by friendly fire at Chancellorsville, dies of pneumonia.

May 19
Grant stages his first unsuccessful assault on Vicksburg's defenses.

May 22
Grant makes a second assault at Vicksburg. When it is unsuccessful, his troops begin siege operations.

May 25
Ohioan Clement L. Vallandigham is banished to the Confederacy.

June 1
General Burnside shuts down the *Chicago Times* for publishing disloyal statements.

June 4
Lincoln rescinds Burnside's order, allowing the *Chicago Times* to renew publication.

June 9
Confederates hold off Union horse soldiers at the Battle of Brandy Station, Virginia, the largest cavalry engagement of the war.

June 20
West Virginia is admitted to the Union as the 35th state.

June 28
General Hooker is replaced by General George G. Meade as commander of the Army of the Potomac.

July 1–3
Lee's invasion of the North is stopped at the Battle of Gettysburg, Pennsylvania.

July 4
Vicksburg, Mississippi, surrenders to General Grant.

July 13–16
Violent draft riots break out in New York City.

July 18
Federals mount an unsuccessful attack on Fort Wagner. The 54th Massachusetts loses more than a third of its troops.

July 26
Former Texas Governor Sam Houston and former Kentucky Senator John J. Crittenden die at their homes.

August 1
In an attempt to strengthen Confederate armies, Jefferson Davis offers amnesty to deserters.

August 21
Confederate guerrillas led by William Quantrill sack Lawrence, Kansas.

August 25
In response to Quantrill's raid, General Thomas Ewing in Missouri orders all civilians to leave the counties of Bates, Jackson, Cass, and part of Vernon.

(Continued on p. 329)

GRANT'S OVERZEALOUS PURGE

★ ★ ★ ★

*When Ulysses Grant issued an order with
anti-Semitic implications, Lincoln immediately
stepped in to right the potential wrong.*

Many of his officers were puzzled by General Ulysses S. Grant's General Order Number 11, issued on December 17, 1862. They were certain that the general had received some bad advice. He was expelling the Jews from the territory he controlled in parts of Kentucky, Tennessee, and Mississippi. He provided part of his thinking in a letter to Assistant Secretary of War Christopher P. Wolcott:

"I have long since believed that...the specie regulations of the Treasury Department have been violated, and that mostly by Jews and other unprincipled traders....The Jews seem to be a privileged class that can travel everywhere....If not permitted to buy cotton themselves they will act as agents for some one else, who will be at a military post with a Treasury permit to receive cotton and pay for it in Treasury notes which the Jew will buy up at an agreed rate, paying in gold.

"There is but one way I know to reach this case; that is, for Government to buy all the cotton at a fixed rate and send it...to be sold. Then all traders (they are a curse to the army) might be expelled."

Fear of Spying Peddlers

The role of independent traders, or peddlers, had always been taken for granted. During peacetime, they crisscrossed the countryside, buying and selling from farmers and towns, but when war came they were viewed with suspicion, particularly by the Union. Federal officers feared that traders could be spies, or worse, that they could be used by Southerners to sell contraband cotton. Since many traders were Jewish, it may have seemed easier to Grant to expel the entire Jewish community from the area. He gave them 24 hours to leave.

Righting an Injustice

Cesar Kaskel was a Jewish merchant and longtime resident of Paducah, Kentucky. This order forced his family and many others out of their homes. But Kaskel knew who could protect the Jewish people: Abraham Lincoln. When Lincoln had been a circuit-riding attorney in his youth, he'd met and made many friends among the Jewish community. Kaskel couldn't believe that Lincoln would condone such an order, so he went east to Washington to take his case directly to the President.

Once notified of the situation, Lincoln moved fast. Through General-in-Chief Henry W. Halleck, he delivered terse instructions to Grant on January 4, 1863:

"A paper purporting to be General Orders, No. 11, issued by you December 17, has been presented here. By its terms it expels all Jews from your department. If such an order has been issued, it will be immediately revoked."

What Was Grant's Motivation?

Was Grant anti-Semitic? It's possible, but more likely he was concerned about stopping the movement of any contraband trading that would benefit the South. Quite possibly he received some bad advice from a subordinate officer who *was* an anti-Semite or he signed an order put in front of him without reading it carefully. But his unfortunate choice of words was remembered.

Grant never discussed this incident in his personal memoirs. In dealing with Jewish officers, and later as president, however, he didn't display the slightest sign of anti-Jewish prejudice, appointing many Jews to positions in his administration.

RATION BASHIN'

★ ★ ★ ★

You think your mother-in-law's cooking is bad?
Try living with the average Civil War soldier's rations.

Ask any soldier to name the top five gripes with the service, and food will always appear in the list. Ever since the armies of Alexander the Great, soldiers have complained about rations—or the lack thereof.

During the Civil War, many soldiers sent letters to their families complaining about the food and begging for packages to be sent from home. "I'll bet when I get hom [*sic*]," a Vermont soldier wrote to his sister, "I Shall have an appetite to eat most anything.... If a person wants to know how to appreciate the value of good vituals [*sic*] he had better enlist.... I have seen the time when I would have been glad to [have] picked the crusts of bread that mother gives to the hogs."

Confederate Rations Lagged Behind the Union

It was hard for all soldiers during the war, but in truth, the rations for Union soldiers were much better in both quality and quantity than those of the Confederates. At the start of the war, the size of the Confederates' rations was equivalent to what Union troops got. Within six months, however, the amount began to drastically decrease. Logistical problems plagued the Confederates throughout the war. There were many instances when ample food supplies were available, but officials didn't have the transportation necessary to get the rations delivered to the soldiers.

The Union camp daily rations included a pound or more of meat; a pound or more of flour, cornmeal, or hard bread (called *hardtack*); salt; beans or peas; rice or hominy; and coffee or tea. When on the march, the troops were given a pound of hardtack, and about a pound of meat, sugar, coffee, and salt. Both Union and Confederate soldiers ate beef or salted pork, which were boiled, broiled, or fried. In the West, soldiers often ate buffalo meat. When necessary, mule meat was cooked.

A Cup of Coffee?

Unlike the South, the North had access to items shipped from foreign ports. The blockade of Southern ports was so effective that many items came up in very short supply as the war progressed. Though coffee was available to Union troops throughout the war, Confederates weren't so lucky. They could sometimes trade with Union soldiers, but when that source was not available, Southerners had to be creative in their choice of coffee substitutes: okra coffee, war coffee (one spoonful of real coffee mixed with a spoonful of toasted cornmeal), chinquapin coffee (dried and ground nuts from a chinquapin tree), grape coffee (boiled grape seeds), pea coffee (brewed from English peas roasted until dark brown), potato and persimmon coffee (persimmon seeds boiled and parched with mashed potatoes or dried sweet potatoes added), and rye coffee (rye boiled and then left in the sun to parch).

Canning for the War Effort

Canned goods became a staple of the Union soldier's food ration, preserving various food items such as cakes, pies, and meats. Borden's Condensed Milk grew in popularity, and the company eventually found it difficult to meet the Union army's demand for its canned milk throughout the war. In general, the annual production of canned goods increased from 5 million to 30 million by the end of the war.

"Pray excuse me. I cannot take it."
Jefferson Davis's last words, in response to his wife's attempt to give him medicine

"Oh my God! Lay me down again!"
Stonewall Jackson's troops after one of their many forced marches

DAMMING THE RED RIVER

★ ★ ★ ★

*A combination of ingenuity and sheer brawn saved
the day for Union soldiers stuck in an embarrassing
jam on Louisiana's Red River in 1864.*

Great battles are decided in many different ways. Acts of bravery
and courage under fire often determine the outcome of armed
conflict. Other struggles end in defeat through the folly or indecision of a commander. Only 14 people were given the official
Thanks of Congress for their services to the Union during the
Civil War, and all but one—Lieutenant Colonel Joseph Bailey—
were commanders in the armed forces. As the chief engineer of
the 19th Corps, Bailey saved a Union gunboat fleet trapped on
Louisiana's Red River in May 1864 using a single formidable
weapon—his brain.

Revered River

The Red River, a tributary of the Mississippi, was highly prized by
Union forces as a channel by which to capture Shreveport and
establish their control over northern Louisiana. The plan was that
Shreveport and the surrounding area would then serve as a spring-
board to launch excursions into Texas and Arkansas. In April 1864,
General Nathaniel Banks led a Union force of 32,000 soldiers and
13 gunboats, including 6 formidable ironclads, northward up the
Red River.

Stuck in the Mud

A series of skirmishes with a determined Confederate opposition
slowed the Union advance. At Alexandria, Confederate defenders
had been busy digging channels to divert the river. They succeeded in lowering the water level to a depth of less than four
feet, which created quite a problem for the Northern fleet. The
smallest Union gunboats required seven feet of water to travel,
and the larger craft needed a depth of more than ten feet.

The Union advance was stalled. The gunboats were at risk of becoming stranded on the river as the waters continued to recede, which would make them sitting ducks for either capture or destruction by Confederate artillery. On May 1, Chief Engineer Bailey was authorized to take any actions necessary to free the boats and permit the advance to continue. To the amazement and consternation of the Union leadership, he resolved to build a dam.

Dam It All

Bailey had worked in the Wisconsin woods in his youth, and he sought out lumbering experience among the approximately 3,500 soldiers he had at his disposal. He then directed the felling of hundreds of trees in the Red River's adjacent forests and had the cut timber fashioned into cribbing. Other soldiers were detailed to gather rock and earth to fill the cribbing that would be used in the makeshift dam. All the while, Bailey's lumberjacks and laborers were subject to continuous Confederate sniper fire.

To complete the dam, Bailey intended to have four barges deliberately overloaded and sunk midstream above the rapids. He would then connect the cribs to the barges, creating two 300-foot wing dams jutting into the river from each bank. This backup would force the water level up to a point at which the gunboats could maneuver. The remaining open water in the middle of the river would form an ingenious spillway through which the gunboats could pass over the rapids.

Cleverness Lauded

In just ten days, the dam was built. The Red River water level rose to almost 13 feet because of Bailey's dam, which allowed the gunboats safe passage into navigable water. The last boat passed over just as the dam itself was breaking due to the water pressure in the river. In his report to the War Department, General Banks lauded Chief Engineer Bailey as the person who both saved a Union fleet worth more than $2 million (a value of approximately $200 million today) and permitted the Red River Campaign to continue.

Fast Facts

- *Virginia honors Robert E. Lee and Stonewall Jackson's birthdays on Lee-Jackson Day. Originally created in 1889 to celebrate Lee's birthday, Jackson's name was added in 1904, and it has been observed as a state holiday ever since. The holiday is the Friday before Martin Luther King Jr. Day.*

- *When the Lincolns' third son, Tad, died of tuberculosis, Mary went into a depression. Historians argue about whether she ever recovered from it.*

- *After the attack on Fort Sumter, Lincoln declared a state of insurrection and called for 75,000 volunteers to serve three months' service.*

- *Many Civil War battles have two names, such as Bull Run/ Manassas or Stone's River/Murfreesboro. Confederates often named the battles after the nearest settlement or town, whereas the Yankees typically named them after the nearest body of water or other geographical feature.*

- *In 1864, 109 Union officers made a famous escape when they tunneled their way out of Richmond's Libby Prison. Of this count, 59 reached Union lines, 48 were recaptured, and 2 drowned.*

- *The Augusta Powder Works supplied the Confederacy with gunpowder as well as all kinds of arms and equipment. It was a two-mile-long factory with some 26 buildings. From 1862 to 1865, it produced more than 2,750,000 pounds of gunpowder. But it was also the Confederacy's single largest producer of curry combs and brushes. Colonel George Rains built it in about seven months using a pamphlet that described the machinery and processes of the English powder plant that was the best in the world at the time.*

CRAZY LIKE A FOX

★ ★ ★ ★

*Using a secret code and other methods to gather information
from prisoners, Elizabeth Van Lew risked her life
to send messages to the Union army.*

When Union General Ulysses S. Grant visited Richmond after the Confederate surrender at Appomattox Court House, one of his first visits was to a magnificent mansion southeast of the city in which a middle-aged spinster sat awaiting his arrival. During the few minutes he spent in her home, Grant told the woman, "You have sent me the most valuable information received from Richmond during the war." Who was this Richmond socialite who played such an important part in the Union victory?

Southern Belle Turned Abolitionist

Elizabeth Van Lew, known to friends as Miss Lizzie, was the daughter of a wealthy merchant. In addition to a beautiful home in Richmond, her father also owned a farm in City Point, Virginia, with 12 slaves to work the land. Miss Lizzie was often at odds with her father about continuing to possess slaves. Her beliefs on slavery only became stronger after she was sent to school in Philadelphia. She wrote in her diary, "Slave power is arrogant, is jealous and intrusive, is cruel, is despotic."

After her father died in 1843, 25-year-old Miss Lizzie convinced her mother to set the slaves free and use their home as a station on the Underground Railroad. She and her mother found it difficult to hide their Northern leanings after war was declared. They were particularly disheartened when the Union army was routed at Bull Run.

Friends Behind Bars

When Libby Prison opened near her home, Miss Lizzie made frequent visits to Union prisoners to provide medicine, food, and books.

She befriended prisoners, guards, and the prison commander—Lieutenant David H. Todd, Mary Todd Lincoln's half brother.

She made a point of interviewing new arrivals, learning as much as she could about what they had seen behind Confederate lines, and then used former slaves who had remained with her after being set free to carry the information to Union camps.

Over time, Miss Lizzie became more and more clever in gathering information. She had prisoners underline specific words in books to reveal key bits of information. The deception became even more sophisticated when she developed a secret code to mask her messages.

"Crazy Bet"

Throughout the war, Miss Lizzie made no effort to hide her allegiance to the Union and her disdain of the Confederacy. To hide her true mission, however, she sometimes acted as if she were mentally unstable, walking around the city in disheveled clothing and talking or singing to herself. She gained the nickname "Crazy Bet."

When the war was over, Miss Lizzie remained in Richmond even though she and an invalid niece were shunned by their neighbors. "No one will walk with us on the street," she wrote. "No one will go with us anywhere; and it grows worse and worse as the years roll on." Miss Lizzie had long since spent her inheritance freeing slaves, providing essentials to prisoners, and giving money to escaped prisoners. All she had left were her house and furnishings.

A Friend Revered

In later years, Miss Lizzie had to sell many belongings to get by. Fortunately, the son of Union Colonel Paul Revere (and great-grandson of the more famous American with that name) came to her aid. Miss Lizzie had developed a friendship with Colonel Revere at Libby Prison. His son returned the favor by providing an annuity for the rest of her life. After she passed away in 1900, the Revere family paid for her headstone, which reads, "Elizabeth L. Van Lew, 1818-1900: She risked everything that is dear to man—friends, fortune, comfort, health, life itself, all for the one absorbing desire of her heart—that slavery might be abolished and the Union preserved."

DOTS AND DASHES

★ ★ ★ ★

The telegraph was a vital part of the war effort on both sides, changing not only the way battles were fought, but also the way information was relayed back to the home front.

Recognizing the importance of the telegraph to the Union war effort, in August 1861, Assistant Secretary of War Thomas Scott sent out a call to the best telegraphers in the Northern states to help create the U.S. Military Telegraph. Some of these telegraphers would be right on the front lines, reporting the progress of troops and results of battles back to Washington. The Army took advantage of the existing infrastructure of telegraph wires, but it had to install new lines when fighting moved into virgin territory.

The operators of the quickly assembled Military Telegraph Corps stood out in stark contrast to their blue-uniformed counterparts on the battlefield. They were and remained civilians, so they were never under the control of Army officers. Photographer Mathew Brady captured a few images of them dressed in suits with bowties and straw hats, smiling as if they were at a summer garden party and not on the front line. A good operator could send about 43 words per minute and up to 2,000 words per hour, leading newspaper reporters to nickname the new system "The Lightning."

Floating Telegraph

The use of the telegraph in the war zone was tested in a number of new ways. One controversial plan was to trail telegraph wires from hot air balloons to observe and report troop movements. President Lincoln strongly supported the idea, but his administrators didn't. Thaddeus Lowe was one balloonist who tried to float the idea of hot air balloons in Washington, but after being rebuked a number of times, he had the President personally walk him to the War Department. With Lincoln's clear backing, the plan was quickly pushed forward. Balloons appeared at the battlefront, and within a year seven balloons were being used successfully.

Keeping the President Connected

Always a supporter of new technology, Lincoln was especially enamored of the telegraph. The White House had not yet been equipped with its own receiver, so the President could often be found in the telegraph office reading dispatches. He was known to stand directly behind clerks as they deciphered messages, reading the scribbled words over their shoulders. During the Battle of Gettysburg, a fatigued Lincoln spent most of the three-day fight pacing the floor of the office waiting for any word on the outcome.

Hand-to-Hand Communication

In the field, some operators used smaller pocket telegraph keys in cases roughly the size of a bar of soap. These small handheld communication stations had originally been used by telegraph repair personnel, or "linewalkers." Now they gave field commanders the ability to tap into any telegraph line and send or receive instructions. However, this same technology allowed enemy agents to eavesdrop through telegraph lines and even send fake messages.

Reporters Get in on the Action

At the beginning of the conflict, "The Lightning" also allowed reporters to send dispatches directly to their newsrooms. This led to a great deal of misinformation being relayed to civilians back home as eager reporters raced to the wire with any nugget of information, much of it full of factual errors if not completely false altogether. At one point, reports circulated that the First Battle of Bull Run was an unmitigated victory for Union troops.

As the army took stronger control of the telegraph and realized its true potential, reporters faced censorship or flat-out refusal to transmit their dispatches. Military officials wanted to control not only the flow of information but the technology, as well. With the telegraph just out of the grasp of reporters, it became easier for them simply to catch a train back to the newsroom to file a story.

Overall, the plan to use telegraphy in the war was a good one, and by the end of the war, the Union operated 15,000 miles of telegraph lines, with the Confederacy utilizing 1,000.

WINNING ALWAYS HAS A PRICE

★ ★ ★ ★

The Battle of Chancellorsville may have been the rebel forces' most spectacular victory, but it also saw one of their greatest losses.

On the night of May 1, 1863, the future of General Robert E. Lee and his Virginia Confederates looked bleak. Just to the northwest, near a crossroads mansion called Chancellorsville, was sprawled Joseph Hooker's better-armed, better-fed federal force of nearly 100,000, which outnumbered the rebels by roughly two to one. These soldiers had been on the march and seemed on the verge of maneuvering around the Confederates and into their rear. As Lee sat on an empty hardtack box conferring with General Stonewall Jackson about their predicament, the question came down to whether or not there was any way out of it.

Lee Takes the Offensive

Lee had an idea he thought might work. Actually, it turned out to be a bold and daring plan that has since become part of Civil War lore. The general was well aware that the Union left and center were heavily defended and that any attack on those parts of the line would be a disaster. But he found out from a scout, his nephew Fitzhugh Lee, that the far right of the Union flank was "in the air," or not entrenched at all. A military push there might start a headlong panic that could roll up the rest of the Union army.

Lee's plan was to stay right where he was with a small token force. Hooker would no doubt remain focused on him, but Lee would also send Jackson and the bulk of his own troops—about 30,000— on a 12-mile march in front of (but out of sight of) Union lines. That force would traverse the thick underbrush of a forest called the Wilderness and ultimately curl around the Union's right flank for a surprise attack. This plan was a real gamble. If Hooker pushed out of his trenches with a frontal assault after most of Lee's troops had moved, Lee and the remainder of his army would be destroyed.

Hooker Hesitates

Lee and the Confederates caught a break. Like his predecessor, George McClellan, Hooker hesitated and became cautious. In fact, Hooker saw Jackson's force on the move, but he misread this evidence as a retreat that required no counteraction. Reports later surfaced that Hooker's passivity was induced by alcohol. Captain George A. Custer said that Hooker had been disabled by "a projectile which requires a cork to be drawn before it is serviceable."

Confederates on the Charge

Around dinnertime on May 2, the Union 11th Corps received its only warning of the rebel attack. According to Union General Oliver Howard, "Its first lively effects...appeared in the startled rabbits, squirrel, quail, and other game flying wildly hither and thither in evident terror." No wonder—they were followed by yelling Confederates, waves and waves of them. Their uniforms torn and tattered by the forest, these woebegone attackers caught the Federals from the side and drove them into a wild retreat. Caught while they were eating dinner, the Union troops were totally unprepared and thoroughly surprised—in panic, they were driven almost two miles into the rear. Once the Union lines were abandoned, hordes of hungry Southerners sliced and sampled the fatback beef Union troops had left cooking over the campfires.

Jackson Takes a Hit

In the aftermath of the fighting, Jackson decided to do a little personal reconnaissance to find out how he might capitalize on his advances and whip the Union army even further. When returning to his own lines, however, his small scouting party was mistaken for the enemy by the 18th North Carolina Infantry, which fired and hit the general and some of his staff. Jackson was shot in three places, with one of the bullets shattering a bone in his left arm.

Armies have to go on, of course, so Jackson was given immediate medical attention, and General Jeb Stuart temporarily took over his position to finish the job. On the Union side, Hooker's command had almost completely collapsed. Although his force still outnumbered the Confederates by about two to one, he remained in retreat. Stuart didn't even have a chance to attack before the Union army pulled even further back, giving up territory the rebels had been prepared to fight over. Almost the only place where Union forces showed any aggressiveness was nine miles away from this front at Fredericksburg, where the bluecoats engaged in a bayonet charge through the Confederate line at Marye's Heights. This is where Lee had left only token opposition, and the Union soldiers had broken through and were advancing on Lee's rear. General Lee responded by dispatching another of his divisions, ultimately thwarting the Federals. With a shaken Hooker essentially having given up the fight, however, and no obvious opportunity to press an advantage, Union forces quietly withdrew north, over the Rappahannock River.

The Real Consequences of Chancellorsville

Lee's troops pulled off a great victory—perhaps their most spectacular of the war. But Chancellorsville proved very costly as well. In treating Jackson's wounds, surgeons determined that they had to amputate his left arm. Although it initially appeared that he would survive the surgery, Jackson developed pneumonia and died eight days later.

In addition to losing Jackson, Southerners sustained 13,000 casualties—about 22 percent of their force. Still, the victory made the Confederates extremely confident, and Lee's army would soon embark on its second invasion of the North.

"I see from the number of physicians that you think my condition dangerous, but I thank God, if it is His will, that I am ready to go."
Stonewall Jackson, on his deathbed

SO THEY SAID

★ ★ ★ ★

"My dead and wounded were nearly as great in number as those still on duty. They literally covered the ground. The blood stood in puddles in some places on the rocks; the ground was soaked with the blood of as brave men as ever fell on the red field of battle."
Confederate Colonel William C. Oates

"We have shared the incommunicable experience of war. We have felt, we still feel, the passion of life to its top."
Oliver Wendell Holmes, Jr.

"Sunday last a soldier of Co. 'A' died and was buried with military honors. It was not an unusual scene for us, yet it is always solemn. First came the muffled drums playing the 'Dead March' then the usual escort for a private. Eight privates, commanded by a corporal, with arms reversed. Then an ambulance with the body in a common board coffin covered with the Stars and Stripes. Co. 'A' with side arms only followed while the Company officers brought up the rear. On arriving at the grave the Chaplain offered prayer and made some remarks. The coffin was then low- ered into the grave, and three volleys were fired by the guard, and then the grave was filled up. The procession returned to camp with the drums playing a 'Quick March.' Everything went on as usual in camp as if nothing had happened, for death is so common that little sentiment is wasted. It is not like death at home. May God prepare us all for this event which must sooner or later come to all of us."
Elisha Hunt Rhodes, 2nd Rhode Island Volunteer Infantry

A FAMILY AT WAR

★ ★ ★ ★

John J. Crittenden was a lifelong public official, but for all of his accomplishments, it was his namesake—the Crittenden Compromise—and his hope to reunite not only the nation, but also his own family, that brought him the most notoriety and heartache.

Having served his country in various capacities such as U.S. district attorney, U.S. attorney general, governor of Kentucky, and most prominently, U.S. senator, in 1860 John J. Crittenden was in a good position to help heal the wounds of his broken land. His proposed compromise between Northern and Southern states would have kept the slavery laws drawn up over preceding decades but limited them to the Southern states by adding six amendments to the Constitution. Among other things, these amendments would have supported the South's right to continue the practice of slavery. Crittenden hoped his work would keep the country unified, but as the compromise leaned almost entirely in favor of the South, Northern Republicans in Congress vehemently rejected it. Any hope of keeping the Union together was effectively erased, and America took one more step toward war.

Trouble at Home

Following his defeat on the floor of Congress, Crittenden temporarily returned to Kentucky, working to keep his home state in the Union. He was successful, and Kentucky remained neutral. Crittenden's intentions went beyond the political, however: His two sons commanded troops on opposite sides of the quarrel, an occurrence that was all too common.

Both of Crittenden's sons served in the military prior to the Civil War, having fought in the Mexican War. Thomas, the younger son, shared his father's belief in saving the Union and joined the U.S. Army at the outbreak of the war. Like his father, Thomas was a lawyer by trade. In the army, he rose to the rank of general and served at the bloody battles of Shiloh, Murfreesboro, and Tullahoma. Crittenden's older son, George, chose to follow his Southern loyalties. A West Point graduate and staunch supporter of slavery, he accepted a commission from the Confederates. He actually held commissions in both armies for three months until he resigned from his Union responsibilities in June 1861.

Trouble in the Field

While fighting for their beliefs, both sons faced their share of misfortune on the battlefield. At the Battle of Chickamauga, Thomas's Union troops were overrun, and he was removed from command for ineptitude. He was brought up on charges, and though he was ultimately acquitted, he was demoted and transferred to the Army of the Potomac. He soon resigned and returned to civilian life, where he served as the state treasurer of Kentucky.

The elder son fared no better in the Confederate army. George fought in only one major skirmish, the Battle of Mill Springs, where his forces were outflanked and he was soundly defeated. He was accused of being drunk during the attack and was almost court-martialed on the spot. But, since the Confederate army was in such dire need of soldiers, he was allowed to continue serving.

On April 1, 1862, however, George was discovered drunk on duty, with his troops in complete disarray. He was arrested, court-martialed, and after being forced to give up his command, demoted to colonel. He resigned instead but continued to serve quietly in a supporting role under General John S. Williams. After the end of the war, he worked as Kentucky's state librarian.

An End for Crittenden

John J. Crittenden continued to work for reunification until the day he died. After the Senate, he joined the Unionist party and represented Kentucky in the House of Representatives. There, he spoke out against the Emancipation Proclamation and confiscation acts, which he argued created greater conflict. He died while campaigning for reelection in 1863. Crittenden didn't live to see the reunification of the nation, but he would be renowned for his unsuccessful attempts to prevent the war, both on the battlefield and in his home.

A SINGULAR WOMAN

★ ★ ★ ★

Mary Walker received a Congressional Medal of Honor, had it revoked, and then got it back posthumously. She never wavered in her belief that she'd earned it.

Only one woman has received the Congressional Medal of Honor—Dr. Mary Walker, in 1866. A medical doctor, she insisted her skills matched those of any male physician, but the army refused to accept her as a surgeon. She signed on as a nurse, working her way up to assistant surgeon for an Ohio regiment.

Experiences in War

Working as a battlefield doctor, Walker was captured by the Confederates and held for four months. After the war, she felt she deserved some recognition. Since she was civilian medical personnel, there were only a limited number of official honors available to her, so she lobbied Congress for a Medal of Honor. Her citation was longer than most, explaining that she partly received the medal because, "by reason of her not being a commissioned officer in the military service, a brevet or honorary rank cannot, under existing laws, be conferred upon her." Uncertain of what honor they could legally bestow, Congress decided to give her this one.

Taken Back

Around the time of World War I, Congress changed the rules for the Medal of Honor to strictly recognize valor in combat by military personnel. The medal had been handed out casually, and Congress decided to rescind more than 900. Although a battlefield doctor, Walker wasn't military and never experienced combat, so the government asked for the medal back. She refused and broke the law by publicly wearing her no-longer-valid medal. She died two years later in 1919, the medal still in her possession. After a few decades, her relatives lobbied for the medal to be restored, and in 1977 President Jimmy Carter signed legislation reinstating it.

Fast Facts

- Enfilade *was the action when a battery succeeded in firing upon the length of an enemy body.*

- *Major Albert James developed the "wig-wag" signaling system that used flags by day and torches by night, after observing American Indian smoke signals and sign language during his service as a surgeon in the Indian Wars of the 1850s. He was advocating the adoption of his system by the Army when the Civil War began. The system became important as a lot of battlefield signaling involved flags and torches rather than telegraph operators.*

- *In the years leading up to the war, the U.S. Army was primarily comprised of and led by battle-tested Southerners. These soldiers defected to the Confederate cause in 1861, which gave the rebels an immediate advantage in leadership and trained soldiers.*

- *When 2,989 slaves of the District of Columbia were freed by act of Congress in 1862, $1 million was appropriated to compensate their owners.*

- *The British-built Confederate cruiser* Alabama, *which captured more than two dozen Union merchant ships, never entered an American port, refueling instead in far-flung places such as Singapore.*

- *Lee and Grant served together in the Mexican War, but not actually side-by-side.*

- *The bedridden Mrs. Judith Henry refused to leave her house during the First Battle of Bull Run and was accidentally killed by a bullet intended for a sniper. She was the first female casualty of an all-out Civil War battle.*

SPIES FOR DIXIE

★ ★ ★ ★

Though it lacked many of the resources that the North possessed,
the South had a healthy stable of spies during the Civil War.

The Socialite Spy

Although she was already in her mid-40s by the time the Civil
War erupted, Rose O'Neal Greenhow—a seductive Washington
socialite and widow—used her wiles to keep Confederates
informed of Northern movements.

Before the war, she had been known to entertain international
diplomats and members of Congress, and she had been close to
President James Buchanan. But when the South started to secede,
her Southern sympathies prevailed, and soon she was enlisted to
collect covert intelligence for the new Southern government.
Befriending Colonel E. D. Keyes—who just happened to be the
secretary to Union General-in-Chief Winfield Scott—Greenhow
gained information that led directly to the Southern victory in the
first major action of the war, the First Battle of Bull Run, in July
1861. For her efforts, officials in Richmond sent her a personal
note of thanks.

In January 1862, Greenhow was arrested as a spy and, after a few
months of house arrest, sent to Old Capitol Prison in Washington,
D.C. Even from jail, however, she continued to collect Union secrets
and pass them to the Confederates, hiding messages in a ball of yarn
or a visitor's hair bun to transport the precious information.

Released in exchange for Union prisoners, Greenhow was exiled
to the Confederacy and arrived in Richmond in June to a hero's
welcome. Confederate President Davis personally received her
party upon its arrival. But now that she was known in the North,
her career as a spy in America was over. Davis sent Greenhow to
Europe, where she sought political and financial support for the
Confederacy.

In September 1864, Greenhow was returning to America aboard the blockade runner *Condor.* During a fierce storm, the *Condor* was pursued by a Northern ship and ran aground. Greenhow tried to escape by rowboat but was thrown overboard. Weighed down by more than $2,000 in gold, Greenhow drowned. Her body later washed ashore, and she was buried with full military honors in Wilmington, North Carolina.

The Covert Chaplain

Thomas N. Conrad was one of the Confederacy's most ambitious and effective spies. His initial plans included assassinating Union General-in-Chief Winfield Scott and kidnapping President Lincoln.

Prior to the war, Conrad had been headmaster at Georgetown College in Washington, D.C., but his enthusiasm for the South proved to be too much: He was arrested in June 1861 when he had "Dixie" played as the graduation's processional march. Upon his release, he signed up as a chaplain with General Jeb Stuart's Confederate troops in Virginia. As a man of the cloth, Conrad easily made his way into Union territory, where he was able to garner Union strategies and plans.

As the war wound down, Conrad returned to Washington, where he changed his hairstyle and shaved his beard. It was a look that made him a dead-ringer for John Wilkes Booth; in fact, Conrad was mistaken for Booth and briefly arrested for Lincoln's assassination.

Conrad returned to the academic world after the war, teaching at Rockville Academy in Maryland and at Virginia A & M, becoming president there in 1881. He recorded his adventures in his memoir, *The Rebel Scout,* and died in 1905.

A Confederate Charmer

As a courier for Rose O'Neal Greenhow, Antonia Ford held many parties for Union officers and soldiers at her home in Fairfax Court House, Virginia. Ever the socialite, she would charm her guests, who didn't realize she was collecting military information for the Confederates.

She became a favorite resource for General Stuart and was named an honorary *aide-de-camp.* She also provided Colonel John Mosby and his rangers with timely information that led to the kidnapping of Union General Edwin H. Stoughton in March 1863. Her luck couldn't last, however, and Ford accidentally blew her cover to a member of Pinkerton's Agency. She was arrested only days later.

A charmer to the end, Ford became involved with her Union jailor in the Old Capitol Prison, Major Joseph Willard. He proposed, they married, and she signed a Union loyalty oath in 1864. Prison life had made its mark on Ford, however, leaving her sickly and weak. She died in 1871 at age 33.

The Squirrel Hill Spy

Laura Ratcliffe was also a valuable aide to Colonel John Mosby and his rangers, who often used her home in Squirrel Hill, Pennsylvania, for clandestine meetings. Ratcliffe allowed Mosby to use a large rock there as a rendezvous where Confederates could exchange messages and keep money taken from Union plunder.

Ratcliffe was active in Confederate espionage throughout the war but was never caught. Later in life, she married a Union veteran named Milton Hanna. When she passed away in 1923, Ratcliffe's wake was set up in the front window of her house. Hundreds of people showed up to pay their last respects.

"I see the President almost every day. I see very plainly Abraham Lincoln's dark brown face with its deep-cut lines, the eyes always to me with a deep latent sadness in the expression. None of the artists or pictures has caught the deep, though subtle and indirect expression of this man's face. There is something else there. One of the great portrait painters of two or three centuries ago is needed."
Walt Whitman

CHARITY BEGINS

★ ★ ★ ★

*Civilians on the Union home front gave freely to help soldiers
and the war. But all that generosity needed some organization.*

Throughout the North, local groups raised money and gathered
donations of clothing, food, and other items for soldiers. Pennsylvania had its state agency, for instance, while the Michigan Soldiers'
Relief Association aided soldiers from that state. The single largest
Union relief agency was the U.S. Sanitary Commission, formed in
June 1861 to impose order on all this unorganized benevolence.

Volunteers

From offices across the North, women volunteers funneled donations to Sanitary Commission warehouses for distribution to soldiers. Throughout the war, the commission distributed more than
$25 million in aid. Commission wagon trains followed the armies
and arrived on battlefields as soon as possible to bring medical
supplies and food to wounded soldiers and their surgeons. When
the army couldn't take its wounded to safety, volunteers staffed
hospital boats, railroad cars, and wagons to do it themselves.

Improving Medicine

Although initially opposed by President Lincoln and his Cabinet, the
Sanitary Commission eventually converted doubters into believers.
But its reports embarrassed the Army, particularly in the area of
medicine. To help hard-pressed surgeons improve their care, the
commission's medical experts compiled booklets on a wide range of
topics—scurvy, dysentery, amputation, and more. As a result of commission pressure, the Army replaced aged Surgeon General Clement
A. Finley and grudgingly began reforming the medical department.

A Little R & R

The commission also established "soldiers' homes" as lodging for
troops in transit. One of the best known was the Cooper Shop

Volunteer Refreshment Saloon in Philadelphia. Until it closed in July 1865, the Cooper Shop facility dispensed more than 800,000 meals to regiments passing through. It also provided medical service, washrooms, paper and stamps, and a laundry room.

Raising Money

By October 1862, the U.S. Sanitary Commission was in dire need of money to continue its relief efforts. Without new support, the privately funded civilian aid society would have to consider disbanding.

In response, commission members Mary Livermore and Jane Hoge of Chicago had the idea of a sanitary fair to display relics of battle and war mementos to raise money for charity. Some of these mementos might even go up for sale. The women solicited goods through newspaper ads and church bulletins, offering a gold watch for the largest contribution. In all, they hoped to raise about $25,000.

At the Fair

Their effort to gather items was quite fruitful, and in Chicago in 1863, schools, businesses, and courts shut down for the event. Exhibition halls were filled with captured battle flags, farm machinery, and art. A huge success, the sanitary fair averaged more than 5,000 spectators a day for 20 days at 75 cents admission. Organizers were flooded with donations. By the end of the spectacle, they'd netted not just $25,000, but close to $100,000. President Lincoln won the gold watch for donating his copy of the Emancipation Proclamation, which was auctioned for $3,000. "I had some desire to retain the paper," he admitted, "but if it shall contribute to the relief and comfort of the soldiers, that will be better."

Due to its success, the sanitary fair in Chicago became a model for similar fund-raisers held in cities and small towns throughout the North. The largest fair was held in New York City in the spring of 1864 and raised more than $1 million. By the end of the war, sanitary fairs had generated nearly $5 million in donations.

All in all, the relief drive led by the U.S. Sanitary Commission aroused patriotism, kept up soldier morale, and helped unify the Northern populace behind the war effort.

NOT MUCH TO BRAGG ABOUT

★ ★ ★ ★

This most despised of Confederate generals
was one of the most ineffective, as well.

Irritable, temperamental, and highly contentious, the hard-driving Braxton Bragg routinely antagonized his officers and alienated his troops. He never listened to the constructive advice of others, and he routinely blamed his blunders on everyone else. He was quick to execute soldiers who didn't meet his standards of discipline. Meanwhile, many officers openly rebelled against the Confederate general, his personality, and his erratic decision making. General Nathan Bedford Forrest in particular minced no words. He told Bragg: "I have stood your meanness as long as I intend to. You have played the part of a damned scoundrel.... If you ever again try to interfere with me or cross my path it will be at the peril of your life."

No Winning Record

Some generals, though they lose popularity contests in the ranks, still manage to win battles on the field. That group doesn't include the spindly, frizzy-haired Bragg. Historians put the number of his battle victories at exactly one. Bragg's sole success occurred at Chickamauga, Georgia, in September 1863, when General James Longstreet's corps poured through a hole in the Union line. Bragg failed to turn that victory into the rout that it could have been when he allowed the Federals to retreat to Chattanooga. That misstep later cost the general and his Confederates dearly when the surrounded Union army broke out of Chattanooga and soundly defeated Bragg in one of the most pivotal battles of the war. Bragg's losses and strategic failures would also include Pensacola, Corinth, Perryville, Stones River, Dalton, and finally Wilmington in 1865.

Bragg wasn't totally lacking in good qualities. In addition to being a highly organized administrator, he apparently possessed some level of self-awareness. In a letter to Confederate President Jefferson Davis regarding Chattanooga, Bragg admitted, "I fear we both erred in the conclusion for me to retain command here after the clamor raised against me."

Friends in High Places

The general's biggest problem may have been that Davis himself was his only friend. The President always stood by his friends, no matter what level of competence they may have displayed. Thus, when he finally removed Bragg from his position as commander of the Army of Tennessee, Davis made the fatal mistake of appointing the general to be his military advisor. Bragg suggested nothing to Davis that would work. Later, put back in the field to stop General Sherman's army in North Carolina toward the end of the war, Bragg failed again. He drew vital reinforcements from where they were desperately needed by rebel General Joseph Johnston at the Battle of Bentonville. It would be the last time he was used in the war—and even he couldn't argue with that.

"We are not only fighting hostile armies, but a hostile people, and must make old and young, rich and poor, feel the hard hand of war, as well as their organized armies. I know that this recent movement of mine through Georgia has had a wonderful effect in this respect. Thousands who had been deceived by their lying papers in the belief that we were being whipped all the time, realized the truth, and have no appetite for a repetition of the same experience.... Many and many a person in Georgia asked me why we did not go to South Carolina, and when I answered that I was en route for that State the invariable reply was, 'Well, if you will make those people feel the severities of war, we will pardon you for your desolation of Georgia.'"

General William Tecumseh Sherman, in a letter to General Henry Halleck after his March to the Sea

THE CONFEDERACY'S HIGH-WATER MARK

★ ★ ★ ★

The sleepy Pennsylvania town of Gettysburg found itself in the biggest battle of the Civil War.

General Lee was on a roll in the summer of 1863. He'd taken his army north of the Mason-Dixon Line and was looking to make the North feel the bite of war. His preliminary target was Pennsylvania's state capital, Harrisburg. If he knocked out the rail line at Harrisburg, he thought it would be possible to advance on to Philadelphia and maybe even Baltimore or Washington D.C. These kinds of large successes could bring about much-needed international recognition.

Gettysburg was a drowsy, rural Pennsylvania town of 2,400 on the way to Harrisburg. No one—North or South—intended to fight there, but when the Union and Confederate armies clashed, it turned out to be the biggest battle of the war—with a combined total of 50,000 soldiers killed, wounded, or missing. It also marked the Confederates' last push into the North.

Scrounging for Supplies

Gettysburg was a crossroads village with five large roads meeting in the middle, and many Confederate soldiers went there looking for food and clothes. According to an account written by Tillie Pierce, a schoolgirl who lived in Gettysburg and witnessed the battle, the rebels burst into town on Friday, June 26:

"They wanted horses, clothing, anything and almost everything they could conveniently carry away.

"Nor were they particular about asking. Whatever suited them they took. They did, however, make a formal demand of the town authorities, for a large supply of flour, meat, groceries, shoes, hats, and (doubtless, not least in their estimations), [*sic*] ten barrels of whisky; or, in lieu of this, five thousand dollars."

The Rebels Were Not Alone

While the Confederates scavenged, some of them discovered that a division of Union cavalry, under General John Buford, occupied a ridge near the town. General Lee heard the news and decided that maybe little Gettysburg would be a good place to test federal strength in the area.

An Accidental Start

The battle began on July 1 at 5:30 A.M. when two divisions of Lee's troops met Buford's at Marsh Creek, about two miles west of Gettysburg. Buford's soldiers fought well, so Lee brought in more troops. Soon a full-fledged battle was underway.

Confederates overpowered Union soldiers late in the day, and the Federals retreated through Gettysburg. The quaint town square flooded with bluecoats being chased by rebels. Buford had anticipated the retreat and already had defensive positions set up on ridgelines to the east and south of town. His troops reached these positions and hunkered down. By this time, Union reinforcements were pouring in, and Buford's superiors became involved.

General George Meade had been given command of the Union Army of the Potomac just three days earlier, but he was a talented leader. He built his defenses in a pattern resembling a giant fishhook, which extended roughly along the eastern and southern edges of Gettysburg. It was all high ground—an excellent defensive position.

Lee Presses His Advantage

The next day General Lee wanted to capitalize on the previous day's success by attacking Union lines. It was a risky tactical call, though, because by then the Yankees were well entrenched. Lee decided to attack at both their southern and northern ends.

On the south, Union General Daniel Sickles was unhappy with the position Meade had given him to guard, so he disobeyed orders and moved his force about half a mile ahead of the rest of the line, to a peach orchard on high ground. Confederate General James Longstreet attacked there, and after furious fighting, Sickles' line collapsed. Fortunately though, Union reinforcements held a key high point behind Sickles's line called Little Round Top, and they fought off the Confederate attack.

On the north, Confederate General Richard Ewell didn't attack until much later in the day—after Longstreet's attack on the south end—and was repulsed at Culp's Hill.

Day Three

On the next day of battle, Lee expected that the middle of the "fishhook" would be lightly defended, assuming the Union had sent reinforcements to the battles on either end the previous day. Confederate cannons—140 of them—bombarded the center of the Union lines. Once the smoke cleared, Lee sent 12,000 soldiers, spread a mile wide, on a mile-long charge to the center he hoped had been weakened even further. Although three divisions led by three different generals took part in the assault, the operation took the name of only one—George Pickett—and has become infamous as "Pickett's Charge."

Unfortunately for the rebel troops, Lee's assumption about the weakness in the middle of the federal line was wrong. In fact, it was heavily reinforced, and the artillery barrage had hardly touched it. Pickett's Charge turned into a slaughter. The Confederates had little cover as they marched toward the Union lines, and the well-entrenched Yankees poured lead onto them. In half an hour, nearly half the charging Confederates were dead or wounded.

The Battle of Gettysburg essentially ended here. Lee retreated toward Virginia, and the Union forces licked their wounds. Several months later, President Lincoln visited the site and delivered his most famous speech, the Gettysburg Address, reminding citizens that they were fighting so their "government of the people, by the people, for the people, shall not perish from the earth." These three bloody days in July 1863 forever transformed the quiet farm town of Gettysburg into a focal point of America's struggle to remain united.

Fast Facts

- An estimated 200,000 blacks served in the Union army and Union navy.

- Charles Francis Adams, U.S. Minister to Great Britain and son of John Quincy Adams, helped prevent Britain from entering the war on the side of the Confederacy. With his son Henry, he also monitored the construction of rebel ships in British shipyards to keep Washington up-to-date on any developments and new activity. In 1870, he built the first presidential library in the United States to honor his father.

- Naval personnel used the cutlass sword in hand-to-hand combat because it was good in close quarters and required very little training.

- Pennsylvania's Quakers, Mennonites, and Dunkards refused to serve for reasons of conscience—generally religious convictions. The Pennsylvania legislature was drafting legislation to allow them to avoid service through payment of a commutation fee when the federal government passed the Enrollment Act of 1863. The act did not allow exemption specifically for religious reasons, but a draftee could either provide a substitute or pay a $300 commutation fee.

- Coffee cooler was a northern term for a worthless soldier.

- After the war, Robert E. Lee became the president of Washington College for an annual salary of $1,500. After his death, the college was renamed Washington and Lee.

- General McClellan was twice fired from his command by Lincoln, and he ran for president against Lincoln in 1864 but lost. Lincoln received 212 of 233 electoral votes and 55 percent of the popular vote.

RUNNING THE BLOCKADE

★ ★ ★ ★

When President Lincoln set out to put an end to Southern trade,
blockade running kept the Confederate economy alive.

After the attack on Fort Sumter, President Lincoln moved quickly
to choke off Southern trade in the Atlantic and the Gulf of Mexico. He believed that if he could blockade Confederate ports and
shut down the Southern economy, he could put a speedy end to
the rebellion. The catch was that this plan required a navy, and the
Union had only a few ships at its disposal: just 27 steamships and
44 sailing vessels to guard 3,350 miles of Confederate coastline.

While the North borrowed, built, or bought any ship it could, the
South, realizing trade meant survival, did what it could to slip
through the noose. It wasn't long before mariners stepped forward to
take up the challenge of sneaking in and out of ports such as Galveston, Texas; Mobile, Alabama; and Wilmington, North Carolina.

The Business of Running

While a few blockade runners were commissioned by the Confederate government, most of the ships were owned by their captains
or by syndicates of rich merchants. The most successful captains
were often former officers of the U.S. Navy.

Because the South didn't have a manufacturing base, many of the
runners were built in England. Their specifications combined the
perfect mix of characteristics for a fast ship, sacrificing seaworthi-
ness for speed and mobility. The *Banshee* was a prime example of
this: A length of 214 feet and a width of only 20 feet allowed the
ship to slice through the water. Burning hard Welsh anthracite coal
so it wouldn't make smoke (most Southern mines brought up soft
bituminous coal that left a telltale cloud behind the ship), the *Banshee* could move at speeds as fast as 18 knots, or 20.7 miles per hour.
The ship had telescoping stacks to lower its silhouette and was
painted a dull gray, one of the first instances of naval camouflage.

Cotton Currency

The Southern economy relied on supplying Europe with cotton. Blockade runners would be piled high with baled cotton for a dash to Bermuda or the Bahamas. There the cargo would be traded for Southern necessities, and the runner would speed back to any open Confederate port on the railroad, where those goods would be sold for a huge profit. As long as the system worked, everyone got rich. A captain could make $5,000 for one voyage, and even common sailors were paid $250, a fortune in the 1860s. But due to inflation, prices for goods shot up higher and higher as the blockade tightened. By 1864, it cost $300 Confederate for a barrel of flour and $40 Confederate for a pound of coffee.

While blockade-runner captains such as John Maffitt of the *Cecile* or John Wilkinson of the *R. E. Lee* were patriots who carried only goods the Confederacy needed, others brought in luxury items such as European liquors and linens. Maffitt went on to captain the commerce raider CSS *Florida,* which captured 23 Union merchant ships, or "prizes," as they were called. Wilkinson captained the CSS *Chickamauga,* another raider of Union commerce.

Northern Incentives

Union sailors on the blockade line made only $16 per month, but they could also receive prize money for captured blockade runners and their cargoes, which were auctioned off at prize courts. As the Union navy grew from 264 ships by the end of 1861 to 588 ships by the end of 1863, more and more Southern runners were being captured. Not only were there more Union ships, but they were faster, with more experienced crews. As the Union armies worked their way through the South, fewer and fewer ports were left open to the Confederacy.

By early 1865, the Union took control of the last Confederate port, the one where it had all started— Charleston, South Carolina—and the days of blockade running were over. The *Banshee* was already long gone, captured on her ninth trip in 1863 and added to the Union blockade fleet.

REMEMBERING THE WAR

★ ★ ★ ★

Heartfelt memorials, monuments, and museums devoted to the Civil War dot the United States. Here are a few that stand out.

Most Likely to Test Your Counting Skills
The Carter House
Franklin, Tennessee
Situated on the site of the Battle of Franklin, the Carter House is known as the House with 1,000 Civil War Bullet Holes. Located in central Tennessee, the house is a museum dedicated to the 1864 battle. Now visitors can count the bullet holes for themselves as well as take part in periodic candlelight tours, children's camps, and even an annual reunion of descendants of the soldiers who fought in the battle.

Least Likely to Move
John Brown Wax Museum   *American Civil War Museum*
Harpers Ferry, West Virginia   *Gettysburg, Pennsylvania*
Wax museums have their particular appeal, and it could be said that the John Brown Wax Museum and American Civil War Museum capture history standing still. The Brown Museum reproduces in wax the abolitionist raid that was a major catalyst leading to the war. The American Civil War Museum takes a wider approach, re-creating moments from the war and events that surrounded it, such as the Underground Railroad, the Battle of Gettysburg, and Lincoln's assassination.

Westernmost Battle
Drum Barracks Civil War Museum
Wilmington, California
The Battle of Picacho Pass is considered the westernmost battle of the Civil War, and it is recognized by Drum Barracks Civil War Museum in Wilmington, California. The battle was fought between members of the California Column—Union soldiers based out of Camp Drum—and Confederates from Texas at a site

located between modern-day Tucson and Phoenix, Arizona. Marching east from Wilmington to secure control of the New Mexico territory, the California soldiers fought the Confederates to a draw, losing three of their own. The museum also shows what life was like for soldiers at Camp Drum during the Civil War.

Most Likely to Take Your Breath Away
The Blandford Church and Cemetery
Petersburg, Virginia
Originally built in 1735, the Blandford Church and Cemetery is a stained-glass-lover's paradise. Restored in 1901, 15 memorial stained-glass windows—including one featuring the Confederate flag—were commissioned from Louis Comfort Tiffany's world-famous studio. The cemetery contains graves of more than 30,000 fallen Confederate soldiers. Daily tours are offered, and the chapel is a popular place for weddings.

Most Enlightening
Antietam Memorial Illumination
Antietam National Battlefield, Maryland
Occurring annually on the first Saturday in December, the Antietam Memorial Illumination features more than 23,000 candles—one for each soldier killed, wounded, or missing in action—in the battlefield to commemorate those lost during the bloodiest single day of the Civil War. The event also features reenactments. It is one of the nation's most emotional memorials to the war.

Remembering the Journalists
Correspondents Memorial Arch
Gathland State Park, Maryland
Barely in his 20s, George Alfred Townsend, known by the pen name "Gath," was the youngest journalist to cover the war. Following the conflict, Townsend built a memorial to his fellow correspondents who risked their lives. The Correspondents Arch near Burkittsville, Maryland, is a 50-foot-tall structure that looks more like the wall of a fallen castle than a memorial. Now run by the state of Maryland, it contains the names of 157 correspondents and artists who told tales of the war.

Smallest National Cemetery
Battleground National Cemetery
Washington, D.C.

One acre in size, the Battleground National Cemetery ranks as one of the country's smallest national cemeteries. Created after General Jubal A. Early's attacks on Washington, D.C., in 1864, the cemetery was dedicated by Abraham Lincoln. There are 41 Union soldiers buried within the graveyard, which is watched over by memorials to the units who fought at the Battle of Fort Stevens and by two six-pounder, smoothbore Civil War cannons.

Most Likely to Give You a Crick in the Neck
Atlanta Cyclorama
Atlanta, Georgia

On display since 1893, the Atlanta Cyclorama holds the record as the largest oil painting in the world. Cycloramas have been described as the "movies of the 1800s," and one look at this will reveal why. Telling the story of the Battle of Atlanta, the 360-degree painting measures 42 feet high and 358 feet around. Guided tours are available to explain every part of the painting, which is on permanent display in Atlanta after touring the nation in the late 19th and early 20th centuries.

Strangest Memorial to a Body Part
Ellwood Manor
Fredericksburg and Spotsylvania National Military Park, Virginia

Felled by three bullets at the Battle of Chancellorsville, General Stonewall Jackson was taken away from the fight to be treated for his wounds. Although his left arm was amputated in an attempt to save his life, the general died of complications from pneumonia. While his body eventually came to rest in the Stonewall Jackson Memorial Cemetery in Lexington, Virginia, his amputated arm is not with it. Instead, shortly after it was amputated, the arm was buried by Jackson's chaplain, Reverend Beverly Tucker Lacy, in the family cemetery next to his brother's house in Spotsylvania County. A marker still stands in that cemetery, adorned with the words, "Arm of Stonewall Jackson—May 3, 1863."

NO TIME FOR R & R

★ ★ ★ ★

Civil War soldiers had to be ready to fight at any moment—
no matter what else they were doing!

On July 28, 1863, the Confederate volunteer 24th North Carolina Company B had been ordered to Weldon, North Carolina, to defend an important railroad bridge. The Confederate and Union forces in the region had fought each other on and off since early July with neither side gaining an advantage.

In a way, Company B, raised and first mustered at Weldon, was returning home. As the soldiers moved along the road to their positions at the Weldon railroad bridge, they passed the old grist-mill and pond at Boone's Mill. The mill was likely well known to many in Company B. They probably remembered its cool and secluded pond as a refuge in the heat of the Carolina summer.

A Nice, Relaxing Swim

Experiencing a lull in the fighting, the company commander let the troops relax and indulge themselves with a rare wartime treat—leisurely bathing in a pond. The soldiers eagerly stripped off their uniforms, discarded their weapons, and entered the water.

While the group was enjoying the pond, a Union cavalry unit headed along the road to capture—and possibly destroy—the vital Confederate railroad bridge. So the Confederates faced a few immediate problems. They were stark naked, and their weapons and gear were scattered along the pond's edge. The Union cavalry, bearing down on the pond, were ready to engage. When the two groups met, both sides likely had to overcome quite a surprise.

A brief but savage battle erupted. Once the Confederates recovered their wits and enough of their equipment, they delivered a fierce resistance to the larger Union force. The Union cavalry were driven off, and the security of the Weldon bridge was preserved.

SO THEY SAID

"For a mile up and down the open fields before us the splendid lines of the veterans of the Army of Northern Virginia swept down upon us. Their bearing was magnificent.... They came forward with a rush.... How our men did yell, 'Come on, Johnny, come on.'"

Lieutenant Colonel Rufus R. Dawes, 6th Wisconsin, The Iron Brigade, on the first day of Gettysburg

"Well, it is all over now. The battle is lost, and many of us are prisoners, many are dead, many wounded, bleeding and dying. Your Soldier lives and mourns and but for you, my darling, he would rather, a million times rather, be back there with his dead, to sleep for all time in an unknown grave."

Confederate General George Pickett, in a letter to his fiancée after Pickett's Charge at Gettysburg

★ ★ ★ ★

"It is believed that the enemy suffered severely in these operations, but our own loss has not been light.

"General Barksdale is killed. Generals Garnett and Armistead are missing, and it is feared that the former is killed and the latter wounded and a prisoner. Generals Pender and Trimble are wounded in the leg, General Hood in the arm, and General Heth slightly in the head. General Kemper, it is feared, is mortally wounded. Our losses embrace many other valuable officers and men.

"General Wade Hampton was severely wounded in a different action in which the cavalry was engaged yesterday."

General Lee, in a letter to Jefferson Davis after Gettysburg

WARHORSES—LITERALLY

★ ★ ★ ★

*Horses were critical on Civil War battlefields, and
more than a million gave up their lives for the cause.*

More than a million horses and mules perished
during the war. Horses went through rigor-
ous training to prepare for battle. In something like equine boot camps, they were
taught simple commands, as well as strategies
for protecting their riders under fire. A trained
horse could drop to the ground to shield its rider
from machine-gun fire and provide cover from
where the soldier could return fire. Acting as a shield, of
course, put horses directly into the line of fire.

Horse Heroes

Some horses achieved a level of fame on a par with their human
officers. General Lee's mount, Traveler, was well known for his
stamina and bravery. After the war, people seeing Lee ride by
would pluck hairs from Traveler's tail to have a memento of the
honored veteran. Union General George Meade's horse, Old Baldy,
was a powerful and stubborn steed that accompanied him in his
victory at Gettysburg. Old Baldy took plenty of fire—he is said to
have been wounded as many as 14 times. Despite the beating he
took through those years, he lived to the ripe old age of 30, outliv-
ing his master. Today, his mounted head is on display at the Civil
War and Underground Railroad Museum of Philadelphia.

Equine Value

The Union army bought horses in bulk, but in the Confederacy,
many soldiers had to bring their own, for which they were paid
40 cents a day. At the end of the war, Lee asked Grant to allow
defeated soldiers to keep their horses to help plant crops at home.
Grant didn't hesitate to agree.

INTRIGUE ALONG THE CALIFORNIA COAST

★ ★ ★ ★

*The west coast of the United States saw some action
when the commander of an old Mexican War sloop
saved the day and foiled a Confederate plot.*

 While the majority of fighting during the
Civil War took place in the settled, eastern
half of the country, the far-flung western
territories weren't completely ignored. California had been a state only since 1850, and
travel across the prairies and mountains to
the west coast was dangerous and time consuming. But Secretary
of the Navy Gideon Welles feared the damage that could be done
to the remote ports and cities of the area by an enterprising Confederate ship. He made an effort to base a substantial fleet in the
Pacific to protect American interests from Confederate raiders
and foreign interlopers. The fleet he cobbled together was not
exactly a fearsome force, however. With much of the Navy tied up
enforcing the blockade of Southern ports, the best he could do for
the Pacific was six wooden sloops with inadequate cannons. They
were old ships, past their prime and with several decades of service among them, but Welles felt there was no choice but to trust
them with a scope of service that stretched from Alaska to
Panama.

Super *Cyane*

The most illustrious ship in the Pacific Squadron was a creaky, 25-
year-old sloop called the USS *Cyane.* Sporting 22 guns and plenty
of scars from battles with enemy ships during the Mexican War of
the 1840s, the *Cyane* didn't let its age show. It became involved in
one of the more exciting engagements of the typically quiet Pacific
Theater.

The main duty for the Pacific Squadron was to protect the vital shipments of mail and gold that traveled through the region, a custodial duty that rarely involved any actual shows of force. In the spring of 1863, however, a mariner named E. W. Travers uncovered a bold and ambitious plot aimed at those gold transports. He informed the commander of the *Cyane*, Lieutenant Commander Paul Shirley, of what was to come. On orders from Confederate President Jefferson Davis, a wealthy rebel named Asbury Harpending was funding the launch of a vessel, the *J. M. Chapman*, that was intended to wreak havoc on the California gold shipments that were keeping the Union economy afloat. The *Chapman*'s first sailing target would be the *Golden Gate*, which carried a cargo of $2 million. Shirley was concerned because he knew the *Chapman* was swifter and younger than the *Cyane*. He was afraid that launching a direct assault on the boat would result in failure, so he set out to devise a plan that would foil the *Chapman*'s nefarious intentions.

Foiled Plot

Working with the information provided by Travers, Shirley was able to ascertain that the *Chapman* would be launching from San Francisco, so he enlisted that city's police force in staging an elaborate sting. On March 15, 1863, the *Cyane* coolly pulled into San Francisco harbor as the local police stationed themselves along the wharf. The crew of the *Chapman* was far too excited about their own plot to notice the activity around them, and they continued to load their ship with supplies. When the *Chapman* finally began to depart, sailors from the *Cyane* rowed up in boats and ordered the Confederates to halt. The rebels had only made it 300 yards away from the dock.

In addition to orchestrating a bloodless capture of an enemy ship, Shirley discovered 16 commandos hidden below decks with guns and knives as well as documentary proof that they planned to commit treason against the Union. Harpending and his coconspirators were sent to Alcatraz, where they sat out the rest of the war. The Pacific Squadron, though old and weathered, had proved its worth in achieving the safety and security of the nation.

Fast Facts

- General Daniel Sickles of New York, whose military career ended with the loss of a leg at the Battle of Gettysburg, sponsored congressional legislation in 1895 that created Gettysburg National Military Park.

- In 1862, the New England Freedmen's Aid Society began a school to educate newly liberated blacks in South Carolina.

- Massachusetts Governor John Albion Andrew formed some of the first black regiments, including the famed 54th and 55th Infantry units.

- General Phil Kearney is credited with devising the U.S. Army's first unit insignia patches. In order to identify officers as members of his unit, he issued an order in the summer of 1862 that they should wear a patch of red cloth on the front of their caps. Enlisted soldiers, proud of their association with the popular Kearney, quickly followed suit. Other units began to devise their own insignia, which over time evolved into the modern shoulder patch. Daniel Butterfield, credited as the creator of "Taps," is also credited with taking Kearney's idea and standardizing it for all of the Army of the Potomac corps, as well as with designing most of the corps badges.

- Old Abe, a pet eagle, became the mascot of the 8th Wisconsin Infantry Regiment. During battles the eagle would spread its wings and scream. Old Abe served in 42 skirmishes and battles and lived after the war until 1881.

- Sam Houston was ousted from his post as governor of Texas in 1861 because he refused to back his state's vote in favor of secession. His son, Sam Houston, Jr., was wounded fighting with the Second Texas Infantry of the Confederate army at the Battle of Shiloh.

BELLE BOYD,
CONFEDERATE SPY

★ ★ ★ ★

*After killing a soldier at the young age of 17, Belle Boyd
embarked on a career as a Confederate spy but ended
up falling in love with one of the enemy.*

In February 1865, President Lincoln received a letter from a 21-year-old woman in London asking a favor. The sender was Belle Boyd, the Southern spy also known as "Le Belle Rebelle" and "Cleopatra of the Confederacy." She ended her message with "I am Sir, Yr. obdt. Sevt." This from the same woman who once wrote, "If it is a crime to love the South, its cause and its President, then I am a criminal. I would rather lie down in this prison and die than leave it owing allegiance to a government such as yours." Now she was asking the man she'd despised for a personal favor—the release of her new husband, a soldier who'd betrayed the Union and become a blockade runner after falling in love with her.

A Spy Is Born

Boyd first came to the attention of Union officers when she shot and killed a soldier trying to hang a Union flag from her home near Martinsburg, Virginia, in July 1861. Strangely, the 17 year old was scolded but not imprisoned. Perhaps the chivalry of the time influenced the men to deal leniently with the attractive young woman.

Possibly emboldened by effectively getting away with the killing, Boyd soon began carrying information about Union forces to Confederate authorities. She's given credit for providing information helpful to Stonewall Jackson in his successful Shenandoah Valley Campaign in the spring of 1862.

Caught in the Act

Boyd was eventually imprisoned for a short time in the Old Capitol Prison in Washington, D.C. Once released, she was assigned to carry dispatches between the Confederacy and England. On her first trip, however, her ship, the *Greyhound,* was captured by the Union. While in custody, she fell in love with Union Ensign Samuel Hardinge, the officer bringing her ship back to the United States.

A Strange Proposal

During that journey, Hardinge asked Boyd to marry him. While considering his proposal, however, Boyd also arranged the escape of the *Greyhound's* commander, Lieutenant George Henry Bier. As a result, Hardinge was arrested and dismissed from the Navy for neglect of duty. Still in love with Boyd, he followed her to Canada, where she went after arriving back on Union shores. She remained in Canada only a short time before resuming her travels to England. Hardinge followed, and they married in London on August 25, 1864.

Influenced by his new wife, Hardinge decided to risk running the blockade to travel to the Confederacy. Boyd remained behind in England. Now on his own, Hardinge was captured by Federals and imprisoned, which led to Boyd's letter to Lincoln.

A Plea for Help

Low on funds after her husband left, Boyd wrote a memoir, *Belle Boyd in Camp and Prison.* As one might expect, she was critical of the federal government, but she apparently tried to use the book as leverage, telling Lincoln that she would delay its release if her husband were freed. "My book was not originally intended to be more than a personal narrative," she wrote in her letter, "but since my husband's unjust arrest I had intended making it political, & had introduced many atrocious circumstances respecting your Government with which I am so well acquainted & which would open the eyes of Europe to many things of which the world on this side of the water little dreams." Lincoln never answered the letter, but Hardinge was released from prison in February 1865, possibly even before the letter reached its destination. He returned to England but died in 1866, having been weakened during his imprisonment. Boyd eventually returned to America, where she married twice more. She had some success as an actress and raconteur after the war and died of a heart attack in 1900, unrepentant to the end.

RESISTANCE WAS FUTILE

★ ★ ★ ★

In the Civil War, surrendering wasn't always an obvious choice.

Colonel John T. Wilder commanded the Union garrison at Munfordville, Kentucky, in September 1862. Wilder had 2,000 soldiers hunkered down in extensive fortifications—a solid defense. Unfortunately, Braxton Bragg steadily approached with his army.

First Conflict

On September 14, General James R. Chalmers, acting under Bragg's command, requested that Wilder surrender and save his troops pain and trouble. Wilder refused, defiantly responding that Confederate troops could save themselves from a bloody conflict by staying out of range of the Northern guns. Chalmers chose not to follow this advice, but when he attacked, the Union troops stood firm. The Confederates responded by laying siege.

Two days later, rebel General Simon Bolivar Buckner had come on the scene with a larger force and taken command. He knew a major conflict in Munfordville would kill or injure scores of civilians. His thinking wasn't entirely benevolent—he didn't want to undermine or alienate Confederate sympathizers in the border state of Kentucky. So he issued another demand for Wilder's surrender.

Considering His Options

Wilder was concerned about his position and went to see Buckner under a flag of truce. To Buckner's surprise, Wilder asked his advice—if he were in Wilder's shoes, would *he* surrender? The crafty yet courteous Buckner escorted Wilder to see his 25,000 soldiers and the 45 cannons waiting to attack the Union garrison. Yes, he replied, in Wilder's position, he *would* surrender. And so Wilder did just that.

Although Buckner's advice was self-serving, it was probably also quite wise. He had the larger force, and there is little doubt that he would have overwhelmed Wilder's defenses.

(Continued from p. 284)

1863

September 4
A bread riot erupts in Mobile, Alabama.

September 5
Britain detains two unfinished ironclads built for the Confederacy in Liverpool.

September 7
Union soldiers assault the batteries on Morris Island, only to find them abandoned.

September 9
Union troops occupy Chattanooga.

September 10
Union troops occupy Little Rock, Arkansas.

September 19–20
Bragg defeats Rosecrans and his army at the Battle of Chickamauga, Georgia. Rosecrans retreats back to Chattanooga.

October 3
Lincoln issues a proclamation of thanksgiving, to be observed on the last Thursday in November.

October 18
Grant assumes command of the new Military Division of the Mississippi. He replaces General William Rosecrans with General George Thomas as commander of the Army of the Cumberland.

October 23
Grant arrives at Chattanooga.

November 9
Lincoln sees John Wilkes Booth perform in *The Marble Heart* at Ford's Theatre.

November 17–December 4
Longstreet conducts a siege of Knoxville, Tennessee.

November 19
Lincoln attends the dedication of a national cemetery at Gettysburg, Pennsylvania, and delivers his Gettysburg Address.

November 23–25
The Battle of Chattanooga, Tennessee, results in Grant's army pushing Bragg's rebel forces out of the area.

November 30
Braxton Bragg resigns from command of the Army of Tennessee.

December 1
Meade's campaign in Virginia is unsuccessful. He calls it off, and his army establishes winter quarters.

December 3
Although still unfinished, a Union prison camp at Rock Island, Illinois, accepts its first Confederate prisoners.

December 3–4
Longstreet ends his siege of Knoxville, withdrawing his troops to winter quarters.

December 8
Lincoln issues his Proclamation of Amnesty and Reconstruction.

December 27
Joseph E. Johnston assumes command of the Army of Tennessee.

(Continued on p. 349)

THE CONFEDERACY'S BRITISH SHIPYARDS

★ ★ ★ ★

Despite Great Britain's ostensible neutrality during the Civil War, it nevertheless produced many of the Confederacy's war materials, including military and merchant vessels.

British-built vessels dominated the Confederate navy—at least 11 took a devastating toll on Union ships early in the war, sinking or capturing hundreds. Union merchant vessels lost more than $19 million and saw a 900-percent increase in insurance rates. The Union had to withdraw many warships from the blockade of Southern ports to hunt for the commerce raiders.

Achieving Infamy

One of the most famous of these ships was the steam-powered sailing sloop the CSS *Alabama,* launched as the *Enrica* in May 1862 by John Laird Sons and Company of Birkenhead, just across the Mersey River from Liverpool. Although the U.S. ambassador knew it had been paid for with Confederate funds and vigorously protested, the British government allowed the *Enrica* to take a "trial voyage"—from which it failed to return. It soon turned up in the Azores outfitted as a warship and rechristened the CSS *Alabama.* Over the next two years, the *Alabama* sank or captured as many as 69 U.S. merchant ships in the Atlantic and Indian Oceans and successfully ran the blockade at Galveston. It was finally defeated on June 19, 1864, when it was sunk off the coast of France by the USS *Kearsarge.*

In the years after the war, an international court of arbitration found that Great Britain had, in fact, violated its neutrality during the war by allowing these ships to be manufactured for the rebellion. As punishment, the country was ordered to compensate the United States with $15 million in gold.

DELAY BY QUAKER GUNS

★ ★ ★ ★

*A clever Confederate ruse spelled
humiliation for General George McClellan.*

In deciding how best to attack the Confederate capital of Richmond, Virginia, Union General George B. McClellan decided to transport his army by ship to Fort Monroe near Norfolk. From there, they would rapidly march up the Virginia Peninsula and capture Richmond before the Confederates could construct strong defenses. This plan collapsed in part due to a clever ruse: McClellan had been tricked by a small Confederate force using Quaker guns.

On April 4, 1862, McClellan advanced the 24 miles up the peninsula from Fort Monroe to Yorktown, flanked by approximately 50,000 soldiers. Meanwhile, Confederate General John B. Magruder's small force was ordered to hold off the federal army as long as possible while the bulk of the Confederate army, commanded by General Joseph E. Johnston, strengthened the Richmond defenses. Magruder used a series of deceptions to give McClellan the impression that he faced a force twice as large as was really there. It looked as though the area was heavily fortified with plenty of cannons and artillery. In fact, only 17,000 Southern soldiers held the 13 miles of the Yorktown defenses along the Warwick River.

McClellan decided to use siege operations to avoid a direct assault on the "heavily defended" positions. Union engineers constructed field works along the federal line, but it was a month before McClellan felt that he had enough artillery to begin action of any sort.

McClellan finally fired on Yorktown at midnight on May 5. Federals met no resistance in entering the Confederate works. Magruder had fallen back that evening, leaving behind a number of Quaker guns—logs painted black and mounted on wheels to look like cannons. McClellan had easily been deceived, which marked a poor beginning to what would be a disastrous Peninsula Campaign.

Fast Facts

- At the bloody Battle of Chickamauga in Tennessee, the combined casualties numbered about 35,000. Chickamauga is derived from an ancient Cherokee word meaning "River of Death."

- The National Conscription Act on March 3, 1863, instituted a U.S. national draft. Prior to that, the North had relied on volunteers and state militia. The Confederacy passed the first of its three conscription acts the year before in April 1862.

- In 1832, Abraham Lincoln was a militia captain in the Black Hawk War, but he did not see any action.

- Because Petersburg, Virginia, was the supply center for the Confederate capital, its defense was essential to the defense of Richmond. Robert E. Lee defended Petersburg against an unrelenting ten months of trench warfare. Grant's troops constructed trenches that extended for 30 miles around the outskirts of the city.

- Half of the enlisted troops and many of the officers in the Union Army of the Southwest at the Battle of Pea Ridge spoke German as their first language.

- Soldiers helped popularize photography, as they wanted to leave a picture behind or take one with them as they left for the war.

- The fourth ship in the U.S. Navy named the USS Alligator was the first submarine known to be active in the Civil War. Launched as an experimental vessel in 1862, it was lost while under tow and sank in April 1863.

- On February 1, 1865, Illinois became the first state to ratify the 13th Amendment, which abolished slavery.

THE UNEXPECTED TAKES THE DAY

★ ★ ★ ★

Two important military lessons, the unpredictability of combat and the value of capitalizing on unexpected opportunity, came to vivid life at the Battle of Chickamauga.

The two-day Battle of Chickamauga on September 19 and 20, 1863, demonstrated the importance of flexibility in fighting a war. The outcome turned on one Union general who stubbornly followed an order he knew was wrong and one lucky Confederate general who took advantage of the opportunity that unwise move created.

Coming to a Head

By mid-September, Confederate General Braxton Bragg's subordinate generals were so angry that he'd abandoned Tennessee without a fight that they were starting to ignore his direct orders. On September 10 and again on September 13, several of Bragg's generals refused to follow through on attacking isolated parts of Union General William Rosecrans's army in north Georgia. But on the morning of September 19, Bragg's generals were forced to fight when the Union and Confederate armies began leapfrogging units on the north end of the battlefield, each in an attempt to outflank the other side. Both Bragg and Rosecrans ignored their crafted battle plans and threw units into the fray as they were needed. The day ended with both armies drifting to the north but with no advantage over the other.

Confused Orders

Scattered fighting opened the second day of the battle. Through a series of miscommunications and misunderstandings, Rosecrans believed that his solid line of units had a hole in it. Obviously concerned that this gave the Southerners an opening, he ordered

General Thomas Wood's division to move from its spot in the line to fill in the nonexistent gap. A peevish Wood knew he would create a real gap by moving his division, but he followed his orders to the letter. At the same moment, two divisions of General James Longstreet's 1st Corps, which had just arrived on the scene after a nine-day train trip from Virginia, struck in the hole created by Wood.

Longstreet's troops took full advantage of the hole in the Union line, first smashing the smaller part of the Union army to their left and then turning right to roll up the remaining force. Instead of organizing to address the breech, Rosecrans's army panicked, with most of the bluecoats fleeing for Chattanooga. Only the corps of Virginia-born Union General George H. Thomas and a brigade of mounted infantry armed with repeating rifles stayed behind to defend their ground.

The Rock of Chickamauga

Thomas's troops and a force of stragglers and reserves built their defense atop Snodgrass Hill. Their determination held off the Confederates for the rest of the day, not allowing them to chase the retreating Federals. This renowned defense in the face of chaos earned Thomas a nickname that stuck: "The Rock of Chickamauga."

The Battle of Chickamauga resulted in enormous losses on both sides, estimated by some at more than 25 percent. In actual numbers, there were roughly 35,000 casualties in all, which made this battle second only to Gettysburg in bloodshed in 1863. Even allowing for Thomas's defense, General Bragg could have pursued Rosecrans's force and crushed it before the Union had time to set up a defense in Chattanooga, but he did not. If he had taken the offense, he might have been able to shift the balance of power in the Western Theater, but nowadays that's all just idle speculation. Bragg's negligence caused one of his subordinates to call Chickamauga a "barren victory."

ROLLING ON THE RIVER

★ ★ ★ ★

A city's clean-up attempt turns into a less-than-fantastic voyage.

The Civil War was a breeding ground for disease. Horrific battle-field conditions and a lack of sanitation let sickness run wild. For every soldier lost to wounds, two died of illness. And for those who survived those perils, another snare was waiting: venereal disease.

It wasn't enough to warn soldiers not to gratify their lusts, so officers tried to make the means of gratification unavailable. Nashville, Tennessee, for example, had been taken over by the Union army in February 1862, and though the city was a win for the cause, assuming control also meant taking on its problems—specifically, prostitution.

An Immodest Proposal

By July 1863, prostitution was such problem in Nashville that the authorities decided to solve it once and for all. Lieutenant Colonel George Spalding was ordered to seize all of Nashville's prostitutes and ship them to Louisville, Kentucky.

Spalding sought suitable transportation and found the steamship *Idahoe*, whose captain and owner, John Newcomb, wanted a military contract. He agreed to transport Spalding's mysterious "cargo."

Newcomb, unsurprisingly, got more than he bargained for. Spalding's soldiers marched more than 100 "ladies of the night" onto the *Idahoe*, handing Newcomb orders not to let the women "leave the boat before reaching Louisville." Many of the women were ill, and Newcomb had neither food nor medicine. He was told that he was on his own and that he should sail immediately.

Hard-to-Handle Cargo

On July 9, the *Idahoe* set sail, with 111 angry women aboard. They immediately destroyed furniture and

vandalized the boat. *The Nashville Dispatch* reported the ladies' deportation, smugly noting, "Where they are consigned to, we are not advised, but suspect the authorities of the city to which they are landed will feel proud of such an acquisition to their population."

Throughout their journey, the women plied their trade to both crew and civilians who would swim out to the boat. Newcomb tried to land several times, but he was turned away by each river town where he attempted to dock. He had to buy food, medicine, and ice with his own funds from boats he met along the river.

Turned Away

Finally, on July 15, the battered *Idahoe* arrived at Louisville and was refused permission to land, Spalding's orders notwithstanding. The military commander in Louisville placed a guard aboard the steamboat and sent it to Cincinnati. Meanwhile, a few women escaped, only to be sent back to Nashville by train. At Cincinnati, the *Idahoe* was quarantined for 13 days before it was sent back to Nashville with its cargo intact. General Robert S. Granger, Union military commander for the area of Middle Tennesee, dealt with the prostitution problem in an unlikely—but effective—way: He legalized it. Nashville's prostitutes were examined and treated by doctors for various venereal diseases, and if deemed free of disease, they were granted an official license. Taking "clients" without a license could result in a sentence to the workhouse for up to 30 days.

Never the Same

Meanwhile, the *Idahoe* was in shambles. Newcomb presented a damage claim for $5,000, but it took more than a year for him to be compensated. Eventually, he received two bank drafts: $1,000 "for damage to the staterooms, furniture, bedding, cabin furniture, tableware, etc.," and $4,316 for "subsistence and medicines furnished 111 prostitutes on board the steamer *Idahoe*...at the rate of $1.50 a day for each." By the time he received the money, Newcomb had sold his interest in the *Idahoe,* which sank in 1869 near Columbia, Louisiana. One can only imagine the stories the boat's sailors told when reminiscing about their tumultuous tour with the ladies, or indeed, what the ladies' side of the story might have been.

NOTHING COULD KEEP THIS MAN DOWN

★ ★ ★ ★

*Unlike many whose careers seesawed throughout the war,
Phillip Sheridan enjoyed an almost vertical rise to success.*

To look at Philip Sheridan's unimpressive early career, no one
would have expected greatness. It took him five years to graduate
from West Point. Eight years later, when the Civil War broke out,
he still held the lowest officer grade of second lieutenant.

As a quartermaster in the Army of Missouri, Sheridan lobbied for a
combat command and was finally promoted to colonel and assigned
to lead a cavalry unit. Within days he took his troops into a successful
battle at Booneville, Mississippi, getting himself a quick brigadier
general's star and command of a division in Kentucky and Tennessee.
He led that division to success in three out of four major battles.

To the Shenandoah Valley

Sheridan was moved east in 1864, getting the job of clearing Confederate General Early's army from the Shenandoah Valley. It was
here where he made his most famous stand. On October 18,
Sheridan was away, meeting with Grant. The next morning, Early
staged an initially successful surprise attack at Cedar Creek. Returning from his meeting, Sheridan heard the fighting. Galloping
swiftly to the front, he found his army retreating in panic. He
quickly reorganized them and took the offensive,
turning the tide. The Confederates fled.

He later helped Grant take Petersburg and Richmond, preventing Lee's escape near Appomattox,
which encouraged Lee's decision to surrender.

Sheridan ended the war as a major general, an
amazing climb from second lieutenant. Remaining
in the Army, he died as a full general in 1888.

VIEWING THE CIVIL WAR

★ ★ ★ ★

Since its inception, Hollywood has been enamored with the Civil War. From early silent films to modern-day blockbusters, here are some movies that have featured the war's glory and despair.

Gone With the Wind (1939)—Undeniably the most lavish and bold cinematic statement on the Civil War and Reconstruction period, this movie was based on the Pulitzer-Prize–winning novel by Margaret Mitchell. At its core, the movie follows a love story in the Confederate South. A rising crane shot of hundreds of wounded and dead Confederate soldiers in the Atlanta railroad yard following the crushing siege of the city, stands as one of Hollywood's most memorable scenes. Stars Clark Gable, Vivien Leigh, Olivia de Havilland, Leslie Howard, and Hattie McDaniel.

The Birth of a Nation (1915)—Directed by film pioneer D. W. Griffith and based on the novel *The Clansman, The Birth of a Nation* depicts abolitionist Northerners and slaveholding Southerners in pre-Civil War times. The story journeys through the war and into Reconstruction, where the Ku Klux Klan is born to "restore order" in the South. Regarded by most modern viewers as a divisive film that supports racism and the Klan, this silent classic nonetheless remains a giant among cinema historians and critics for its technical innovations. Stars Lillian Gish, Walter Long, and Henry B. Walthall.

Gettysburg (1993)—Based on Michael Shaara's Pulitzer-Prize–winning novel, *The Killer Angels,* the film *Gettysburg* details the three-day definitive battle. This four-hour film was shot on-site at many of the actual battle locations, including Devil's Den and Little Round Top. Stars Jeff Daniels, Tom Berenger, Martin Sheen, and Stephen Lang.

Glory (1989)—This winner of three Academy Awards highlights the story of the 54th Massachusetts Volunteer Regiment, one of the first formal U.S. Army units to be made up entirely of black soldiers. The climax of the film depicts the Battle of Fort Wagner in July 1863, during which the 54th showed great courage and bravery while suffering heavy casualties, convincing many skeptics that black soldiers had a significant contribution to make toward the war effort. Stars Matthew Broderick, Denzel Washington, Cary Elwes, and Morgan Freeman.

The General (1927)—Starring, cowritten, and codirected by "the Great Stone Face," Buster Keaton, this film is considered one of the greatest silent comedies of all time. Playing a character on the Confederate side of the true Civil War story of Andrews's Raid, Keaton stars as a train engineer who loses his locomotive, the *General,* along with his fiancée to Union spies. One acclaimed scene involves Keaton removing a railroad tie from the tracks while perched on the train's cowcatcher. Also stars Glen Cavender and Marion Mack.

The Horse Soldiers (1959)—Directed by film legend John Ford, this movie stars John Wayne as a Union cavalry colonel who leads his troops deep into Confederate territory to sabotage supply and transportation lines. It is based on the true story of Grierson's Raid in Mississippi in April 1863. Also stars William Holden and Constance Towers.

A Southern Yankee (1948)—This comedy stars Red Skelton as a would-be Union spy who ventures deep into Confederate territory and falls for a Southern belle. One famous sight gag, designed by Buster Keaton, has Skelton walking a battlefield between North and South—half-dressed as a Northerner and half-dressed as a Southerner, carrying a two-sided flag. Once the wind changes direction, however, his cover is blown. Also stars Arlene Dahl and Brian Donlevy.

Cold Mountain (2003)—A romance set at the end of the Civil War, this award-winning film follows a wounded Confederate soldier returning to his home in North Carolina. As he makes his trek to reunite with his sweetheart, he crosses paths with memorable people and events. Stars Jude Law, Nicole Kidman, and Renée Zellweger.

COMBAT BECOMES MORE EFFECTIVE

★ ★ ★ ★

Innovations in warfare advanced at a rapid pace during the Civil War—sometimes more quickly than military planners could take advantage of them.

The Civil War and World War II seem worlds away, but in fact, they are separated by only 75 years. Even more astounding is the number of technological advancements that took place during the Civil War and how many were still in use during the Second World War. These devices ushered in a new age of warfare.

Ironclad Ships

Although both sides worked on their own ironclad ships simultaneously, the North and South came up with radically different designs. The famous showdown between the Confederate *Virginia* and the Union *Monitor* exemplifies the differences. The CSS *Virginia* was partially made from the hull of the Northern frigate USS *Merrimack*. This impressive vessel had 2-inch plates mounted on the 24-foot-high sides of the ship. On the other side, the *Monitor* rode exceedingly low in the water, with only the 9-foot-high turret visible above the waterline. On March 9, 1862, the ships fought to a stalemate. The two vessels served as prototypes for modern warships that appeared in the two world wars.

Underwater Mines

The Confederacy looked for any edge it could gain over the superior Northern forces. The Southern military experimented with a number of innovative weapons to breach the federal blockade and strengthen their coastal and river defenses. For example, mine fields were planted in Confederate harbors, leaving narrow passages open for blockade runners. There were several different types of mines, all of which were essentially containers filled with gunpowder. These included metal mines or wooden kegs. They would either be set to explode on contact or be electrically discharged by someone onshore with a battery that sent an electric charge across a copper wire to the gunpowder inside the mine.

Land Mines

Union officers prefered to stay away from mines, torpedoes, or other such devices, dismissing them as "infernal machines" that were unworthy of a "chivalrous nation." The Confederates, on whose territory the war was mostly fought, had more incentive to explore the technology. They developed two types of land mines: those set off by a tripwire and those detonated by more than seven pounds placed on a pressure-sensitive fuse. The most effective use of mines was during the attack on Fort McAllister near Savannah, Georgia, on December 13, 1864, where most of the 134 federal casualties were from deployed land mines. As one federal officer wrote, these devices worked "as much by their moral[e] effect as by actual destruction of life."

Trench Warfare

It took Civil War generals three years to realize that massive charges toward well-defended positions often resulted in heavy losses by the attacking army. Soon after the slaughter of Union troops at Cold Harbor, Grant and Lee had their troops burrow into the ground facing each other around the city of Petersburg, Virginia. Thus began the trench warfare phase of the Civil War. It foreshadowed the strategy used by forces in World War I. Trench warfare tactics had been employed by Grant in his siege of Vicksburg and in the defenses around Atlanta encountered by William Sherman. These furrows were often bolstered by a fraise, a line of sharpened timber stakes angled toward the enemy. Six- to nine-foot logs studded with sharpened stakes, or chevaux-de-frise, were also placed in front of the trench line. Attacking troops caught in the teeth of these deadly obstacles made easy targets for defenders.

Fast Facts

- *The colorful Zouave uniform adopted by volunteer units of both sides was typified by a short-waisted jacket, a vest, a sash, baggy pantaloons, leggings, greaves, a turban, and a fez. It was based on the French army's elite Zouave battalion, which had in turn based it upon the dress of Algerians who had fought with them during the 1830s' colonial war in North Africa.*

- *Great Britain paid the United States $15.5 million in gold when a postwar international tribunal settled claims arising from depredations of Confederate cruisers built in the island kingdom.*

- *On April 6, 1865, at Sayler's Creek, Virginia, nearly one quarter of the Confederate army was cut off by Union cavalry forces under Philip Sheridan. Several officers and about 7,700 rank-and-file enlisted soldiers surrendered—the largest number of the war.*

- Scalawag *was the title given to white southern Republicans, regarded as traitors by their fellow Confederate citizens.*

- *Flamboyant Confederate General Jeb Stuart kept a banjo player on his headquarters staff and rode into battle wearing an ostrich plume in his hat and a gray coat lined with scarlet.*

- *On Easter Sunday, 1865, the troops of Union General James H. Wilson assaulted and captured Columbus, Georgia, in what is widely regarded as the final battle of the Civil War east of the Mississippi.*

- *About 400,000 British Enfield rifles, which fired a .557 caliber shot, were imported by both sides during the war.*

- *The soldier at parade rest is the dominant design theme for Civil War monuments nationwide.*

THE UNION DRESS PARADE

★ ★ ★ ★

*General Grant used a clever ruse to distract the
Confederate army and win a major Union victory.*

In the early afternoon of November 23, 1863, two divisions of
Union troops left their line around Chattanooga, Tennessee, and
went on the plain between the city and Missionary Ridge, an area
occupied by Confederate infantry under the command of General
Braxton Bragg. For about an hour, the Union troops marched back
and forth as if on dress parade.

The Confederates left their rifle pits to watch the military pageant.
"It was an inspiring sight," observed a federal colonel. "Flags were
flying, the quick, earnest steps of thousands beat equal time....
The ringing notes of the bugles, companies wheeling and counter-
marching and regiments getting into line—all looked like preparations for a peaceful pageant, rather than the bloody work of death."

It's All a Trick

At 1:30 P.M., a cannon fired. This was a signal to the Union troops
to break formation and charge the Confederate position a few
hundred yards away on Orchard Knob, which was a 100-foot-high
hill near the base of Missionary Ridge. Joined by three additional
divisions, the determined Union soldiers stormed the rebel line,
overrunning the surprised enemy defenders. The "pageant" had
been a ruse to catch the Confederates off guard. It succeeded,
driving the Confederates—those who could escape—to the fortifications along Missionary Ridge.

What began as a reconnaissance of the forward enemy position
became a full-scale assault that exceeded General Grant's expecta-
tions. He had used the dress parade trick because the ground in
front of Orchard Knob was relatively flat and treeless and provided little cover for attacking troops. The "parade" allowed the
Union infantry to move closer to the enemy position without

raising their suspicions. Little did Grant and his subordinates realize that this was just the opening act of a spectacle rarely seen in warfare.

On November 25, Grant ordered the troops under Generals Sherman and Hooker to attack both flanks of Bragg's line on Missionary Ridge. When each of those attacks stalled, Grant ordered General Thomas's Army of the Cumberland to seize the rifle pits at the base of the ridge. The Confederates looked to be too formidable for a direct attack, so this was primarily intended as a distraction.

An Unexpected Charge

Before the smoke from the signal guns had cleared, Thomas's force moved forward. "Fifteen to twenty thousand men," a Union lieutenant described the charge, "in well-aligned formation, with colors waving in the breeze, almost shaking the earth with their cadenced tread."

A hail of Confederate artillery and rifle fire pelted the charging federal troops, but this didn't deter them. "A terrific cheer rolls along the line," wrote the Union lieutenant. "The quick step has been changed to the 'double quick.' Another cheer, and the enemy's first line of works...is ours."

Without orders, the massive Union battle line quickly regrouped at the foot of the ridge and surged forward. In his memoir, Grant recorded how "our troops went to the second line of works; over that and on for the crest." Confederate fire was fierce but generally inaccurate. Afraid of hitting their own troops who were retreating from the first two Confederate lines, Bragg's gunners on the crest fired too high. Many Southern soldiers surrendered after being caught in the crossfire.

Bragg, pressured by Sherman on his right flank and Hooker on his left, watched helplessly as the center of his line crumbled. Barely escaping capture, Bragg left nearly 6,700 of his troops behind. What started out as a "harmless" dress parade ended in a major Union victory.

THE WAR WAY OUT WEST

★ ★ ★ ★

*Access to the Santa Fe Trail and the allure of gold made
the New Mexico Territory a much sought-after area.*

When people think about the geography of the Civil War, battle
locations from the Atlantic Ocean to Texas are usually what come
to mind. The truth, however, is that this war was waged from one
coast to the other. The Union and the Confederacy even had
some altercations in California. In the New Mexico Territory,
serious conflict erupted as Confederate forces invaded, seeking to
take all or part of the land away from Union control and add it to
their side.

Before the war, the New Mexico Territory included the modern-
day states of New Mexico and Arizona, as well as part of Nevada.
Many residents in the southern part of that territory were in
agreement with the Confederates and supported the concept of
secession. They proposed splitting the New Mexico Territory into
northern and southern portions (as opposed to the eventual east-
west division between New Mexico and Arizona that occurred
instead) and even selected a southern territorial governor in 1860.
But the U.S. government did not divide the territory in this manner because of fears that the southern area would support slavery
and join the cause of secession.

In July 1861, as the war escalated, Confederate Lieutenant
Colonel John Baylor led the 2nd Regiment Texas Mounted Rifles
from El Paso into New Mexico, capturing Fort Fillmore near the
Las Cruces area. Within weeks, Baylor decreed the formation of
the Confederate Territory of Arizona and installed himself as
governor in the capital of Mesilla. General Henry Sibley soon
brought nearly 4,000 soldiers, called the Confederate Army of
New Mexico, into the area. They hoped to control the Santa Fe
Trail—as well as the riches of gold in California. In response,
federal Governor Henry Connelly issued a statement in both

English and Spanish urging residents of
the territory to take arms and oppose the
Confederate uprising.

Winners Yet Losers

In February 1862, the Confederates scored a
victory at the Battle of Valverde, the first major
conflict in the area. By March, Confederate
troops had also overtaken Santa Fe, but at the Battle of Apache
Canyon, federal troops claimed victory. There they lost only 5
soldiers, with 14 wounded, while the Southerners lost more than
30, with 40 wounded and 70 captured as prisoners.

The decisive battle, however, was at Glorieta Pass—which has
since become known as "The Gettysburg of the West"—where
more than 2,500 soldiers clashed. The Confederates were at a
disadvantage, as supplies from Texas were impossible to move
quickly enough to the front lines, and thus any Confederate offensive was stifled. In the end, they admitted defeat with nearly 200
casualties.

This lack of support forced the Confederates to abandon their
attack on the New Mexico Territory. By April, Southern troops
had left Santa Fe and Albuquerque. By July, all Confederate
troops had left the territory. They were forced to return to Texas
empty-handed, victims of the harsh desert climate and weak
supply lines.

★ ★ ★ ★

"On the Avenue in front of the White House were several
hundred colored people, mostly women and children,
weeping and wailing their loss. This crowd did not appear
to diminish through the whole of that cold, wet day; they
seemed not to know what was to be their fate since their
great benefactor was dead, and their hopeless grief
affected me more than almost anything else, though
strong and brave men wept when I met them."
Gideon Welles, describing the aftermath of Lincoln's death

JUST A FEW REMARKS

★ ★ ★ ★

*In late 1863, President Abraham Lincoln received
an invitation to make "a few appropriate remarks"
at the November 19 dedication of a national cemetery
at Gettysburg. Lincoln accepted the invitation.*

After a long, slow procession to the brand-new cemetery south of the town of Gettysburg, Pennsylvania, Edward Everett, a famous and popular orator of the time, delivered an eloquent two-hour speech describing the Battle of Gettysburg and drawing lessons about it from European military history. After thundering applause from the thousands in attendance, President Lincoln rose, stepped to the front of the platform, and delivered his own brief tribute to those who fought and died there during the first three days of July 1863.

The Gettysburg Address

"Fourscore and seven years ago our fathers brought forth on this continent a new nation, conceived in liberty, and dedicated to the proposition that all men are created equal. Now we are engaged in a great civil war, testing whether that nation, or any nation so conceived and so dedicated can long endure. We are met on a great battlefield of that war. We have come to dedicate a portion of that field as a final resting place for those who gave their lives that that nation might live. It is altogether fitting and proper that we should do this. But, in a larger sense, we cannot dedicate—we cannot consecrate—we cannot hallow this ground. The brave men, living and dead, who struggled here have consecrated it far above our poor power to add or detract. The world will little note nor long remember what we say here, but it can never forget what they did here.

"It is for us, the living, rather, to be dedicated here to the unfinished work which they who fought here have thus far so nobly advanced. It is rather for us to be here dedicated to the great task remaining before us—that from these honored dead we take increased devotion to that cause for which they gave the last full measure of devotion; that we here highly resolve that these dead shall not have died in vain, that this nation, under God, shall have a new birth of freedom; and that government of the people, by the people, for the people, shall not perish from the earth."

The Aftermath

Applause interrupted the speech five times, and a tremendous ovation and three cheers followed its completion. Though Lincoln confided later that he felt the speech a "flat failure," Everett summed up the impact of the President's "few remarks" when he wrote him the next day: "I should be glad, if I could flatter myself that I came as near to the central idea of the occasion, in two hours, as you did in two minutes." This speech is likely Lincoln's most famous—it is engraved into the Lincoln Memorial on the Mall in Washington, D.C.

"As a nation, we began by declaring that 'All men are created equal.' We now practically read it, 'All men are created equal, except Negroes.' Soon, it will read 'All men are created equal, except Negroes, and Foreigners and Catholics.' When it comes to this, I should prefer emigrating to some country where they make no pretense of loving liberty. To Russia, for instance, where despotism can be taken pure and without the base alloy of hypocrisy."
Abraham Lincoln

"In giving freedom to the slave we assure freedom to the free—honorable alike in what we give and what we preserve. We shall nobly save, or meanly lose, the last, best hope of earth."
Abraham Lincoln, to Congress, 1862

(Continued from p. 329)

1864

February 27
Andersonville Prison opens near Americus, Georgia.

March 9
President Lincoln commissions Ulysses S. Grant as lieutenant general, the first American to achieve that rank since George Washington.

April 12
Nathan Bedford Forrest's troops attack and capture Fort Pillow, near Memphis, Tennessee. Controversy still remains as to how many black soldiers were slain as they tried to surrender after the shooting stopped.

April 17
Grant halts all prisoner-of-war exchanges to exacerbate the Confederacy's shortage of fighting personnel.

April 22
Congress authorizes the phrase "In God We Trust" to be stamped upon coins.

April 30
Jefferson Davis's five-year-old son Joe dies after a fall from the veranda of the Confederate White House.

May 5–6
Inconclusive fighting at the Battle of the Wilderness, Virginia, results in at least 8,000 Confederate casualties and a Union loss of 17,666.

May 7
General Sherman's Union armies set out on their southward march as the Atlanta Campaign begins.

May 8–19
For 12 days, the armies of Grant and Lee fight around the village of Spotsylvania, Virginia. Casualties total about 18,000 Union and 12,000 Confederate.

May 11
In the cavalry Battle of Yellow Tavern, Virginia, Union horse soldiers strike north of Richmond. Jeb Stuart is mortally wounded in the fighting.

June 1–3
The Battle of Cold Harbor, Virginia, is a Union defeat. Attacks against entrenched Confederates fail, resulting in 12,000 Union casualties over three days of fighting.

June 8
Meeting in Baltimore, the National Union convention (essentially the Republican party convention) nominates Lincoln for a second term, with Andrew Johnson as his running mate.

June 15–18
Union troops attack the defenses of Petersburg, Virginia, failing to achieve a decisive breakthrough. Grant begins a siege of the city that will last until April 1865.

June 28
Lincoln signs a bill that repeals all fugitive slave laws.

(Continued on p. 385)

ALLAN PINKERTON—SPYING FOR THE UNION CAUSE

★ ★ ★ ★

The exploits of Allan Pinkerton during the Civil War helped pave the way for the modern Secret Service.

In a letter to President Lincoln dated April 21, 1861, detective Allan Pinkerton offered his services and commented on one of the traits that would make him an icon of law enforcement for generations. "Secrecy is the great lever I propose to operate with," he wrote.

Establishing the Eye

Born in Scotland in 1819, Pinkerton came to the United States in 1842. He originally was a barrel builder by trade, but his skills at observation and deduction led him to a career fighting crime. By age 30, he'd joined the sheriff's office of Cook County, Illinois, and been appointed Chicago's first detective. He later joined attorney Edward Rucker to form the North-Western Police Agency, forerunner of the Pinkerton Agency. As his corporate logo, Pinkerton chose an open eye, perhaps to demonstrate that his agents never slept. Clients began calling him "The Eye."

Pinkerton and his operatives were hired to solve the growing number of train robberies, which became more and more of a problem as railroads expanded across the nation. George B. McClellan, president of the Ohio and Mississippi Railroad, took particular notice.

Wartime Duties

In 1861, Pinkerton's agency was hired to protect the Philadelphia, Wilmington, and Baltimore Railroad. In the course of their duties, Pinkerton and his agents learned of a preinaugural plot to kill President-elect Lincoln. The detectives secretly took Lincoln into Washington before he was scheduled to arrive, thwarting the conspirators. Lincoln was inaugurated without incident.

When the war began, Pinkerton was given the duty of protecting the president as a forerunner of today's Secret Service. He was also put in charge of gathering intelligence for the army, now run by his old railroad boss, McClellan. The detective and his operatives infiltrated enemy lines. Using surveillance and undercover work, both new concepts at the time, agents gathered vital information. Pinkerton tried to get details any way he could. His people interviewed escaped slaves and tried to convince literate slaves to return to the South to spy. He used female spies, and he even infiltrated the Confederacy himself several times using the alias Major E. J. Allen.

Uncertain Information

While much of this was invaluable, his work was tarnished by a seeming inability to identify enemy troop strengths. His reports of enemy troops were detailed, including notes on morale, supplies, movements, and even descriptions of the buttons on uniforms. Yet the numbers of troops he provided were highly suspect.

In October 1861, as McClellan was preparing to fight, Pinkerton reported that Confederate General Joseph Johnston's troops in Virginia were "not less than 150,000 strong." In reality, there were fewer than 50,000. The next year he reported the strength of Confederate General John Magruder at Yorktown, putting troop numbers at about 120,000 when the true number was closer to 17,000.

After the true strength of these forces was discovered, Pinkerton was ridiculed. Some historians believe that Pinkerton was unaware of the faulty information, but others insist he intentionally provided inflated figures to support McClellan's conservative battle plans. The truth will likely never be known, as all of Pinkerton's records of the war were lost in the Great Chicago Fire of 1871.

Return to Civilian Life

After McClellan, one of Pinkerton's staunchest supporters, was relieved of his command by Lincoln, Pinkerton limited his spying activities and shifted his work back toward criminal cases, which included the pursuit of war profiteers. He ultimately returned to Chicago and his agency, working until his death in 1884.

THE KINGDOM OF JONES

★ ★ ★ ★

A county in Mississippi became known for its resistance against what its residents considered "a rich man's war."

It is fitting that southern Mississippi's Jones County was named for Revolutionary War hero John Paul Jones. His famous declaration, "I have not yet begun to fight," was suited to this county that became the scene of its own civil war during the War Between the States.

Mississippi's secession from the Union had been a hotly debated political issue in Jones County prior to 1861. The county was torn socially and politically between two diametrically opposed factions. On one side were the prosperous plantation owners for whom slavery was an economic imperative. On the other side were the generally poorer, landless classes who regarded both secession and the war as having no benefit for them.

Unfair Policies

The Civil War brought conscription (and ways to avoid it) to the South. The Confederacy enacted the first-ever American conscription laws in April 1862 to counter the Union army's 3–1 numerical advantage of available soldiers. In agricultural regions such as Jones County, the Confederate legislation known as the "Twenty Negro Law" exempted plantation owners and overseers from military service if they owned more than 20 slaves. It was believed that the agricultural output of the plantations was vital to the Confederate war effort. The Confederacy also permitted draft-eligible men to hire substitutes to serve. The going rate for a substitute was $3,000 or more, making it an option only for the wealthy. Poorer, nonslaveholding Southerners saw conscription as a benefit to the rich alone, with the interests of the plantation owners seemingly advanced over those of the poorer classes. The maxim "rich man's war, poor man's fight" came from the discontent that flowed from these conscription policies.

A Knight Rises

Against this backdrop, Newton Knight rose to prominence in Jones County in 1863. Knight was descended from one of the families that first settled Jones County. The family didn't own slaves, and Knight hadn't supported war when it was declared in 1861. Conscripted into the Confederate army in 1862, he served with other Jones County soldiers in Vicksburg, 100 miles to the northwest. In the aftermath of the Union siege and subsequent victory at Vicksburg in July 1863, Knight and thousands of other Confederates abandoned the army. He returned to Jones County along with many other deserters, and the county quickly became known as a haven for deserters from other parts of Mississippi.

The Confederate army sent a small force under the command of Major Amos McLemore to capture the Jones County deserters, but McLemore was killed—reputedly at Knight's hands. This was Knight's springboard to the leadership of a loose-knit band of guerilla fighters known as the "Knight Company." From an island base in the Leaf River, Knight and more than 100 guerillas conducted quick-hitting, successful raids against Confederate targets. The Knight Company captured Confederate supplies, destroyed wagons and buildings, and generally disrupted the Confederate war effort in south central Mississippi. Knight and his group became folk heroes to the people of Jones County.

War Within a War

Between December 1863 and the end of the war, a virtual civil war within a war existed in Mississippi. Knight had regular contact with Union commanders at Vicksburg, although it is unlikely he ever received formal military support from Union forces. There's no hard evidence that Knight or his troops actually entered the formal service of the Union army. Rather, they perceived their action to be against the privileged plantation owners as much as toward Confederate military targets in Jones County.

Two cavalry units commanded by Confederate Colonel Robert Lowry were dispatched to Jones County to eliminate the guerilla leader. Knight and his raiders were kept in check by Lowry's Confederate regulars, but despite intense efforts, the Knight Company was never conclusively defeated, and Knight was never

captured. The closest the rebels came was the seizure of Ben Knight, Newton Knight's cousin, who was hanged in 1864 by Confederates who mistakenly believed they'd captured the guerilla leader. Knight's guerillas continued their operations until the end of the war.

A Free State

Knight wasn't the only Jones County symbol of defiance in the Civil War. In late 1862, county representatives issued a purported declaration of independence from both the state of Mississippi and the Confederacy. It's clear that many in the fractious county saw themselves not as allied to the Union but as independent of any government. The county became known locally as "The Free and Sovereign State of Jones" or "The Kingdom of Jones." The precise scope of their declaration is difficult to ascertain, as most records of the period were burned in a Jones County courthouse fire in 1880.

In 1865, Reconstruction loomed, and there was fear that Jones County would suffer from the stigma associated with Knight and his Union sympathizers. A group of county citizens seeking favor with the Mississippi government successfully petitioned to change the county's name to Davis, in honor of the Confederate president, in 1866. The name was changed back a short time later.

Knight continued to carry out his political battle against Mississippi's wealthy landowners into the postwar era. More remarkably, he helped create an unusual mixed-race community in Jones County that defied the general racial divisions in the state— Knight had several children by both his white wife and a black woman. His mixed-race descendants lived in Jones County for a number of generations following the Civil War.

SO THEY SAID

★ ★ ★ ★

"Grant began by expressing a hope that the war would soon be over, and Lee replied by stating that he had for some time been anxious to stop the further effusion of blood, and he trusted that everything would now be done to restore harmony and conciliate the people of the South. He said the emancipation of the Negroes would be no hindrance to the restoring of relations between the two sections of the country, as it would probably not be the desire of the majority of the Southern people to restore slavery then, even if the question were left open to them."
Union General Horace Porter, on the surrender at Appomattox Court House

"You cannot make soldiers of slaves, nor slaves of soldiers.... The day you make soldiers of them is the beginning of the end of the revolution. If slaves will make good soldiers our whole theory of slavery is wrong."
Confederate General Howell Cobb

"I appear this evening as a thief and robber. I stole this head, these limbs, this body from my master and ran off with them."
Frederick Douglass

"Future years will never know the seething hell and the black infernal background of countless minor scenes and interiors...of the Secession war; and it is best they should not—the real war will never get in the books."
Walt Whitman

THE BATTLE OF SPOTSYLVANIA

★ ★ ★ ★

Grant proves that great loss of life would not prevent him from hammering his attack on the Confederates.

In early May 1864, General George G. Meade's Union Army of the Potomac had been pummeled in the thick underbrush of a Central Virginia area called the Wilderness. They'd already lost 18,000 troops, compared to two-thirds of that many for the Confederates. The soldiers thought they would be able to fall back and lick their wounds for a while, as had been normal after a major Union defeat.

Grant's Way of Doing Things

General Ulysses S. Grant, recently promoted to commander of all Union forces, had a different idea. He ordered his soldiers to take the offensive and quickly march to Spotsylvania Court House, due east of the Wilderness. He wanted to get in between Confederate General Robert E. Lee's army and the Confederate capital of Richmond, Virginia. If the maneuver was successful, Lee would be forced to attack Grant's entrenched troops, and Richmond would be largely undefended.

Lee learned about the plan, however, and quickly marched his own force the ten miles to Spotsylvania. They made it by morning and beat the Yankees to the strategic crossroads village. Lee had his 50,000 troops build a series of earthworks, or mounds used as rudimentary forts. One, called the Mule Shoe because of its shape, was strategically placed in the center of the lines.

Grant and the first of his troops arrived later that morning and launched an attack, even before his full army was in place. The Confederates, digging themselves in for a better position, thwarted it. All day the blue-coats probed Confederate lines, and all day they were driven back.

The Fighting Continues

Light combat ensued the following day, but on the third day, May 10, General Grant ordered several attacks on the Confederate left and center lines. These were not successful, but Grant sensed that a larger attack could be. May 11 was cold and stormy. The Union generals used the lull to move the 2nd Corps into position to attack the Mule Shoe. Lee anticipated a different move and pulled most of his artillery from that area. The stage was set for carnage.

At 4:30 A.M. on May 12, a solid mass of screaming Union soldiers stormed the Mule Shoe. The early morning attack surprised the Confederate defenders, and their line collapsed in minutes. Lee's army was split in two.

Lee wasn't about to give up. He personally led reinforcements in an attack and recovered a lot of lost ground. The Federals were driven back to a thin wall of logs and earth. Fierce hand-to-hand combat lasted until almost dawn of the next day, earning the Mule Shoe its nickname, "The Bloody Angle."

All Those Dead for a Stalemate

Lee finally pulled his troops back half a mile to a line of hastily constructed fortifications. One Northern soldier observed, "Hundreds of Confederates, dead or dying, lay piled over one another in those pits. The fallen lay three or four feet deep in some places, and... they were shot in and about the head." The Union troops suffered even more losses.

The battlefield lay quiet for the next few days, with only minor skirmishes. A final Union attempt to crack Lee's defenses on May 18 was repelled by Confederate artillery. On May 19, Grant officially pulled his army away from Spotsylvania. Roughly 18,000 Union soldiers had been killed or wounded, and around 12,000 Confederates had fallen.

Fast Facts

- *The marching ration of a Union soldier consisted of one pound of hard bread (aka hardtack), in addition to meat, sugar, coffee, and salt.*

- *The ironworks of Pittsburgh, Pennsylvania, was the major Northern center for manufacture of heavy mortars.*

- *Indignant members of the Massachusetts 54th and 55th black regiments protested the difference in pay between white and black Union infantry. After they refused pay for 18 months, legislation passed in 1864 to bring equivalent pay to black and white soldiers.*

- *Future U.S. Supreme Court justice Oliver Wendell Holmes, Jr., was wounded three times during the Civil War: in the chest at Ball's Bluff, in the back at Antietam, and in the heel at Chancellorsville.*

- *The strongest concentration of Unionists in the South was in East Tennessee.*

- *Confederate General John Bell Hood fathered 11 children, including three sets of twins. When he died along with his wife and eldest daughter during a yellow fever epidemic in 1879, he left behind ten children ranging in age from nine-year-old twins to a one-month old. A Hood Relief Committee managed to raise $28,0000 for the children, who were ultimately adopted by seven different families in five different states.*

- *The Confederate submarine* H. L. Hunley *was the first sub to sink a warship, the USS* Housatonic, *a 1,800-ton sloop of war. The* Hunley *itself sank shortly after the torpedo attack, and its crew was lost. In August 2000, the submarine was recovered in Charleston Harbor.*

THE GREAT LOCOMOTIVE CHASE

★ ★ ★ ★

Part low-speed chase, part mercenary adventure, and part Civil War legend, Andrews's Raid in Georgia is a sensational footnote.

In the spring of 1862, civilian spy James J. Andrews appealed to Union General Ormsby Mitchel with an unusual and ambitious proposition. He wanted to creep behind enemy lines, hijack a train, and destroy the railroad supplying rebels in Chattanooga.

Mitchel approved, and Andrews assembled a crew of 23. Although two of the crew were caught slipping into rebel territory, the rest made it to Marietta, Georgia, dressed in plainclothes. Over time, the group's ranks would continue to dwindle. On the morning of the operation, two of the would-be raiders overslept.

Dine and Dash

On April 12, as the crew of the *General* ate breakfast, Andrews's raiders commandeered the train. The conductor, William Fuller, noticed the *General* had pulled away. The chase was on!

Fuller and his assistants pursued the raiders for seven hours over 87 miles. Aware they were being pursued, the raiders disrupted the rail track and cut telegraph lines. Fuller continued his chase, first pursuing the steam engine on foot, later by handcar, and finally—successfully—using the locomotive *Texas*.

Running Out of Steam

The *General* ran out of steam at Ringgold, Georgia, near the Tennessee border. Confederate authorities rounded up the Northerners, and Andrews and seven of his crew were tried as spies and hanged.

Though of little military value, the episode was hailed as heroic in the North. Six of the raiders were the first soldiers to receive the Congressional Medal of Honor.

LINCOLN RUNS AGAIN

★ ★ ★ ★

What was once believed to be a lost election for Lincoln turned in his favor as the Union gained ground on the battlefield.

By 1864, the United States had been at war with itself for more than three years and had seen defeat, horror, and death. Many Northerners were looking to place blame for the losses, and they were looking squarely at President Abraham Lincoln.

Newspapers reported tales of bloodshed and war atrocities such as Confederates deliberately bayoneting surrendering black Union soldiers at Fort Pillow. The battles of 1864 were some of the bloodiest of the war, and rumors that Lincoln would be turned away from a second term were growing. "Mr. Lincoln is already beaten," said Horace Greeley, editor of the *New York Tribune* and one of the founders of the Republican Party. "He cannot be elected."

A Sure Loss

Even Lincoln believed the election was lost. His fear was that a Union general, such as John C. Frémont or even Ulysses S. Grant, would ride his celebrity to a Republican nomination and split the party vote. An even greater fear was that the war-weary American people would elect a general who would settle for compromise, such as his eventual Democratic opponent General George McClellan.

So concerned was Lincoln that on August 23 he wrote a secret note, sealed it, and asked all of the members of his Cabinet to sign the back. They all obliged without knowing the contents, which would only be revealed at a later date. "This morning, as for some days past, it seems exceedingly possible that this administration will not be re-elected," Lincoln had covertly written. "Then it will be my duty to so co-operate with the President elect, as to save the Union between the election and the inauguration, as he will have secured his election on such ground that he can not possibly save it afterwards."

To strengthen his appeal, Lincoln reached out to a possible Democratic running mate in war hero General Benjamin Butler. Butler turned him down, so Lincoln asked the military governor of Tennessee, Andrew Johnson, also a Democrat. They ran as the Union party.

The Tides Turn

Just as it seemed darkest for Lincoln and his administration, the tide turned on the battlefield. On September 2, 1864, Atlanta fell to General William Tecumseh Sherman. Coupled with Admiral David G. Farragut's triumph at Mobile Bay and General Philip Sheridan's victory in the Shenandoah Valley, suddenly the strongest plank in the Democrats' platform—that the war was a stalemate and couldn't be won—had disintegrated. As candidates campaigned to crowds on this idea, they were met with chants of "Sherman and Sheridan!"—the military heroes of the hour.

In addition to the victories on the battlefield, Lincoln's opponent was having troubles of his own. McClellan had connections to some of the more radical Peace Democrats and Copperheads. These didn't play well with voters, especially a group McClellan believed he could easily deliver: the army itself. "Not that the soldiers dislike the man so much as the company he keeps," one soldier said to explain his vote against the general.

The Votes Are Counted

On election night in 1864, a powerful rainstorm opened up on Washington, D.C., as the votes were being tallied. Braving the storm, Lincoln walked from the White House to the telegraph office to wait for returns. That night he was rewarded for his perseverance. Of the 4.2 million votes cast, Lincoln received 55 percent, winning the Electoral College in a landslide of 212–21. Except in Kentucky, where anger over emancipation still lingered, Lincoln even won the Union soldiers' vote in every state by a 4–1 margin. The soldiers wanted the war to end, but they wanted it to end in victory.

SUNKEN DEFEAT

★ ★ ★ ★

When a Union captain became negligent, Virginians took over an important naval shipyard.

It was 2:30 A.M. on April 21, 1861, when the USS *Cumberland* and USS *Pawnee* sailed away from Gosport Naval Shipyard (today called the Norfolk Naval Shipyard). They carried Union Captain Charles Stewart McCauley and the last of the Union troops protecting the facility. Behind them, they could see the naval yard in flames, along with the 11 ships that remained docked there.

Within minutes of the Union force's escape, townspeople and members of the Virginia militia broke into the yard and began putting out the flames. How could the officers abandon their most important shipyard, leaving behind 11 ships, 1,000 cannons, thousands of rounds of ammunition, and tons of powder?

Laying Low

In the days following the firing on Fort Sumter, the Navy Department was unsure how to handle the defense of Gosport. As commander of the yard, McCauley, a 67-year-old Navy veteran with a reputation for reliable command, had received orders to "do nothing to upset the Virginians." Secretary of the Navy Gideon Welles believed McCauley was just the man for this sensitive mission of protecting the nation's largest and most expensive naval shipyard.

Civilians were not McCauley's only worry, however—there were a number of officers and sailors at the shipyard who were known to have Southern leanings. It was even speculated that the order not to upset the civilians was actually itself part of a Confederate plot to buy time until the Virginia militia could capture Gosport intact.

Fleeing the Scene

Meanwhile, a 40-gun steam frigate, the USS *Merrimack*, was docked at the facility for repairs. Nervous about the *Merrimack*'s safety, Welles secretly ordered McCauley to speed up repairs on the ship. After McCauley estimated it would take at least one month to finish the job, Welles rushed the Navy's chief engineer to Gosport to supervise the work.

McCauley's estimate proved to be incorrect, as the chief engineer completed repairs in only three days. By this time, however, McCauley seemed to have lost touch with the events happening around him, because his information was largely coming to him from secessionist officers purposely deceiving him. Once the *Merrimack* was repaired, it was readied to leave Gosport, along with three other warships. Inexplicably, McCauley instead ordered all ships to remain docked.

Following Virginia's secession on April 17, a number of naval officers and sailors resigned from the service. When word reached McCauley that the state militia was headed to Gosport, the captain ordered the yard's ships and buildings destroyed and the cannons spiked. McCauley and the remaining Federals then made their hasty getaway.

A Heavy Price to Pay

The Virginians who broke into and commandeered the yard were able to salvage $3 million of property, including approximately 1,000 cannons and 2,000 barrels of gunpowder. They were also able to raise and repair four of the ships that had been scuttled by the departing forces, including the USS *Merrimack,* whose hull was used to build the CSS *Virginia,* the Confederacy's first ironclad. The *Virginia* later faced the federal ironclad USS *Monitor* in battle at nearby Hampton Roads, Virginia, in March 1862.

A Senate inquiry found that McCauley was "highly censurable for neglecting to send the *Merrimack* out of the yard.... And for scuttling the ships and preparing to abandon the yard before any attack was made or seriously threatened." Following this finding— and additional charges that he had been drunk the night of the fire—McCauley retired from the Navy soon after the inquiry was completed.

BLOODY BILL

★ ★ ★ ★

Missouri Confederate guerilla "Bloody Bill" Anderson
left much destruction in his wake before Union forces
beat him at his own game... or did they?

Although many Civil War histories emphasize the valor and the honor exhibited in this terrible conflict, the exploits of Confederate "Bloody Bill" Anderson and his guerillas are a stark and fearsome example of war without limits.

The Life of the Lawless

Captain William Anderson achieved infamy in the two years leading up to his death at age 24. He'd joined the Missouri partisans shortly after federal forces occupied the state in 1861. When his father was killed by a pro-Union neighbor in 1862, Anderson joined the guerilla forces of Captain William Quantrill, representing the most lawless edge of the Confederate army in Missouri. The guerillas placed pressure on Union forces by raiding supply lines and attacking small Union units in hit-and-run sorties.

In July 1863, three of Anderson's sisters were imprisoned by Union forces in Kansas City with other civilian relatives of known guerillas. The building where they were held collapsed on August 12, killing Anderson's sister Josephine and crippling another sister. When he learned of Josephine's death, Anderson swore to exact a dreadful revenge on all Union soldiers he encountered.

Delivering Vengeance

His first chance at revenge came quickly with Quantrill's infamous raid on Lawrence, Kansas, on August 21, 1863. The raiders killed 183 men and boys, many executed in front of their horrified families. After looting and setting fire to much of the town, the guerillas fled to Texas and re-formed into smaller raiding units, one of which was headed by Anderson. Anderson's raiders returned to Missouri in late 1863 to attack Union rail and communications lines. In each case, the guerillas struck, seized what they could carry, and killed anyone in their way before hiding among the pro-Confederate civilian population.

Centralia Carnage

"Bloody Bill" Anderson ignored all military conventions. In one infamous raid on September 27, 1864, his troops wore stolen Union army uniforms and captured 25 Union soldiers at the Centralia, Missouri, railway station. The Federals pleaded their surrender as Anderson summarily executed each one. He and his raiders took scalps from the dead soldiers and attached them to their horses' bridles as trophies. They then ran riot through Centralia, killing innocents, attacking women, and looting buildings.

At the same time, a Union cavalry company had been pursuing Anderson without success. Outside Centralia, Anderson became aware of his pursuers and ambushed a Union patrol, killing each soldier and taking more scalps. When the horrors of Centralia became public knowledge, Bloody Bill's Confederates became the most feared fighters in the Midwest.

A Wanted Man

Anderson was a prime Union target. Union Captain S. J. Cox led a force tasked to pursue and neutralize the raiders. On October 27, 1864, Cox used his own guerilla tactics by luring Anderson and a group of guerillas into an ambush in Orrick, Missouri. Anderson and several fighters were killed. Union hatred of Anderson was so profound that he was decapitated and his head was spiked to a telegraph pole for public viewing.

The End?

A legend endures that Anderson actually escaped to live in Texas under an assumed name until his death in 1927. An old photograph of three of Anderson's sisters is said to have been found with the dead Texan. The official Union reports concerning his death renders Anderson's escape unlikely but not impossible. This tantalizing possibility is the subject of historical debate to this day.

Fast Facts

- In 1861, Jefferson Davis issued Letters of Marque to privately owned vessels authorizing them to prey on Northern ships sailing the high seas. Lincoln responded by saying that any captured crews of these "privateers" would hang as pirates.

- Shinplasters, a type of promissory note, were one of four basic types of widely circulated currency during the war. They could only be used to buy goods from the merchant who issued the note.

- Confederate General Earl Van Dorn survived many battles only to be killed by a jealous husband who accused the general of having an affair with his wife.

- Of 14 national cemeteries managed by the National Park Service, only one is not related to a Civil War battlefield park.

- Lincoln suspended the writ of habeas corpus in some areas of the country in 1861 and throughout the entire country in 1862 and again in 1863. He ignored a ruling by Roger Taney, the Chief Justice of the Supreme Court, that this suspension was unconstitutional. Congress backed the President by authorizing his actions in 1863.

- In 1859, Ulysses S. Grant freed the one slave he owned.

- Free blacks made up 1.5 percent of the population of the Northern states.

- During Sherman's March to the Sea, soldiers needed to render the Confederate rail lines unusable and unrepairable. To do so, they heated the rails on bonfires until they were red hot and then wrapped them around trees. These became known as "Sherman's Bowties."

LESS-THAN-STERLING REPUTATIONS

★ ★ ★ ★

If you think driving while intoxicated is dangerous business,
try leading hundreds of troops while under the influence.

Charges for being drunk while on duty have often been leveled against Union and Confederate officers who had somehow failed in command, particularly if that failure occurred in battle. Drunkenness is an easy accusation to make, and in instances when it turns out to be true, it provides an easy explanation for an officer's losing record.

Perhaps the most famous officer alleged to have been drunk during many engagements is Ulysses S. Grant. Early in his career, while stationed at Fort Humboldt, California, in July 1854, he resigned from the Army under rumors of alcoholism. This haunted him throughout the Civil War. The influence of alcohol has often been used to explain setbacks he experienced in battle or command. While his successes during the war didn't stop the rumors, they did make them irrelevant. Still, reports of Grant's drinking continued to resurface during his postwar political career.

A Grave Mistake

Grant's story is hardly unique. Nathan Evans graduated from West Point in 1848, where he earned the nickname "Shanks" because of his long, slender legs. Evans served on the frontier until he resigned from the U.S. Army in 1861 in order to serve in the Army of South Carolina. The brigade under Evans's command is given some of the credit for the Confederates' win at the First Battle of Bull Run. It was reported, however, that during that battle he had an aide carry a small whiskey keg, providing him with drinks throughout.

His success on the battlefield continued throughout the early stages of the war with victories at Ball's Bluff, Virginia, in October

1861, and at the Battle of Secessionville in South Carolina in June 1862. Evans's commanders were well aware of his fondness for alcohol, but as long as he won battles, it never became an issue. Their views changed, however, after the Battle of Kinston on December 14, 1862.

On that day, Union troops under the command of General John Foster advanced on Kinston, North Carolina. Evans, with a brigade of 2,014 troops, met Foster on the south side of the Neuse River but was overwhelmed and forced to retreat. Only a single bridge crossed the river to the north side, and Evans ordered his brigade to cross the bridge and then burn it so they couldn't be followed. Unfortunately, more than 400 of his command somehow did not receive the order to fall back, and they were left on the wrong side of the burning bridge. For most of them, there was no choice but to surrender.

Allegations arose of Evans having been drunk during the battle, and he was charged with being intoxicated while on duty. Although he was later acquitted, Evans lost the confidence of his commanders and never again held a position of independent command during the war. After suffering serious injuries from falling off a horse in the spring of 1864—an incident also rumored to have been caused by alcohol—Evans was not able to return to the war until about a month before its end.

Lookin' for a Fight

A Union general whose ability to command was hindered by the use of alcohol was Thomas Sweeny. Called "Fighting Tom" during his service in the Mexican War, he lost his right arm during the Battle of Churubusco in Mexico. Sweeny remained in the regular Army until he was commissioned brigadier general of the 90-day Missouri troops. Being wounded a number of times did not hinder his advancement in rank and command. He particularly distinguished himself as commander of the 2nd Division of the 16th Corps, brawling outside of Atlanta.

Despite this, Sweeny was dissatisfied with his corps commander, General Grenville Dodge, and his fellow division commander,

General John Wallace Fuller. He considered both of them to be political generals, in their positions only as political favors. During a battle outside Atlanta, Dodge gave direct orders to one of Sweeny's regiments, a violation of chain of command. That evening Sweeny invited Dodge and Fuller to his tent to celebrate the victory of the day. Already intoxicated by the time the two officers arrived, Sweeny confronted them both, calling them cowards and striking Dodge, his superior. When Fuller attempted to intervene, Sweeny wrestled him to the ground. Dodge preferred charges of assault against the hot-tempered general, but a military court acquitted him, most likely due to his excellent record.

Even though he was cleared of the charges, Sweeny never regained his command. General Oliver Howard, commander of the Army of the Tennessee, told General Sherman, "Sweeny has been cleared, but I don't want him. . . . [He] might be mustered out, with a view to the interest of the service." The dismissal marked the end of the war for Sweeny.

Alcohol-Fueled Courage?

Another general whose career was affected by alcohol was John Dunovant. Though he was not a graduate of West Point, Dunovant had advanced to captain of the regular Army. Resigning his commission after South Carolina seceded from the Union, he was appointed colonel of the First South Carolina Regulars but was ultimately dismissed in June 1862 for drunkenness. That didn't prevent him, however, from becoming colonel of the 5th South Carolina Cavalry.

Dunovant's gallant performance in battle led to his appointment as a general, but his impaired judgment resulted in an ambush by Union cavalry and an ill-advised charge through a swamp on an entrenched Union line on October 1, 1864, during the siege of Petersburg. Despite his superior officers' objections, Dunovant led the attack and was one of the first killed. It was believed that alcohol contributed to his ill-advised behavior, which ultimately led to his death.

WANTON WASTE
AT COLD HARBOR

★ ★ ★ ★

*On June 3, 1864, mistakes and miscommunication led to
one of the bloodiest and most lopsided battles of the war.*

At the end of May 1864, Grant and Lee were ready for a showdown. By this time, the Army of the Potomac had been fixated on
taking Virginia, attempting to do so nearly a half-dozen times
within the last three years. And each time they were thwarted by
Lee's Confederate forces.

Eyes on the Prize

Grant was ready to take Richmond once and for all. This time, as
commander of all Union forces, he'd lead the charge himself,
with the help of General George Meade. The previous battles of
Spotsylvania Court House and the Wilderness had been stale-
mates, and Grant was determined to avoid yet another setup by
maneuvering his army around Lee's right flank, toward the southeast. Lee tried to figure out Grant's intentions, figuring correctly
that the Union army would attempt to secure the crossroads at
Cold Harbor, which featured a network of roads with access both
to Richmond—only ten miles from Cold Harbor—and to Lee's
rear areas.

On May 31, Union General Philip Sheridan brought his troops to
Cold Harbor to join Grant's. Lee's forces failed to retake the crossroads, but while decisions were being made, Confeder-
ate reinforcements were arriving. Soon, Lee's
Army of Northern Virginia had
59,000 soldiers, while Grant's boasted
108,000. Despite the overwhelming ratio,
the numbers were evened out by experience: Grant's army included many fresh
recruits and troops inexperienced with

infantry tactics, while Lee's soldiers were experienced combat veterans.

The Seven Days Battles of 1862 had been fought at the same site, and as soldiers hunkered down, they found a disturbing sight: the skeletal remains of the soldiers who had died there two years before. Smaller skirmishes were underway—2,200 Union troops died on June 1 alone. The next day, Grant decided to launch an attack, but because Winfield Scott Hancock's troops were late arriving to the scene, that battle was rescheduled for the next morning.

Digging In

Meanwhile, as Union soldiers waited to make their move, the Confederates took the opportunity to build fortifications and dig trenches. They erected large, labyrinthine barricades of earth and logs. Stakes were posted to aid in the accuracy of the sharpshooters' range estimates. The Union delay was one of the key elements of their ultimate loss at Cold Harbor: It gave the Confederates an entire extra day to prepare, whereas the Union troops remained disorganized and exhausted.

By the morning of June 3, the number of mistakes the Union commanders were making continued to snowball. Terrain was improperly scouted or not scouted at all. Grant left many important decisions up to his commanders rather than taking the lead. A sense of fatalism spread among the troops, many of whom were reported to have pinned their names to the inside of their coats so their bodies could be identified later. One soldier wrote (accurately) in his diary prior to the battle, "June 3, 1864, Cold Harbor, Virginia. I was killed."

At dawn, Grant and Meade ordered an attack but failed to specify their orders. Rather, they left it up to the corps commanders to decide when and where to hit the Confederate lines. Making matters even worse, they had also neglected to gather any reconnaissance of the Confederates' position. Due to lack of coordination and rough terrain, the first Union lines were broken from the beginning, appearing not as a unified assault but as smaller regiments operating alone. General William "Baldy" Smith later wrote that he was "aghast at the reception of such an order, which proved conclusively the utter absence of any military plan." To his troops at the time, he said, "It is simply an order to slaughter my best troops."

As three of the Union corps began to advance, they were gunned down from the Confederate lines. Most of the soldiers never even made it close to the Confederate entrenchments. Within a half hour, those still alive and able to walk went back to their lines or took shelter where they could. Though one of Hancock's corps was able to successfully get through a part of the front line, his other corps, led by General John Gibbon, became mired in swampy ground and could not advance. Other Union soldiers were trapped in front of the Confederate lines and began digging entrenchments with anything they could find: their hands, cups, bayonets—they even stacked the bodies of fallen soldiers. Although the Union army was in disarray and suffering from massive casualties, Grant still ordered further assault. His commanders refused, having had enough of this, as Smith later called it, "wanton waste of life."

A Regrettable Day

Within a single hour, the Union lost 7,000 soldiers, while the Confederates lost a comparatively minor 1,500. At 12:30 P.M., Grant conceded that he had lost the day. Still, it took the two armies four more days—until June 7—to agree to the terms of a truce. By then, many of the wounded soldiers from both sides had died in the fields, due to lack of medical care, food, or water. In just a little over a month, the Union army under Grant had suffered a loss of nearly 50,000 in his campaigns against Lee, and yet no real advance had been made. Although Grant reported to Washington, D.C., that his "losses were not severe," he later wrote in his memoirs, "I have always regretted that the last assault at Cold Harbor was ever made. I might say the same thing of the assault of the 22d [sic] of May, 1863, at Vicksburg. At Cold Harbor no advantage whatever was gained to compensate for the heavy loss we sustained."

RECRUITING SLAVES FOR THE CONFEDERATE ARMY

★ ★ ★ ★

Faced with a losing battle, the Confederate Congress made a decision toward the end of the war to recruit black slaves to join the ranks.

If the phrase "black Confederate" makes about as much sense as "light heavyweight," "jumbo shrimp," "friendly fire," or even "civil war," then consider yourself in good scholarly company. According to Civil War historian Eric Foner, "Apart from a handful who 'passed' for white," no blacks actually fought for the Confederacy. Indeed, arming blacks to fight for the Southern homeland would seem to undermine the very ideology of slavery on which the Confederacy was largely based.

A Numbers Game

Ideological inconsistencies aside, the decision to arm slaves became an unavoidable—and highly controversial—topic toward the end of the war. By late 1863, after the battles of Gettysburg and Vicksburg had turned the tide of the war in favor of the Federals, it was becoming increasingly clear that the Confederates would have to resort to extreme measures to keep up.

General Patrick Cleburne, who commanded troops in the Western Theater, suggested that the rebels arm slaves to compensate for the Union's superior numbers. The argument quickly became energetic, as each side wondered if fighting slaves would allow themselves to remain in servitude. One officer said that arming slaves "contravene[s] the principles on which we fight." Samuel Clayton, a private citizen from Cuthbert, Georgia, had none of that argument, writing to President Davis, "Giving up slavery to have slaves defend [the institution]? To have them shoot down the enemies of slavery? Strange notion, indeed! From the outset of the war, we have used the negro to defend the institution by making him raise provisions for the Army, &c. Let him be used still further, and put the sword and musket in his hand, and make him hew down and shoot down those who come to destroy the institution and enslave us. Would this be giving up the question? I opine not."

Putting It to a Vote

By March 1865, however, the recruiting situation had become so dire for the rebels that the Confederate Congress voted to go ahead and do what many still considered unthinkable. Robert E. Lee supported the decision, and some have argued that this policy shift was more a testament to Lee's political clout than anything else. Ironically, the fighting ended before the Negro Soldier Bill was put into practice. Even so, the Confederate army had used and continued to use blacks as laborers, cooks, and musicians. These positions were considered far less significant than soldiering, however, so this use of slaves did not constitute slaves fighting for the South.

Battlefield Backlash

The reaction of Confederate soldiers to the announcement that blacks would join their ranks illustrates how different the roles of laborer and soldier were assumed to be. "I did not volunteer my services to fight for a free negroes country, but to fight for a free white mans country & I do not think I love my country well enough to fight with a black soldier," wrote one Confederate soldier to his mother. Those who accepted the Confederate Congress's plan did so grudgingly. As one Tennessee officer put it: "We can certainly live without negroes better than with Yankees and without negroes both."

- *It is estimated that between 60,000 and 93,000 blacks served the Confederacy in some capacity.*

HOW NAPOLEON
AFFECTED THE CIVIL WAR

★ ★ ★ ★

The little general had a big impact on American fighting.

In the mid-19th century, French General Napoleon Bonaparte was regarded as one of the greatest military geniuses in history. Everyone wanted to emulate his tactics. Civil War generals on both sides had been trained at West Point, and one of their primary textbooks was a book on Napoleonic tactics written by Antoine Henri Jomini. Many of these officers absolutely revered the French general and emperor. Thomas J. Jackson, who was later nicknamed "Stonewall," traveled to Europe to study Napoleonic battlefields firsthand. George McClellan proudly carried the nickname "The Young Napoleon."

Building on Napoleon's Ideas

Outflanking was one of the most important Napoleonic principles taught to Civil War generals. When an attacking force gets around the side of its enemy, it forces the defender to turn its lines to face the attacker, rush reinforcements to that side, and disrupt the battle plan. How did Sherman conquer Atlanta? Not by facing the rebel army head on, but by executing a string of flanking maneuvers that forced the rebels to fall back slowly until Atlanta was vulnerable.

Sherman took another page from Napoleon's playbook after capturing Atlanta. In his March to the Sea across Georgia, he fed his army by ransacking farms along the way. Living off the land was Napoleon's strategy for maintaining an army far from home.

Not all the general's tactics worked, though. He advised keeping troops in straight formation. That's fine for enemies with bad aim, but Civil War rifles were more accurate than Napoleonic muskets, and soldiers lined up in neat formation were sitting ducks for sharpshooters. Overall, though, Napoleon's lessons made Civil War armies much more effective—and deadly—than previous American forces.

ADVANCING ON ATLANTA

★ ★ ★ ★

*The Union armies turned the corner on defeat when
General Sherman took the war into Georgia.*

As late as the scorching summer of 1864,
victory didn't seem to be moving fast
enough in the Union's direction. Federal
forces faced inertia on the map and crippling
casualties in the field.

By September 1, however, tides were turning.
The Union recaptured glory when its forces marched into Atlanta
and raised the American flag over City Hall. General William T.
Sherman had defeated General John Bell Hood, seizing a crucial
railroad that was a supply and manufacturing lifeline of the South.

Taking the Fight South

An earnest call for action had come in the spring, less than a month
after Sherman took control of the western armies. His friend General Grant directed him "to move against Johnston's army, to break it
up and to get into the interior of the enemy's country as far as you
can, inflicting all the damage you can against their war resources."

Undaunted by the ambitious orders so soon into his post and
relying on strength of numbers, Sherman designed a vigorous plan
to outflank the Army of Tennessee. General Joseph Johnston had
assumed command of the Southern army the previous December
with a goal of restoring order to a force teetering on collapse after
its brutal defeat at Chattanooga. In conquering Johnston, Sherman
figured he could position his soldiers between the Army of Tennessee and Atlanta, taunting Confederate forces to attack.

Though President Davis wanted Johnston to strike Sherman near
Chattanooga, Johnston knew his army was outnumbered two to
one and preferred a strategy of defense. He'd hoped that the

rugged terrain of northern Georgia would impede a strong federal advance, but this notion fell by the wayside when Sherman launched an offensive at Dalton. A force of 110,000 Federals struck north and west of Johnston's position, while Union General James McPherson was sent to cut off Southern supply lines to Atlanta.

The Confederate Mountain Stand

Ultimately, Johnston retreated south in haste, with Union troops on his trail. A succession of Confederate withdrawals brought the two armies face-to-face at Kennesaw Mountain near Marietta, Georgia, in June. Temperatures reached 100 degrees as columns of federal troops slammed rebel lines like human battering rams. They were repelled again and again. After three savage hours of battle, the Confederates drove back the Union soldiers. Sherman later wrote, "By 11:30 the assault was in fact over, and had failed."

Five days later, Sherman tried another approach. He moved around Johnston's left flank and forced the Confederates to fall back to entrenchments along Peachtree Creek, just four miles from Atlanta. Though fighting was indecisive, this action had an important result: Davis tired of Johnston's seemingly losing defensive strategies and replaced him with the bold General John Bell Hood.

Into Atlanta

As expected, Hood immediately struck Sherman's army. On July 20, he attacked a two-mile-wide gap in the Union line. Although this seemed like a good opportunity to cause some damage, Hood was soon distracted when Union artillery in another part of the line moved within range of Atlanta. Though the artillery was not yet mounting a full-scale attack, gunnery officers had started to lob shells into the city.

Hood attempted another attack two days later, but it was a bloody defeat. Unhindered, Union troops devastated Atlanta with artillery throughout August, completely cutting the two remaining railroads into the city. Desperate Confederate attacks could not halt Sherman's dogged onslaught, and Hood marched out of Atlanta under cloak of night on September 1.

Fast Facts

- *Julia Ward Howe wrote the words to "Battle Hymn of the Republic" after a visit to a Union camp in wartime Washington. The Atlantic Monthly paid her five dollars for her poem, which was subsequently set to the tune of the popular song "John Brown's Body."*

- *Of the more than 2.7 million men in the U.S. armed services during the war, 42,000 were younger than 18 or older than 46 at the time of their enlistment.*

- *Denmark was the first nation to abolish its slave trade in 1792.*

- *Alexander Stephens, Confederate vice president, is believed to have coined the phrase "War Between the States."*

- *John B. Turchin, a Russian army colonel, served in the Union army from 1861 to 1864 and advocated a more vigorous campaign against the South. Turchin was an early advocate of the total war concept that William Tecumseh Sherman later became famous for—destroying the infrastructure and terrorizing the civilian population.*

- *When David D. Porter of the U.S. Navy built a dummy warship in a bid to dupe the Confederates, it was armed with large logs made to look like cannons. This was an old trick used in many forts on both sides and even in the field.*

- *The average Union soldier carried about 50 pounds of equipment and clothing, which cost the federal government roughly $42 per person in 1861.*

- *Confederate cotton exports were reduced 95 percent from 10 million bales in the three years prior to the war to just 500,000 bales during the Union blockade.*

THE FOLLY OF GRANT'S CANAL

⋆ ⋆ ⋆ ⋆

In an effort to sidestep a Confederate blockade on the Mississippi River, Union engineers came up with an ill-fated plan.

The target in the Western Theater during the summer of 1862 was Vicksburg, the last major Confederate fortress on the Mississippi. The Union advanced by land and river, but rebel guns lined the bluffs above the river, blocking any attempt by Union ships to pass.

If the River's a Problem, Just Move the River

To avoid running their ships through that gauntlet, Union commanders ordered a canal to be built to cut off an outcropping in the river across from Vicksburg and away from the bluffs. Engineers believed that the river's current would follow the shorter path and divert the flow of the river away from Vicksburg.

On June 27, 1862, Flag Officer David Farragut's ships shelled the Confederate gun positions as General Thomas Williams's brigade of 3,200 began work on the canal. They dug desperately, but summer conditions soon became unbearable, and disease and heat devastated the soldiers. The task far from done, Williams withdrew his troops at the end of the month.

If at First You Don't Succeed...

Although he wasn't confident of success, Grant ordered work to resume in January 1863. Lincoln enthusiastically supported the project and requested almost daily updates on its progress. Work actually *was* progressing when, on March 5, the river broke through into the construction area. Water engulfed the canal and flooded nearby land, destroying several encampments. Grant had no choice but to finally abandon the doomed project.

A HOUSE DIVIDED

★ ★ ★ ★

Although her loyalty was to her husband and the Union government he served, Mary Todd Lincoln couldn't ignore the ties she still held to her relatives in the Confederacy.

Mary Todd Lincoln was a Northerner by marriage but a Southerner by birth and upbringing. Raised in a Kentucky slaveholding family, Mary Todd moved to Illinois at the age of 20 to live with her sister Elizabeth. She was a hit within the Northern social circles, and various men—including Stephen A. Douglas—courted her. Abraham Lincoln was the new legal partner of her cousin, who spoke highly of the lanky lawyer and helped make the introduction between Mary and Abe. Despite her sister's objections, Mary Todd married Lincoln three years later.

A Family Apart

Like many families in the nation, the Todd family was torn apart by the Civil War. Most of the family supported the Confederacy—one of Mary's brothers, three half-brothers, and three brothers-in-law actively fought for the South. Mary's stepmother was related to John C. Breckenridge, former U.S. vice president and Confederate general. Only Mary and a few other family members supported the Union. Her sister Elizabeth, however, had opposed her marriage to Lincoln and thus offered her no political support. Of the Kentucky Todds, only Mary's older brother Levi was a staunch Unionist, but his health was poor, and he never served in the Union army.

Mary Lincoln remained loyal to the North and to her husband, of course, but newspapers and Washington society regularly used her Confederate family ties against her. Southerners called her a traitor to her roots, and Northerners suspected her tangled allegiances. Though she did sometimes arrange for her family to get travel passes to cross the enemy lines in both directions, there is no evidence of her ever having aided the Confederacy. Mary

Lincoln was caught between a rock and a hard place—she couldn't publicly mourn her Confederate family members without seeming disloyal to the Union, but she couldn't ignore them without seeming disloyal to her family.

Death Tolls in the Todd Family

In such a large family, tragedies were plentiful. Levi died of illness in 1864. Mary's half-brother Samuel died at Shiloh. A second half-brother, David, was wounded at Vicksburg and died a few years after the war. A third, Alexander, was killed at Baton Rouge.

Most newsworthy of all was the death of her brother-in-law, Benjamin Hardin Helm, a West Pointer married to her sister Emilie. He was offered a high-ranking paymaster post by Lincoln but refused it, instead accepting a field position in the Confederate army. He rose to the rank of general before his death at the Battle of Chickamauga. Helm was the son of John Helm, a well-known Kentucky politician who was not pleased at his son's decision to fight, much less with his choice of sides. Like many Kentucky politicians, the elder Helm favored the Union, or at least neutrality in the war.

When Benjamin Helm died, Emilie had trouble going to visit either Mary in Washington, D.C., or her mother in Kentucky. Because she had gone to the South with her husband, traveling to either place involved crossing Union lines, and because she was the widow of a Confederate officer, local commanders would not give her permission. To make matters more difficult, Emilie refused to take an oath of loyalty to the Union, saying it would be an insult to her late husband. Lincoln gave her a special pass to permit her and her young daughter Katherine to travel to Washington, where she stayed with the Lincolns at the White House. Despite the fact that Emilie was a family member, the Lincolns were strongly criticized for "giving aid to the enemy" in this fashion.

The family conflict even filtered down to succeeding generations. Katherine Helm and the Lincolns' son Tad would argue about the war. As they played together at the White House, Katherine would yell, "Hurrah for Jeff Davis!" Tad would yell in reply, "Hurrah for Abe Lincoln!"

WHAT WERE THEY READING?

★ ★ ★ ★

Uncle Tom's Cabin is probably the most famous best seller from the Civil War era. Here's a list of some of the other popular reading of the time.

Ten Nights in a Bar Room and What I Saw There
Timothy Shay Arthur

Considered the *Uncle Tom's Cabin* of the temperance movement, this novel set out to convince people of the evils of liquor. The story is told from the point of view of Simon Slade, an ambitious tavern owner who relates the sad and disturbing effects alcohol has on his patrons. Arthur believed that alcohol and drunkenness were the first steps on a slippery slope that could ultimately lead to degeneracy, gambling, and murder.

The Sword and the Distaff
William Gilmore Simms

Later published under the title *Woodcraft,* this book was the most successful of about two dozen so-called "anti-Tom novels." Written to counterpoint *Uncle Tom's Cabin,* these books portrayed loving relationships between slaves and their masters and tried to put a happy face on the South's peculiar institution. Set during the Revolutionary War, the novel centers around Captain Porgy, a benevolent master whose obedient slave (also named Tom) helps him in his patriotic duties.

The Planter's Northern Bride
Caroline Lee Hentz

Another "anti-Tom novel," this book tried to win over Northerners with a protagonist from their own backyard. The novel focuses on a Northern abolitionist's daughter who marries a Southern plantation owner and quickly learns the "truth" about slavery. While Hentz pushes the notion of a familial relationship between the slave and the slave owner, she also introduces the specter of slave rebellions, bringing in several evil, homicidal characters in an effort to show that blacks could not be trusted to mind their own affairs.

Beulah
Augusta J. Evans

This Alabama author portrays the coming of age of the unusually independent Beulah Benton in a huge best seller shortly before the war. The orphaned Beulah survives a troubled childhood determined never to marry or accept the traditional woman's role. Beulah and author Evans give in by the end of the book, however, when Beulah finds true love and settles down.

"Paul Revere's Ride"
Henry Wadsworth Longfellow

Narrative poetry was a popular form that readers would memorize and recite for others. First published in *The Atlantic Monthly* in January 1861, the poem told the exciting story of Paul Revere, who warned Massachusetts colonists that the British army was coming at the start of the American Revolution. Revere had been a minor historical figure before this time, but this transformed him into a national legend and a symbol of Northern patriotism at a time when a new call to arms was needed.

"Barbara Frietchie"
John Greenleaf Whittier

This was another narrative poem that first saw life in *The Atlantic Monthly*. It ostensibly told the tale of an elderly woman in Frederick, Maryland, who refused to be cowed by Stonewall Jackson and his invading troops. When they took down the Union flag flying at her home, she replaced it. When they fired upon it, she called out to them. "'Shoot, if you must, this old gray head, / But spare your country's flag,' she said." In response, Jackson ordered his troops to let the flag continue flying. There really was a Barbara Frietchie (whose name was sometimes spelled *Fritchie* or *Frietschie*), but although poet Whittier claimed to be relaying what he had been told, the story itself is apocryphal.

THE DOUBLED-UP NAMES OF CIVIL WAR BATTLES

★ ★ ★ ★

Antietam or Sharpsburg, Pittsburg Landing or Shiloh.
There's a reason so many battles have more than one name.

One of the most striking aspects people notice when reading about the Civil War is the fact that key battles are often called by more than one name. Sometimes the earliest major battle between the North and the South is referred to as the First Battle of Bull Run, while other times it is called the First Battle of Manassas (not to mention the sources that refer to the Battle of First Bull Run or the Battle of First Manassas). This same situation of more than one common name exists for at least 15 other major battles of the war. Why do the names of Civil War battles seem so inconsistent? The reason, as in so many other instances in this conflict, comes down to the difference between the North and the South. Some names are Union names, and some are Confederate.

Urban Versus Rural

The most common explanation for this phenomenon comes out of the background of Northern and Southern soldiers. Many Union troops came from cities, towns, or villages and noticed the things they considered more unusual, namely natural objects such as bodies of water. Bull Run was a stream near the battlefield, so the Northerners referred to the Battle of Bull Run. Southerners, on the other hand, came from a more rural background and were more impressed with settlements or other evidence of people. They named the Battle of Manassas after the train station that was close by. Likewise, Antietam was a creek that ran through the battlefield, and Sharpsburg was a nearby town. Pittsburg Landing was a natural object—a landing on the banks of the Tennessee River—while Shiloh, a church building on the battlefield, was built by people.

(Continued from p. 349)

1864

July 11–12
General Jubal Early and his Confederates probe the defenses of Washington, D.C. President Lincoln comes under fire at Fort Stevens on July 12.

July 17
General John B. Hood replaces General Johnston in command of the Confederates at Atlanta.

July 22
Hood launches a major attack on Sherman's troops east of Atlanta. Known as the Battle of Atlanta, this engagement costs Hood 8,499 casualties while inflicting 3,641 casualties on Sherman's forces.

July 30
At 4:45 A.M., a huge blast from a gunpowder-packed tunnel under a Confederate fort at Petersburg launches a day of fighting as Union troops try to crack the rebel lines. The Battle of the Crater, however, is another Union failure.

August 5
Union Admiral David G. Farragut leads his fleet past defending rebel forts and ships in the naval Battle of Mobile Bay, Alabama.

August 31
The Democratic national convention in Chicago nominates George B. McClellan as its presidential candidate.

September 2
Union troops occupy Atlanta.

October 19
At dawn, Jubal Early's Confederates launch a surprise attack on Sheridan's army in their camps along Cedar Creek, Virginia. After initial Southern success, Sheridan regroups and heads a devastating counterattack that forces the Confederates to retreat.

October 31
Nevada is admitted to the Union as the 36th state.

November 8
Lincoln is reelected President, receiving 55 percent of the popular vote, 400,000 more votes than McClellan.

November 15
Sherman leaves Atlanta to advance on Savannah, Georgia. This comes to be known as Sherman's March.

November 25
A Confederate plot to burn New York City fails.

December 13
General Sherman's troops capture Fort McAllister, Georgia, near Savannah.

December 15–16
General George H. Thomas launches an attack on General Hood's outnumbered troops at Nashville. In two days of fighting, Hood's army is completely defeated and heads south.

December 21
Union troops occupy Savannah, Georgia.

(Continued on p. 405)

THE MUD MARCH

★ ★ ★ ★

Downpours and thick mud put an end to Union General Ambrose Burnside's hopes of a winter attack.

Winter and early spring were difficult times for a Civil War army to fight. Instead of marching and battling, troops hunkered down in their camps to await the end of the rainy season. Storms that ruined gunpowder and turned roads into muddy traps for wooden wheels usually started to diminish by mid-spring.

Retaliation Time

In the middle of January 1863, General Ambrose Burnside was on thin ice with President Lincoln, having been stung by his disastrous defeat at Fredericksburg, Virginia, the previous month. In that botched assault on the Southern army entrenched on the opposite side of the Rappahannock River, Burnside crossed the river only to have Robert E. Lee's soldiers cut down thousands of his federal troops. Desperate to turn the tide of the war and repair his damaged reputation, once he felt a warming in the weather, Burnside ordered his Army of the Potomac to strike "a great and mortal blow to the rebellion."

Bogged Down

Burnside's second plan for crossing the river singled out Banks' Ford, a bit upriver from Fredericksburg, as the spot from where he would launch a surprise flank attack on Lee. The plan was to build five floating pontoon bridges to cross the Rappahannock and come up beside and behind Lee's force. On January 20, as Burnside's army of 100,000 blue-clad soldiers began their march west along the river, the ground was dry underneath their feet. But soon dark clouds formed, and before long it would not stop drizzling. The rainfall increased throughout the day, and the ground became muddier and muddier. After very slow progress—one regiment reported marching only a mile and a half for the whole day—the troops set up camp. Rain continued all night, pelting the tents and turning the landscape to muddy goo.

All the activity had not been ignored on the Confederates' side of the river. Lee had been monitoring Burnside's moves, speculating that the Federals might try to cross the Rappahannock in such a way.

Second Time's a Charm?

The next morning, the sun returned, the ground dried out a bit, and Burnside's army set out anew. But then the sky opened again. Muddy confusion reigned—in addition to the rain itself, the thousands of marching feet and the heavy wagons churned the mud to unmanageable levels. Military formations gave way to chaos as troops simply tried to make any progress at all. Wheeled weaponry and supply wagons sank to their wheel hubs in the muck. With the rain driving at them, determined teams of soldiers and mules strained to pull the wagons and cannons along the roads but couldn't make them budge. More teams of horses and mules were added to the wagon trains but could get no additional traction. Stopping in the afternoon of the second day, Burnside resolved to try again tomorrow.

As a new day dawned and the rain continued, determination gave way to a mood of wild despair. Supplies were bogged down, and engineers who had been able to get to Banks' Ford didn't have enough supplies to build even one pontoon bridge, let alone five. Ordering a whisky ration for his troops to raise morale, Burnside—himself caked with mud—strained to push a cannon into position. The alcohol simply added to the frustration, so not only did Burnside have troops that were stuck, many were now drunk, too. Tempers already at a fever pitch began to boil even more. There were reports of a massive fistfight between regiments and of a drunken artillery captain cutting down a sergeant with his sword. Across the river, the rebels did what they could to ridicule the Union effort, planting mocking signs that read, "This way to Richmond" and "Burnside stuck in the mud." By this time, soldiers were getting sick and hundreds of horses and mules had died.

Sloppy Defeat

On the afternoon of the third day, Burnside finally recognized the futility of the situation and ordered everybody back to where they had started. Conditions weren't any better on the way back, of course, so the Union army still had to withstand a great deal of suffering to return to the place they'd left a few days earlier. Over two days, the Union leader's troops slogged away to return to their original positions, defeated without a fight. The loss of equipment was as terrible as if they had been in a real lost battle. Illness and desertions made the march's casualties as high as if the army had experienced combat. To Union soldiers, the Mud March embodied the incompetence of its commanders. "Hell with Burnsides," one trooper said. To others, it became a symbol of the army's will to press on, whatever the elements.

Lee might have seized the moment to crush the federal army, already shattered without a battle, but he was wary of following Burnside's lead and rushing into the same kind of swamp himself. He later reported that the weather turned cold a week after the Mud March's first day, and two days later he was in six inches of snow. By this time, however, he was no longer facing Burnside. Before the month of January was out, Burnside had already been sacked and replaced by General "Fighting Joe" Hooker.

"The hoarse and indistinguishable orders of commanding officers, the screaming and bursting of shells, canister and shrapnel as they tore through the struggling masses of humanity, the death screams of wounded animals, the groans of their human companions, wounded and dying and trampled underfoot by hurrying batteries, riderless horses and the moving lines of battle—a perfect Hell on earth, never, perhaps to be equaled, certainly not to be surpassed, nor ever to be forgotten in a man's lifetime. It has never been effaced from my memory, day or night, for fifty years."

A Massachusetts private

Fast Facts

- Grant was an excellent horse rider by age 12. Although not a great student—he was 21st out of his 39-member West Point class of 1843—he was one of the academy's most skilled riders ever. His favorite and most famous horse during the Civil War was Cincinnati, the son of Lexington, the fastest four-mile thoroughbred in the United States.

- In September 1862, approximately 72,500 troops guarded Washington, D.C.

- Southerners called the period of Reconstruction of the South "Yankee Rule."

- The cruiser CSS Florida was illegally seized in neutral Brazilian waters and then towed to Hampton Roads and sunk. This caused an international incident.

- The surrender terms at Appomattox in 1865 permitted every Confederate cavalry soldier to take his horse home with him. This provision, requested by Lee, was accepted by Grant who realized that, once they returned to civilian life, former soldiers wouldn't be able to work their farms without the horses they'd used in war.

- Union General Winfield Scott served under every president from Jefferson to Lincoln and was on active duty as a general from 1808 to 1861—longer than any other person in American history.

- President Abraham Lincoln issued General War Order No. 1 on January 1, 1862, calling for a Union offensive and for all U.S. naval and land forces to begin a general advance by February 22, George Washington's birthday. His order was ignored by General McClellan.

WHEN THEY REALLY DIDN'T WANT TO FIGHT

★ ★ ★ ★

The North and the South each struggled to deal with conscientious objectors to the war.

The Civil War posed a dilemma to members of pacifist religious groups such as Mennonites, Quakers, Seventh Day Adventists, and hundreds of others throughout the North and South. These groups were against violence of any kind and wished to be left alone, but as the number of available soldiers, particularly in the South, reached critical levels later in the war, this became more and more difficult.

The South Poses an Exemption Tax

The Confederate government passed its first Conscription Act in April 1862, but it didn't address how to deal with conscientious objectors. In October 1862, the Confederate Exemption Act was passed, allowing pacifists to escape service if they paid a $500 exemption tax. This seemed to solve the problem until the later months of the war when many people could not afford the exemption tax. A number of families were forced into hiding to escape punishment.

Noncombatant Roles in the North

As in the South, the Union government didn't know how to handle conscientious objectors. When Congress called for a draft of 300,000 from state militias in 1862, it made no provision for pacifists. The Draft Act of 1863 included exemptions for conscientious objectors but neglected to define the term. The act left it up to individuals to submit petitions for conscientious objector status.

Congress passed an 1864 law allowing pacifists subject to the draft to fill noncombatant roles, such as hospital orderlies. Those who were drafted could also avoid military service by paying $300 specifically to be applied to the hospital care of wounded or sick soldiers.

LAYING SIEGE TO PETERSBURG

★ ★ ★ ★

Northern and Southern soldiers settled in for a long wait as the Union gradually cut communication and supply routes around this Virginia city near the Confederate capital of Richmond.

After extended fighting in some of the most vicious battles of the war, Grant's Army of the Potomac and Lee's Army of Northern Virginia were exhausted. Although both sides needed to rest, they couldn't have been very comfortable in the early form of trench warfare that developed around Petersburg.

On to Richmond

Grant had launched his Overland Campaign in May 1864 with the aim of finally destroying the Army of Northern Virginia. He wanted to maneuver his 120,000 soldiers of the Army of the Potomac between the rebels and the Confederate capital of Richmond. Grant knew that if he squeezed his troops into that space and dug them into defensive positions, Lee would have to attack in defense of the capital. Lee's army was half the size of Grant's, so an attack against Grant's entrenched troops could be extremely costly to the rebels.

Things didn't work out as planned for the Union army. Grant tried to outflank Lee for a month, but each time the rebels held fast. Grant's force found itself fighting against entrenched Confederates instead of the other way around. At tremendous cost, the Federals had advanced to Cold Harbor on the outskirts of Richmond, but Grant's plan didn't seem to be working. He decided that, rather than trying to slip between Lee and Richmond, he'd isolate the Confederate capital by capturing the vital railroad and communication center at nearby Petersburg.

A Change of Plan

By midnight of June 14, the Federals had ferried one corps across the James River beside Petersburg. Grant's engineers built a 2,000-foot-long pontoon bridge across the river so the rest of the army could march across the river.

Once they made it across, though, the Union general did not put together a coordinated assault, and his haphazard attacks proved ineffective. Even though Petersburg was only lightly defended by a hastily assembled group of defenders under General P.G.T. Beauregard, the Confederates again held fast. Lee's army joined Beauregard a few days later, and they settled into a ten-mile-long chain of trenches, breastworks, and redoubts. (Breastworks were chest-high fortifications made of dirt and wood, and redoubts were mini forts, large enough for a few soldiers and cannons.) The defensive positions ran south of Richmond and were anchored on the east and west by the Appomattox River.

In the Trenches

Union troops built their own network of fortifications opposite the Confederates. But the Southerners held tight, fending off attack after attack. Grant realized that breaking through their lines would be a major struggle, so he decided that it would be better to wait.

And wait they did. Not much happened during the next several months. The Union forces' one hope of breaking the stalemate, the Battle of the Crater turned into a disaster and changed nothing.

Waiting It Out

The Union absorbed the loss, and the situation around Petersburg remained unchanged. As the scorching summer wore on, disease, boredom, and constant skirmishing took their toll on both armies. Grant's trench works edged steadily westward. Though he failed to inflict a decisive blow against Lee, attrition stretched Confederate strength to the limit. By October, the Weldon Railroad was in federal hands, leaving Lee with a single rickety rail line to supply his army, as well as the city of Petersburg, through the bitter winter months. The standoff didn't substantially change until early 1865.

FIGHT FIRST, EAT LATER

★ ★ ★ ★

A Union officer is accused of having misplaced priorities.

Many commanders on both sides of the Civil War engaged in behavior that ranged from the unsavory to the downright bizarre, for which they were constantly being reprimanded. One Union commander, however, was actually charged with eating in lieu of leading his troops.

Early in the war, William Dwight served his country with honor. He was severely wounded as commanding lieutenant colonel of the 70th New York Volunteer Infantry during the Battle of Williamsburg in May 1862. Dwight was captured but later released in a prisoner exchange. Soon, he was promoted to general and served with distinction in the Western Theater of operations.

What About Lunch?

Even the best and the brightest have their bad days, however. Dwight's alleged actions as commander of the 1st Division of the U.S. 19th Army Corps during the Battle of Winchester were far less than gallant. On September 19, 1864, Dwight, it was charged, "did, while the troops of his command were engaged with the enemy and hard pressed and in a critical part of the day, go to the rear beyond the presence of his troops and beyond the falling of the shot of the enemy, and in a place of comparative safety, and did remain there . . . and eat his dinner or lunch."

The actual validity of these charges is questionable. The witnesses against him were officers whose own conduct during the battle General Dwight had complained about in his official report. Dwight ultimately withdrew his report, and his name was eventually cleared in the charges against him. He continued to serve in the U.S. Army. After the war, Dwight went on to a successful career in manufacturing—during which, presumably, he could take his meals whenever he wished.

ACCORDING TO ABRAHAM LINCOLN

★ ★ ★ ★

"I believe this government cannot endure permanently half slave and half free."

★ ★ ★ ★

"If we do not make common cause to save the good old ship of the Union on this voyage, nobody will have a chance to pilot her on another voyage."

★ ★ ★ ★

"Although volume upon volume is written to prove slavery a very good thing, we never hear of the man who wishes to take the good of it, by being a slave himself."

★ ★ ★ ★

"Human nature will not change. In any future great national trial, compared with the men of this, we shall have as weak and as strong, as silly and as wise, as bad and as good."

★ ★ ★ ★

"As I would not be a slave, so I would not be a master. This expresses my idea of democracy. Whatever differs from this, to the extent of the difference, is no democracy."

★ ★ ★ ★

"I claim not to have controlled events, but confess plainly that events have controlled me."

★ ★ ★ ★

PIRATES OF THE CONFEDERACY

★ ★ ★ ★

Daring raids didn't only take place on land during the Civil War—
there was plenty of action and adventure on the sea, as well.

Though the Civil War army generals and their soldiers get most of the attention, the most successful
raider of the war may well have been a sailor—
Lieutenant Charles Read. Read, from Mississippi, was determined to show the Union that
the fledgling Confederate navy wasn't the joke
it had been made out to be. During a three-
week period in June 1863, he made a daring
and dauntless push up the eastern seaboard,
jumping from ship to ship and generally
wrecking havoc on both military and civilian shipping. Read
started with the CSS *Clarence* and burned or captured 22 ships in
only 21 days.

Read knew his profile was too high on a Confederate ship, so he
commandeered the Northern *Tacony* and used it to stage his raids.
Before too long, however, the *Tacony* had been identified by the
Union navy, so continued use of it was too dangerous. On June 25,
1863, he seized and took control of the *Archer,* another Northern
vessel. Looting Union ships, he'd discovered, was a great way of
taking advantage of the generally superior quality of Northern
ships and supplies.

Going Too Far

His boldness ultimately led to his downfall, however, when he
decided to hide his Confederate allegiance and dock the *Archer* in
Portland, Maine, only two days after he had commandeered it. He
had run out of ammunition and so needed to resupply. While in
the harbor at Portland, Read grew ambitious—instead of con-

stantly switching ships, he wondered what it would be like if he could amass a small fleet powerful enough that he wouldn't have to slink across the seas in fear of being discovered. Nearby, a fast and fresh ship known as the *Caleb Cushing* caught his eye. He ordered a few of his crew to hijack it.

As dawn rose over Portland, the *Archer* and the *Caleb Cushing* sailed to the open seas together, but they were betrayed by the rising sun. In the light, the harbormaster noted the absence of the *Cushing* and sounded the alarm. Soldiers joined private citizens in taking to the sea in pursuit. The Confederates were ready to fight them off, but Read found only a small amount of ammunition on the *Cushing.* In his official report, he wrote, "After firing five rounds from the pivot gun I was mortified to find that all projectiles for that gun had been expended." Read attempted to destroy the *Cushing* as a diversion to allow himself to escape, but he was captured anyway. In truth, there was more ammunition aboard the *Cushing,* and one Union commander later suggested that Read surely would have escaped if he'd only found it. Read was imprisoned in Fort Warren on George's Island in Boston Harbor. But in those three weeks he had averaged capturing or destroying just over a ship a day, Read became the most famous naval raider of the Confederacy.

- Cotton clads *was the name given to Confederate riverboats "armored" with bales of cotton.*

- *In June 1861, Frederick Douglass called for an emancipation proclamation. Lincoln issued the Emancipation Proclamation in January 1863. Lincoln and Douglass met privately for the first time in August 1863.*

- *Many soldiers carried a "housewife" in their knapsacks. This kit contained scraps of fabric, thread, buttons, and a needle for mending their uniforms.*

GALLANT ADVENTURE AT THE BATTLE OF MOBILE BAY

★ ★ ★ ★

"Damn the torpedoes!" saves the day.

The legendary saying "Damn the torpedoes!" sounds like something that would have originated during the great sea battles of World War II. But that isn't the case. The speaker was Union Rear Admiral David G. Farragut, and he made the proclamation during one of the great sea battles of the Civil War, the Battle of Mobile Bay.

By the summer of 1864, Mobile Bay, Alabama, was the last major port still open against the Union blockade. The bay, which sits about 50 miles northeast of New Orleans on the Gulf of Mexico, was protected by Fort Morgan, Fort Gaines, and Fort Powell. The bay itself was full of floating mines, which were then called *torpedoes,* as well as pilings and other obstructions. A narrow channel was the only relatively clear path through the bay, but it passed close to the guns of Fort Morgan.

Closing Down the Port

Mobile Bay was widely used by blockade runners to supply the Confederacy, so Union officials placed a priority on shutting it down. Admiral Farragut steamed to the bay with 14 wooden warships, 4 ironclad monitors, and 1,500 marines. When this force appeared, Confederate Admiral Franklin Buchanan moved his meager force of three wooden gunboats and one ironclad, the *Tennessee,* into the channel to confront them.

Farragut's leading ironclad, the *Tecumseh,* charged up the channel and positioned itself to take on the *Tennessee.* That maneuver swung the craft out of the safe zone, though, and it struck a mine. The explosion ripped the bottom of the ship—it sank in minutes. In the ensuing confusion, the rest of the Union line halted, making the federal ships sitting ducks for the Confederate cannons of Fort Morgan.

A Legend Is Born

That's when Farragut saw the chance to be a hero, or so some say. Legend has it that he lashed himself to the rigging of his flagship, the *Hartford,* and yelled out, "Damn the torpedoes! Full speed ahead!"

The rallying cry evidently worked, because the rest of the Union fleet sped into the harbor and neutralized the three wooden warships. Only the *Tennessee* remained. Its armor withstood cannon fire, so Farragut ordered his ships to ram the ironclad repeatedly. Eventually the ship's steering was wrecked, its smoke-stack was knocked off, and its gunport shutter chains were cut, making it impossible for the Confederates to return fire. After an hour of this battering, Admiral Buchanan, who had been wounded in the battle, raised the white flag. It would take another two weeks to capture Fort Morgan, but the naval battle for Mobile Bay was over.

- *According to some analysts, the most significant single federal operation of the war was the blockade of Southern ports.*

- *Some federal warships used on inland waters were converted riverboats protected only by thin coats of iron, hence their nickname* tinclads.

- *The two warring capitals, Washington, D.C., and Richmond, Virginia, were less than 100 miles apart.*

- *There were 53 Confederate and 67 Union generals at the Battle of Gettysburg.*

Fast Facts

- Late in 1862, Illinois voters adopted a constitutional provision that barred the immigration of blacks into the state.

- Daniel Butterfield, the creator of "Taps," based the song on "Tattoo," the lights-out call adapted from a French bugle call. He ordered that his new call be used instead of "Tattoo." After the Civil War, "Taps" was established as the official military bugle call for the end of the day. Although Butterfield did not attend the school, he was buried at West Point by special order.

- The completion of the transcontinental telegraph in October 1861 made the Pony Express obsolete. The Express was important in keeping communications open with California during the early days of the Civil War.

- The gigantic 20-inch Rodman smoothbore gun could project a shell about 3.5 miles.

- Years before the war, Jesse Grant, Ulysses S. Grant's father, worked for Owen Brown, the father of notorious abolitionist John Brown.

- President Johnson granted amnesty to all Southerners in 1868, but Jefferson Davis declined to accept it.

- Union General Ambrose Burnside is perhaps most well-known for his facial hair—side whiskers connected to a moustache with a clean-shaven chin, a style that became known as Burnside's and later sideburns. He was also credited with patenting the Burnside carbine, which after the Sharps and Spencer carbines, was the third most-used carbine by Union cavalry.

- The largest predominantly cavalry engagement of the Civil War was at Brandy Station, Virginia, on June 9, 1863.

AN UNLIKELY FIGURE TO WIN A WAR

★ ★ ★ ★

*Ulysses S. Grant didn't get the nickname
"Unconditional Surrender" for nothing.*

General Ulysses S. Grant was an average student at West Point,
had a moderately successful early military career, and was long out
of the army—working instead as a clerk in his father's leather
goods store—by the time the Civil War broke out. When he
returned to the Union army to defend his country, however, he
discovered his true calling.

Grant graduated from West Point in 1843, ranking 21st out of 39
students. During the Mexican War, he was a regimental quartermaster, a supply position that normally doesn't see combat but did
in this case. He served under General Zachary Taylor, a future U.S.
president, and General Winfield Scott, who was the top U.S. military leader when the Civil War began. He demonstrated skill under
both men and won brevets, which were pseudo-promotions handed
out in lieu of medals, for two campaigns during the Mexican War.

Peacetime Disappointment

Unfortunately for Grant, peacetime was not good for his military
career, and amid rumors of heavy drinking, he quit the army in
1854. To support his wife and children, he took up farming on his
father-in-law's land. He was not successful at this venture, so he
tried real estate, engineering, and finally, clerking in the family
business in Galena, Illinois. Try as he might, he just couldn't get a
foothold in the business world.

A Return to War

Grant's military career had been the high point of his professional
life, so it made sense for him to return to it when war broke out in
1861. He applied for a position with the Union army, but his appli-

cation was ignored. So instead, he organized Illinois volunteers and established himself as a colonel of the 21st Illinois Infantry.

Grant started to lead troops in low-profile maneuvers on the western edge of the war in northwestern Kentucky and southeastern Missouri. These early excursions demonstrated his leadership abilities as an action-oriented individual, making bold, decisive moves against the Confederates. His successes resulted in his promotion to general. The first chance he had at a high-profile battle came in February 1862 at Fort Donelson, Tennessee, where he led his army against a strong, entrenched Confederate force. Although neither side managed to take the upper hand over two days of battle, the two top Confederate officers abandoned the fort, leaving third-in-command Simon Boliver Buckner, an old West Point classmate of Grant, to surrender. When Buckner asked for lenient terms, Grant famously replied that he would accept nothing less than an unconditional surrender, earning him the nickname "Unconditional Surrender" Grant. For a country unhappy with military setbacks, the capture of Fort Donelson was big news. And Grant was the new hero.

Two months later, he was leading troops at Shiloh. This battle was a disaster for the Union on its first day, but Grant confidently predicted that he would "whip" the rebels the next day. He did. The Union army regained the ground it had lost, but the effort resulted in the bloodiest battle of the war so far, with 23,000 soldiers lost in total on both sides.

Despite Grant's success, his superior, General Henry Halleck, soon arrived on the field and took over command, which bumped Grant down to number two. Grant was unhappy having less responsibility, but he was soon put back in charge to lead the attack on Vicksburg, a vital city on the Mississippi River. Capturing Vicksburg would effectively slice the Confederacy in half and give the Union control of the mighty river.

Success Breeds Success

Vicksburg was easy to defend from the north and east, and the rebels had the river covered by artillery on the west. So Grant expertly led his army on an attack from the only exposed side. He defeated the smaller forces guarding the southern route and laid a 47-day siege of the city. The bloody struggle ended on July 4, 1863, when the Confederates surrendered the city. It was a gigantic victory for the Union, and Grant was again the hero.

After fighting a few more successful battles across Mississippi, Grant was placed in charge of all Union armies in the West. In that role, he broke the Confederate hold on Chattanooga and Knoxville, Tennessee, further cementing his reputation as a powerhouse general.

Heading East

With Grant's victories in the West, the powers in Washington decided it was time to bring him east to face General Robert E. Lee. He set up his headquarters with the Army of the Potomac and began pounding Lee's forces in Virginia.

In the bloody Battle of the Wilderness, Grant led Union troops to victory at an extremely high cost in dead and wounded. After it was over, the weary troops believed Grant would give them time to lick their wounds, but unlike the previous eastern generals they were used to, Grant ordered the army to load up and immediately pursue the whipped Confederates. Again, Grant's boldness shone brightly, and it was just the type of fighting required to win the war. But Lee and his rebels were tenacious and not easy to defeat. Grant's army chased them almost all the way to their capital, Richmond, Virginia. The Union laid another siege at Petersburg, a stronghold south of Richmond. As he had shown in Vicksburg, Grant knew how to execute a siege, and he slowly tightened a noose around Lee and his troops. It took ten months, but this siege worked as well, and Grant captured Petersburg and Richmond beyond it. Lee and some of his remaining soldiers broke out and fled south, but a week later Lee surrendered at Appomattox Court House. The war was essentially over.

Grant proved that success in war requires fearless, rapid action. He stepped up when it counted and earned the love of the Union along the way.

THE UNION ARMY'S AMBULANCE CORPS

★ ★ ★ ★

What do people do when they need to go to the hospital?
They call an ambulance. But that was considered
a luxury for the Civil War wounded.

Having access to a dedicated ambulance service is a relatively modern development. Early in the Civil War, wounded soldiers were typically removed from the battlefield by drummer boys and carried to the rear of the action on stretchers. This practice didn't allow for transportation over long distances, obviously, and it wasn't an efficient means of dealing with the unprecedented number of wounded soldiers, either.

A Rough Ride

To remedy the situation on the Union side, the army deployed field ambulances, developing two- and four-wheel versions. Two-wheel ambulances provided a bumpy ride, and many severely wounded soldiers became worse as a result. Four-wheel ambulances were more comfortable. Supply wagons were also sometimes pressed into service to carry the wounded.

Initially, Union ambulances were controlled by the Quartermaster Corps, which made them a lower priority than other transportation tasks. The Quartermaster Corps assigned the soldiers who had been ineffective in battle to drive ambulances and tend to the wounded, but bad soldiers usually made bad orderlies, as well, so the care they rendered was generally second-rate at best.

A New Ambulance Corps

Despite the drawbacks of this system for removing the helpless wounded from battlefields, nothing substantive was accomplished until August 1862. That's when General George B. McClellan issued General Order Number 147, which established an ambulance corps for the Army of the Potomac. The corps would operate according to a plan devised by McClellan's medical director, Jonathan Letterman.

Under the Letterman Ambulance Plan, each division would have a corps equipped with dedicated vehicles, draft animals, supplies, and personnel—consisting of two stretcher-bearers and one driver per ambulance—that could not be used for anything else. All such ambulances would then travel together under the supervision of a mounted noncommissioned officer to collect the wounded from the battlefield, bring them to dressing stations, and then take them to field hospitals.

Letterman's scheme worked well and, despite turf-based opposition in the various major commands, it was emulated in other field armies. His plan received the ultimate endorsement in March 1864 when Congress passed legislation creating an ambulance corps for all Union armies.

"On they come, with the old swinging route step and swaying battle flags. In the van, the proud Confederate ensign. Before us in proud humiliation stood the embodiment of manhood; men whom neither toils and sufferings, nor the fact of death could bend from their resolve; standing before us now, thin, worn, and famished, but erect, and with eyes looking level into ours, waking memories that bound us together as no other bond; was not such manhood to be welcomed back into a Union so tested and assured? On our part not a sound of trumpet more, nor roll of drum; not a cheer, nor word, nor whisper or vainglorying, nor motion of man, but an awed stillness rather, and breath-holding, as if it were the passing of the dead!"
General Joshua Lawrence Chamberlain, 20th Maine, on the Confederate surrender at Appomattox Court House

(Continued from p. 385)

1865

January 31
The House of Representatives passes the 13th Amendment.

February 18
Sherman's Union troops occupy Charleston, South Carolina.

March 4
Lincoln is inaugurated for his second term as President.

April 2
Union troops attack and break the Confederate lines at Petersburg, forcing Lee to begin evacuating from Petersburg and Richmond.

April 3
Union troops occupy Petersburg and Richmond.

April 9
Lee surrenders to Grant at Appomattox Court House, Virginia.

April 13
Sherman's troops enter Raleigh, North Carolina.

April 14
Lincoln is shot by John Wilkes Booth as the President watches the play *Our American Cousin* at Ford's Theatre in Washington.

April 15
President Lincoln dies in the Petersen House, across the street from Ford's Theatre. Andrew Johnson is sworn in as President.

April 18
General Sherman and General Joseph E. Johnston sign a surrender agreement near Durham, North Carolina. Washington refuses the agreement as too lenient.

April 26
Johnston surrenders his troops to Sherman in an agreement acceptable to Washington.

April 27
The USS *Sultana* explodes on the Mississippi River, resulting in the deaths of at least 1,238 crew members and soldiers, the worst maritime loss in U.S. history.

May 10
Union cavalry captures Jefferson Davis near Irwinville, Georgia.

President Andrew Johnson declares armed resistance at an end.

May 12–13
The last major military action of the war occurs at Palmito Ranch, Texas.

May 22
Jefferson Davis is imprisoned in solitary confinement at Fort Monroe, Virginia.

May 26
Confederate troops west of the Mississippi agree to surrender at New Orleans.

November 6
The CSS *Shenandoah* arrives in Liverpool, England, the last Confederate commerce raider to surrender.

December 6
In his annual message to Congress, President Johnson announces that the Union has been restored.

(Continued on p. 439)

SHERMAN'S SOFT SURRENDER

★ ★ ★ ★

Attempting to carry out the wishes of President Lincoln regarding the terms of surrender, General Sherman's approach was a bit too forgiving for some politicians.

The April 14, 1865, assassination of Abraham Lincoln, coming just days after Robert E. Lee surrendered at Appomattox Court House, left the Union with no strong leader and incomplete instructions for how generals should dictate peace to the collapsing armies of the South. Lincoln had left them with a plea to end this war "with malice towards none," and new president Andrew Johnson leaned toward treating Southerners like wayward brothers. But a hard-line faction, led by powerful Secretary of War Edwin M. Stanton, wanted total capitulation followed by punishment.

Work of Forgiveness

On April 17, when General William Tecumseh Sherman found himself facing a defeated Confederate General Joseph Johnston under a flag of truce, he stated it was "a perfect furor, of rejoicing." But what terms should he offer? Weeks earlier, he'd walked away from a meeting with Lincoln aboard the White House steamer, the *River Queen,* convinced that he'd been authorized to begin the work of forgiveness. Reflecting on Lincoln's wishes in his memoirs, Sherman wrote, "All he wanted of us was to defeat the opposing armies, and to get the men...back to their homes, at work on their farms and in their shops."

During armistice talks at a farmhouse near Durham, North Carolina, the Confederates offered the surrender of all their armies. Sherman, who has since become vilified for his march through Georgia to Savannah and the sea, wrote out the terms, "which I thought concisely expressed [Lincoln's] views and wishes." By merely laying down their guns and signing promises not to oppose the United

States, Sherman agreed, Southern soldiers could go home undisturbed. So far, that was in keeping with what fellow Union General Ulysses S. Grant had already offered Lee a few days earlier.

Taking Things Too Far

But then Sherman went beyond Grant's already lenient terms and accepted the surrender of all Southern states and leaders, promising that the Southern states themselves could rejoin the United States, no questions asked, if only their troops would deposit all weapons in armories and vow to uphold the Constitution. When news of the agreement reached War Secretary Stanton, he and other politicians were livid over what they perceived as Sherman's meddling in political affairs. Stanton sent Grant to North Carolina to "assist" Sherman with a second version of the agreement. Sherman, seen as a hero in the North for his "March to the Sea," was briefly pilloried in Northern newspapers. For his part, Grant didn't understand what the fuss was about. He later wrote about Sherman and the incident in his own memoirs: "Some people went so far as to denounce him as a traitor—a most preposterous term."

In the end, it was back to the drawing board. The April 26 agreement returned to the terms originally stated by Grant to Lee. It would be months before the final surrender of all Confederate armies had taken place, and the readmission of all Southern states would take years longer than Sherman expected. It wasn't until 1870 that the last state, Georgia, returned to the Union.

★ ★ ★ ★

- *Secretary Edwin Stanton was named to the Supreme Court by President Grant, but he died before he could be sworn in.*

- *Reno, Nevada, is named after Union General Jesse Lee Reno, who was shot from his horse and mortally wounded at the Battle of South Mountain at Fox's Gap, Maryland.*

CONFEDERATES SOUTH OF THE EQUATOR

★ ★ ★ ★

"Confederados," they call them in Brazil: Southerners who fled farther south, into the tropics, after losing the Civil War.

In the southern Brazilian state of São Paulo, there survives a town named Americana where the great-great-grandchildren of Confederate rebels speak in a Georgia drawl with a Portuguese accent. They are descendants of the *"Confederados"*, a group of Southerners who settled in Brazil after the Civil War ended. Every year, a diminishing number of offspring reunite for the *Festa Confederada*, a celebration of Dixie culture. They serve deep-fried chicken, fly the Confederate flag, dress in antebellum fashion, and downplay the issue of slavery.

Fleeing the South

In the post-Civil War upheaval, a Confederate migration found tens of thousands of people escaping to Europe, Mexico, and beyond. While the 2,500 who settled in Mexico ultimately saw their hopes dashed and were forced to return to the United States, the 9,000 who continued "way, way down South" to Brazil found a dependable protector in its emperor, Dom Pedro II. He wanted the Southerners to bring state-of-the-art cotton-farming know-how to his country.

Pedro was gradually phasing out slavery in Brazil. His daughter, Princess Isabel, would end the institution with the stroke of a pen, ushering in the Golden Law of abolition in 1888. But with a few exceptions, the *Confederados* didn't appear to have brought all the practices of their antebellum plantations to the tropics. A recent study by Brazilian researcher Alcides Gussi was able to find evidence of only 66 slaves owned by four families of *Confederados* in Brazil. Many of the immigrants were too poor to own slaves, and the rest relied largely on cheap local labor.

A New Home

By the end of the 1860s, Southerners were steaming for Brazil from the ports of New Orleans, Charleston, Newport News, Baltimore, and Galveston to settle in towns such as Americana and nearby Santa Bárbara D'Oeste. "My grandfather came from Texas and built his house in the middle of a forest," 86-year-old Maria Weissinger told the *Atlanta Journal-Constitution* in 2003. The new land was fertile but rife with insects that carried deadly tropical diseases. Many refugees gave up and returned to the Reconstruction South, but about two in five stayed in their adopted homeland, intermarried with Brazilians, grew pecans and peaches, and built schools and universities.

Weakened Roots

After nearly 150 years, most of the *Confederados* have been absorbed into the populations of big cities, but in the industrial town of Americana, traces of the South survive, kept alive in part by a group called the Fraternity of American Descendents. Multiple generations in, the lines between *Confederados* and Brazilians have become more blurred than ever. Many of the observant *Confederados* in Americana no longer speak English, but many continue to travel to a cemetery in nearby Santa Bárbara D'Oeste, where the graves tell the stories of their families' fading Confederate roots. In 1972, the cemetery was visited by one settler's great-niece: Rosalyn Carter, wife of future president Jimmy Carter, then governor of Georgia.

- *General Philip St. George Cooke served in the U.S. Army for 50 years. During the Civil War, he saw active service only in the Peninsula Campaign before being assigned to administrative duty. He is remembered more for his family, which was the subject of national gossip because of its division over the war. His son, John R. Cooke, became a Confederate general. Of three daughters, only one remained loyal to the Union. Another was married to General Jeb Stuart of the Confederate cavalry.*

WHERE WAS THAT AGAIN?

★ ★ ★ ★

Match these Civil War battles to the state in which they took place.

Battle	State
Bayou Fourche	Alabama
Big Black River Bridge	Arkansas
Boonsborough	Arkansas
Cheat Mountain	Florida
Dallas	Georgia
Devil's Backbone	Georgia
Garnett's & Golding's Farm	Kansas
Grimball's Landing	Kansas
Griswoldville	Kentucky
Hanover	Louisiana
Irish Bend	Maryland
Ivy Mountain	Mississippi
Lexington	Mississippi
Little Blue River	Missouri
Marais des Cygnes	Missouri
Middle Boggy Depot	North Carolina
Mine Creek	Oklahoma
Mossy Creek	Pennsylvania
Natural Bridge	South Carolina
Okolona	South Carolina
Plymouth	Tennessee
Saint Mary's Church	Virginia
Secessionville	Virginia
Spanish Fort	Virginia
Wilson's Wharf	West Virginia

Spanish Fort—Alabama; Bayou Fourche, Devil's Backbone—Arkansas; Natural Bridge—Florida; Dallas, Griswoldville—Georgia; Marais des Cygnes, Mine Creek—Kansas; Ivy Mountain—Kentucky; Irish Bend—Louisiana; Boonsborough—Maryland; Big Black River Bridge, Okolona—Mississippi; Lexington, Little Blue River—Missouri; Plymouth—North Carolina; Middle Boggy Depot—Oklahoma; Hanover—Pennsylvania; Grimball's Landing, Secessionville—South Carolina; Mossy Creek—Tennessee; Garnett's & Golding's Farm, Saint Mary's Church, Wilson's Wharf—Virginia; Cheat Mountain—West Virginia

MATHEW BRADY, DEAN OF THE PHOTOGRAPHERS

★ ★ ★ ★

Acting more like a director than a photographer, Mathew Brady was the first to provide visual documentation of war.

The connection between Mathew Brady and Civil War photography isn't completely accurate—his assistants captured the immortal images attached to his name. He had a drive to propound his own myth, seeking personal glory and fortune as chronicler of the war. But Brady was an innovator—prior to his time, no one else had even done as much as consider how to take pictures of a war.

An Entrepreneur Is Born

Even before the war, Brady was no ordinary entrepreneur. Born in upstate New York, he arrived in the big city in 1840 as a teenager and trained in basic photography with Samuel Morse, the inventor of the telegraph. Just five years later, Brady launched his own empire. Never without ambition, Brady styled himself as photographer to the illustrious, from chronicling leaders such as Andrew Jackson and the Prince of Wales to entertainers and writers such as singer Jenny Lind and Edgar Allen Poe. His Broadway gallery became a compulsory stop for both those who were seeking immortality and those who merely wished to observe it.

Documenting History

With the country poised to erupt in flames in 1861, Brady prepared himself to document history. Brushing aside concerns for his personal safety, he parlayed his connections into a ringside seat at the country's darkest hour: President Lincoln signed a note reading "Pass Brady" to smooth any obstacles he might encounter.

The resourceful Brady put together rolling horse-drawn dark-rooms staffed by his best photographers. Possibly due to failing eyesight, he worked more as a director than a hands-on camera operator. Two of his associates, Alexander Gardner and Timothy O'Sullivan, were responsible for the lion's share of what we know today of the war's horrific images.

Seeing the war's carnage up close awakened Brady to the commercial possibilities of putting it on public display. Antietam provided his first opportunity for an exhibition of the photographic documentation. Recording an endless array of images of corpses on the battlefield, Brady's team caused a media sensation when the series "The Dead at Antietam" played to packed houses at his New York City gallery shortly after the battle. Viewers were horrified by the compelling photographs, but they kept coming. As *The New York Times* wrote, "Mr. Brady has done something to bring home to us the terrible reality and earnestness of war." The net effect of Brady's work galvanized public opinion in the North against the war.

Brady's penchant for claiming all the credit galled his associates, and soon Gardner and O'Sullivan struck out on their own. Gardner in particular prided himself on his technical innovations. Undeterred, Brady hired others who in time made their own mark in photography. By war's end, he had an inventory of some 10,000 images.

Interest Wanes

When the fighting ended, however, interest in Brady's work quickly dissipated. The public was weary of the war in all its aspects. Brady had spent himself into oblivion, and competitors soon wrested his share of the market away. It took him ten years and much quibbling to convince Congress to buy out his negatives for a paltry $25,000. Pushed by Representative James Garfield, a Union vet, the government eventually ponied up, but not before Brady had sold off most of his assets, including his New York City gallery.

Brady's wife died in 1887, and he never recovered. He became an alcoholic and died penniless and forgotten in 1896. Not until the next century would historians take stock of his achievement and restore his name to its place in photographic history.

MISGUIDED INTENTIONS

★ ★ ★ ★

President Lincoln issued the Emancipation Proclamation in September 1862, and it became federal law on January 1, 1863. However, Northern leaders and military commanders had made their own attempts to "free the slaves" prior to Lincoln's edict.

There is such a thing as overstepping your boundaries. Lincoln trusted Union General John C. Frémont and named him commander of the Western Theater only a few days after the Northern defeat at the First Battle of Bull Run in July 1861. Once he wielded power, Frémont wasted little time putting it to use. Soon, he boldly and blindly announced that Missouri was now under martial law and, consequently, under his complete control. What's more, Frémont declared that all slaves of Missouri Confederates were now free. Lincoln remained tactful, asking the arrogant Frémont to "modify" his edict to only that of Union confiscation of Confederate property—which included slaves. In response, Frémont sent his wife, Jessie, to Washington to put the President back in his place.

Left with no choice, Lincoln on September 11 officially directed Frémont to change the order of emancipation. The President relieved Frémont of his command two months later, bringing in General David Hunter as a replacement.

Let Them Have Guns

Another attempt at emancipating the slaves occurred in late 1861. Lincoln named Simon Cameron to be secretary of war as a political favor for Cameron's help in the 1860 election. In an end-of-the-year report, Cameron called for freeing the slaves of those making war against the United States and arming those slaves to fight for the Union. Unfortunately, Cameron had prepared and released this report without sharing it with the President. When the report was made public, Lincoln was upset enough to order copies of the report to be collected and returned for correction.

Simon Cameron was relieved of his Cabinet position within a month. He was later named minister to Russia, getting him off the American continent altogether.

Hunter Becomes the Hunted

By March 1862, General David Hunter had been named commander of the Department of the South. Ironically, Hunter followed the path of his predecessor, Frémont and "freed" slaves. From his South Carolina headquarters, Hunter issued this order: "Slavery and martial law in a free country are altogether incompatible; the persons in these three States—Georgia, Florida and South Carolina—heretofore held as slaves, are therefore declared forever free."

Again, Lincoln had to command his general to rescind the order, fearing that emancipation would influence border state slave owners to join the Confederacy. Privately, Lincoln was furious. He wrote to Treasury Secretary Salmon Chase, "No commanding general shall do such a thing, upon *my* responsibility, without consulting me." Jefferson Davis and other Southern leaders were also furious at Hunter's bold action. Davis ordered that, if captured, General Hunter was to be considered a felon who should be executed. Hunter eventually resigned his commission.

★ ★ ★ ★

"There are times when a corps commander's life does not count."
Union General Winfield Scott Hancock, Commander II Corps, July 3, 1863

"The warlike scene was fascinatingly grand beyond description. The battlefield presented a scenic view that the loftiest thought of my mind is far too low and insignificant to delineate, describe, or portray."
Confederate Corporal George M. Neese, Stuart's Horse Artillery, on the Battle of Brandy Station

ACHIEVING THE GRATITUDE OF YOUR COUNTRY

★ ★ ★ ★

Now the military's highest, most coveted honor, the Medal of Honor was generously passed out during the Civil War.

During the four years Americans fought in World War II, 464 men—out of about 16 million who served—won the Medal of Honor. Only 245 received it during the Vietnam War. Just one member of the Coast Guard has ever received one, and only 17 members of the Air Force. It's a rare, highly respected honor, given only to service members who do something dramatically courageous during combat.

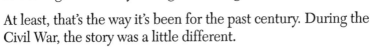

At least, that's the way it's been for the past century. During the Civil War, the story was a little different.

Establishing the Medal

No medal for valor existed when the Civil War started. Army General-in-Chief Winfield Scott didn't like medals—he felt they smacked of show-off European armies. Others felt individual medals discouraged unity among the troops.

But Navy leaders believed that recognizing bravery was motivational, so they proposed a medal of valor "to be bestowed upon such petty officers, seamen, landsmen, and Marines as shall most distinguish themselves by their gallantry and other seamanlike qualities during the present war." Lincoln agreed and authorized the medal on December 12, 1861. When General Scott resigned from the Army, the new Army leaders decided they wanted a medal, too. The Army version of the Navy medal was approved on July 12, 1862.

The new medal was handsome—a five-pointed star hanging from a ribbon resembling the American flag. Soldiers wore it around their necks.

The First Honorees

The stage was set for recognizing outstanding soldiers. So to whom did the first medals go? Well, they were brave men, but the event didn't involve dramatic hand-to-hand combat. Rather, they were soldiers led by Union spy James J. Andrews who snuck behind Confederate lines in Georgia to destroy railroad tracks, bridges, and telegraph lines. They failed and most were captured, but the six who survived the raid were awarded with Medals of Honor in 1863.

At least those honorees did something fearless and dramatic. Because it was the only medal around, leaders started handing the Medal of Honor out somewhat indiscriminately. Consider the case of the 27th Maine Infantry Regiment. All 864 members won the medal. That's more than all the winners from World War I, World War II, and the Vietnam War combined! One might think those Maine boys did something heroic—won a major battle against tremendous odds, captured the Confederate capital, or something along those lines. Well, one would be wrong. This regiment received the medal because it did a stellar job sitting around the barracks in forts near Washington, D.C. Offered as an incentive for troops to stay to protect the capital after their enlistment was up, a clerical error resulted in the entire regiment sharing the honor.

Of course, many Civil War Medal of Honor winners did actually risk their lives. A number of winners were cited for capturing Confederate battle flags. These flags inspired and guided troops in battle, so a soldier risked serious personal damage sneaking behind enemy lines to snag one of these prizes. Of course, some battle flags were just dropped in the heat of combat or lay with dead or wounded color bearers, so the first lucky Union soldier to come across one and hurry it back to his lines could be awarded a shiny new Medal of Honor.

The rules for winning a Medal of Honor were tightened in the early 20th century. Now soldiers must risk their lives in combat "above and beyond the call of duty." When the restrictions were enacted in 1917, a panel of generals reviewed all previous winners and revoked 911 medals, including those given to the brave protectors from Maine. The final total of Civil War Medals of Honor awarded is 1,522.

Fast Facts

- *The exact number of Confederate enlisted men during the war years is unknown. Authoritative estimates range from as many as 1.4 million to as few as 600,000.*

- *Almost 39 percent of the Confederacy's population were slaves.*

- *After the war, Confederate General Longstreet became a Republican. He renewed his friendship with Grant and served as Grant's minister to Turkey.*

- *Postage service was abolished between the North and South in 1861. At the time, the basic postal rate was 3 cents, with adjustments for distance. The South established a higher 5-cent rate for distances less than 500 miles but standardized its rate at 10 cents for all distances in 1862. The North standardized the 3-cent rate in 1863. Express service cost from 15 to 25 cents.*

- *Typical Union gear included a musket, a bayonet, a cartridge box with 40 rounds, a belt, a cap pouch, a haversack, a canteen, a knapsack, a ground blanket, a shelter half, a winter greatcoat, a tin cup and plate, and leggings.*

- *Abraham Lincoln credited his first presidential victory to two things: a speech he gave at Cooper Union in 1860 and a widely distributed portrait taken by Mathew Brady.*

- *Benjamin Harrison, the 23rd president and the grandson of 9th president William Henry Harrison, entered service as a second lieutenant of the 70th Regiment of Indiana Volunteers and rose to the rank of brigadier general by the end of the war.*

- *After the Union defeat at Bull Run, enlistment periods for Union troops were increased from three months to two years.*

SHERMAN'S MARCH

★ ★ ★ ★

*Union soldiers made their presence known as Sherman's
army marched its way through Georgia to the sea.*

An army lives on its supply lines. Food, ammunition,
fresh troops, and horses are all necessary for an army
on the march. But when Union General William
Tecumseh Sherman began his march across Georgia,
he knew that he would quickly outrun his supply lines.

In late autumn 1864, Sherman conquered Atlanta,
and he believed he could break the will of the
Southern people by traveling the remaining 300 miles
through Georgia to the seaport of Savannah. "If the North can
march an army right through the South," he wrote to General
Ulysses Grant, "it is proof positive that the North can prevail."

Breaking the Supply Line

The only drawback to this plan, however, was that such a march
would thoroughly cut Sherman's army off from the North, meaning that no supply lines could keep them connected to the necessities of life. To follow through with his plan, he had only one
choice: His soldiers would have to appropriate food and supplies
from the Southern civilians along the way.

With 60,000 troops to feed, it would be necessary to find a lot of
food. The plantations along the route were obvious targets. Soldiers would march through and grab all the meat, bread, dairy
products, and other supplies they could. But sometimes they
didn't stop there. Many civilians reported that the soldiers stole
valuables that had no real military use.

Living off the Land

"They robbed every house on the road of its provisions, sometimes taking every piece of meat, blankets and wearing apparel,

silver and arms of every description," wrote Dolly Sumner Lunt, a widow who lived on a plantation near Covington, Georgia, and whose diary was later published. "They would take silk dresses and put them under their saddles, and many other things for which they had no use. Is this the way to make us love them and their Union? Let the poor people answer whom they have deprived of every mouthful of meat and of their livestock to make any!"

Merry Christmas

This unpopular method of resupplying the army worked, though, and Sherman easily defeated the meager defenses between Atlanta and Savannah. He captured that port city on December 22, five weeks after his march began. Just in time for the holidays, he wired President Lincoln: "I beg to present you, as a Christmas gift, the city of Savannah."

"I know the hole he went in at, but I can't tell you what hole he will come out of."
Abraham Lincoln, when asked about the destination of Sherman's destructive March to the Sea

"If you don't have my army supplied, and keep it supplied, we'll eat your mules up, sir."
William Tecumseh Sherman to an army quartermaster before his army's departure from Chattanooga toward Atlanta

"I hate newspapermen. They come into camp and pick up their camp rumors and print them as facts. I regard them as spies, which, in truth, they are. If I killed them all there would be news from Hell before breakfast."
General William Tecumseh Sherman

SENDING THE WAR INTO OVERTIME

★ ★ ★ ★

Limited communication meant that a ship at sea might not hear of the Confederacy's downfall for ages. The CSS Shenandoah *kept the cause alive for several months after Appomattox Court House.*

"The Confederate flag no longer floated on the land," the deposed Confederate President Jefferson Davis wrote in his memoirs, "but one gallant sailor still unfurled it on the Pacific." The last of the Confederate army may have surrendered on May 26, 1865, but one Confederate warship, the CSS *Shenandoah,* refused to surrender until November. As long as it patrolled the Pacific Ocean, it provided a last glimmer of hope to Davis, who was now residing in a Union prison.

The *Shenandoah* began life as the *Sea King,* a British commercial steamer designed to carry British troops to India. In October 1864, Confederate agents secretly bought the vessel. It set sail under the cover of a commercial voyage but actually journeyed to the Portuguese island of Madeira, where it was outfitted as a warship and rechristened the CSS *Shenandoah.* Under the command of First Lieutenant James Waddell, the crew was ordered to "seek out and utterly destroy" Union commerce ships in waters not yet patrolled by Confederate vessels.

Mission Accomplished

In late January 1865, the *Shenandoah* arrived at Melbourne, Australia, for repairs. When the repairs were completed, it left Melbourne to attack American whaling ships in the South Pacific. Alerted to the danger, the whaling fleet dispersed. Undeterred, Waddell set course for the North Pacific to attack whaling ships there. As the warship sailed north during April and May, Waddell had no way of knowing that the Confederate army was surrendering. By the time the *Shenandoah* reached the Bering Sea in June, the ship had captured 24 Union ships, destroying most of them.

While sailing the Bering Sea, Waddell read of Lee's surrender and Lincoln's assassination in American newspapers gathered from captured ships. Still, he believed the printed word was less than reliable, and so, satisfied that his work was completed in the North Pacific and concerned about the potential damage of arctic pack ice, Waddell continued to sail and steered the ship south. He expected that San Francisco would be lightly defended and decided to shell the city. Before the ship reached the California coast, however, on August 2 the *Shenandoah* met a British merchant ship whose captain confirmed that the Confederacy had indeed surrendered. Waddell was on the brink of attacking San Francisco, but he realized that if his ship was no longer affiliated with an existing Confederate nation, he and his crew would be considered nothing more than pirates.

No Alternatives

Waddell's first task was to dismantle the ship and disguise its true function as a vessel of war. Guns were dismounted and placed below deck, and the ship was painted to resemble a merchant ship. Waddell's next task was to determine a port at which to surrender. He ruled out Cape Town in Africa because of the difficulties the crew would have when trying to go home. He finally steered the ship toward Liverpool, England.

The voyage from the west coast of the United States to the United Kingdom, even making no stops, took more than three months. By the time the *Shenandoah* had sailed the 17,000 miles to reach Liverpool on November 6, 1865, its supplies had dwindled, and some of the sailors had developed scurvy. Waddell negotiated for the freedom of his crew with British authorities before he agreed to surrender, though he and other officers were unable to return to the United States for several years until they received pardons.

In only 13 months, the *Shenandoah* had sailed more than 58,000 miles and had captured 38 enemy ships and 1,053 seafarers, while Waddell's crew had only lost two sailors to illness. In 1866, the *Shenandoah* was sold to the Sultan of Zanzibar and was renamed *El Majidi.* It was damaged in a hurricane near Zanzibar in 1872, and it sank in the Indian Ocean later in the year.

SO THEY SAID

"Our Southern brethren have done grievously, they have rebelled and have attacked their father's house and their loyal brothers. They must be punished and brought back, but this necessity breaks my heart."

Major Robert Anderson, defender of Fort Sumter in April 1861

"I have heard of 'the dead lying in heaps,' but never saw it till this battle. Whole ranks fell together."

Union Captain Emory Upton, 2nd Artillery, at Antietam

"They will attack you in the morning and they will come booming—skirmishers three deep. You will have to fight like the devil until supports arrive."

Union General John Buford, June 30, 1863, before Gettysburg

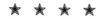

"Whether the Union stands or falls, I believe the profession of arms will henceforth be more desirable and more respected than it has been hitherto."

Senator Charles Sumner of Massachusetts, April 1861

★ ★ ★ ★

"When news of the surrender first reached our lines our men commenced firing a salute of a hundred guns in honor of the victory. I at once sent word, however, to have it stopped. The Confederates were now our prisoners, and we did not want to exult over their downfall."

Ulysses S. Grant, on the Confederate surrender at Appomattox Court House

TREASURES LOST AND FOUND

★ ★ ★ ★

Millions of dollars worth of treasure was pillaged, buried, sunken—you name it—during the riotous days of the Civil War.

Treasures of coin, bullion, and other valuables had already been traveling along America's waters, rails, and roads before the Civil War began. Once that conflict erupted, these stores of wealth became targets for pirates, outlaws, and soldiers to intercept either for personal gain or to hit the enemy in the pocketbook—or both. The paths this loot took on the high seas, on the tracks, and in the backwoods of the country became more and more treacherous as the war developed.

The Sources of Treasure

As early as January 1861, the Union's secretary of the Navy sent word to his commanders stationed along the water route from New York to California to "be vigilant and if necessary be prompt to use all the means at your command for the protection of the California steamers and their treasure." Commodore Cornelius Vanderbilt recommended adding guns on passenger ships because "our steamers may be seized or robbed on their voyage." Treasury Secretary Salmon Chase and others also begged for strong cannons to be mounted on merchant boats to protect them from Confederate bandits. One group of merchants petitioning for such assistance estimated that $40 million in gold traveled from San Francisco to New York every year.

The Confederate navy simply didn't match up to that of the Union, so the South hired private raiders to attack Northern merchant ships in an effort to stop general trade and the transport of items that assisted the Union war effort. In the first half of the war, Confederate-sponsored raiders captured 40 Northern ships. The South eventually commissioned about 200 warships that had been built in England. Many carried British sailors driven by the promise of reward. One daring raider, the *Tallahassee*, had a field day sinking ships off the coast of New Jersey and New York. It sank six ships in six hours before moving northward to attack coastal and transatlantic trading vessels.

Weather Woes

Other Union merchant ships were subject to damage from the weather. The SS *Republic*, a twin-paddlewheel steamer reportedly carrying $400,000 in coins, sailed from New York to New Orleans in 1865 and was pounded not by a Confederate attack but by a powerful hurricane. The *Republic* disappeared beneath the waves many miles off the coast of Georgia.

After more than a decade of failing deep-sea hunts and haggling with the government over proper rights and authorization, two modern undersea explorers, John Morris and Greg Stemm of Odyssey Marine Exploration, hit the jackpot in 2003 when they discovered more than 50,000 coins and 13,000 artifacts totaling $75 million. Such excavations and treasure hunts are expensive, though, leaving much underwater Civil War loot out there waiting to be discovered.

Bury the Loot

Money and assets on land during the war were also precious and subject to soldiers' looting. Notorious Confederate General John Hunt Morgan pillaged Union towns in Kentucky and throughout the Ohio River Valley. This harsh Southerner rode with his raiders up to wealthy homes and threatened to burn them down unless the owner could pay the ransom. With a command of more than 2,000 troops, Morgan ravaged towns, stole from businesses, and even took collection plates from churches.

After Morgan's force conducted a tour of robberies in central Kentucky, which included a hit on a bank for $80,000, Union cavalry came upon the raiders. The cavalry dispersed Morgan's troops, but their plunder was never found—was it buried in the Kentucky hills? The total wealth Morgan looted on his infamous raids will never be known, but it is likely that much of it was dispersed and hidden throughout the area along the trails and roads his forces traveled. One estimate is that Morgan accumulated nearly $1 million in gold and silver bullion.

The Treasury's Depleting Treasure

Perhaps the largest stash that traveled through Confederate hands was the Confederate Treasury after Union soldiers encroached on the Southern capital of Richmond, Virginia. Nearing the point of surrender, President Jefferson Davis ordered the area evacuated and assigned the Treasury to Captain William Parker. Parker and his soldiers loaded the sum, which totaled upward of $1 million, onto boxcars and sent it as far as Danville, Virginia, the new Confederate capital for the next eight days. Already on the run and trying to evade capture, several Southern leaders chose to distance themselves from the loot in favor of their own safety.

After the money bounced from town to town, it landed in Washington, Georgia. Here, Confederate troops charged with protecting the wealth feared for their safety and demanded payment on the spot. The military escort dwindled, as did the Treasury itself. As the loot traveled from farmhouse to farmhouse, it shrunk to $288,022.90 by the time it reached President Davis and what was left of the acting government. Some believe Davis took a large chunk of the money himself and buried it in several locations before he was captured.

On May 14, 1865, two Virginia bankers arrived in Washington with a federal order to commandeer the money, and Clark gave it up. The party carrying the money back to Richmond pulled over for the night 12 miles outside of the city only to be robbed. The outlaws, understanding that both law enforcement and Confederate soldiers were on their trail, buried their take before Confederates shot and killed them. Some believe the loot was buried on the south bank of the Savannah River.

Secret Society

According to legend, documented history, and some modern-day discoveries, rebels buried much more wealth than this. The mysterious Knights of the Golden Circle likely left behind millions in coin and precious metals. This secret society, explains historian and Knights of the Golden Circle detective Bob Brewer, grew out of anti-Union, proslavery sentiment and had several chapters by 1855. Famous politicians and rank-and-file composed the secret membership society, helping foster the ideas behind nullification and secession. Through a complex system of Masonic codes, secret signals, handshakes, and other rites, the organization, it is believed, buried much of the South's wealth in the hopes of financing a later uprising to reassert and complete the goals of the temporarily defeated South.

Some of this loot has been found. Brewer discovered a pint jar with coins and gold pieces—worth about $28,000 by today's values—at a location 65 miles from Oklahoma City called Buzzard's Roost. Treasure hunters report that four caches of booty have been unearthed over the years near this location, totaling more than $1 million. Those who study the Knights predict a lot more is out there. The organization likely developed some type of grid system marked with tree and rock carvings directing fellow Knights to the wealth. While little or no known record of the alleged postwar scheme fully defines its scope, it is believed that information to locate the money and the group's cause has been handed down by word of mouth, from father to son, in the hopes that one day the South will rise again.

"The edge of the conflict swayed to and fro, with wild whirlpools and eddies. At times I saw around me more of the enemy than of my own men; gaps opening, swallowing, closing again with sharp convulsive energy. All around, a strange, mingled roar."

Colonel Joshua Lawrence Chamberlain, 20th Maine, at Little Round Top

THE BATTLE OF NASHVILLE

★ ★ ★ ★

A Union general proved the old saying true:
Slow and steady wins the race.

Several high-ranking Union generals were notorious for moving into battle like tortoises—shyly, slowly, and conservatively. In fact, some were fired because of that tendency. But once in a while that approach worked perfectly.

A Tennessee Diversion

By late November 1864, Union General Sherman was marching through Georgia. Confederate General John Bell Hood tried to lure him north to fight near Nashville, Tennessee. Sherman didn't take the bait, leaving the battle to Union General George Thomas. A good commander, Thomas was certainly in the tortoise category. Instead of attacking Hood immediately, as President Lincoln wanted, he waited until reinforcements brought his troop strength to 70,000.

Lincoln told General Grant to get Thomas moving. Grant threatened to fire Thomas if he didn't attack at once. Thomas insisted that he was almost ready and would attack as soon as possible.

As luck would have it, when Thomas was finally poised to attack, freezing rain and snow bombarded the area. The slippery hills were a tactical disadvantage to the troops, so Thomas kept waiting. Grant knew that Lincoln was fed up, so he planned to travel to Nashville and take command of the army himself.

Decisive Victory

Before he could, however, a warm rain on December 15 melted the ice. Thomas attacked, smashing Hood's lines and driving the dispirited Confederates into retreat. Hood's army was routed, and the remains of it fled Tennessee. It was the first time a Union victory was so complete that the defeated army virtually ceased to exist. General Thomas's tortoise-like strategy had paid off.

Fast Facts

- *Many underage youths slipped into military service on both sides by signing on as volunteer musicians and then later shifting into service as soldiers.*

- *Among the many other names for the Civil War are: the War Between the States, Mr. Lincoln's War, the War Against Northern Aggression, the Second American Revolution, the Lost Cause, the War of the Rebellion, the Brothers' War, the Late Unpleasantness, the Uncivil War, the War of the Southrons, the Great Rebellion, the War for Southern Independence, and the Second War for Independence.*

- *Three out of four medical operations during the Civil War were amputations.*

- *Initially all but defenseless, Washington, D.C., had seen its defenses grow to 68 forts, 93 unarmed batteries, and 20 miles of rifle trenches by the time General Lee surrendered to General Grant in April 1865.*

- *General Thomas J. "Stonewall" Jackson was featured on the highest denomination bill issued by the Richmond government. He was the only general pictured on its currency.*

- *Alexander Hamilton Stephens of Georgia, vice president of the Confederacy, was called "Little Ellick" by his colleagues because of his small stature and slightness. He never weighed more than 100 pounds throughout his entire life.*

- *The Confederacy had 1.2 million men of combat age compared to the Union's 4 million.*

- *In August 1862, Abraham Lincoln became the first president to welcome a black delegation to the White House.*

THE COST OF
THE CIVIL WAR

★ ★ ★ ★

The national trauma of the Civil War could be felt
in the losses of both life and treasure. Its repercussions
would be felt for generations to come.

The Human Cost

The Civil War was the bloodiest conflict in American history. If we combined all the deaths from all conflicts in U.S. history, nearly half would come from the Civil War. But because of fragmentary records, it can never be known precisely how many people served on both sides of the war nor how many were killed, wounded, or captured.

Officially, the U.S. Army recorded 2,778,304 enlistments, although many soldiers enlisted more than once in different regiments. Of this, 178,975 were black and 3,530 were American Indian. The U.S. Navy and Marine Corps enlisted 105,963.

Northern casualties can be tallied as follows:

Total deaths	359,528
Killed in battle	67,088
Mortally wounded	43,012
Died of disease	199,720
Died as prisoners of war	24,866
Killed by accident	4,114
Died from other causes	20,728
Wounded	275,175
Navy killed and mortally wounded	1,804
Navy died of disease and accidents	3,000
Navy wounded	2,226

Since many Confederate records were burned when Richmond fell in 1865 or were otherwise misplaced or destroyed during the war itself, exact numbers of Southern enlistments and casualties will always remain something of a mystery. It is estimated that Confederate enlistments fell somewhere between a low of 600,000 and a high of 1.4 million, with a widely accepted estimate being 1 million. The gray armies included more than 1,000 regiments, battalions, independent companies, and artillery batteries.

The best estimate of Southern deaths include 94,000 killed in battle or mortally wounded, with another 164,000 deaths from disease, for a total of 258,000. One incomplete summary of the Confederate wounded included 194,026 names. The number of soldiers who died in Northern prison camps has been estimated to be somewhere between 26,000 and 31,000. Figures for losses in specific battles change over the years, however, as historians discover new muster rolls or casualty lists and must revise the figures from earlier research.

Statisticians adding up the fighting in the war came up with 1,882 incidents in which at least one regiment was engaged. In 112 of these battles, one of the two sides had at least 500 combatants killed or wounded.

★ ★ ★ ★

Monetary Costs

In addition to the human toll, the Civil War cost quite a bit of cash, too. Here are some estimates, figured in 1879 dollars, about 15 years after the war, and adjusted for inflation to modern-day dollars in 1999.

	1879 Estimate	1999 Estimate
Union	$3.2 Billion	......$27.3 Billion
Confederacy	$2.0 Billion	......$17.1 Billion

THE WAR'S LAST LAND BATTLE

★ ★ ★ ★

Seeking glory, a Union colonel picked a fight at Palmetto Ranch, Texas, after the war was over. Unfortunately, his plan backfired.

Throughout most of the war, things had been very quiet in Texas. Both the Union and Confederacy had neglected the state in order to support more vital movements farther east. What few troops remained in the region in 1865 knew the end was near and largely avoided unnecessary conflict. That is, until ambition and insecurity got the better of Union Colonel Theodore Barrett.

Missing Out on the Action

Barrett had seen very little action during the war, and his lack of experience haunted him. He feared his political aspirations would be smashed by the legions of war heroes who would certainly be running against him. Lee's surrender confirmed his fears: The war had ended, and he had nothing to show for it.

Picking a Fight

In May 1865, a full month after the recognized end of open hostilities, Barrett started a fight at the inconsequential outpost of Palmetto Ranch, about as far south as one could go and still be in Texas. Perhaps inspired by Andrew Jackson, whose victory at New Orleans came after the end of the War of 1812 and catapulted him into the presidency, Barrett set out to build a legacy.

Confederate soldiers (who knew the war was over) didn't realize the Union troops were spoiling for a fight. Once shots were fired, however, the rebels closed ranks and called for reinforcements. Major John "Rip" Ford organized the counterattack and handily repelled the Union without losing a single life. By contrast, Barrett's losses were 118 dead or wounded. Less than a month later, all Confederate forces in Texas were disbanded, and Barrett retreated into obscurity.

GENERAL SHERMAN MARCHED STRAIGHT INTO HISTORY

★ ★ ★ ★

A man who couldn't settle down before the war gained national recognition for keeping his army on the move.

William Tecumseh Sherman seemed to come alive on the battle-field. Before the war and at its beginning, he was viewed as a man unsure of himself, but before the war was over, he had evolved into a general full of bravado, one of the most fearsome warriors this country has ever seen.

A Disappointing Beginning

Sherman was born in 1820 in Lancaster, Ohio. When he was only nine years old, his father died, and his mother, overwhelmed, put him in the care of Thomas Ewing. Ewing later became a U.S. senator and secretary of the interior and used his influence to get Sherman into West Point at age 16. Sherman graduated sixth in his class in 1840. His military career thereafter was lackluster, however. He served mostly in Southern states, and he regretted missing the action of the Mexican War. He wrote to his future wife, "I feel ashamed having passed through a war without smelling gunpowder."

Seeing little future in an army career, Sherman quit and became a banker in 1853, running the San Francisco branch office of Lucas, Turner and Company of St. Louis. Accounts differ concerning his success; some historians say he was cautious and prudent in the role, while others call him a failure. In any case, he soon left banking to become a lawyer, a field in which he didn't gain much more success: He lost his only case. Tired of moving from one place to another and being too often separated from his wife and children, Sherman once wrote, "I am doomed to be a vagabond, and shall no longer struggle against my fate." In 1859, he finally settled for a short time into the job of superintendent of Louisiana State Seminary of Learning & Military Academy (which later changed its name to Louisiana State University). He proved himself an efficient administrator there, and he became a popular storyteller among young professors and students.

Taking a Stand with the Union

Though Sherman enjoyed his job and loved the South, he knew that he could not follow Louisiana out of the Union if it came to that. When Louisiana seceded in 1861, he went north and took a position with a street railway company in St. Louis. Two months later, when he realized war was inevitable, he volunteered to return to his Army uniform.

Sherman continued his mediocre career performance through the first half of the Civil War. He was made a colonel and saw his brigade routed along with everyone else in the Union defeat at Bull Run, although he himself was said to have performed well. Transferred to Kentucky, he blundered politically by stating that it would take a force of 60,000 to hold that state and another of 200,000 to open the Mississippi Valley. Newspapers and Northern politicians called him insane for these estimates. By the end of the war, however, his estimates had been proven right.

Sherman had backed himself into a corner and was relieved of his Kentucky post, but he'd made an important friend while in the West: General Grant. In Sherman's next few battles—Vicksburg, Jackson, and Chattanooga—he had minor success but was highly praised by Grant. His career was on the upswing.

Sherman Steps Into His Own

When Grant was called to take command of all military operations for the war, Sherman took over command of the West. As was the case for many Union generals, his early, less successful battles had served as a training ground. In his new position, Sherman understood that his objective went beyond the military force opposing his vast army. "War is cruelty and you cannot refine it," he wrote, "and those who brought war into our country deserve all the curses and maledictions a people can pour out." Militarily, Sherman led his army against that of Confederate General Joseph E. Johnston. He pushed Johnston all the way to Atlanta and crushed Johnston's successor, John Bell Hood, in three battles outside that pivotal city. Then began his famous March to the Sea, which cemented his reputation and his place in American history. Sherman finished the war marching north through the Carolinas until hostilities ended.

He accepted the surrender of Johnson's army a little more than two weeks after Lee surrendered to Grant.

After the War

Sherman remained in the army after the fighting was finished, but his activity in the last year of the war had made him a high-profile political figure. Because he had spent so much of his time in the South before the war, he had a lot of friends in the areas undergoing Reconstruction. He always advocated a light Reconstruction policy, falling on the side of those who preferred to "welcome back" the seceding states. When Ulysses Grant was elected to the office of president, Sherman took his place as general of the army, the top military officer of the day. He continued to hold that position until his retirement in 1883.

Sherman remained popular after the war, even—surprising as it may sound today—in the South. In 1879, he toured the sites of many of his Southern victories, such as Atlanta and Savannah, and received a friendly reception. Many expected that he would follow in Grant's footsteps and run for president, but Sherman never had any interest. When supporters threatened to draft him as a Republican candidate in 1884, he wired back a famous response: "I will not accept if nominated and will not serve if elected." The nomination that year went instead to James G. Blaine, who lost to Grover Cleveland. Sherman died in 1891. Joseph E. Johnston, the Confederate general who surrendered to him in North Carolina, served as a pallbearer at his funeral.

Fast Facts

- In 1862, the U.S. income tax was at a rate of 3 percent for incomes of $600–$10,000 and 5 percent for higher incomes.

- Harriet Tubman, the one-time slave who helped hundreds of other slaves escape via the Underground Railroad, has been called "The Moses of Her People."

- During the war, James Butler Hickok, aka "Wild Bill" Hickok, was a Union spy in Missouri.

- City Point, a small Virginia community, was completely transformed by General Grant, when he made it his headquarters and the "nerve center" of the Union for the final ten months of the war.

- Jefferson Davis denied POW status to captured black soldiers.

- The Model 1861 Springfield Musket was the most common firearm of the Civil War. It was actually a rifle because the bore was rifled. Manufactured at the Springfield Armory in Massachusetts, it cost between $15 and $20. Soldiers were drilled endlessly in the complex procedure for loading and firing, but in the heat of battle they would either forget to prime or they would over-prime, either way causing a misfire. Soldiers would often reload without clearing the misfire, and many a dead soldier was found with six or seven "loads" stuck in his musket from continuing to reload a fouled weapon.

- George Armstrong Custer disdained the clothing issued by the Union quartermaster and instead wore a uniform he'd had tailored. It was blue velvet, heavily trimmed with gold.

- More than 10,000 military engagements occurred during the course of the Civil War.

HORSE SOLDIERS

★ ★ ★ ★

Soldiers in the Civil War often literally lived or died by the horse they were riding. Identify the favorite horses of these generals.

1. Robert E. Lee

   A. Babieca   B. Trigger
   C. Traveller   D. Arlington

2. Ulysses S. Grant

   A. Cincinnati   B. Man O' War
   C. Lucky   D. Champion

3. George B. McClellan

   A. Kentuck   B. Tony
   C. Seattle Slew   D. Ruffian

4. Stonewall Jackson

   A. Elijah   B. Bonaparte
   C. Fred   D. Little Sorrel

5. Nathan Bedford Forrest

   A. Andy Jackson   B. King Philip
   C. Tennessee   D. Paleface

6. George Meade

   A. Champion   B. Cadiz
   C. Old Baldy   D. Scout

7. Philip Sheridan

   A. Comet   B. Winchester
   C. Pegasus   D. Big Sky

Answers: 1. C, 2. A, 3. A, 4. D, 5. B, 6. C, 7. B

ON TO THE WHITE HOUSE

★ ★ ★ ★

Six Civil War soldiers not only survived the bloody conflict but went on to become the leader of the country.

Fought primarily by young people, wars exert great influence in shaping a person's character and sometimes even his or her life path. The Civil War was no exception, serving as a proving ground for no fewer than six U.S. presidents.

Ulysses S. Grant

Grant rose to prominence during the war and was elected president in 1868 based on his service. He ran as a Republican in the first presidential election to follow his victory at Appomattox.

Rutherford B. Hayes

Almost 40 when the war broke out, Hayes volunteered and nearly lost his left arm to a musket ball in 1861. Following a miraculous recovery, he saw action in the Shenandoah Valley and ended the war as a major general. In 1877, he became president.

James Garfield

Garfield served under General Don Carlos Buell in Kentucky and at the Battle of Shiloh. In early 1862, he personally led a charge that drove Confederate troops out of the eastern part of the state. He left the army after the Battle of Chickamauga to take a seat in Congress in 1863, and he was elected president in 1880. Shortly after he took office, however, he was assassinated.

Chester A. Arthur

Although Arthur served the Union cause, he was nowhere near the front lines. He served as quartermaster general for the state of New York and was thus responsible for obtaining and delivering supplies to New York soldiers. He was ultimately awarded the rank of brigadier general. Elected vice president in 1880, he became president upon James Garfield's death.

Benjamin Harrison

Harrison raised a unit of volunteers in the Indiana Infantry and served as their colonel, later receiving a brevet promotion to general. Harrison was elected president in 1888, interrupting Grover Cleveland's two nonconsecutive terms.

William McKinley

The bloodiest single day of the war occurred at Antietam in 1862. Serving as a wagon driver under heavy enemy fire was one Sergeant William McKinley from Ohio. In the heat of the battle, he coolly drove two mule teams into the field at considerable personal peril to disperse food rations to hungry troops. His bravery that day won him a promotion to second lieutenant by his commanding officer—Rutherford B. Hayes. He was elected president in 1896 and 1900.

Grover Cleveland

The one president during the postwar years who didn't serve in the military was Grover Cleveland. His widowed mother's sole support, Cleveland hired a substitute to serve in his place. Although perfectly legal, this didn't endear him to Grand Army of the Republic veterans who were quite politically influential during Cleveland's burgeoning political career. Nevertheless, he won election in 1884 and 1892.

- *Ten of the first twelve U.S. presidents owned or had owned slaves. George Washington, Thomas Jefferson, James Madison, James Monroe, and John Tyler each came from Virginia plantation aristocracy. William Henry Harrison did too, although he moved to the free-soil Northwest Territories and changed his slaves' status to indentured servants. Andrew Jackson and James K. Polk became wealthy as Tennessee lawyers; Jackson was even a slave trader for a time. Zachary Taylor owned a Mississippi plantation. The one Northerner among these Southerners, Martin Van Buren of New York, owned one slave before the practice was outlawed in his state. Of the early presidents, only John Adams and his son John Quincy Adams never owned slaves.*

TIMELINE

(Continued from p. 405)

1866

March 13
Congress passes the Civil Rights Act, which is designed to protect the rights of newly enfranchised African-Americans.

May
The Ku Klux Klan is organized in Pulaski, Tennessee.

June 16
The 14th Amendment is submitted to the states for ratification.

July 24
Tennessee becomes the first former Confederate state readmitted to the Union.

July 25
Congress establishes a new military rank above all others, General of the Army. It is immediately bestowed upon Ulysses S. Grant.

1867

May 13
Jefferson Davis is released from prison on bail.

1868

June 22–25
Congress enacts the Omnibus Act, in which the Southern states of Arkansas, Alabama, Florida, Georgia, Louisiana, North Carolina, and South Carolina are readmitted to the Union.

July 28
The 14th Amendment becomes law after being ratified by three-fourths of the states.

November 3
Ulysses S. Grant is elected president of the United States.

1869

February 26
Congress passes the 15th Amendment, guaranteeing African-American men the right to vote.

December
In response to trouble on a number of fronts, Congress reimposes military rule in Georgia.

1870

January–March
Virginia, Mississippi, and Texas are readmitted to the Union.

March 30
The 15th Amendment to the Constitution is officially declared ratified.

July 15
Georgia is again readmitted to the Union.

1872

May 22
The General Amnesty Act paves the way for many former Confederate leaders to resume their political careers, restoring complete civil rights to all but about 500 Southerners.

1877

April 10
Union troops are withdrawn from South Carolina.

April 24
Union troops are withdrawn from Louisiana. They are the last occupation troops to leave the former Confederacy.

UNLIKELY ENDS

★ ★ ★ ★

A few Union and Confederate military leaders had less-than-heroic ends—to their careers and even sometimes their lives.

Earl Van Dorn

Confederate General Earl Van Dorn's notoriety wasn't due to success on the battlefield—his efforts to defend Missouri from Union forces had gone about as well as can be expected from a man at the bottom of his West Point class. His incompetence was on display at Pea Ridge, Arkansas, in March 1862—Van Dorn lost 4,600 troops, and Arkansas and Missouri were left defenseless against Union forces.

Van Dorn was known as an unrepentant womanizer, wrecking homes not with cannonballs but with his charming demeanor. He also had a reputation for being hot-blooded and impulsive. After an argument over supplies for troops in 1863, Van Dorn pulled a pistol on his superior, General Nathan Bedford Forrest, to challenge him to a duel. Forrest—older, wiser, and more experienced—turned up his nose and told Van Dorn that he had enough Union soldiers to fight without worrying about his own troops, too.

Ultimately, Van Dorn proved affairs of the heart could be just as dangerous as matters of war. In 1863, he and Forrest had routed a Union force into surrender, and Van Dorn made his headquarters in Spring Hill, Tennessee, where he could settle in with his soldiers and reconstitute his forces while awaiting further orders. During this time of rest, his wandering eye caught sight of Mrs. Jesse Peters, the wife of a local doctor. Van Dorn wooed the woman, taking her on romantic rides in his carriage and even visiting her in her home, barely concealing his improper intent.

So self-assured and without fear of discovery was Van Dorn that he barely batted an eye when Mr. George Peters, her husband, appeared at his headquarters on May 7, 1863, requesting a pass to travel to the front lines. Perhaps figuring it might be a good way to get the man killed, Van Dorn happily bent over his desk to scrawl out the permission slip. Mr. Peters calmly walked up behind the lascivious general and put a bullet in his head. Peters argued in court that he acted in defense of the sanctity of his home, and the court agreed, giving him no punishment. He even reconciled with his wife.

William "Bull" Nelson

When Van Dorn threatened to shoot Forrest, cooler heads prevailed and both men emerged unscathed. But when Union General William "Bull" Nelson had a run-in with one of his peers, General Jefferson C. Davis, no such luck was with them.

Nelson had ordered Davis to organize a militia of citizens to help defend Kentucky from the Confederates. Davis's work was apparently unsatisfactory and took too much time, so Nelson angrily dismissed him and ordered him shipped off to Ohio, effectively cutting Davis out of the thick of the war. Davis took this as an insult and was determined to take revenge on Nelson. On September 29, 1862, he strolled down Main Street in Louisville and entered the Galt House, a hotel where Union officers had been meeting. Davis confronted Nelson, angrily asking why he had been treated so shabbily. Nelson slapped Davis in the face, and before anyone could step in to diffuse the situation, Davis's pistol flew up and a single round was fired, killing Nelson.

Killing a superior officer is generally not acceptable in the military, and this should have been a career-ending decision for Davis. But with the Confederates bearing down on Kentucky and a significant lack of experienced generals, no one pressed charges against him. He returned to combat, and though he never was punished, he was never afforded any promotions or honors, either.

John Reynolds

While Van Dorn got into trouble by sleeping around, Union General John Reynolds got into trouble by just sleeping. A well-respected commander, Reynolds fought bravely until his death by a stray bullet at Gettysburg. His troops saw him as a competent and exceptional leader who rode hard with them and had a consummate knowledge of military strategy. His first few months on the job, however, were not quite as impressive.

Reynolds had been separated from his troops after intense fighting at Gaines' Mill, Virginia, in 1862. Taking refuge in a nearby community named Boatswain's Swamp, he intended to rest and rally with his unit later. Unfortunately for Reynolds, a crew of Confederates snuck into town while he slept and captured him with ease. His embarrassment was only compounded by the fact that the Confederate general to whom he was presented was an old friend from before the war, General D. H. Hill. After a few weeks in awkward captivity, Reynolds was traded for Confederate prisoners of war and returned to duty.

Edwin Stoughton

Union General Edwin Stoughton was also enjoying a pleasant night's sleep when he was abruptly roused with a slap to his backside. He was furious, kicking away the sheets and confronting his assailant with a bellow, asking, "Do you know who I am?" The unfamiliar voice replied that yes, he did know the general and then asked Stoughton whether he was familiar with a reviled Confederate raider named John Mosby. Suddenly, Stoughton's anger turned to optimism. "Have you got the rascal?" he asked, excitedly. "No," replied the voice, "but he has got you." Mosby had made a daring raid deep into Union-controlled territory, picking up Stoughton in Fairfax County, Virginia.

While his victory was a great morale boost for the Confederacy, Mosby had not captured a very popular general. Stoughton was the youngest general in the army at only 24 years old. His inexperience, coupled with a preoccupation with his appearance and a finicky personality, made his troops wary of him. Even Abraham Lincoln hardly cared when he was captured, expressing more concern over the loss of 60 horses. When Stoughton was released back to the North, he was immediately discharged to civilian life.

A UNION LEADER BY MARRIAGE

★ ★ ★ ★

As the wife of one of America's greatest leaders, Mary Todd Lincoln had to fight rumors—and reality.

Mary Todd Lincoln was a Southerner born into a slaveholding family, and she had very little interest in being a role model for keeping the Union together. But that was the position she held due to the man she married.

By all appearances, the marriage of Abraham and Mary Todd Lincoln was an unlikely one. By the time he met Mary Todd, the future president made little secret of his frontier upbringing and his lack of any significant formal education. Throughout his life, Lincoln carried himself with the bearing and demeanor of the quintessential common man.

By contrast, the early life of Mrs. Lincoln, née Mary Todd, was one of refinement and culture. Raised by a large and wealthy family in a genteel Kentucky home, Mary Todd was as well educated as it was possible for a young woman at that time in America to be. She moved to Springfield, Illinois, at age 20 and was a society belle when she first met the older Lincoln in 1841.

The Heat Is On

Mrs. Lincoln's Kentucky roots and her closeness to her family members—some of whom owned slaves—stirred the Washington gossip mill as Lincoln ascended to the presidency in 1860. As fear of an imminent war between the states became more pronounced in the capital, Mrs. Lincoln's loyalties were repeatedly questioned by various elements of Washington society. She particularly felt heat from those who opposed her husband's efforts to find some sort of agreement on states' rights issues and questions concerning slavery. Although Mrs. Lincoln several times pledged her support for the Union cause both publicly and privately, rumors continued that she was a Southern spy.

There's no denying that Mrs. Lincoln had a strong connection to the Confederacy. She kept excellent relations with her brother-in-law, Confederate General Benjamin Helm. Her father had married again after her mother's death and had fathered several more children. By 1861 Mary Lincoln's extended family included several brothers and half brothers who'd enlisted in the Confederate army. In 1861 and early 1862, the Union military was bogged down, and a Confederate attack on Washington was a constant concern to the populace. Union forces seemed unable to deal decisively with the enemy, and the gossip about Mrs. Lincoln's true loyalties and her influence over the conduct of the war never lessened.

As the war effort deepened in Washington, Mrs. Lincoln's detractors turned their attention from her suspected Union disloyalty to her spending habits in the White House. From 1862 to 1864, she exceeded her permitted White House domestic budget, often going so far as to hide the true cost of purchases from her husband. She told a confidante about her utter relief at Lincoln's reelection victory in 1864—not from any sense of sharing a political triumph with her husband, but because her personal debts far exceeded his annual presidential salary of $25,000. Her husband's victory would give her a longer grace period with her many creditors. The accumulation of such debts by the President's wife—especially during wartime—was ripe for scandal.

After the Fall

Few women in American public life have sustained the personal tragedies that Mrs. Lincoln did. She and her husband had four children, but only one survived to adulthood and outlived both his parents. The death of their 11-year-old son Willie in 1862 caused great depression for Mrs. Lincoln—in many ways, she never fully recovered. She had a reputation for being tempestuous, a trait that led Lincoln's private secretary John Hay to call her a "hell-cat" in his published private diaries. Her emotional troubles became worse after President Lincoln's assassination in April 1865.

Mrs. Lincoln left Washington with very little fanfare after her husband's murder. It's inconceivable to us in our media-drenched age that a former first lady could exit public life so quietly. The combined effect of her Confederate connections and her reckless spending, however, proved extremely difficult for her in the summer of 1865. She lived in Europe for a time, dreading the possibility of a life of poverty. Her fears were not rational, however, as she often had more than $50,000 in securities and cash in her skirt pocket. Despite her pleas to the federal government for financial support befitting a presidential widow, Mrs. Lincoln got nothing from the government until 1870, when she received a $3,000-a-year pension. The amount was increased in 1882, and she received a one-time gift from the Senate of $15,000.

In 1867, Mrs. Lincoln tried to sell her entire White House wardrobe and most of her jewelry through a New York estate agent. Although she intended to make the sale anonymously, her identity became known, and she was the subject of both ridicule and disgust. One of the dresses she tried to sell was the dress she'd worn the night of Lincoln's assassination, still stained with her husband's blood. The entire transaction took on a macabre tone, and the sale of these possessions was never completed.

Mrs. Lincoln's mental health continued to deteriorate, and in 1875 a court committed her to an asylum in Batavia, Illinois. Her son, Robert Todd Lincoln, had arranged this against her will, and Mrs. Lincoln fought to be released. She remained in the asylum for only a short time and was helped in her efforts to be released by attorney Myra Bradwell, one of the first women licensed to practice law in the United States.

In part to escape her son's efforts to have her recommitted, Mrs. Lincoln lived for a few years in France. She returned to Springfield, Illinois, in 1880 and lived with her sister Elizabeth Edwards and her family until her death two years later. Until she died, she signed every letter she wrote as "Mrs. A. Lincoln."

AN END IN SIGHT

★ ★ ★ ★

When Petersburg and Richmond fell, the North and South each realized the ordeal was nearly over.

Throughout the war, Richmond was consistently well defended, so General Grant turned to Petersburg, a smaller city 20 miles to the south, where five railroads and several important roads converged. If Petersburg fell, Richmond couldn't survive for long.

Under Siege

Petersburg was no easy victory—Grant laid siege to the city for almost 300 days. By February 1865, Lee had only 60,000 soldiers against Grant's 110,000. Weary Confederates were stretched thin over 37 miles of trenches. If Lee did nothing, the Yankees would eventually encircle Petersburg or burst through the Confederate line. He decided to try to break the Union lines for a clean escape, perhaps joining Confederate armies in North Carolina. So he sent about half his forces against Union Fort Stedman in early March. Taking the Yankees by surprise, the Confederates captured it, but before they could establish their position, Union artillery and soldiers took the fort back. This had been, essentially, Lee's last major stand.

Grant had the upper hand. On April 1, he attacked the South Side Railroad, the last line still coming in to Petersburg, and crushed the weakened defenders. The next day Lee's entire right flank collapsed.

Escaping the Capital

With the fall of Petersburg and Richmond, the war was nearly over. Jefferson Davis escaped with his government and set up a new capital in Danville, Virginia. It was only the capital for eight days, however. On April 10, his Cabinet was at dinner when word reached them that Lee was forced to surrender at Appomattox Court House.

SO THEY SAID

★ ★ ★ ★

"I think I understand what military fame is; to be killed on the field of battle and have your name misspelled in the newspapers."
General William Tecumseh Sherman

★ ★ ★ ★

"I remarked, in Mrs. Jackson's hearing, 'General, how is it that you can keep so cool, and appear so utterly insensible to danger in such a storm of shell and bullets as rained about you when your hand was hit?' He instantly became grave and reverential in his manner, and answered, in a low tone of great earnestness: 'Captain, my religious belief teaches me to feel as safe in battle as in bed. God has fixed the time for my death. I do not concern myself about that, but to be always ready, no matter when it may overtake me.' He added, after a pause, looking me full in the face: 'Captain, that is the way all men should live, and then all would be equally brave.'"
John D. Imboden, relating an exchange with General Stonewall Jackson

★ ★ ★ ★

"The enemy has assailed my outposts in heavy force. I have fallen back on the line of Bull Run and will make a stand at Mitchell's Ford."
General P.G.T. Beauregard, July 17, 1861

★ ★ ★ ★

"The dead covered more than five acres of ground about as thickly as they could be laid."
A Confederate soldier describing the Union dead after the battle of Cold Harbor in 1864

WHERE DID THEY FIGHT?

★ ★ ★ ★

*Although three times more battles occurred in Virginia
than the second busiest state, Civil War battles
were spread throughout the country.*

Civil War battles were fought in 20 states, the District of Columbia, and several territories. Here is a list of present-day states and the number of battles that took place in them. Battles in some of the western states include campaigns directed against Native Americans, not all of whom were affiliated with the Confederacy.

Alabama	7	Mississippi	16
Arkansas	17	Missouri	27
Colorado	1	New Mexico	2
District of Columbia	1	North Carolina	20
Florida	6	North Dakota	5
Georgia	31	Ohio	2
Idaho	1	Oklahoma	7
Indiana	1	Pennsylvania	2
Kansas	4	South Carolina	11
Kentucky	11	Tennessee	38
Louisiana	23	Texas	5
Maryland	7	Virginia	123
Minnesota	2	West Virginia	15

Fast Facts

- A 25-pound barrel of flour selling for $6 in New York during the war would have cost $25 in New Orleans.

- Famous international banker Baron Rothschild of London once predicted the North would win the war because it had the "larger purse."

- When an individual medal for valor—the Medal of Honor—was proposed to Winfield Scott, the commanding general of the U.S. Army, he did not approve it because he opposed the European practice of awarding medals for heroism. Lincoln signed it into law for the Navy in 1861. Scott was relieved of command at the end of 1861, and in 1862 the medal was approved for the Army as well.

- On April 12, 1861, at 4:30 A.M., Confederates under the command of General P.G.T. Beauregard opened fire with 50 cannons on Fort Sumter in Charleston, South Carolina, and proceeded to bombard it with more than 3,000 shells.

- During the war, Macon, Georgia, housed a hospital for wounded Confederate soldiers, a prison for Union soldiers, and a center for the manufacture of Confederate weapons.

- When Confederate ships came out to meet Union vessels attacking Galveston, they were shielded with dozens of bales of cotton.

- Historians have determined that approximately 3.5 million soldiers actually fought in the Civil War.

- In 1863, Major General Benjamin F. Butler used his personal funds to purchase 12 of the newly invented Gatling machine guns and 12,000 rounds of ammunition for $12,000.

AN END AT LAST

★ ★ ★ ★

*After four long years of bloody chaos, the
Civil War ended in a quaint country living room.*

After the fall of Petersburg and Richmond in Virginia, General
Robert E. Lee's fatigued and retreating Confederates found themselves in a viselike grip: Union forces in front of them and Union
forces behind them. In fact, Palm Sunday, April 9, 1865, dawned
with Federals in possession of the Appomattox train station, which
the Confederates had seen as their last avenue of retreat.

Out of Options

Where else could the Southern army go? One of Lee's subordinates suggested that Confederates sneak off into the Virginia
woods and operate against the Union as guerillas, but Lee would
have none of it. A guerilla war "would bring on a state of affairs it
would take the country years to recover from," said Lee. "There is
nothing left for me to do but go and see General Grant, and I'd
rather die a thousand deaths."

Making It Official

Lee officially surrendered to Grant later that day in Appomattox
Court House, Virginia. More specifically, it was in the parlor of the
home of Southern businessman Wilmer McLean, who had moved
his family to the town from Manassas Junction, site of the First
Battle of Bull Run. The generals talked briefly before Lee agreed
to Grant's generous surrender terms. The Union granted Southern
soldiers immunity from prosecution for treason and allowed them
to keep any horses they owned "to put in a crop to carry themselves and their families through the next winter."

As word of Lee's surrender spread, soldiers who'd fought each other
hard for four long years could hardly believe it. When Lee rode
through his army, "whole lines of battle rushed up to their beloved
old chief," recorded an onlooker, "and struggled with each other to

wring him once more by hand. . . . Not an eye that looked on that scene was dry."

The reaction was just as emotional on the Union side. "Such yelling and cheering I never heard," wrote General Meade's son George to his mother. There was a lot of yelling and crying, and General Meade was the man of the hour among his troops.

Ironing Out the Details

On Monday, April 10, Meade and his staff passed through the enemy line in search of General Lee. Seeing Lee approaching on horseback, Meade bowed and removed his cap in solemn respect. Lee, who had known Meade but had not seen him in 18 years, barely recognized him at first. Once he realized that it was his old friend, Lee asked, "What are you doing with all that gray in your beard?" Meade responded, "You have to answer for most of it."

After the two generals convened in Lee's tent to discuss recent operations, Meade also searched out his brother-in-law, former Virginia governor and Confederate General Henry A. Wise. The in-laws conversed, and Meade loaned Wise 50 dollars and ordered two mules and an ambulance loaded with supplies to be sent back to the Wise family in Richmond. It appeared to be a day of reconciliation, repair, and closure.

Ironically, the ending at Appomattox also left at least one surprising figure with a profound sadness. Grant later wrote that the occasion had left him depressed. "I felt like anything rather than rejoicing at the downfall of a foe who had fought so long and valiantly, and had suffered so much for a cause, though that cause was, I believe, one of the worst for which a people ever fought."

- *Coal became so scarce that Southerners mixed coal dust, sawdust, sand, and wet clay, hardened it into lumps, and used it for burning and heating. These lumps were called* fireballs.

A LITERARY LOOK
AT THE WAR

★ ★ ★ ★

*Walt Whitman, one of America's most famous writers, had
unique experiences during the Civil War. He left behind
his interpretation of the conflict in his poetry.*

Walt Whitman was born in 1819 and lived most of his life in New
York. Early in his career, he worked as a printer, a journalist, and an
occasional teacher. In the 1850s, Whitman embarked on a path as a
poet among transcendentalists, publishing the first version of *Leaves
of Grass* in 1855. (He continued to add to and revise it throughout
the rest of his life.) As the Civil War approached, Whitman believed
it was more important to preserve the Union than to emancipate
slaves. He hated both the fire-eaters of the South and the aggressive
abolitionists of the North, feeling that extremists threatened the
harmony of the Union. The South's greatest sin, Whitman felt, was
secession, and the North's greatest virtue was devotion to the Union.

A Lasting Impression

The Civil War fascinated Whitman, and his experiences during the
conflict transformed him as a writer: He left behind a catalog of
colorful descriptions of both the political dispute and the conflict
on the battlefield. For example, after the First Battle of Bull Run,
he penned "Beat! Beat! Drums!" In this poem, Whitman calls on
the drums and bugles to "scatter the congregations" and to take
groom away from bride and "peaceful farmer [from] any peace" so
they will serve in the war.

In the Thick of Things

In late 1862, Whitman learned through newspaper reports that his
brother, George, was wounded in battle at Fredericksburg, Virginia.
He immediately left New York for Virginia. While looking for his
brother, he passed through a makeshift field hospital where he saw a

heap of amputated human limbs and wondered if
any of these belonged to his brother. He finally
found George—all in one piece—with his regiment, recovering from a bullet wound that had
pierced his cheek. Spending time with his brother
and the war-hardened soldiers, Whitman was enrap-
tured by the stories he heard. He also helped the young
soldiers of the ranks bury the dead.

From the field in Virginia, Whitman decided to take up residence
in the nation's capital and take a job copying material in the Army
Paymaster's Office. He also volunteered as a nurse's assistant in the
local hospitals, performing small acts of kindness to the wounded:
reading to them, writing letters for them, and bringing them small
gifts. It was this experience that inspired *Drum-Taps,* Whitman's
collection of 43 poems that captures the emotional experiences of
the war. These poems, such as "The Wound Dresser," show the
nation's transformation from patriotic militarism to a sense of
compassion and grief for the wounded and dead.

An Ode to Lincoln

Also among Whitman's most celebrated writings are those that
define the commander in chief, Abraham Lincoln. While in Washington, D.C., Whitman lived within walking distance of the White
House and crossed President Lincoln's path several times. He
even attended the reception for his second inauguration, but he
never actually met the President.

Although Whitman was unable to express his fondness for Lincoln
in person, he left a written record of poetry that shows a great deal
of respect and admiration for his President. He confirmed their
common ideology, "We are afloat on the same stream—we are
rooted in the same ground." Whitman understood Lincoln's struggle
and witnessed what the war did to him on a personal and physical
level, writing that the president looked "worn and tired; the lines,
indeed, of vast responsibilities, intricate question, and demands of
life and death, cut deeper than ever upon his dark brown face; yet
all the old goodness, tenderness, sadness, and canny shrewdness,

underneath the furrows." He also complimented Lincoln's "purest, heartiest tenderness, and native western form of manliness."

After the Union victory and Lincoln's assassination, Whitman wrote what is probably his most famous ode to his hero Lincoln.

"O Captain! My Captain!"

1

O Captain! my Captain! our fearful trip is done;
The ship has weather'd every rack, the prize we sought is won;
The port is near, the bells I hear, the people all exulting,
While follow eyes the steady keel, the vessel grim and daring:
    But O heart! heart! heart!
      O the bleeding drops of red,
        Where on the deck my Captain lies,
          Fallen cold and dead.

2

O Captain! my Captain! rise up and hear the bells;
Rise up—for you the flag is flung—for you the bugle trills;
For you bouquets and ribbon'd wreaths—for you the shores a-crowding;
For you they call, the swaying mass, their eager faces turning;
    Here Captain! dear father!
      This arm beneath your head;
        It is some dream that on the deck,
          You've fallen cold and dead.

3

My Captain does not answer, his lips are pale and still;
My father does not feel my arm, he has no pulse nor will;
The ship is anchor'd safe and sound, its voyage closed and done;
From fearful trip, the victor ship, comes in with object won;
    Exult, O shores, and ring, O bells!
      But I, with mournful tread,
        Walk the deck my Captain lies,
          Fallen cold and dead.

INDEX

★ ★ ★ ★

Contributing Writers

Michael Amedeo has written for *Encyclopaedia Britannica, Chicago Sun-Times, Screen Magazine*, and a wide variety of other publications.

Ed Avis, a freelance writer and editor, is the author of two books: *Come On, Dad! 75 Things for Fathers and Sons to Do Together* and *The Lobster Kids' Guide to Exploring Chicago.*

Michael Patrick Brady is an editor and freelance writer whose cultural criticism has appeared in numerous publications, including *Pop Matters, ALARM Magazine,* and *Brainwashed.*

Bryan Davies has written more than 800 published articles, including an analysis of the Civil War and its impact on Canada.

Tom DeMichael has authored several books on American history. He has also published books and magazine articles on the subjects of American film and collectible toys.

Eric Paul Erickson is a freelance writer, photographer, and cultural explorer whose work has been featured in the *Chicago Tribune, Chicago Sun-Times,* the Associated Press, and other outlets.

William and **John Gorenfeld** are a father-son team who have written for *Wild West Magazine.* William is an attorney, and his son John is a journalist and author.

Martin F. Graham is coauthor of seven books on the Civil War, including *The Civil War Chronicle* and *The Blue and the Gray,* and has contributed to *Civil War Times, Blue and Gray,* and *World War II* magazines.

Kathryn Holcomb is a writer who has written a number of articles on little-known events, particularly Chicago's *Eastland* disaster.

Sarah Milov graduated from Harvard University in 2007 and is a history graduate student focusing on the modern South at Princeton University.

Richard Mueller is a novelist and historian who also writes for television. His documentaries have appeared on A&E and The History Channel.

Nick Smith is president of the Civil War Round Table of the San Gabriel Valley and performs as a storyteller at libraries, museums, and festivals.

Michael J. Varhola is a writer, editor, and lecturer who has authored or coauthored a dozen books, including *Everyday Life During the Civil War,* and written for *Civil War Times Illustrated* and other publications.

Jacob Wheeler is an author and freelance journalist who founded the *Glen Arbor Sun,* is an editor at *In These Times,* and is completing a book on the Guatemalan adoption industry.

David Wolfford teaches American government and history at Mariemont High School in Cincinnati. He has published articles in historical journals and teachers' magazines.